AUSTRALIAN TRAVELLERS
IN THE
SOUTH SEAS

AUSTRALIAN TRAVELLERS
IN THE
SOUTH SEAS

NICHOLAS HALTER

PRESS

PACIFIC SERIES

Published by ANU Press
The Australian National University
Acton ACT 2601, Australia
Email: anupress@anu.edu.au

Available to download for free at press.anu.edu.au

ISBN (print): 9781760464141
ISBN (online): 9781760464158

WorldCat (print): 1232438742
WorldCat (online): 1232438653

DOI: 10.22459/ATSS.2021

This title is published under a Creative Commons Attribution-NonCommercial-NoDerivatives 4.0 International (CC BY-NC-ND 4.0).

The full licence terms are available at creativecommons.org/licenses/by-nc-nd/4.0/legalcode

Cover design and layout by ANU Press. Cover photograph reproduced courtesy of the Fiji Museum (Record no. P32.4.157).

This edition © 2021 ANU Press

Contents

Acknowledgements vii
List of Figures ix
Preface xi
Note xiii
Introduction 1
1. Fluid Boundaries and Ambiguous Identities 25
2. Steamships and Tourists 61
3. Polynesian Promises 109
4. Degrees of Savagery 145
5. In Search of a Profitable Pacific 187
6. Conflict, Convicts and the Condominium 217
7. Preserving Health and Race in the Tropics 255
Conclusion 295
Appendix: An Annotated Bibliography of Australian Travel Writing . . . 307
Bibliography 347

Acknowledgements

This book took life as a doctoral dissertation in Pacific History at The Australian National University under the supervision of Brij Lal, to whom it is dedicated. Brij has been a generous mentor and friend from the beginning. I credit my personal and professional development to Brij's inspirational example. I would not be where I am today without the love and support of Brij, Padma and his family.

This research was made possible with financial support from The Australian National University and the Australian Government. Thank you to my friends and colleagues at the ANU School of Culture, History and Language, who shared their ideas and experiences with me. In addition, I am grateful to a number of scholars who generously gave their time to assist me—thank you Angela Woollacott, Vicki Luker, Max Quanchi, Ryota Nishino, Kirstie Close, Paul D'Arcy and Stewart Firth.

The support services provided by the staff of archives and libraries in Australia and the Pacific have been crucial to this research. This includes the National Library of Australia, the State Library of New South Wales, the Noel Butlin Archives Centre, the Barr Smith Library and the National Archives of Fiji, in whose spaces I spent countless hours. A special thanks also to Kylie Moloney and Ewan Maidment of the Pacific Manuscripts Bureau for providing inspiration along the way.

I have been fortunate to continue my research while working at the University of the South Pacific for the last five years. I am grateful to the staff and students of the School of Social Sciences and the Faculty of Arts, Law and Education for this precious time. *Vinaka vaka levu* and *fa'afetai tele lava* for the memories.

Thank you to my ever supportive family, my grandparents, Aunty Joyce, Mum, Dad, Emily and Stephen. You have always encouraged me to chart my own path, even if it has taken me far from home. Finally, to my wife Makayla, I owe everything. Thank you for your compassion, patience and unwavering love on this journey.

List of Figures

Figure 1: Routes Map Torres Straits—Tahiti. xiv
Figure 2: Map of the Pacific Islands 30
Figure 3: New Guinea Native. 39
Figure 4: Let's Explore in New Guinea Wilds Australia's Mandated Territory 40
Figure 5: Burns, Philp & Company Publication. 72
Figure 6: Rear Cover of a Union Steamship Company Publication. . . 73
Figure 7: Translate Your Precious Holiday Moments into Pathescope Home Movies 74
Figure 8: Australasian United Steam Navigation Co. Travel Guide . . . 83
Figure 9: Australian Samoans 101
Figure 10: Pearls of the Pacific 113
Figure 11: Cruise to the Solomon Islands. 119
Figure 12: Memories of Moorea 127
Figure 13: How a Lady Travels on Ocean Island. 142
Figure 14: The Author, Recruiter, Captain, and Boat's Crew of Natives. 155
Figure 15: Front Cover of a Book in 'The Vagabond' series published by *The Australian* 156
Figure 16: Old Cannibal Chief of the Island of Aoba, New Hebrides 180
Figure 17: Products of the Pacific Islands 189

Figure 18: Canaques Are After Them 243

Figure 19: On the Quayside, Noumea 249

Figure 20: One of the Wards of the Methodist Mission Hospital,
    Ba, Fiji 277

Preface

> How superb in reality, fragrant in retrospect, for those who love and understand.[1]

Daniel Defoe, Robert Louis Stevenson, Herman Melville, Robert Michael Ballantyne and Louis Becke—as a young man, I had never read these authors' famous and fantastical tales of adventure and savagery in the Pacific Islands. On the contrary, my Pacific education was based on the American film *Castaway* (2000) and a *Lonely Planet* guidebook. Yet, for Australians of the early twentieth century, these writers loomed over the Pacific, overshadowing the accounts of explorers before them and informing and inspiring new generations of Australian-born who were more literate and more mobile than their forebears. As I read the novels and magazines that those Australian children would have consumed, as well as the subsequent travel accounts of Australians who had realised their dreams of a Pacific odyssey, I was captivated by their recollections. I was especially fascinated by the moments of expectations meeting reality, and the subsequent choices that were made to reconcile fact with fiction.

My travel experience in the Pacific Islands was profoundly liberating. Eager to leave behind the familiar for an adventure promised by the unknown, I went to Weno Island (in Chuuk Lagoon, in the Federated States of Micronesia) to volunteer at a Catholic high school for 12 months. I relished my isolation and freedom from the outside world. I was energised by my new-found independence. I was only 18 years old and was naive and impressionable, and I remember the joys and frustrations of cross-cultural exchange. It was a formative period in my life and, like

---

1 Alan John Marshall, *The Black Musketeers: The Work and Adventures of a Scientist on a South Sea Island at War and in Peace* (London: William Heinemann, 1937), 295.

Australian zoologist Alan John Marshall, in 1937, I strove to convey to my family and friends the powerful influence of my Pacific encounters and the depth and intensity of the emotions that moved me.

Writing was an important process during my travels: the nightly ritual of reflection in my journal, the weekly emails to parents, the monthly letters to grandparents and the periodic updates to my online blog. For me, writing was a simultaneous activity of reflection, communication and chronicling. Each text served a specific purpose—to reassure, to document, to argue, to entertain, to advertise, to question and to project— and each was always written with a certain audience in mind. I struggled to articulate my personal experiences in a way that moved others to empathise and understand. As the years passed, my reminiscences became romanticised and nostalgic. I travelled further afield, beyond the Pacific Islands, to chase those fragrant memories. In doing so, I returned with a desire to search for that same sense of connection in Australia that I had found elsewhere. It is this experience that underscores my passion for the Pacific Islands and writing.

Note

I refer to authors by their published names, with their initials expanded if known. I also refer to islands as they were named at the respective time. The following names listed in Table 1 were used by an Australian shipping company in its 1903 route map (see Figure 1) published in *All about Burns, Philp & Company, Limited*.[1]

Table 1: Route Map Names

Island (s)	Present Name
Caroline Islands	Federated States of Micronesia
Ellice Group	Tuvalu
Fiji Group	Fiji
Gambier Group, Marquesas Group, Paumotu or Tuamotu Group or Low Archipelago, Society Group, Tubuai or Austral Group	French Polynesia
Gilbert or Kingsmill Group, Phoenix Group	Kiribati
Hawai'i, Sandwich Islands	Hawai'i
Hervey or Cook Group, Manahiki Group	Cook Islands
Marshall Islands	Marshall Islands
New Caledonia and Loyalty Group	New Caledonia
New Guinea, Bismarck Archipelago	Papua New Guinea
New Hebrides	Vanuatu
Niue or Savage Island	Niue
Ocean Island	Banaba
Pleasant Island	Nauru
Samoa or Navigator Group	Samoa and American Samoa
Solomon Islands, Santa Cruz Group	Solomon Islands
Tokelau or Union Group	Tokelau
Tonga or Friendly Group	Tonga

Source: Table created by the author, based on information from Burns, Philp & Company, *All about Burns, Philp & Company, Limited*.

---

1   Burns, Philp & Company, *All about Burns, Philp & Company, Limited* (Sydney: John Andrew & Co., 1903).

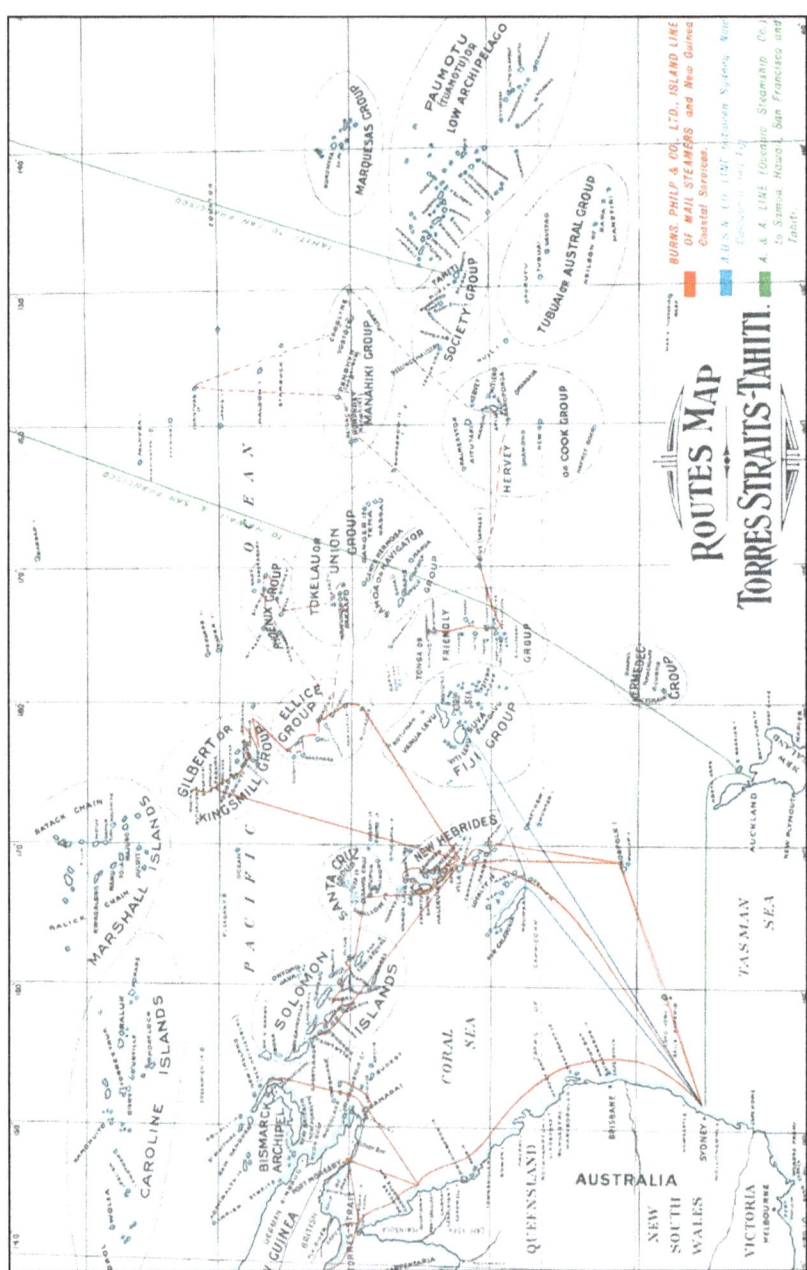

Figure 1: Routes Map Torres Straits—Tahiti.
Source: Burns, Philp & Co., *All about Burns, Philp & Company, Limited*.

Introduction

> The truth is that in the places where 'every one' goes, almost no man sees with his own eyes … The celebrated spot … is like a photograph which a countless number of others, all more or less similar, have been superimposed in the well known 'composite' style … In the whole blurred, worn-out picture, each man's personal impression counts for just another touch of shade set upon a shadow that has long been there … It is impossible to admire by the battalion, and yet enjoy to the full that sense of an individuality enlarged by experiences absolutely new, that is the real heart of travel-pleasure.[1]

Beatrice Grimshaw is known as one of Australia's most famous travel writers of the early twentieth century. Beginning as a sports journalist in Dublin in 1891, Grimshaw then found success as a prolific travel writer of the Pacific Islands. She travelled from 'Fiji to the Cannibal Islands' and across the 'Strange South Seas' before settling in the territory of Papua for 27 years and ultimately retiring to a small town near Bathurst, New South Wales. Although Grimshaw's career followed an unusual trajectory, her experience of travel resonates with countless global travellers who have described crossing unfamiliar landscapes and oceans and who have faced the choice of following well-worn routes or forging their own path—or, as she has explained, the choice between the collective memory or knowledge of 'the celebrated spot' and 'that sense of an individuality enlarged by experiences absolutely new'. However, her observations were also mediated through a particular cultural and historical lens. A close reading of her observations may tell us something about the individual that she was, the time in which she lived and her distinct view of the world and place in it, but can she be claimed as 'Australian' if her national identity was rendered ambiguous and fluid by her mobility? A similar question

---

1   Beatrice Grimshaw, *From Fiji to the Cannibal Islands* (London: Eveleigh Nash, 1907), 168.

could be asked of the 'Australian' audience who consumed her books for education and entertainment and of the literary context in which her accounts emerged. More importantly, what can travel writing tell us about the collective 'Australian' knowledge of the region, and how did travellers like Grimshaw shape popular notions about the Pacific Islands?

Grimshaw's contribution forms part of a more extensive collection of Australian travel writing about the Pacific Islands that has yet to be studied in detail. Whether used to describe an individual or a body of literature, the category of 'Australian' is contested, and its origins may not be simply traced to the nation's formal independence in 1901. In fact, notions of a distinctive national identity emerged well before the federation of the six colonies—the settlements that owed much to the British colonisers who claimed the continent in 1788 and less to the first inhabitants who had lived there for approximately 50,000 years. It is generally acknowledged that Australians have always been, and continue to be, exceptionally mobile. Despite the relative proximity between Australians and their Pacific neighbours, their relationship has not been studied by historians to the same extent that Australia's relationship with Asia or Europe has warranted. This may be due to the immense diversity of Pacific Island cultures and the complex web of European colonial masters who tried to control them. Or perhaps it reflects the dominant European narrative of the Australian colonies and the predominance of Asia in Australian perceptions of the Asia-Pacific region. This book re-centres the spotlight on the Pacific Islands, which have played as important a role as Asia or Europe in shaping Australians' notions about the world and their place in it.

Australian engagement with the Pacific Islands intensified during a crucial period of Australia's formation and growth, from c. 1880 to 1941. Situated on the periphery of the British empire, colonial Australian travellers began to consider themselves the centre of an emerging Australian–Pacific empire. A growing body of literature that was produced in the Australian colonies during the late nineteenth century reveals the development of a more robust national consciousness (politically and culturally), with the Pacific Islands featuring in public debates about federation, nationhood and regional expansion. However, the Pacific War, which commenced in 1941, has tended to overshadow Australians' much longer-standing relationship with the Pacific Islands. This historic period also coincides with the expansion of steamship routes between Australia and the

Pacific Islands. These routes responded to, and facilitated, the growth of Australian engagement with the Pacific region, including in the areas of trade, business, Christian outreach and colonial administration in the region. Consequently, more Australians than ever before came into contact with the Pacific region and its peoples, which created new possibilities for encounters and exchange. It is surprising that no historian has considered the corpus of travel writing itself to understand Australia–Pacific relations.

The travel accounts that were produced demonstrate that Australians were more closely connected to the Pacific Islands than had previously been acknowledged. The level of engagement was much deeper and more widespread than a purely political or economic relationship. It infiltrated popular language and literature, as well as public discourse. Travel writing reflected how close Australians living on the eastern seaboard were to their Pacific neighbours, the constant exchange of goods, peoples and notions across the Pacific Ocean, and a broader awareness within Australia of how significant the Pacific Islands were in their national history, as well as in European fantasy. These travel writing texts provide a reminder of the historical legacy of early European and Australian encounters in the Pacific Islands, signifying that these places and people were as familiar, if not more so, than other exotic backdrops of Africa or Asia.

Travel Writing, the Pacific and History

'Travel writing' remains a highly contested term, reflecting ambiguous literary content and form. The purpose and style of travel writing have changed over time, and the category today can encompass both records of exploration and more modern tourist reflections. Prior to 1900, travel writing was more commonly termed 'voyages and travels' in the English vernacular—and, to this day, library catalogues continue to offer a diverse set of categories and subjects for this corpus. This is reflected in the use of terminology such as 'travel memoir', 'travel narrative', 'travelogue', 'travel magazine', 'travel guide' or simply 'travels'. The ambiguous status of travel writing has left the category open to different interpretations from the disciplines of literature, history, anthropology, linguistics, geography and sociology. It has thus been labelled as a 'genre of genres', a 'hybrid genre', a 'subspecies of memoir' or, alternatively, as a theme or discourse rather than a genre. Its diversity is reflected in the numerous edited collections dedicated to the subject, which have demonstrated that efforts to define and limit travel writing to a set of specific criteria are fraught.[2]

Efforts to articulate what exactly constitutes travel writing have often focused on the category's intellectual or literary value. Once regarded as a sub-literary genre, travel writing began to feature in the works of historical and cultural revisionists, such as in analyses of discourse and representations of Roland Barthes, Hayden White, Michel Foucault and Edward Said.[3] Finally accepted as a historical source, travel writing was adopted as a useful tool for postcolonialists who were interested in revealing the processes and structures that underpinned imperial endeavours. Said's landmark study of European colonial discourses about Asia identified travel writing to be a major, influential component in the construction of a 'second-order knowledge'—a term Said used to explain 'Europe's collective day-dream of the Orient'.[4] Following this cultural turn, the literary criticisms of notable scholars such as Peter Hulme and Mary Louise Pratt have highlighted the colonial discourse that is inherent in the language and judgements of European travellers. Travel writing is now commonly acknowledged as having played an informal yet significant role in European colonial exploits overseas, not only revealing the activities and attitudes of the travellers abroad but also creating a sense of excitement about European expansionism.[5]

---

2   Joan-Pau Rubiés, 'New Worlds and Renaissance Ethnology', *History and Anthropology* 6, nos 2–3 (1993): 157–97; Patrick Holland and Graham Huggan, *Tourists with Typewriters: Critical Reflections on Contemporary Travel Writing* (Ann Arbor: University of Michigan Press, 1998), doi.org/10.3998/mpub.16396; Paul Fussell, *Abroad: British Literary Travelling between the Wars* (New York: Oxford University Press, 1980); Jan Borm, 'Defining Travel: On the Travel Book, Travel Writing and Terminology', in *Perspectives on Travel Writing*, ed. Glenn Hooper and Tim Youngs (London: Routledge, 2004), 13–26, doi.org/10.4324/9781315246970-2. See also Ros Pesman, David Walker and Richard White, eds, *The Oxford Book of Australian Travel Writing* (Melbourne: Oxford University Press, 1996); Peter Hulme and Tim Youngs, eds, *The Cambridge Companion to Travel Writing* (Cambridge: Cambridge University Press, 2002), doi.org/10.1017/ccol052178140x; Tim Youngs, ed., *Travel in the Nineteenth Century: Filling the Blank Spaces* (London: Anthem Press, 2006); Carl Thompson, *Travel Writing: The New Critical Idiom* (New York: Routledge, 2011); Tim Youngs, *Cambridge Introduction to Travel Writing* (Cambridge: Cambridge University Press, 2013); Carl Thompson, ed., *The Routledge Companion to Travel Writing* (New York: Routledge, 2016).
3   See Mary Blaine Campbell, 'Travel Writing and Its Theory', in *The Cambridge Companion to Travel Writing*, ed. Peter Hulme and Tim Youngs (Cambridge: Cambridge University Press), 262.
4   Edward Said, *Orientalism* (London: Pantheon Books, 1977), 52.
5   Peter Hulme, *Colonial Encounters: Europe and the Native Caribbean, 1492–1797* (London: Methuen, 1986); Mary Louise Pratt, *Imperial Eyes: Travel Writing and Transculturation* (New York: Routledge, 1992).

The first Europeans who traversed and described the Pacific Ocean in the sixteenth century were influenced by a long tradition of travel accounts with biblical and classical origins. As Neil Rennie demonstrated, popular notions of the Pacific Islands in European literature and mythology can be traced back to Greco-Roman texts and concepts (e.g. Elysium, Atlantis or the Golden Age), evidencing the 'desire of men to locate the imaginary historical past in the real geographical present'.[6] In addition to the more well-known accounts of explorers, the reports of itinerant merchants, pirates, captives, castaways, diplomats and scholars were influential in reshaping European ideals. Their voyages to the Pacific Islands formed part of a broader narrative about the discovery of the 'new world' that, according to Eric Leed, stimulated a 'cultural reorientation' in Renaissance Europe; it shifted the focus away from the traditional centres of Western civilisation (Greece, Rome, Egypt, India and Palestine) to the new-found peripheries. These peripheries 'became the site of cultural origins, in contrast to which Europeans defined themselves and crystallized a cultural self-image', and the information that was produced 'ultimately transformed ancient categories of order'.[7]

In light of these encouraging voyages of discovery outside Europe, this period encapsulates the time when travel writing as a genre began to form. The chronological report emerged as a common format and symbolised a new systematic form of observation among travellers—one that would soon become the primary method for Europeans to investigate and observe the world. The work of English philosopher and scientist Francis Bacon was especially influential in the sixteenth century, as he was one of the first to advocate a scientific methodology for travel that would become increasingly regulated and disciplined in the seventeenth and eighteenth centuries. Discoveries in the Pacific Islands profoundly influenced scientific thinking in Europe, arguably more so than any other continental expeditions at the time. With the drive for colonial competition and expansion in the Pacific, a more precise, scientific and utilitarian form of writing was adopted not only by Pacific explorers and colonial administrators, but also 'ordinary' travellers such as sailors, missionaries and traders.

---

6   Neil Rennie, *Far-Fetched Facts: The Literature of Travel and the Idea of the South Seas* (Oxford: Clarendon Press, 1995), 6.
7   Eric J Leed, *The Mind of the Traveler: From Gilgamesh to Global Tourism* (New York: Basic Books, 1991), 135.

The sixteenth century also witnessed the emergence of tourists within Europe, a new group who travelled for pleasure rather than necessity and who shaped travel writing accordingly. Although pilgrims may also be considered the ancestors of modern tourists, scholars have typically attributed the 'grand tour' as evidence of this shift in the form and content of travel writing. Extending from previous traditions that were established by errant knights and wandering scholars of medieval Europe, the grand tour was a social ritual in which young English male elites travelled Europe along well-worn routes after university to visit the centres of civilisation and engage in sexual encounters. These young elites were often required to keep a journal, which introduced the new philosophical notion that knowledge was rooted in experience and that travel was considered a method of self-improvement.[8] It was not until the late eighteenth and early nineteenth centuries that the emergent middle classes in Europe increasingly engaged in tourism (corresponding to a growth in travel writing), and only in the late nineteenth century that a similar process began to develop in the Pacific Islands. Since these tropical destinations were relatively new and unknown, the ensuing travel accounts were initially valued as a form of education and were widely considered valid contributions to the public record. Yet, when faced with the unknown, European travellers continued to rely on European conventions and traditions to observe and describe the Islands.

The tension between conformity and individuality underscores many travel accounts and is often expressed in the distinction between 'traveller' and 'tourist'. John Urry, Dean McCannell and James Buzard have unpacked the processes of tourism and the 'tourist' label, explaining the gradual development of a distinction between *reactive* tourists who were associated with conventional sightseeing and *proactive* travellers who were considered superior because they followed their own routes rather than the 'beaten track'.[9] A similar distinction emerged in the Pacific in the early twentieth century in response to greater numbers of people travelling in the region recreationally, thus increasing fears of homogenisation among travellers and placing pressure on travel writers to validate and distinguish

---

8 Leed, *The Mind of the Traveler*, 184; James Buzard, 'The Grand Tour and After (1660–1840)', in *The Cambridge Companion to Travel Writing*, ed. Peter Hulme and Tim Young (Cambridge: Cambridge University Press), 37–52.

9 John Urry, *The Tourist Gaze: Leisure and Travel in Contemporary Societies* (London: Sage Publications: 1990); Dean MacCannell, *The Tourist: A New Theory of the Leisure Class* (New York: Schocken Books Inc., 1976); James Buzard, *The Beaten Track: European Tourism, Literature, and the Ways to Culture, 1800–1918* (Oxford: Clarendon Press, 1993).

their accounts from others. These structural processes have since been illuminated by sociological and anthropological approaches, many of which have informed the field of tourism studies by using quantitative methods to test social and cultural theories of change. Although they have been useful for understanding the universal experiences of travel, tourism studies in the Pacific Islands context have tended to concentrate on contemporary trends. They have been criticised for traditionally focusing on static destinations rather than mobilities and for relying on reified notions of tourism rather than for acknowledging complexity.[10] In her work on Hawaiian tourism, Jane Desmond called for 'the need for greater specificity in situating acts of tourist consumption within a wider frame of historical relations between specific groups of consumers and the places and populations they visit'.[11]

The changing nature and purpose of travel over time has complicated attempts to locate and define the narratives that are produced from it, particularly when the literature has so often incorporated fictional elements. The ambiguous relationship between fact and fiction is a common feature of most travel writing and its criticisms; Thompson argued that 'a degree of fictionality is thus inherent in all travel accounts', and White regarded most travel narratives as 'fictions of factual representation'.[12] The Pacific was no exception to the rule—it was torn between popular European imagination and a growing desire to explore and categorise the Islands scientifically.[13] In some cases, the manuscripts of Pacific explorers returning home to Europe were rewritten and embellished to make them more interesting and adventurous. In other cases, a physical journey was not always a prerequisite, and narratives of discovery provided material for philosophers and so-called 'armchair travellers' to adapt. The publication

---

10 Jane C Desmond, 'Afterword: Ambivalence, Ambiguity and the "Wicked Problem" of Pacific Tourist Studies', in *Touring Pacific Cultures*, ed. Kalissa Alexeyeff and John Taylor (Canberra: ANU Press, 2016), 444, doi.org/10.22459/tpc.12.2016.31. See also John K Walton, 'Histories of Tourism', in *The SAGE Handbook of Tourism Studies*, ed. Tazmin Jamal and Mike Robinson (London: Sage Publications, 2009), 115–29, doi.org/10.4135/9780857021076.n7.
11 Jane Desmond, *Staging Tourism: Bodies on Display from Waikiki to Sea World* (Chicago: University of Chicago Press, 1999), xix.
12 Thompson, *Travel Writing*, 28; Hayden White, 'The Fictions of Factual Representation', in *Tropics of Discourse: Essays in cultural criticism* (Baltimore: Publisher, 1978), 121–34.
13 For further discussion of European literature about the Pacific Islands, see Bernard Smith, *European Vision and the South Pacific* (Sydney: Harper & Row, 1985); Bernard Smith, *Imagining the Pacific: In the Wake of the Cook Voyages* (New Haven: Yale University Press, 1992); Rennie, *Far-Fetched Facts*; Vanessa Smith and Rod Edmond, eds, *Islands in History and Representation* (New York: Routledge, 2003); Rod Edmond, *Representing the South Pacific: Colonial Discourse from Cook to Gauguin* (New York: Cambridge University Press, 1997).

of Daniel Defoe's *Robinson Crusoe* (1719) is conventionally regarded as the defining moment of Pacific Island travel writing, as his work stimulated a new interest in adventure and the exotic. Prior to Defoe's publication, literary interest in mythical and exotic islands was mainly utopian and influenced by fictional or satirical works, such as Thomas More's *Utopia* (1516–1519), William Shakespeare's *The Tempest* (1611) and Francis Bacon's *New Atlantis* (1627). The emergence of a new survival literature (the 'Robinsonade') included first-person narratives of shipwrecks, castaways and mutinies that offered the illusion of truth by sometimes being based on real shipwreck narratives, while also incorporating mythical creatures, pygmies and giants.[14] Legitimated by the 'pseudoscience of observation', the heroic figure of the Robinsonade was modified to the form of the gentlemanly naturalist or scientist, and the use of scientific language and detailed observations increasingly featured in fictional works.[15]

Given this entangled web of discourses, it is unsurprising that scholars have been reluctant to pursue travel writing as a reliable source for historical analysis. As Ryota Nishino noted, the dangers with travel writing are that it can easily be dismissed as a 'genre of "pseudos"—pseudo-ethnography, pseudo-biography, pseudo-literary and pseudo-historical' and that, in this dismissal, we lose a more 'textured' appreciation of these genres.[16] Or, as Carl Thompson expressed, much academic discussion of travel writing has tended to focus on critique: 'They regard the form as typically seeking not to reflect or explore contemporary realities, but rather to escape them'.[17] This trend towards critique has overlooked travel writing's potential to inform our understanding of mobility as a central force in historical transformations. Cultural histories of travel—notably those by Jas Elsner, Joan-Pau Rubiés and Eric Leed—have identified global trends and patterns to expose the cultural paradigms that travel writing has built and challenged over time. Large-scale studies of travel in the African and Asian regions also highlight similarities in the experiences of colonial

---

14   Chris Ballard, 'The Art of Encounter: Verisimilitude in the Imaginary Exploration of Interior New Guinea, 1725–1876', in *Oceanic Encounters: Exchange, Desire, Violence*, ed. Margaret Jolly (Canberra: ANU E Press, 2009), 224, doi.org/10.22459/oe.07.2009.08.
15   Holland and Huggan, *Tourists with Typewriters,* 24; Pratt, *Imperial Eyes*, 26.
16   Ryota Nishino, 'The Self-Promotion of a Maverick Travel Writer: Suzuki Tsunenori and His Southern Pacific Islands Travelogue, *Nanyō tanken jikki*', *Studies in Travel Writing* 20, no. 4 (2016): 379, doi.org/10.1080/13645145.2016.1264356.
17   Thompson, *Travel Writing*, 5.

travellers.[18] In the Pacific, Ngaire Douglas's *They Came for Savages* (1996) is one of the few histories of tourism that refocuses on tourism's origins in the colonial period.[19] Although the subfields of transportation and technology history occasionally draw on travel writing as a source, it is the social histories of colonialism and empire that have greatly benefited from acknowledging these mobilities—and these subfields now present imperialism more accurately as a contested and fluid network rather than a static and monolithic system. Historian Tony Ballantyne suggested that 'webs of empire' is a more suitable and integrative notion of colonialism that also acknowledges the imperial connections between multiple nodes and localised encounters that existed outside the metropole.[20] Nicholas Thomas advocated a similar approach by identifying colonialism as a cultural process that was often disputed and conflicted; he noted that travel reinforces colonialism at the same time that it is 'an enlarging and liberating process that unsettles the confidence of authority'.[21] Travel writing is thus increasingly identified as a vehicle for colonialism and as a highly contested and contradictory space in which European travellers, authors and audiences negotiated colonial legacies. The same argument can be applied to individual travellers who cannot always be compartmentalised into convenient categories and whose intentions were not always exploitative.

Although historians have more frequently discussed the subject of travel in the Pacific Islands in recent years, none have made travel writing their primary focus. Conversely, this book's focus on a specific corpus of Australian travel writing locates authors and their texts within certain historical contexts and discourses and compares key experiences in the hope of revealing underlying issues. It does not concern itself with

---

18 Jas Elsner and Joan-Pau Rubiés, *Voyages and Visions: Towards a Cultural History of Travel* (London: Reaktion Books, 1999); Leed, *The Mind of the Traveler*. See also Joan-Pau Rubiés, 'Travel Writing as a Genre: Facts, Fictions and the Invention of a Scientific Discourse in Early Modern Europe', *Journeys* 1, nos 1–2 (2000): 5–35, doi.org/10.3167/146526000782488036; Johannes Fabian, *Out of Our Minds: Reason and Madness in the Exploration of Central Africa* (Berkeley, CA: University of California Press, 2000), doi.org/10.1525/california/9780520221222.001.0001; Steve Clark and Paul Smethurst, eds, *Asian Crossings: Travel Writing on China, Japan and Southeast Asia* (Hong Kong: Hong Kong University Press, 2008).
19 Ngaire Douglas, *They Came for Savages: 100 Years of Tourism in Melanesia* (Lismore: Southern Cross University Press, 1996); Ngaire Douglas and Norman Douglas, 'P and O's Pacific', *Journal of Tourism Studies* 7, no. 2 (1996): 2–14.
20 Tony Ballantyne, *Webs of Empire: Locating New Zealand's Colonial Past* (Wellington: UBC Press, 2012).
21 Nicholas Thomas, *Colonialism's Culture: Anthropology, Travel, and Government* (Princeton: Princeton University Press, 1994), 5.

the achievements or failings of individual writers, nor with providing a comprehensive history of Australian tourism or colonialism in the Pacific. The discipline of history is well placed to situate travel writing more meaningfully within the contexts in which it arises, in which the lives and experiences of travel writers are connected to broader trends and patterns over time. A historical approach to travel writing offers a suitable compromise between the universal experiences of travel that sociologists and anthropologists attempt to define and the specific textual analysis of a work and its author that is espoused by literature studies. Such an approach recognises that travellers, in the act of writing, also seek to maintain a balance between past and present, between the 'desire to come to terms with a complex world in transformation and its nostalgic need to restore the imaginary site of a "simpler" past'.[22] Eric Leed described this as a 'tendency of modern Europeans to equate differences in space with differences in time—to "historicize"'.[23] If we consider travel writing a form of memory through which people construct and legitimise cultural identity, then history is apropos to studying these cultural interactions. As Jeannette Mageo described it:

> Too often cultural identity is conceived as flat—as an ideological presentation of culture. When one re-examines cultural identity in light of memory, however, these identities appear as sites of transit between layers of historical experience.[24]

These tensions between past and present, fact and fiction, and individual and collective travel experience are an inherent part of travel writing and will thus be a constant theme throughout this book. Studying Australia, as a periphery of empire and as an emerging colonial power, offers the opportunity to examine some of these ambiguities and complexities of travel and the European colonial experience in a new light.

Australian Travel Writing

The emergence of travel writing in Australia is significant because travel has been a pivotal force in shaping the continent's history. The *Oxford Handbook of Australian Travel Writing* noted that 'travel has always been

---

22   Holland and Huggan, *Tourists with Typewriters*, 24.
23   Leed, *The Mind of the Traveler*, 172.
24   Jeannette Mageo, ed., *Cultural Memory: Reconfiguring History and Identity in the Postcolonial Pacific* (Honolulu: University of Hawai'i Press, 2001), 2, doi.org/10.1515/9780824841874.

central to the experience of living in Australia'.²⁵ Post-structuralist and postcolonial studies that encourage an exploration of cultural transmission, flexible identity, mobility and dissolving borders are especially relevant to Australians, whose experiences of travel have often been shaped by an ambiguous sense of place. From the first inhabitants of the continent to its more recent European colonisers, Australians have been defined by journeys of migration and are distinguished by their exceptional mobility. In literature, Australians idealised the explorer and the wanderer, acknowledging a proud maritime heritage and celebrating the pioneers of the inland frontier.²⁶

Although Australian historiography has been previously criticised as isolationist, Australian historians have slowly adopted a more regional focus that acknowledges the international encounters and exchanges that shaped the country, including those connections with the Pacific Islands.²⁷ Building on earlier political and economic histories of Australia's relationship with the Pacific Islands,²⁸ these regional or 'transnational' histories have been useful in highlighting the crucial role that the Pacific Islands played in the development of an Australian cultural identity. Similar conclusions have been made by scholars who have explored Australian connections with

---

25   Pesman, Walker and White, *The Oxford Book of Australian Travel Writing*, ix.
26   Pesman, Walker and White, *The Oxford Book of Australian Travel Writing*, xii; Richard White, 'Travel, Writing and Australia', *Studies in Travel Writing* 11, no. 1 (2007): 6, 10, doi.org/10.1080/13 645145.2007.9634816.
27   Donald Denoon, 'The Isolation of Australian History', *Australian Historical Studies*, 22, no. 87 (1986): 252–60, doi.org/10.1080/10314618608595747; Donald Denoon, Philippa Mein-Smith and Marivic Wyndham, *A History of Australia, New Zealand and the Pacific* (Oxford: Wiley, 2000); Donald Denoon, 'Re-Membering Australasia: A Repressed Memory', *Australian Historical Studies*, 34, no. 122 (2003): 290–304, doi.org/10.1080/10314610308596256; Marilyn Lake, 'Colonial Australia and the Asia-Pacific Region', in *The Cambridge History of Australia*, ed. Alison Bashford and Stuart Macintyre (Port Melbourne: Cambridge University Press, 2015), 535–59, doi.org/10.1017/cho9781107445758.025. See also the first seven articles from *Australian Historical Studies* 46, vol. 3 (2015): 337–439.
28   Clinton Hartley Grattan, *The Southwest Pacific Since 1900, A Modern History: Australia, New Zealand, the Islands, Antarctica* (Ann Arbor: University of Michigan Press, 1963); William Roger Louis and William S Livingston, *Australia, New Zealand and the Pacific Islands since the First World War* (Austin: University of Texas Press, 1979); Roger C Thompson, *Australian Imperialism in the Pacific: The Expansionist Era, 1820–920* (Carlton: Melbourne University Press, 1980); Roger Thompson, *Australia and the Pacific Islands in the Twentieth Century* (Melbourne: Australian Scholarly Publishing, 1998).

Asia.²⁹ Richard White's work was crucial in this cultural turn because it encouraged an examination of how collective and individual identities of Australians are shaped by travel.³⁰ The significance of mobility was well known to Pacific historians—many of whom trained in the first school of Pacific history that was established in Australia in the 1960s and who continued to study the early colonial contacts that constituted 'Australia's Pacific Frontier'. It resonated with Pacific historians such as Donald Denoon, who argued that 'the essence and the implications of many Australian ideas became manifest *only* [his emphasis] in those extreme situations which Australians encountered abroad'.³¹

Of course, national identity is an elusive and fluid concept that historians find challenging to articulate. In her review of travel writing theory, Mary Blaine Campbell noted that travel literature was significant not only for highlighting multiple different views that challenged conventional or official narratives but also for revising theoretical approaches that have been based on 'locatable cultures, bounded nations, and the imperial past'.³² This is especially true for colonial Australia prior to federation, as demonstrated by the maritime histories of Frances Steel, Cindy McCreery and Kirsten McKenzie. Steel's history of the Union Steamship Company in New Zealand extended beyond conventional business histories of shipping to explore the problems of national identity and colonial power in light of the regional connections that were facilitated by steamships in the Pacific. This was an approach that consciously sought to avoid the 'conceptual and spatial narrowing' of a nationalist history and to decentre

---

29   For more information on Australia's relationship with Asia, see Neville Meaney, *The Search for Security in the Pacific 1901–1914* (Sydney: Sydney University Press, 1976); Neville Meaney, *Australia and the Wider World: A Documentary History from the 1870s to the 1970s* (Melbourne: Longman Cheshire, 1985); David Walker, Julia Horne and Adrian Vickers, eds, *Australian Perceptions of Asia* (Kensington: UNSW Press, 1990), 65–79; Alison Broinowski, *The Yellow Lady: Australian Impressions of Asia* (Melbourne: Oxford University Press, 1992); David Walker and Agnieszka Sobocinska, eds, *Australia's Asia: From Yellow Peril to Asian Century* (Crawley: UWA Publishing, 2012); Agnieszka Sobocinska, *Visiting the Neighbours: Australians in Asia* (Sydney: NewSouth Publishing, 2014); Agnieszka Sobocinska, 'Innocence Lost and Paradise Regained: Tourism to Bali and Australian Perceptions of Asia', *History Australia* 8, no. 2 (2011): 199–222, doi.org/10.1080/14490854.2011.11668380.
30   Richard White, *Inventing Australia: Images and Identity, 1688–1980* (Sydney: Allen & Unwin, 1981); Richard White, *On Holidays: A History of Getting Away in Australia* (North Melbourne: Pluto Press, 2005); White, 'Travel, Writing and Australia', 1–14; Richard White, 'Time Travel: Australian Tourists and Britain's Past', *Portal* 10, no. 1 (2013): 1–25.
31   John MR Young, *Australia's Pacific Frontier: Economic and Cultural Expansion into the Pacific: 1795–1885* (Melbourne: Cassell Australia, 1967); Denoon, 'The Isolation of Australian History', 258.
32   Campbell, 'Travel Writing and Its Theory', 262.

imperial history.³³ Although this book shares many similarities with Steel's subject matter and recognises the contested, transnational space in which Australians were moving, it makes the individual travellers its central focus, rather than the ships that carried them. These 'ordinary' travellers, as depicted by the work of Agniescka Sobocinska in her study of Australians in Asia, highlight 'the ways in which personal experience intersected with broader political patterns'.³⁴

Australian accounts are distinct in a broader travel writing context because they offer insights from the periphery of empire. Studies of colonisation in the Pacific Islands have tended to focus on how the colonised were represented by the colonisers, with little recognition of how the colonisers imagined themselves as conforming to this racial and cultural hierarchy.³⁵ This is the point at which Australians, simultaneously coloniser and colonised, can offer a more nuanced perspective of colonialism and the racial hierarchies that underpin it. This is especially significant in terms of the 'White Australia' policy—a term referring to a series of immigration and quarantine legislation that was introduced by the national government from 1901 and that lasted until the mid-twentieth century. One of the first policies of its kind in the world, it formally enshrined the superiority of white Australians and implemented protective measures that were designed to promote racial segregation.³⁶ The undesirability of Asian immigration was an important political motivation at the time. Writing in 1912, Australian journalist Frank Fox warned that 'Australia is at once the fortress which the White Race has thinly garrisoned against an Asiatic advance southward, and the most tempting prize to inspire the Asiatic to that advance'.³⁷ Race was a persistent underlying theme in Australian travel writing of this period, as revealed in Sobocinska's study of Australian travellers to Asia; Australians believed that they were inferior to the British at home, yet they were considered Europeans and

---

33   Frances Steel, 'Oceania under Steam: Maritime Cultures, Colonial Histories 1870s–1910s' (PhD thesis, Australian National University, 2007), 22; Frances Steel, *Oceania under Steam: Sea Transport and the Cultures of Colonialism, c. 1870–1914* (Manchester: Manchester University Press, 2011); Cindy McCreery and Kirsten McKenzie, 'The Australian Colonies in a Maritime World', in *The Cambridge History of Australia*, ed. Alison Bashford and Stuart Macintyre (Port Melbourne: Cambridge University Press, 2015), 560–84, doi.org/10.1017/cho9781107445758.026.
34   Sobocinska, *Visiting the Neighbours*, 2.
35   Nicholas Thomas and Richard Eves, *Bad Colonists—The South Seas Letters of Vernon Lee Walker & Louis Becke* (Durham: Duke University Press, 1999), 79.
36   Marilyn Lake, 'The Australian Dream of an Island Empire: Race, Reputation and Resistance', *Australian Historical Studies* 46, no. 3 (2015): 410–24, doi.org/10.1080/1031461x.2015.1075222.
37   Frank Fox, *Problems of the Pacific* (London: Williams & Norgate, 1912), 107.

were reassured of their white superiority abroad.[38] Similar tensions and experiences can be found in accounts of the Pacific Islands, with travel accounts confirming and contradicting notions of racial superiority and progress.

The benefits of studying the periphery perspective also apply to the understanding of class and gender. Studies of the Australian version of the grand tour (often framed as Australians' return to their ancestral origins in Europe) have revealed that women travelled as frequently as men, unlike the conventional European tradition, and that travel was not just for the aristocracy, but for all classes.[39] Geographically far from Europe, the Australian and Pacific colonies were consequently less restricted by social requirements or expectations, so they attracted a diverse group of travellers.[40] Of the 81 travel writers whose ages are known, 16 were in their 20s, 21 were in their 30s, 17 in their 40s, 14 in their 50s and 12 were older than 60 years. Travellers were also diverse in occupation: they were businessmen, politicians, academics, journalists, artists, opportunists, soldiers, seamen, traders and teachers. 'Opportunists'—a term used here to describe wanderers without any particular aim, or those travelling in search of employment or residence—constituted the highest proportion of travel writers in this book's study (with 18 in total, followed by journalists, who numbered 12). Travel accounts reveal that travellers to the Islands were not restricted to a specific class or social group, and the relative isolation of the region did not discourage those with limited means. In fact, the Pacific was often considered a land of opportunity for those seeking to climb the social ladder. Male travel writers may have outnumbered their female counterparts in the Pacific Islands (they represented over 80 per cent), but it is unclear whether this bias reflects travel patterns in general or the nature of the publishing industry at the time. For certain, the development of trans-Pacific cruises rendered travel much safer and more accessible to a greater number of female travellers. The few female

---

38   Sobocinska, *Visiting the Neighbours*, 28.
39   Ros Pesman, *Duty Free: Australian Women Abroad* (Melbourne: Oxford University Press, 1996); Anne Rees, 'Ellis Island in the Pacific: Encountering America in Hawai'i, 1920s–1950s' (paper presented at the Travel, The Middlebrow Imagination, Australasia-Pacific 1918–50 Colloquium, James Cook University, Queensland, 29 November 2013); Angela Woollacott, '"All This Is the Empire, I Told Myself": Australian Women's Voyages "Home" and the Articulation of Colonial Whiteness', *The American Historical Review* 102, no. 4 (1997): 1003–29, doi.org/10.2307/2170627; Angela Woollacott, *To Try Her Fortune in London: Australian Women, Colonialism, and Modernity* (New York: Oxford University Press, 2001); Laura Olcelli, *Questions of Authority: Italian and Australian Travel Narratives of the Long Nineteenth Century* (New York: Routledge, 2018), doi.org/10.4324/9780203709719.
40   Penny Russell, *Savage or Civilised?: Manners in Colonial Australia* (Sydney: UNSW Press, 2010).

travel accounts that do exist confirm that Australian women in the Pacific were resilient and intrepid travellers. This further evidences the need for a more nuanced understanding of Australian travellers—one that does not bind them to a specific group or category.

The Australian perspective of the Pacific changed considerably between c. 1880 and 1941, which must be considered in the context of changing patterns of mobility, political and economic changes in the Pacific and Australia, and cultural shifts in literature and publishing. Some travel writing accounts were produced by colonial Australians before 1880, but they were intermittent and limited in scale compared to those written after the 1880s, when the Australian colonies' interest in the Pacific Islands peaked. Three general phases can be discerned in this 60-year period, though they often overlap.

The few accounts that were written in the late nineteenth century continued to exhibit European myths and stereotypes of a romanticised and alluring Pacific, in which the Islands were appropriated as settings for fantastical tales of savagery and adventure. Travel was irregular and intermittent at this time, so these accounts were influential sources of information to the Australian colonial reader, even if they relied on stereotypes. Deeply entrenched tropes of the 'noble savage' and 'ignoble savage' persisted well into the early twentieth century, influencing public opinion and underscoring domestic and regional issues such as the Queensland labour trade and the White Australia policy.

Travel writing increased dramatically from the 1890s to 1914, encouraged by economic prosperity in Australia, the growth of publishing, steamship and tourism industries, and a national self-confidence and optimism that followed the federation of the colonies in 1901. Travellers from the Australian continent in the decades before and after Federation began to identify themselves as being distinct from their European origins. Possessing their own ideological baggage regarding a distinctively Australian form of masculinity, progress, purity and innocence, these travellers began to write accounts that were distinct from conventional European observations. They were also aware of the colonial rivalries in the region since the late nineteenth century, their descriptions often containing judgements regarding the successes or failures of colonial rule and, in some cases, the potential benefits of a new Australian imperialism.

The bulk of Australian travel writing was produced during the interwar period that followed World War I. Tourism industries responded to the new demand for travel in, and through, the Pacific Islands and increasingly more travellers produced travel accounts, in which they attempted to distinguish themselves in a competitive commercial market. Some of the accounts began to question previously held assumptions about the Pacific and Australia's role within the region. These accounts evidence the gradual shift away from conventional stereotypes that emphasised Islander inferiority and savagery to a more humanistic identification with them. This change may represent a 'cultural maturity' in Australian literature that was prompted by the massive social and economic upheaval after World War I and Australia's newly acquired mandates in the Pacific.[41] A close study of travel writing provides additional evidence of a general weariness of exaggerated and overused Pacific tropes, compounded by the proliferation of travellers whose experiences did not match their expectations. Travel writers who challenged conventional perspectives of the Pacific were still a minority by 1941, but their critical attitude would reappear with greater frequency in subsequent decades. The beginning of the Pacific War in 1941 restricted Australian mobility in the region and the construction of island airstrips facilitated the growth of air transportation after the war, which permanently changed subsequent Australian travel to the region. After 1945, popular literature about the Pacific increasingly focused on war themes, with sites of conflict becoming memorials and tourist attractions.

Sources and Categories

Strict definitions of travel writing are subjective and problematic, and they risk excluding valuable sources. A historical approach to travel writing should be inclusive and flexible, which is why this book prefers the 'guiding principle' proposed by Tim Youngs:

> Travel writing consists of predominantly factual, first-person prose accounts of travels that have been undertaken by the author–narrator. It includes discussion of works that some may regard as genres in their own right … but it distinguishes these from other types of narrative in which travel is narrated by a third party or is imagined.[42]

---

41   Andrew Hassam, *Through Australian Eyes: Colonial Perceptions of Imperial Britain* (Carlton: Sussex Academic Press, 2000), 167.
42   Youngs, *Cambridge Introduction to Travel Writing*, 3.

Such a broad approach is important because how texts are read has changed over time, as is reflected in the different catalogues of archives and libraries in Australia, New Zealand and Fiji that were consulted during research. Such texts included published memoirs, autobiographies, travelogues and unpublished accounts (e.g. letters, diaries, notebooks and draft manuscripts). The classification of texts was not always clear—some were clearly labelled by the authors as 'notes', 'observations' or 'accounts' of travel, while others were described as 'reminiscences', 'musings', 'opinions', 'reflections', 'confessions' or 'memories'. Interested only in the personal and 'ordinary' experiences of travel, I avoided texts that were written by authors with a vested interest (e.g. missionaries, scientific researchers and government officials) or by authors who had resided in the Islands for longer than six months. Other travel narratives were also scattered throughout guidebooks, newspapers, travel magazines and encyclopaedic and educational materials that are too numerous to count.

Determining who was 'Australian' was equally problematic, given that a sense of distinctive Australian identity was not clearly articulated between 1880 and 1941 and that travellers did not often explicitly describe themselves as 'Australian' in their texts. Mobility often prompted many travellers to avoid national labels, instead preferring to present themselves as romantic and heroic wanderers or explorers and using terms such as 'globetrotter', 'vagabond', 'wayfarer', 'sundowner', 'beachcomber', 'shell-back', 'troubadour' and 'pilgrim'. Several bibliographies and dictionaries of Australian literature provide some guidance in this regard, though they have different criteria.[43] The crucial criterion in this book is whether Australia was the writer's natural comparison or reference point. Of course, blurred lines exist, especially given that more emphasis was placed on being Anglo-Saxon than on being British or Australian during most of the nineteenth century. Before 1871, over half the Australian population was born elsewhere and by 1901, 18 per cent of Australians in

---

43   In fact, a body of 'Australian literature' was not identified until 1927, when Sir John Quick published *A Classified Catalogue of Books and Writing by Australian Writers*. See John Arnold and John Hay, eds, *The Bibliography of Australian Literature* (St Lucia: Australian Scholarly Publishing, 2001); Terri McCormack et al., eds, *Annotated Bibliography of Australian Overseas Travel Writing, 1830 to 1970* (Canberra: ALIA Press, 1996); Edmund Morris Miller, *Australian Literature from Its Beginnings to 1935: A Descriptive and Bibliographical Survey of Books by Australian Authors in Poetry, Drama, Fiction, Criticism and Anthology with Subsidiary Entries to 1938* (Melbourne: Melbourne University Press, 1940). Online databases include the *Australian Dictionary of Biography*, National Centre of Biography, The Australian National University, adb.anu.edu.au; and *AUSTLIT*, University of Queensland, www.austlit.edu.au.

the census were born in the United Kingdom (UK).[44] Some travellers thus referred to themselves as 'British', 'Britisher', 'Colonial' and 'Australasian' to express a shared colonial identity under the British empire. Due to this colonial legacy, national identity continued to be ambiguous and contested in the early twentieth century. Passports did not distinguish between the two nationalities until 1949, and Australians' upbringing and education prepared them to believe Britain was 'home', with travellers who visited Europe finding their British identity being strengthened (as well as their own Australian identity).[45]

Between c. 1880 and 1941, approximately 130 travel accounts about the Pacific Islands were produced by 'Australian' authors. This is only an approximation due to the ambiguities within the texts themselves, which sometimes obscured the texts' authorship, nationality and dates of travel or publication. These accounts represent just over 10 per cent of the 1,000 travel books that were written by 'Australians' between 1830 and 1970.[46] Of the 130 sources that were examined, 23 were 'personal recollections'—that is, they were written by travellers who did not travel on a steamship tour, but who sailed their own vessels or who visited the Islands for a purpose other than tourism. Their accounts usually had more detailed descriptions of the Islands (and of the authors themselves) compared to the 65 'tourist recollections' that contained momentary observations. There were 18 memoirs and autobiographies, and 18 texts were written for a specific purpose (though often disguised as travelogues): personal treatises, promotional material commissioned by governments or businesses and reports to specific communities or organisations at home. There were 20 unpublished materials, including the diaries of businessmen, Australian naval seamen, missionaries' wives, as well as the logbooks of traders and sailors and other travel ephemera (e.g. scrapbooks, postcards and letters).

The study of this corpus as a whole has never been undertaken before. Instead, more general bibliographies of Australian literature or non-indigenous literature about the Pacific Islands were written; rarely have

---

44 White, *Inventing Australia*, 47–8; 'A Snapshot of Australia, 1901', Australian Bureau of Statistics, www.abs.gov.au/websitedbs/D3110124.NSF/24e5997b9bf2ef35ca2567fb00299c59/c4abd1fac53e3df5ca256bd8001883ec!OpenDocument.
45 Hassam, *Through Australian Eyes*, 15.
46 McCormack et al., *Annotated Bibliography of Australian Overseas Travel Writing*.

scholars considered Australian travellers a collective group.[47] Popular individual Australian travellers such as Louis Becke, Frank Clune, Beatrice Grimshaw, Frank Hurley and Ion Llewellyn Idriess have thus far occupied the attention of scholars.

The vast archives of photographs and films related to the Pacific Islands were also an important feature of many travel writing accounts. Images were no longer a luxury by the 1900s; they not only featured in monographs, but were also reproduced in photo albums, encyclopaedias, guidebooks, magazines, newspapers, stamps and postcards, and were presented at exhibits, museums and lantern shows. Up until the 1930s—after which camera technology became more accessible—few travellers took their own photographs. Popular images were instead reproduced and widely circulated, such as the works of Australian artist Norman Hardy and those of Australian photographers John Watt Beattie, Frank Hurley, John William Lindt and Thomas McMahon. As such, reprints often reduced the quality and resolution of the original photographs, and authors could misappropriate images for their own purposes. As the cinema industry developed from the early 1900s, several Australians were influential in the production of cinematic works as writers, actors, actresses and directors. Notable Australian contributors to cinema include Charles Chauvel (director), Errol Flynn (actor and author), Beatrice Grimshaw (author), Frank Hurley (director), Annette Kellerman (actress and author) and Raymond Longford (director). Amateur films were even taken aboard cruise ships by travellers in the 1920s—two of which are currently preserved at the National Film and Sound Archive of Australia.[48] American films dominated the commercial market, preferring Hawai'i as an ideal location. The visual imagery of the Pacific reinforced and contributed to the persistent tropes about the Pacific Islands, which are discussed in the following chapters. Although the proliferation of images, both static and moving, did not wholly displace travel writing, it did alter the market for travel literature—in some cases even subordinating travel writing as

---

47 The exceptions to this include McCormack et al., *Annotated Bibliography of Australian Overseas Travel Writing*; Pesman, Walker and White, *The Oxford Book of Australian Travel Writing*; Hank Nelson, 'Lives Told: Australians in Papua and New Guinea', in *Telling Pacific Lives: Prisms of Process*, ed. Brij V Lal and Vicki Luker (Canberra: ANU E Press, 2008), 243–76, doi.org/10.22459/tpl.06.2008.18.
48 Title #64121 *[Pacific Islands Leg of Boat Trip to U.S.; Sydney to Los Angeles by Boat]*, (National Film and Sound Archive of Australia: c. 1927), home movie; Title #37863 *[New Zealand, Pacific Island and Canadian? Holiday]* (National Film and Sound Archive of Australia: c. 1928), home movie.

a form of communication that was less 'real'. Subsequent travel writing had no choice but to incorporate, and respond to, this new collection of images that was perpetuating certain tropes about the Islands.

The proliferation of texts and images regarding travel in the Pacific presents a formidable challenge to those wishing to study and understand this period in history. It would be futile to try and provide a complete list of every piece of travel writing, or to offer a conclusive analysis of every Australian who lived in, or travelled through, the Pacific Islands. Their lives were often fragmented and intermittent, and the evidence they left behind reflected this accordingly. Instead, these travel accounts have been read as a collective so that general trends in Australian representations of the Pacific Islands can be discerned, and the momentary glimpses that individual travellers provide highlight the key themes and issues that shaped Australian notions about the region. Like many of the texts that these Australians wrote, the chapters in this book are arranged thematically. They signpost a set of themes that persisted in Australian travel writing from c. 1880 to 1941 and question how these themes changed over time and why individual Australian travellers chose to reinforce or undermine them.

In some cases, these themes are located within a specific location or region. The following chapter situates Australia within this complex region of diverse indigenous peoples and mutable colonial networks. It explores the fluid geographical boundaries and ambiguous national identities found within the Pacific and considers the changing uses and meanings of terms such as 'South Seas', 'Australasia', 'Melanesia' and 'Polynesia'. These terms are useful for situating the Australian continent within the Pacific region, as well as for acknowledging Australia's historic maritime connections to the Pacific. Understanding these terms is also important for determining who was an 'Australian' travel writer and for understanding how 'Australians' identified themselves in relation to others.

Chapter 2 charts the rise of steamship travel and Pacific Islands tourism, as well as the effect that this rise had on the individual experiences of travel and the Islands. It examines the processes of travel—the excited anticipation, disappointed realisation and remembered nostalgia—as Australian travellers read, observed and wrote about the Pacific Islands. As steamship companies grew in size, trading operations expanded from cargo to passengers, and tourism became an increasingly viable source of revenue by the early 1900s. Islands responded to the new influx of visitors, and the influence of tourism became visible in stopover destinations such as Suva, Papeete, Apia, Pago Pago, Honolulu and Nuku'alofa. Travel accounts describe life aboard these modern ships as new communities were temporarily created, with the experience of cruising shaping travellers' expectations and impressions of the Pacific Islands. The voyage culminated with the moment of first arrival, a point on which travel accounts often focused, describing the inevitable clash of expectation and reality. As the Islands became increasingly consumed by the 'tourist gaze' in the 1920s and 1930s, travel accounts grappled with the commercialism and popularism of travel, with many choosing to reject the 'tourist' label because it contradicted the values of adventure and exploration that were traditionally associated with the Pacific.

These popular ideals were frequently associated with Polynesia—a region historically imagined by Europeans as utopian and romantic. Chapter 3 considers the Polynesian ideal and its sustained use by Australian travellers throughout the early twentieth century. For those Australians who sought escape and freedom, Polynesia was the preferred choice; it was enshrined as alluring, available, feminine, pure and idyllic. Australian representations specifically focused on Tahiti and remained relatively unchanged from 1880 to 1941, despite the increasing number of travellers who expressed disappointment with the sought-after paradise that had been tarnished by European residents, tourists and modernisation. Rather than deconstructing the problematic trope, representations of Tahitian fragility and corruption only enhanced Tahiti's desirability, and its geographical isolation from Australia facilitated the continuation of European myths and romanticisms. The accounts of those Australian idealists and escapists who chased the utopian lifestyle in Tahiti reveal the limitations of the Polynesian ideal—namely the difficulties of interracial romance and of abandoning 'civilisation', as well as the role that gender played in shaping experiences of travel in the Pacific.

In contrast to Polynesian femininity was Melanesian masculinity—specifically the Islander 'savage' that was a persistent and complex trope in Australian travel writing. Chapter 4 tests the savage–civilised dichotomy as it was applied by Australian travellers to Melanesia, identifying four perceived traits of the savage—the bestial, infantile, primordial and cannibal—and revealing how these were modified and adapted over time. Popular notions of the savage were influenced by the representations of those involved in the Queensland labour trade who emphasised the brutality of the savage until the early 1900s; by the missionaries who stressed childlike characteristics to further their evangelising goals; and by the tourists who tolerated the savage in their search for an idealised, natural primitivism. Representations of the Islander cannibal were consistent throughout the first half of the twentieth century, albeit increasingly formulaic and commodified over time. The changing emphasis on certain traits of the savage, those that shifted the category away from the barbaric image portrayed in adventure fiction and pioneering accounts, suggest that Australian representations of the savage softened over time as travellers expressed an awareness of the category's contested nature.

Despite the dominance of the savage trope, the Pacific also presented opportunities for employment and investment. Chapter 5 focuses on the commercial motivations of travel writers and discusses the difference between emotive travel impressions and accounts written by those with vested interests in the Pacific (e.g. to evangelise, propagandise, make an official report or substantiate a scholarly theory). The economic idealisation of the Pacific Islands was a key component of travel writing, symbolised by the romantic figure of the 'enterprising Australian' who was based on nineteenth-century tales of traders, overseers and miners in the Pacific. Australian travellers contributed to a narrative that imagined the Pacific Islands as a region for Australian investment and profit, and they negotiated the disjuncture between the romanticised Pacific trader/planter and the stark realities of making a living in the Islands.

Commercial endeavours in Melanesia also encountered French colonial expansionism in the Islands of New Caledonia and the New Hebrides. Chapter 6 discusses how both Island groups were the subject of intense debate in Australia before World War I, which formed an integral part of the Australian Federation movement and shaped early Australian perceptions of the Pacific Islands. These island groups were distinct from other French possessed lands in the eastern Pacific, with their proximity to the Australian coast driving alarmist public sentiment. New Caledonia was chiefly known for its convicts and violent conflicts with Islanders, while descriptions of the New Hebrides were characterised by uncertainty and confusion. Although concern about the French annexation of New Caledonia subsided after World War I, the British and French governments' shared custodianship of the New Hebrides continued to stimulate public debate throughout the 1920s and 1930s.

Chapter 7 traces the genealogy of 'scientific' racial theories and how Australian travellers used these theories in their representations of the Pacific Islands—particularly their judgements regarding the perceived progress and stasis of particular places and peoples. Racial theory was a persistent undercurrent in Australian travel writing that informed popular notions about disease, depopulation and ethnic diversity in the Pacific. Australians expressed concern about disease and the assumed dangers of a tropical environment; they commented on the alleged depopulation and degradation of Pacific Islanders (and queried the role of Australians in protecting and civilising); and they questioned the presence of other races in the Pacific (especially Indian, Chinese and Japanese peoples). Travel provided opportunities for face-to-face encounters that challenged assumptions of the passive and primitive Islander, as well as drew attention to the diverse racial makeup of the Pacific. It also fuelled growing speculation regarding the superiority of Australian civilising agents and their role in the development of the Pacific Islands.

The questioning of popular stereotypes and preconceptions is ever present in travel writing—it is an inevitable product of the tension between the individual traveller and travellers as a collective group. Yet the Australian experience of travel in the Pacific is a topic that has not been sufficiently explored. It can offer a perspective from the periphery that counters dominant European narratives, as well as enriches our understanding of how Australia expanded its presence in the region. The risk of generalisation when drawing together a diverse collection of travel accounts about a vast geographical area over a long period is far outweighed by the valuable insights that are garnered—insights that reveal how ordinary Australians understood concepts such as science, race, gender, commerce, nation, empire and mobility as they were applied to the Pacific Islands. Ultimately, this discussion is rooted in the accounts of individual travellers. From these individual reflections, impressions and glimpses of the Pacific Islands, historians can make connections to broader historical themes and issues and better inform and expand our understanding of Australia's relationship with the Pacific Islands.

This diversity can also be applied to Australian authors and the islands they visited. Australians were not a uniform set of travellers—they carried their own ideological baggage with them, influenced differently by their own backgrounds and upbringings, education, gender, class, religious and political affiliations, professions and different motives for travel. Just as this book displaces the formulaic stereotypes of Pacific Islanders, it also displaces a specific Australian type. Regional Australian diversity among the different colonies, states and towns shaped travellers' impressions of the Pacific, as well as influenced how readers responded to travel literature. Ultimately, individual Australians forged their own paths, even when travelling along others more well-worn. For this reason, it is important to recognise how Australians in the past perceived the Pacific Islands with their own eyes.

1

Fluid Boundaries and Ambiguous Identities

> At Suva you pass from Polynesia into Melanesia and into the Australasian sphere of influence. The Fijis are ruled from London, but one begins to be aware of Sydney and Wellington west and south.[1]

Australia's place in the region has changed over time. In the 1880s, it was part of a collection of British colonies referred to generically as the 'antipodes' or 'Australasia'. In 1912, an Australian shipping company portrayed the country as 'the greatest of the South Sea Islands, the centre around which the smaller constellations are scattered'.[2] By 1942, an Australian journalist described the Pacific Islands in the quotation above in terms of a collection of 'spheres of influence'. This latter description may more accurately conceptualise the fluid political and cultural boundaries within the Pacific—boundaries with spheres of influence radiating from specific Islands and Island groups, from villages and towns, from trading posts and missionary stations, and from traditional political centres and colonial administrative nodes. These spheres of influence shaped the routes and experiences of the travellers who crossed them, and transnationalism was tied to the specific political identification with these Islands. In this ambiguous and contested geographical region, travel writing can indicate to us the changing meanings and uses of terms. This is ultimately necessary for understanding how travellers conceived the world beyond their own, a world to which they compared and defined themselves.

---

1 Paul McGuire, *Westward the Course: The New World of Oceania* (Melbourne: Oxford University Press, 1942), 59.
2 Burns, Philp & Company, Limited, *Picturesque Travel*, no. 2 (1912), 54.

Most travellers who embarked on their voyages to the Pacific Islands used terms such as 'South Seas', 'South Pacific', 'Polynesia', 'Melanesia' and 'Australasia' to describe their routes and destinations. These general terms were the products of literary fiction and scientific classifications, variously appropriated and misappropriated by travellers for different purposes and contexts. The preference for these generalised descriptors instead of specific Island names and cultures reflects the ambiguous nature of European geographical knowledge of the Pacific Islands, as well as the dominance of imagined ideals and stereotypes. These terms may have been preferred due to the constantly shifting boundaries of colonial influence over time, as well as the popular belief in the immutability of race. A similar issue of terminology can be applied to the Australian continent and its inhabitants; although the official history of the nation-state began in 1901, naming conventions and boundaries continued to shift in the twentieth century. How did Australians identify and locate the South Seas, and how did they situate themselves within the region? This chapter will first consider colonial Australia's own oceanic connections and internal differences, and then it will explore how Australians demarcated the South Seas region. It will trace how an Australian literary culture and publishing industry emerged, as well as analyse the role that it played in shaping an Australian perspective of the Pacific that was distinct from those of other nations.

Oceanic Imaginary: A Land Girt by Sea

The immense size and geographical diversity of the Australian continent have at times obscured its Oceanic characteristics: it is an island bordering the Pacific Ocean, with more than 85 per cent of its population currently living within 50 kilometres of the coastline. Before it was claimed as a British colony in 1788, there was an estimated Indigenous population of 750,000 people who spoke over 700 languages and dialects.[3] Termed 'Aboriginals' by the British settler colonials, they were considered culturally and racially distinct from Pacific Islanders. Comparisons between the two were rare in travel writing, despite the fact that Aboriginal Australians were connected beyond continental boundaries, including the islands between Australia and New Guinea, which is why they are presently referred to as

---

3   'Aboriginal and Torres Strait Islander Population', Australian Bureau of Statistics, last modified 3 June 2010, www.abs.gov.au/ausstats/abs@.nsf/0/68AE74ED632E17A6CA2573D200110075?opendocument.

Aboriginal and Torres Strait Islanders.[4] Even the terms 'Australian' and 'native' have assumed multiple meanings over time, being variously used to refer to Aboriginal Australians or European colonists.[5] The European inhabitants of the country before the federation of the colonies in 1901 are more accurately referenced as colonial Australians (although national identity after this time remained contested and ambiguous). Unless referring to a specific historical period, the term 'Australia' in this book is used to generically refer to the literature or people produced by the continent during the late nineteenth and twentieth centuries.

Like Frances Steel's history of New Zealand shipping in the Pacific, Australian history can benefit from a more 'multi sited (-sighted) gaze' that looks to the sea as much as it does to the land.[6] Colonial Australians have historically shared a strong connection to the Pacific Islands and the maritime world in general, displaying pride in the British traditions of seamanship and navigation. For example, the initial composition for 'Advance Australia Fair' in 1879 included the lyrics 'Britannia rules the wave' and revered 'gallant' Captain James Cook as a popular hero who was emblematic of 'British courage' and naval skill.[7] Sydney, in particular, was a port city built on sea trade and harbour life—'waterborne and waterbound', according to Grace Karskens. Rather than being a barrier, the ocean provided a connection to England and to the rest of the world.[8] Sydney Harbour and its visiting seamen inspired popular writers such as Joseph Conrad, Henry Lawson and Kenneth Slessor. Ian Hoskins noted how the regular arrival of the HMS *Powerful* (the flagship of the British navy's Australia station), the visit of the American Great White Fleet in 1908 and the reception of Australia's first naval fleet in 1913 all attracted wide attention.[9] Popular interest in sailing and navigation resurged in the 1920s and 1930s, which is evident in several accounts of travel on private sailing vessels that were inspired by Jack London's *The Cruise of the Snark* (1911).

---

4   In this book, reference to Aboriginal Australians does not include Torres Strait Islanders unless specifically mentioned.
5   Denoon, 'Re-Membering Australasia', 296.
6   Steel, *Oceania under Steam*, 9.
7   Peter Dodds McCormick, *Advance Australia Fair* (Sydney: Reading & Co, 1879).
8   Grace Karskens, *The Colony: A History of Early Sydney* (Crows Nest: Allen & Unwin, 2010), 161, 166.
9   Ian Hoskins, *Sydney Harbour: A History* (Sydney: UNSW Press, 2011), 232.

Australia's oceanic origins were constrained by a turn to the interior, particularly from the 1820s onwards. A national character was beginning to form on the Australian colonial frontier, yet the ocean remained a vital link and an important part of the lifestyle and culture of many people. Early trading ventures between the Australian continent and the Pacific cemented this bond—so important was the Pacific in colonial Australia that John Young described it as 'Australia's Pacific Frontier'.[10] The Australian colonial gaze was torn between the sea and the land, with both domains being perceived as pathways for returning 'home', as escape destinations, as opportunities for social betterment, as spaces of danger and threat or as spaces to be explored, known, owned and colonised.

For the first colonial settlers in Australia, knowledge of the Pacific Islands was influenced by the popular imagination of Europe. Few of the settlers travelled through the Pacific Islands before the 1880s, and the Pacific Islands were frequently identified as the 'South Seas', a term coined by Spanish explorer Vasco Núñez de Balboa in 1513. The term was derived from the classical Greek myth of an antipodean southern landmass that counterbalanced the north.[11] Fictional tales of adventure incorporated the accounts of returning travellers and continued to place protagonists on an unspecified 'cannibal', 'savage', 'coral', 'tropical' or 'treasure' island within the South Seas, cementing the Pacific Islands as a generic and exotic backdrop upon which European actors played. These ambiguous descriptors persisted in Australian travel accounts and were more prevalent than terms such as 'Pacific' or 'Oceania'. The Islands continued to serve as ideal settings for boyhood adventure tales in the late nineteenth century, which were popular, influential and valued in Australia for their educational content and entertainment.[12]

---

10   Young, *Australia's Pacific Frontier*. See also Bill Gammage, 'Early Boundaries of New South Wales', *Australian Historical Studies* 19, no. 77 (1981): 524–31, doi.org/10.1080/10314618108595657; DR Hainsworth, 'Exploiting the Pacific Frontier: The New South Wales Sealing Industry 1800–1821', *Journal of Pacific History* 2, no. 1 (1967): 59–75, doi.org/10.1080/00223346708572102; John Young, *Adventurous Spirits: Australian Migrant Society in Pre-Cession Fiji* (St Lucia: University of Queensland Press, 1984).

11   Bronwen Douglas, *Science, Voyages, and Encounters in Oceania, 1511–1850* (Basingstoke, UK: Palgrave Macmillan, 2014), 4.

12   Henry Maurice Saxby, *A History of Australian Children's Literature 1841–1941* (Sydney: Wentworth Books, 1969), 24; Bill Pearson, *Rifled Sanctuaries: Some Views of the Pacific Islands in Western Literature to 1900* (Auckland: Auckland University Press, 1984), 58.

Another popular regional term that encompassed the Australian colonies and the South Seas was 'Australasia'. First coined in 1756 by the French philosopher Charles de Brosses as one of his three divisions of 'Terra Australis', the term initially categorised the lands south of Asia. It was then defined in 1890 by the Victorian parliament as including the Australian mainland, New Zealand, Tasmania, Fiji 'and any other British colonies or possessions in Australasia now existing or hereafter to be created'.[13] Not only did Australasia express a collective British identity of shared 'migration … similar social structures, economic enterprises and political institutions', it also described a network in which colonies supported, competed and compared themselves to one another.[14]

Significant diversity was found within these Australasian colonies, including different relationships with, and attitudes to, the Pacific Islands. Roger Thompson's history highlights the discord over foreign policy and trade in the Pacific between the eastern Australian colonies and the British Colonial Office, as well as the role of particular businesses, religious groups and individuals who lobbied the government when public interest waned.[15] Of all the Australian colonies, those on the eastern seaboard were more closely connected to the Pacific Islands. New South Wales benefited from Sydney's strategic location at the centre of Pacific trade and advocated a free-trade ideology, displaying less interest in annexation and protectionist policies than the other Australian colonies. Victoria was the seat of the national government from 1901 to 1927, with its Presbyterian Church being a dominant lobbyist for the annexation of the New Hebrides (where their missions had vested interests). This call for annexation was not heeded as strongly by the Catholic population of Sydney. Queensland's close proximity to the Pacific Islands entailed a closer exchange of people and goods than other colonies. The demand for cheap labour to maintain the colony's sugar plantations drove the Queensland labour trade from 1869 to 1906. Variations between rural and urban communities were also present within these colonies, not to mention that many travellers to the Pacific were frequently mobile and shifted between different homes.

---

13   Denoon, 'Re-Membering Australasia', 293.
14   Denoon, Mein-Smith and Wyndham, *A History of Australia, New Zealand and the Pacific*, 32.
15   Thompson, *Australian Imperialism in the Pacific*.

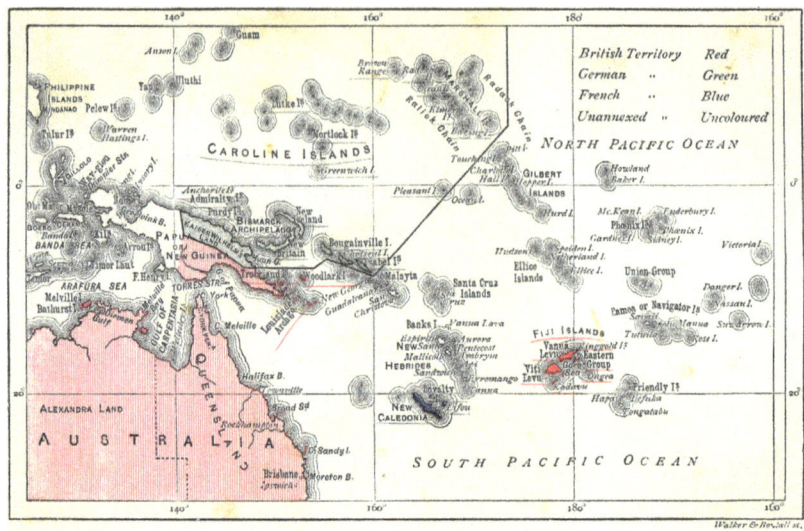

Figure 2: Map of the Pacific Islands.
Source: Julian Thomas, *Cannibals and Convicts: Notes of Personal Experiences in the Western Pacific* (Melbourne: Cassell & Company, 1886).

The realities of colonial competition in the region from the 1880s onwards brought specific Islands into focus for certain members of the Australian colonies. Australian public interest in the Pacific Islands reached its peak during the 1880s and, rather than an empty South Sea, the imagined Pacific was filled with islands that were mapped in colour according to their colonial masters (see Figure 2). By 1885, a well-attended town hall meeting in Australia could be held on a Pacific issue.[16] Concern about foreign threats was generated by German expansion throughout Tonga, Samoa and New Guinea, the transportation of French convicts to New Caledonia and overseas conflicts involving Britain, such as the 'Russian war scare' of 1884/1885. Among the many perceived external threats, the French presence in New Caledonia and the New Hebrides prompted considerable debate in Australia during the late nineteenth century. These issues were used by the Australian federation movement to highlight the need for a foreign policy that was independent of Britain and, in some cases, for the formation of Australian imperialism in the Pacific that was based on the United States' (US) 'Monroe Doctrine'. This policy, which prohibited foreign annexations in the Americas, was adapted by Australians

---

16   Luke Trainor, *British Imperialism and Australian Nationalism: Manipulation, Conflict, and Compromise in the Late Nineteenth Century* (Melbourne: Cambridge University Press, 1994), 18.

and applied to the region of Melanesia. As early as 1869, *The Age* had declared 'the manifest destiny of Australia, to employ an Americanism, is to colonise and subdue the islands of Melanesia'.[17] In addition to the contested Pacific Island territories, the Australian colonies were interested in strengthening pre-existing relationships in the more secure British territories of Papua, Fiji and the Solomon Islands—relationships that were based predominantly on trade and commerce.

The Australasian colonies discussed the political future of the Pacific Islands during periodic meetings, such as the Colonial Conferences held in London in 1887, 1894 and 1897. These negotiations between the colonies and the British Colonial Office included topics such as political alliances and treaties, trade agreements and financial support, in which the Pacific Islands became important bargaining chips. These inter-colonial alliances were fluid and fragile, especially while the Australian colonies and New Zealand competed for greater influence in the region. Individual politicians could also play leading roles in advancing colonial ambitions in the Pacific. Notable Australian examples include Queensland premier Thomas McIlwraith, who ordered the annexation of New Guinea without permission on 4 April 1883, or Victorian premier James Service, who possessed an imperialistic vision for the country in the early 1880s. Some politicians even travelled to the Islands in pursuit of this cause, as New Zealand Prime Minister Richard John Seddon did in May 1900 to solicit agreements for New Zealand annexation.[18]

With Australia's Federation in 1901, the newly formed national government could begin to implement a distinctively Australian foreign policy; however, it remained constrained by interstate rivalries, economic pressures and allegiance to Britain.[19] Australasia's relevance may have diminished, but the term continued to be appropriated by Australians to either articulate a British colonial affinity (a trans-Tasman relationship with New Zealand) or to describe Australia itself or an Australian sphere of influence in the region. In fact, Denoon, Mein-Smith and Wyndham argued that 'as Australian federation rendered "Australasia" obsolete, the continent and the seas and islands were more firmly cemented in

---

17 *The Age*, 14 August 1869, 2, nla.gov.au/nla.news-article188570311.
18 Steel, *Oceania under Steam*, 36; Richard John Seddon, *The Right Hon. R. J. Seddon's (The Premier of New Zealand) Visit to Tonga, Fiji, Savage Island, and the Cook Islands, May 1900* (Wellington: New Zealand Government, 1900).
19 Thompson, *Australia and the Pacific Islands*, 65.

the colonists' imaginations as a region, and indeed as *their* region'.[20] In this region, the wider identity of Australasia was still being expressed well into the twentieth century. It included the Australian colony of Papua (then New Guinea), as well as the future possibility of New Zealand, the New Hebrides, Fiji and the Solomon Islands. This contested colonial relationship was visible to war correspondent Charles Bean in 1909 when he visited Fiji:

> Fiji is really an Australian colony, though it does not care to be called so. The white men who govern Fiji come mostly from England; the white men who trade there, except a few English and British-Canadians, come all from Australia … Now all the trade goes to Australia and New Zealand in two sharply-divided compartments. Red-funnelled Union boats take it, and bring next to nothing back. Nearly all the bananas and all the copra … go in black-funnelled A.U.S.N. steamer Suva to Sydney; and nearly everything that Fiji uses comes from Sydney. That is Australia's interest in Fiji.[21]

Therefore, not only did the political legacy of the British empire influence Australian foreign policy and trade, it also continued to shape the paths that Australian travellers followed and the judgements that they made during their journeys. These travellers increasingly noted the strategic importance of certain Islands, with their observations specifying deep harbours, military fortifications and native police as evidence of growing colonial power and might. Further, improvements in technology not only encouraged colonial mobility—they also fostered colonial suspicions.

The borders defining spheres of influence in the Pacific Islands shifted over time, yet the most pervasive, persistent and unchanging conceptualisation of the Pacific Islands was a racialised one. The terms 'Melanesia' and 'Polynesia' were firmly rooted in Australian understandings of the Pacific region, denoting race rather than geographical location.[22] The Islands of Melanesia included Papua and New Guinea, the Bismarck Archipelago, the Solomon Islands and Santa Cruz group, the New Hebrides, New Caledonia and Fiji. The Islands of Polynesia stretched from New Zealand

---

20   Denoon, Mein-Smith and Wyndham, *A History of Australia, New Zealand and the Pacific*, 186.
21   Charles Edwin Woodrow Bean, *With the Flagship of the South* (Sydney: William Brooks, 1909), 62–3.
22   Serge Tcherkezoff, 'A Long and Unfortunate Voyage Towards the "Invention" of the Melanesia/Polynesia Distinction 1595–1832', *The Journal of Pacific History* 38, vol. 2 (2003): 176, doi.org/10.1080/0022334032000120521.

in the south, to Easter Island in the east and to Hawai'i in the north. Twentieth-century Australians frequently described the Pacific in terms of this racial binary, omitting the original categories of Malaysia (which was considered part of Asia) and Micronesia (which was too distant). This racialised conception of the Pacific Islands was reflected in Australian travel accounts; they increasingly advocated a scientific understanding of race as being immutable and situated Pacific Islanders as being inferior and static. This resonated with early European conceptions of the Pacific Islands as being a space for scientific discovery, which described the Pacific Islander as a 'passive receptacle of observation'.[23] It also encouraged stereotyping. Science and race permeated Australian travel writing, particularly in the texts describing Melanesia, and were convenient tools for justifying colonial exploitation and governance. Travel writing informed, and was in turn informed by, a series of domestic racial policies that were designed to protect the nation from foreign immigration, known collectively as the White Australia policy. Historians have tended to focus on how this policy was informed by fears of Asian immigration; presently, less research has been conducted to explore the Pacific evidence. The *Immigration Restriction Act* (1901) and the *Pacific Island Labourers Act* (1901) outlined Australia's official policy towards Pacific Islanders—and the consequences of these regulations were most keenly felt in the shipping trade, which was forced to privilege white labour over Islanders on government ships and ships with government contracts.[24] A more balanced account of the White Australia policy must acknowledge the role that Polynesian and Melanesian tropes played in shaping popular public opinion about race.

Australian travellers continued to imagine the Pacific Islands according to the literary and scientific legacies that were left by their European predecessors, and popular notions of the South Seas, Polynesia and Melanesia remained unquestioned by most. However, an increasing number of travellers during the interwar period began to undermine popular tropes about the Pacific Islands. As more Australians travelled further abroad, there were more possibilities for cross-cultural encounters that undermined conventional stereotypes of the Pacific. The acquisition of the New Guinea mandate in 1920 also redefined Australia's geographical conception of the Pacific and demanded the growth of a greater international consciousness within Australia. Travel writing during the

---

23 Paul Sharrad, 'Imagining the Pacific', *Meanjin* 49, no. 4 (1990): 597.
24 Lake, 'The Australian Dream of an Island Empire', 410–24. For more information regarding the importance of Pacific Islander labour on the shipping trade, see Steel, *Oceania under Steam*.

1920s and 1930s witnessed the term 'Pacific' being used more commonly than previous regional descriptors such as 'South Seas' or 'Australasia'; this evidences a greater recognition of the Pacific Islands being a shared and contested colonial space, especially in light of Japanese imperial ambitions in the region. This claim has been supported by recent studies of Australians' participation in pan-Pacific organisations in the 1920s and 1930s, which originated from US efforts that encouraged the notion of a 'new Pacific' as being a sphere of influence that was separate from Europe—one in which the US could play a leading role.[25]

Looking Beyond the South Seas

Some parts of the Pacific Island region did not feature as prominently in popular Australian perceptions of the South Seas, such as the North Pacific, New Zealand, Papua and New Guinea. With the exception of Hawai'i, the North Pacific region was rarely the subject of Australian travel writing, reflecting the minimal level of Australian engagement with, and interest in, the region. Intermittent Australian business ventures in the Marshall Islands and Kiribati failed to gain traction because of the region's geographical distance from Australia and its closer colonial associations with Japan and the US.

Across the Tasman Sea, New Zealand grew distinct from Australia in its relationship with the Pacific Islands and its indigenous Maori population. Having chosen not to be part of Australia's Federation in 1901, New Zealand articulated its own Pacific destiny in the early twentieth century. New Zealand nationalists advocated a nation that was superior to Australia— one born of free settlers rather than convicts and one with an indigenous people who were considered superior to the Aboriginal Australians.[26] Having gained the Cook Islands in 1901, New Zealand aspired to add Fiji, Samoa and Tonga to its colonial acquisitions in the Pacific due to claims of scientific evidence of Polynesian homogeneity (with New

---

25 Tomoko Akami, *Internationalizing the Pacific: The United States, Japan, and the Institute of Pacific Relations in War and Peace, 1919–45* (New York: Routledge, 2002); Fiona Paisley, *Glamour in the Pacific: Cultural Internationalism and Race Politics in the Women's Pan-Pacific* (Honolulu: University of Hawai'i Press, 2009).

26 Denoon, Mein-Smith and Wyndham, *A History of Australia, New Zealand and the Pacific*, 32–3; Angus Ross, *New Zealand Aspirations in the Pacific in the Nineteenth Century* (Oxford: Clarendon Press, 1964); Angus Ross, ed., *New Zealand's Record in the Pacific Islands in the Twentieth Century* (London: Hurst, 1969).

Zealand located at the southernmost tip of the 'Polynesian triangle'). New Zealand colonialists established a more equitable relationship with the Maori population than Australians did with their country's Indigenous population; New Zealand 'became the growth pole for Polynesia South of the equator, as well as that region's leading centre for technical and higher education', with its openness to Polynesians starkly contrasting the racialised immigration policies of Australia.[27] By comparison, Australians displayed little political interest in the Polynesian Islands, with many travelling to this region as tourists.

For Australian travellers, New Zealand was not often considered part of the South Seas, despite its location and Maori cultural origins. Chemist Charles Agar Atkin exemplified many Australian travellers who overlooked the island characteristics of New Zealand during his travels up the east coast to Fiji. He instead focused on the country's European architecture, public works and modern transportation, comparing its rate of progress to that of the Australian colonies.[28] In addition to its cities, New Zealand's natural scenery (particularly Rotorua's thermal springs) provided popular tourist attractions. Maori were occasionally mentioned, though usually in comparison to other Pacific Islanders and in reference to their assumed superior status as Polynesians. For example, when John Cromar visited Honolulu, he noted that 'the Hawaiians were a very superior type of native, and similar to the Maoris of New Zealand, being light-skinned, and having long straight hair and perfect physique'.[29] Strangely, Australian travellers were more willing to compare Maori with Pacific Islanders than to draw similar comparisons with Aboriginal Australians. In fact, comparisons between Aboriginal Australians and Pacific Islanders rarely appeared in Australian travel writing. It is unclear whether this was because Aboriginal Australians did not fit into the exotic stereotypes or racial hierarchies of the Pacific, or because of the official government policies in Australia that encouraged the segregation and displacement of Indigenous communities.

---

27 Denoon, 'Re-Membering Australasia', 301; Kerry R Howe, *Race Relations: Australia and New Zealand: A Comparative Survey 1770's–1970's* (Wellington: Methuen Publications, 1977).
28 Charles Agar Atkin, *A Trip to Fiji via East Coast of New Zealand* (Melbourne: Massina, 1885).
29 John Cromar, *Jock of the Islands: Early Days in the South Seas: The Adventures of John Cromar, Sometime Recruiter and Lately Trader at Marovo, British Solomon Islands Protectorate, Told by Himself* (London: Faber & Faber, 1935), 20. The only exceptions to this are George Robertson Nicoll, *Fifty Years' Travels in Australia, China, Japan, America, Etc., 1848–1898* (London: George Robertson Nicoll, 1899) and Arnold Safroni-Middleton, *Tropic Shadows: Memories of the South Seas, Together with Reminiscences of the Author's Sea Meetings with Joseph Conrad* (London: The Richards Press, 1927).

The only other times that Australian travel accounts mentioned New Zealand involved the intention to observe (or challenge) the country's role as a colonial power in the Pacific. In Percy S Allen's 1920 handbook, New Zealand's colonial rule of Samoa was deemed ineffective due to its poorly trained officials:

> The average New Zealand official in Samoa does not command the respect of the natives. He lacks prestige, has little education, and is without that traditional upbringing and savoir vivre that, for example, usually distinguishes the British Colonial Office official.[30]

Perhaps New Zealand's omission from the accounts of the South Seas was because it was perceived as less exotic—whether due to its European features, its location, its climate or its more developed tourism industry. Travel writer Elinor Mordaunt simply chose to avoid discussing New Zealand because it 'has been too much written about for me to tackle it'.[31]

In contrast, Australians' significant long-term contact with Papua and New Guinea since the late nineteenth century has created a vast archival record of Australian travel, some of which has been explored by Nigel Krauth, Clive Moore and Hank Nelson.[32] The greatest test of Australia's colonial abilities was in the territories of Papua and New Guinea, which were limited realisations of a much broader Australian imperial vision. The territory of Papua comprised the south-eastern quarter of the island of New Guinea, which became a British protectorate in the year 1884 and

---

30 Percy S Allen, *Stewart's Handbook of the Pacific Islands: A Reliable Guide to All the Inhabited Islands of the Pacific Ocean—For Traders, Tourists and Settlers, with a Bibliography of Island Works* (Sydney: Steward McCarron, 1920), 13.

31 Elinor Mordaunt, *The Venture Book* (New York: The Century Co., 1926), 298. See also Lydia Wevers, *Country of Writing: Travel Writing and New Zealand, 1809–1900* (Auckland: Auckland University Press, 2002).

32 Nigel Krauth, ed., *New Guinea Images in Australian Literature* (St Lucia: University of Queensland Press, 1982); Nigel Krauth, 'The New Guinea Experience in Literature: A Study of Imaginative Writing Concerned with Papua New Guinea, 1863–1980' (PhD thesis, University of Queensland, 1983); Clive Moore, James Griffin and Andrew Griffin, eds, *Colonial Intrusion: Papua New Guinea, 1884* (Port Moresby: PNG Centennial Committee, 1984); Clive Moore, *New Guinea: Crossing Boundaries and History* (Honolulu: University of Hawai'i Press, 2003); Hank Nelson, 'European Attitudes in Papua, 1906–1914', in *The History of Melanesia*, ed. KS Inglis (Port Moresby and Canberra: University of Papua and New Guinea and The Australian National University, 1969); Hank Nelson, 'Our Boys up North: The Behaviour of Australians in New Guinea', *Meanjin Quarterly* 32, no. 4 (1973): 441–3; Hank Nelson, *Black, White and Gold: Goldmining in Papua New Guinea, 1878–1930* (Canberra: ANU Press, 2016), doi.org/10.22459/bwg.07.2016; Hank Nelson, 'Looking Black: Australian Images of Melanesians', in *The Pacific War in Papua New Guinea: Memories and Realities*, ed. Yukio Toyoda and Hank Nelson (Tokyo: Rikkyo University, Centre for Asian Area Studies, 2006).

was then formally annexed as British New Guinea four years later. In 1906, Australia became responsible for British New Guinea's administration. The north-eastern part of the island of New Guinea and several outlying Islands (including the German-named Bismarck Archipelago, New Britain and New Ireland) were known as German New Guinea. It was a protectorate from 1884 to 1914, when it fell to Australian forces following the outbreak of World War I. From then, it was known as the Trust Territory of New Guinea, given to Australia as a League of Nations mandate (along with Nauru) in 1920. In 1949, the territories of Papua and New Guinea were combined. The Dutch claim to the western half of New Guinea remained unchallenged by Germany, Britain and Australia.

The first large-scale movement of Australians to Papua and New Guinea began due to the search for gold. Initial prospecting in the 1870s offered mixed rewards, but by the 1890s, greater numbers of Australian diggers were sailing north. Gold was the main export of the territories of British New Guinea and Papua until 1916, and by 1940, it constituted 80 per cent of the mandated territory of New Guinea's exports.[33] In the footsteps of these Australian diggers followed colonial officials, traders, agriculturalists, opportunists and tourists. By 1906, approximately 700 Europeans resided in the Australian territory—mostly miners, missionaries or government officials, whose contradictory interests were the source of frequent comment.[34] These travellers wrote accounts that informed Australians about the country, complementing other news articles and official reports. Included in these accounts were the adventure literature of frontier patrols, the propaganda of Sunday school literature, the memoirs of missionaries and public officials, several handbooks and promotional materials, and a growing body of literature written by professional travel writers.[35] So vast is the scale and diversity of the literature and the region it describes that it warrants its own dedicated study—and in this book, only a brief summary is provided of the significant role that Papua and New Guinea played in contributing to Australian perceptions of the broader Pacific Islands (particularly the evaluations of Australian colonial rule).

---

33 Nelson, *Black, White and Gold*, vi, 114.
34 Nelson, 'European Attitudes in Papua', 593.
35 For a bibliography of Australian biographical writing about Papua and New Guinea, see Nelson, 'Lives Told: Australians in Papua and New Guinea'.

Papua and New Guinea occupied their own place in European and Australian imagining, distinct from the South Seas, partly due to their geography and political status. Due to their difficult terrain and relatively late contact with Europeans compared to the Islands of the eastern Pacific, early narratives of Papua and New Guinea instead transplanted descriptions of the interiors of Africa, Asia and South America, describing mythical creatures, savage inhabitants and hidden fortunes.[36] Australian representations of Papua and New Guinea shared close similarities with the depictions and tropes of Melanesia in general, which are discussed in detail throughout this book. Images of 'New Guinea natives', either elaborately decorated or brandishing weapons, were regularly reproduced in books and magazines to emphasise Pacific exoticism and masculine savagery (see Figure 3). In other cases, this was juxtaposed with images of women and children (see Figure 4) to suggest innocence and justify patriarchal colonialism in the region. Max Quanchi's comprehensive study of images of the territory outlines the ways in which people, objects and designs were indiscriminately attributed to other Islands in the Pacific in print culture and in film.[37] But unlike the smaller islands of the South Seas, many of which could be easily crossed or circumnavigated, the New Guinean mainland could only be probed by arduous journeys up rivers or across mountain ranges. Papua and New Guinea was thus popularly regarded as the 'last unknown'—a phrase that was coined in Karl Shapiro's wartime poem and that was later used as the title of a history by Australian Gavin Souter in 1963.[38] Consequently, Papua and New Guinea were places of extremes within the broader Pacific imagining, lands 'of phantasmal imaginings and unexplainable nightmares'.[39]

---

36 See Chris Ballard, 'Collecting Pygmies: The "Tapiro" and the British Ornithologists' Union Expedition to Dutch New Guinea, 1910–1911', in *Hunting the Gatherers: Ethnographic Collectors, Agents and Agency in Melanesia, 1870s–1930s*, ed. Michael O'Hanlon and Robert L Welsch (New York: Berghahn Books, 2000), 127–54, doi.org/10.2307/j.ctt1x76fh4.11; Chris Ballard, 'Strange Alliance: Pygmies in the Colonial Imaginary', *World Archaeology* 38, no. 1 (2006): 133–51, doi.org/10.1080/00438240500510155; Chris Ballard, 'The Art of Encounter', 221–58.

37 Max Quanchi, *Photographing Papua: Representation, Colonial Encounters and Imaging in the Public Domain* (Newcastle: Cambridge Scholars Publishing, 2007), 93.

38 Karl Shapiro, *V-Letter and Other Poems* (New York: Reynal & Hitchcock, 1944), 10; Gavin Souter, *New Guinea: The Last Unknown* (Sydney: Angus & Robertson, 1963).

39 Arnold Safroni-Middleton, *In the Green Leaf: A Chapter of Autobiography* (London: Fortune P, 1950), 125.

Figure 3: New Guinea Native.
Source: Front cover of *Walkabout* 2, no. 7 (May 1936). Image courtesy of the Australian National Travel Association.

In New Guinea Wilds
Australia's Mandated Territory

NORTH of Australia lies the enchanted land of Papua and New Guinea, where strange native races still follow quaint customs. Waving coconut palms, blue lagoons and grim, rugged mountain ranges lend beauty and mystery to their surroundings. From Australian ports comfortable steamers carry tourists for winter cruises around these islands of the Pacific, visiting Port Moresby, Samarai, Rabaul, Salamoa, Woodlark Island and innumerable places of interest.

The Mandated Territory includes 72,000 square miles of the mainland of New Guinea and thousands of islands large and small. New Britain covers 13,000 square miles, while the very smallest are mere specks of coral, a few square yards in extent.

The most important article of food and commerce is the product of the coconut. The natives are engaged in preparing the copra and are employed loading the vessels.

Mother and baby enjoy their morning dip together at Talasea, New Britain.
Photo: H. L. Downing.

Port Moresby, the capital, is built near a beautiful harbour, and behind the township towers the great peak of Mt. Victoria (13,200ft.), in the Owen Stanley Range. Not far from the town are the beautiful Rona Falls and the tree houses of the Ikeri villages.

Samarai is the second largest township and is situated on an island a short distance from the mainland. Beautiful crotons grow in profusion and bright many-coloured trees line the road.

Rabaul, the capital, lies on the shores of a pretty bay, at the entrance of which are hot sulphur springs and nearby are the islands of Matupi.

Woodlark Island is another lovely spot. Gold mining has been carried on in this district.

Salamoa is the port of call for the goldfields of Edie Creek and Bulolo, which are seven days' march inland, over mountainous country. Native boys, who carry loads of 50lbs. each are employed for transport work, and when the weather permits the aeroplane service is used. The goldfield was discovered in 1921.

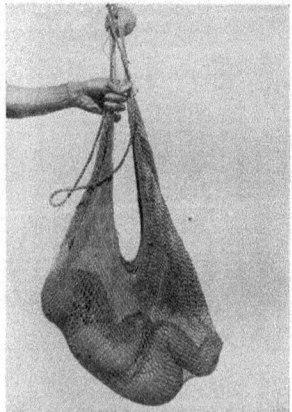

A New Guinea baby's cradle, woven from special grasses which are mosquito proof.
Photo: H. L. Downing.

Figure 4: Let's Explore in New Guinea Wilds Australia's Mandated Territory.
Source: *BP Magazine* (June–August 1930): 51.

As Australian narratives of settlement gradually replaced those of exploration, Papua and New Guinea became a 'testing-ground for the strength of the Australian character' in the 1900s.[40] It was also in these territories that Australian imperial ambitions were most fully enacted until 1975. As a result, there was a proliferation of accounts by government officials and district officers and these territories became a standard by which Australian rule was appraised. Australian parliamentarians emphasised a clear responsibility for the territory in 1901, eager to secure the transfer of British New Guinea to Australian control. In the first session of Parliament, Prime Minister Edmund Barton hoped that 'New Guinea is to be a territory, perhaps, a State of this Commonwealth'.[41] In contrast to the attitudes towards the Northern Territory, an optimism existed for the notion that white settlement and indigenous protection could occur simultaneously. As Charles McDonald, a parliamentarian, noted in 1901: 'We know that the treatment of the aborigines in Australia has been a blot upon Australian history. I hope that it will not be repeated in the case of British New Guinea'.[42] Such comparisons made by Australian government officials regarding the Indigenous inhabitants of Australia and those of British New Guinea have likely influenced travellers' observations of the territory. These observations are distinct from travel writing about the rest of the Pacific region, which rarely mentioned Australian Aboriginals.

Australia's responsibility in New Guinea was re-emphasised in 1920 with the award of the League of Nations mandate, which made Australia accountable to a global audience. For example, this meant that, in practice, only colonial officers who worked in Papua and New Guinea received specialised training in anthropology, geography and hygiene from 1925, despite the welfare of Papuans and Aboriginal Australians frequently coming under the control of the same ministerial office.[43] Despite this positive rhetoric, racial discrimination continued to underscore Australia's relations with Papua and New Guinea, as Alfred Deakin acknowledged in 1901: 'A "White Australia" may exist across the straits, but a "Black New Guinea" the territory now is and must always remain'.[44]

---

40   Krauth, *New Guinea Images in Australian Literature*, xiv. See also Lake, 'The Australian Dream of an Island Empire', 410–24.
41   *Australian Parliamentary Debates,* House of Representatives, Vol. 6 (1901–02), 7079–91.
42   *Australian Parliamentary Debates,* House of Representatives, Vol. 6 (1901–02), 7411–2.
43   Thompson, *Australia and the Pacific Islands*, 74–5.
44   *Morning Post*, 31 December 1901.

Although Australian politicians may have been confident about the role that Australians played in Papua and New Guinea, individual travellers were much more uncertain. As Hank Nelson argued, many people believed in the racial dogma of the day, yet few had the experience of close contact with other people; their understanding of the territory and their responsibilities compounded this rift, making many uncertain about whether Papua and New Guinea constituted a foreign country or an Australian frontier.[45] This uncertainty was reflected in travellers' observations of the indigenous peoples and in their superficial comparisons with Australian Aboriginals. In general, Australians were assured of their superiority to the indigenous people and were confident that they were better and more humane colonisers than other Europeans. Realistically, they were inexperienced and unsure about how to handle the supposed 'inferiors'.[46] Therefore, for the post–World War I Australian travellers who increasingly questioned the merits of their 'civilisation' and the allegedly 'superior' Australian coloniser, Papua and New Guinea presented the clearest opportunity for evaluating Australian efforts.

Texts and Contexts

Individual experiences of travel abroad could have a marked effect on travellers, but the process of writing and, in some cases, publishing an account of one's travels could introduce another set of constraints. An emerging literary culture in Australia was responding to the new notions and demands of Australian audiences, while also remaining aware of the popular conventions and accepted truths that were exhibited in European and US markets. Travel writing offers numerous examples of how travellers were aware of the popular genres of the day, the key texts that preceded them and the shifting demands of the Australian audience. Therefore, contextualising the experiences of travellers within their appropriate literary contexts is important. Jonathon Lamb's literary history of Pacific voyages emphasises the context of the metropolitan audience who consumed the narratives, highlighting how the accounts were dramatised and distorted. Rather than detailing scientific truth, firsthand impressions magnified the uncertainties and anxieties

---
45 Nelson, 'Our Boys up North', 433.
46 Nelson, 'Our Boys up North', 440.

of European society.⁴⁷ Robert Dixon has been influential in addressing the discourse of travel writing as part of his advocation for a 'stronger postcolonial perspective in interdisciplinary Australian studies'. Dixon argued that text cannot be reduced only to ideology or to the nation-state and highlighted the role that commercial entertainment markets play in shaping texts. His text-based analyses demonstrate the hybridisation of Australian texts, acknowledge the discernment of Australian audiences and argue for a more nuanced understanding of the relationship between culture and governance that is 'contingent and mediated'.⁴⁸

Publishing in books, magazines or newspapers was a convenient method for travellers to make a living, which likely explains the high proportion of journalists and professional writers within the corpus of Australian travel writers (approximately 20). Newcomers to the publishing industry would circulate multiple copies of the same or similar stories to various magazines so that they could establish a reputation. Publishers were aware of popular trends and current affairs and could satisfy periodic peaks of demand for news about the Pacific Islands with reports from recently returned travellers. Authors such as Frank Hurley, Ion Llewellyn Idriess and Frank Clune were clever marketers and capitalised on sponsorship and publicity on radio and in print. Others such as Grimshaw earned commissions from governments and businesses for their travel writing. It is thus important to consider these authors' revealing literary aspirations, though this is not the central focus of this book. Australian novelists who wrote about the Pacific were confident about a market in Australia, England and the US for sensational accounts of mysterious Islands. The international success of Australia's first Pacific travel writer at the turn of the century, Louis Becke, was a testament to this. Most writers were conscious of the characteristics of popular genres at the time, and the abundance of travel writing produced a need for travellers to distinguish themselves, even if this tended towards sensationalism.⁴⁹

---

47 Jonathan Lamb, *Preserving the Self in the South Seas, 1680–1840* (Chicago: University of Chicago Press, 2001), 6, 83.
48 Robert Dixon, *Prosthetic Gods: Travel, Representation, and Colonial Governance* (St Lucia: University of Queensland Press and API Network, 2001), 9. See also Robert Dixon, *Writing the Colonial Adventure: Race, Gender, and Nation in Anglo-Australian Popular Fiction, 1875–1914* (New York: Cambridge University Press, 1995), doi.org/10.1017/cbo9781139085038; Robert Dixon, 'What was Travel Writing? Frank Hurley and the Media Contexts of Early Twentieth-Century Australian Travel Writing', *Studies in Travel Writing* 11, no. 1 (2007): 59–81, doi.org/10.1080/13645145.2007.9634819.
49 Broinowski, *The Yellow Lady*, 23; Wevers, *Country of Writing*, 156.

Whether writing for family, friends, validation, fame or fortune, travellers returning home who wished to publish their diaries or notes had to negotiate a competitive market in Australia. The changing literary landscape between 1880 and 1941 correlates with shifting representations of the Pacific Islands in Australian travel writing. As national literacy improved and printing became cheaper, the 1870s and 1880s witnessed a growing mass market for books in Australia and an increasing number of professional writers.[50] Since few book publishers existed in Australia, periodicals were often de facto publishers. A trans-Tasman print culture entailed that writing was regularly shared between Australia and New Zealand, as was authorship. For both Australian and New Zealand writers of this period, literature was closely tied to British publishers and themes.[51]

There were several consequences to being situated on the periphery of the British publishing empire. Helen Bones' analysis of newspaper literary reviews reveals that the reception of travel writing at home and overseas affected the way that it was interpreted, which is especially significant for Australia and New Zealand, as the two countries 'have historically been anxious about forging an independent, authentic, national identity'. She thus argued that 'fictionality or authenticity is dependent on identity politics as well as genre'.[52] This may explain why travellers were reluctant to self-identify as Australian, or why they would sometimes call themselves British, Britisher, colonial or Australasian. This shared identity was encouraged by the books and magazines about the Pacific Islands that were distributed among the colonies, which included Australian, New Zealand and British authors.

Several authors recognised that the chances of succeeding as a professional writer were greater in London. Many Australian authors chose to move to Europe in search of employment and often stayed there—such as Jack McLaren, a Melbourne-born author who wrote extensively about his Pacific travels in the late 1890s and who moved to London in 1925 when he was 39 to pursue his writing career. McLaren found success in London and established his reputation as an author, publishing most of his fictional work about the Pacific and working for the British Broadcasting

---

50 White, *Inventing Australia*, 89.
51 As discussed by Elizabeth Morrison in Dixon, *Writing the Colonial Adventure*, 197. See also Helen Bones, 'New Zealand and the Tasman Writing World, 1890–1945', *History Australia* 10, no. 3 (2013): 129–48, doi.org/10.1080/14490854.2013.11668484.
52 Helen Bones, 'Travel Writers and Traveling Writers in Australasia: Responses to Travel Literatures and the Problem of Authenticity', *Journeys* 17, no. 2 (2016): 74–94, doi.org/10.3167/jys.2016.170205.

Corporation. In fact, some Australian authors were considered British by their readers because their books were published in London.[53] One example is Eric Muspratt, a twice-serving Australian war veteran and one-time plantation manager in the Solomon Islands in 1920, whose death went unnoticed in Australia yet was remembered in England. According to the biography by Bruce Grant, this was likely because 'Muspratt played up to the wealthy and influential English, especially in the newspapers, in a manner they expected. He wanted the publicity and they were happy to give it'.[54] Muspratt's life is one example that reveals how the cultural isolation of Australia affected its writers, though Helen Bones cautions against assuming that all writers in the 'Tasman writing world' were disadvantaged by distance.[55]

Pressure from British publishers could also alter the content of the texts, though it was uncommon to acknowledge this explicitly. One rare example is provided by Caroline David in a collection of her personal papers, in which she commented on having to remove 'a heap of nice but naughty things' during the publishing process for her 1897 diary about a trip accompanying her husband's scientific mission to Funafuti. David's experience was consequently modified for British audiences, which she noted disparagingly: 'The worst of it is that in considering the delicacy of the spiritual and moral constitution of the Brit. Public, one is apt to lose the vividly truthful picture of the island as it really is'.[56] Publishing under her own name, it is likely that David's gender played a part in the choices made by the editor. David was one of a small group of female travel writers of the Pacific, but this imbalance may reflect the gender bias of the publishing industry rather than the travel patterns of Australians.

The publishing context within the Australian continent can also explain some of the general trends of Australians' Pacific travel writing. The number of travel accounts significantly increased from the 1890s onwards, which may be explained by the expansion of steamship routes in the Pacific Islands and the economic growth and national optimism

---

53   David Carter, 'Transpacific or Transatlantic Traffic? Australian Books and American Publishers', in *Reading Across the Pacific: Australia–United States Intellectual Histories*, ed. Robert Dixon and Nicholas Birns (Sydney: Sydney University Press, 2010), 345.
54   Bruce Grant, ed., *Arthur and Eric: An Anglo-Australian Story from the Journal of Arthur Hickman* (Melbourne: Heinemann Australia, 1977), 211.
55   Helen Bones, 'New Zealand and the Tasman Writing World', 129.
56   Caroline David, 'Letter to Mrs Scott, 1898', Papers of the David Family, NLA MS 8890, Series 2, Folder 25, Canberra, National Library of Australia.

exhibited up until 1914. A new literary culture was developing in Sydney at this time, led by *The Bulletin* and the establishment of new publishers.[57] These included the Sydney bookstore Angus and Robertson (established in 1888) and the New South Wales Bookstall company, which began publishing around the same time. By 1922, Bookstall alone had published 120 authors and 200 titles and had sold 4.5 million copies, at a time when Australia's population numbered 5 million.[58] In this environment, Australian literature presented the newly federated nation as being young, pure and innocent, and—through the figure of the 'coming man'—idealised a people who were superior to the British stock, who were shaped by the Australian climate and who were proven in sports and war. This idealisation was also shaped by popular racial assumptions regarding the superiority of Australians, both at home and abroad. Australian travellers in the Pacific influenced and incorporated these popular notions about race and nation that were circulating in Australian literature at the time.

Following the upheaval of World War I, a new urban and cosmopolitan middle class in Australia drove a simultaneous demand for travel and literature. Despite the economic impact of the Great Depression, approximately 24,000 Australians were travelling the world annually after World War I.[59] This was the 'age of the tabloid press', as argued by Peter Kirkpatrick, when newspapers had to excite and entertain rather than simply inform.[60] Facing increasing competition and a new 'segmented hierarchy of taste cultures', Australian publishers had to market their materials to a more diverse public, as argued by David Carter.[61] This shift is evident in the use of titles that are distinctive from the traditional

---

57   Peter John Kirkpatrick, *The Sea Coast of Bohemia: Literary Life in Sydney's Roaring Twenties* (St Lucia: University of Queensland Press, 1992), 52.
58   Toni Johnson-Woods, 'Popular Australian Writing', in *A Companion to Australian Literature Since 1900*, ed. Nicholas Birns and Rebecca McNeer (Rochester: Camden House, 2007), 394. See also White, 'Travel, Writing and Australia'; R Wynn, ed., *The Late Alfred Cecil Rowlandson: Pioneer Publisher of Australian Novels* (Sydney: J. Sands, 1922); Jennifer Alison, *Doing Something for Australia: George Robertson and the Early Years of Angus and Robertson, Publishers: 1888–1900* (Melbourne: Bibliographical Society of Australia and New Zealand, 2009); Linda S Crowl, 'Politics and Book Publishing in the Pacific Islands' (PhD thesis, University of Wollongong, 2008); Carol Mills, *The New South Wales Bookstall Company as a Publisher: With Notes on Its Artists and Authors and a Bibliography of Its Publications* (Canberra: Mulini Press, 1991).
59   Richard White, 'The Retreat from Adventure: Popular Travel Writing in the 1950s', *Australian Historical Studies* 28, no. 109 (1997): 92, 101, doi.org/10.1080/10314619708596045.
60   Kirkpatrick, *The Sea Coast of Bohemia*, 111.
61   David Carter, '"Literary, but Not Too Literary; Joyous, but Not Jazzy": Triad Magazine, Modernity and the Middlebrow', *Modernism/Modernity* 25, no. 2 (2018): 245–67, doi.org/10.1353/mod.2018.0018. See also David Carter, *Always Almost Modern: Australian Print Cultures and Modernity* (North Melbourne: Australian Scholarly Publishing, 2013).

cannibal or coral stereotypes of previous decades, such as *South Sea Foam, Sinabada, The Black Musketeers, Stormalong, Backwash of Empire, No Longer Innocent* and *Wine-Dark Seas and Tropic Skies*. These titles may also reflect a broader weariness of overused and exaggerated Pacific tropes that existed during the interwar period. This resonates with Andrew Hassam's claim that the Depression of the 1930s stimulated a more critical attitude in Australia and that it produced a literature that was marked by a greater cultural maturity.[62]

This cultural shift during the interwar period is also evident in the diverse content of magazines. An analysis of Australian magazines of the twentieth century reveals that 22 out of 85 titles were established during the interwar period.[63] The Pacific content of Australian magazines in the early twentieth century generally focused on Australians' economic or social opportunities in the region, which was in addition to travel magazines that specifically promoted popular tourist destinations. Illustrations played an important role in these publications and travel writing. Max Quanchi has written extensively on the twin-barrelled effect of text and image in magazines and in illustrated weekend newspapers.[64]

Two magazines, *BP Magazine* and *Walkabout,* featured the most Pacific content. *BP Magazine* was unabashedly promotional material published by the Australian shipping company, Burns, Philp and Company, and emphasised the comfort and luxury of ocean travel while simultaneously publicising the experience as exotic and adventurous. Although directed at tourists and, in some cases, potential investors and settlers, the magazine's editors also marketed it as educational and informative material. For this reason, *BP Magazine* may be considered closely related to travel writing in style and purpose, especially since many of its articles were written by individual travellers who reported the observations that they made during their holidays in the region. Further details about the publication and its parent company will be discussed later in this book.

---

62 Hassam, *Through Australian Eyes*, 167.
63 'Australian Magazines of the Twentieth Century', *AUSTLIT*, www.austlit.edu.au/specialist Datasets/BookHistory/AustMag. See also Toni Johnson-Woods, *Index to Serials in Australian Periodicals and Newspapers* (Canberra: Mulini Press, 2001).
64 Max Quanchi, 'The Power of Pictures: Learning-by-Looking at Papua in Illustrated Newspapers and Magazines', *Australian Historical Studies* 35, no. 123 (2004): 37–53, doi.org/10.1080/10314 610408596271.

Walkabout was a monthly geographic magazine that was published by the Australian National Travel Association from 1934 to 1974. It has been the subject of several studies—most recently by Anna Johnston and Mitchell Rolls, who argued that the magazine reveals key issues in Australia's cultural history and that it shaped understandings of Australia's place in the region.[65] *Walkabout* published an equal number of images and stories about the Pacific as it did about Australia (nearly 400), and like other geographical magazines at the time, it blended anthropological information and tourism promotions. Images of Papua and New Guinea featured more frequently on the front covers of *Walkabout* than any other Pacific Islands, and the magazine reflected a general preoccupation with Australia's colonial mandate. Johnston and Rolls recognised that many of the magazine's contributions were travel accounts, and their conclusions echo the findings of the study in this book—although 'paternalist and assimilationist policies are regularly reflected' in the Pacific content of *Walkabout*, the Pacific Islands were given 'varied, often conflicting treatment by different writers'.

Walkabout was notable because it was one of the few travel magazines that regularly featured Pacific and Australian content together. Frequent images of Aboriginal Australians placed next to Pacific Islanders prompted Johnston and Rolls to identify a 'rhetoric of neighbourliness' that permeated *Walkabout*, but they provided limited evidence of explicit comparisons between the two.[66] Although pictorial comparisons may have been common in *Walkabout*, writers rarely compared Indigenous Australians and Pacific Islanders, or their environments, in the written text of the 1930s volumes—which is a surprising omission, given the magazine's educational and anthropological overtones. Nonetheless, the case of *Walkabout* highlights how travel writing was intertwined with illustrated magazines and newspapers and how it produced diverse and, at times, ambiguous results.

Magazines are also useful indicators of readership and circulation, which are difficult details to determine in travel writing monographs. For example, Victorian Kuttainen and Sarah Galletly used *Walkabout* to make broader generalisations about 'middlebrow orientalism' in

---

65 Anna Johnston and Mitchell Rolls, *Travelling Home, Walkabout Magazine and Mid-Twentieth-Century Australia* (London: Anthem Press, 2016).
66 Johnston and Rolls, *Travelling Home*, 174–6.

Australian interwar magazines and its reception by Australian readers.[67] The notion of the 'middlebrow' can apply to the texts themselves and to a collective readership; it is also useful for considering the inherent tensions within travel writing, as writers blended genres and styles from lowbrow and highbrow literature. Lowbrow literature drew from popular fictional tales and stereotypes to offer the unexpected and fantastical, while highbrow literature claimed an authority that was gained from firsthand experience and objective observations, justifying travel as an educational and informative activity of self-improvement. This middlebrow ideal was typified by statements like those made by *BP Magazine*, which claimed to 'phrase the fascination from these varying activities and cull from the Markets of the World the best in Literature and Art for the entertainment and interest of its readers'.[68] Richard White has described this preoccupation with 'respectability as rational recreation' as being a clear marker of the middlebrow.[69] The Pacific Islands (as well as the vessels that transported people to them) may have been settings that encouraged this middlebrow sensibility in travel texts.[70]

The middlebrow readership should not be confused with the middle class, though middlebrow content may have reflected certain class issues or biases. Most authors in the study presented in this book belonged to the middle class; however, this may reflect the composition of the publishing industry rather than the travel patterns at the time. Australian travel writers were more likely to be middle- and upper-class Australians because they were well educated and literate and because they had the networks and means to access publishers. Whether this signifies that a Pacific consciousness was more prevalent among certain classes in Australia is unclear. There is some evidence to suggest so. Warwick Anderson highlighted this in his research on a group of Australasian liberal intellectuals who were obsessed

---

67 Victoria Kuttainen and Sarah Galletly, 'Making Friends of the Nations: Australian Interwar Magazines and Middlebrow Orientalism in the Pacific', *Journeys* 17, no. 2 (2016): 23–48, doi.org/10.3167/jys.2016.170203.
68 'Editorial', *BP Magazine* 1, no. 1 (1928): 1.
69 Richard White, 'Armchair Tourism: The Popularity of Australian Travel Writing', in *Sold by the Millions: Australia's Bestsellers*, ed. Toni Johnson-Woods and Amit Sarwal (Newcastle upon Tyne: Cambridge Scholars Publishing, 2012), 183. See also Holland and Huggan, *Tourists with Typewriters*, 10; Richard White, 'Australian Journalists, Travel Writing and China: James Hingston, the "Vagabond" and G. E. Morrison', *Journal of Australian Studies* 32, no. 2 (2008): 238–9, doi.org/10.1080/14443050802056755; Christina Klein, *Cold War Orientalism: Asia in the Middlebrow Imagination, 1945–1961* (Berkeley: University of California Press, 2003), 64.
70 Nicholas Halter, 'Ambivalent Mobilities in the Pacific: "Savagery" and "Civilization" in the Australian Interwar Imaginary', *Transfers* 7, no. 1 (2017): 34–51, doi.org/10.3167/TRANS.2017.070104.

with the Pacific in the 1920s and 1930s, seeing the region as a place to learn about Australia's population problems.[71] The emergence of a local literary bohemia in Sydney in the early twentieth century also suggests that class played a role in the development of literature about the broader Pacific region.[72]

Articulating Australianness

So, what can travel writing tell us about what it means to be Australian? Historians have highlighted the 'bushman', the soldier (also known as the 'digger'), the sportsman and the 'larrikin' as emblematic figures of Australian values; however, the way that the Pacific Islands reflected aspects of Australian character and concerns has yet to be fully explored. Setting aside the fact that travel writing highlights the diversity and individuality of Australians—and that the process of travelling abroad amplified the ambiguities and insecurities of individual and national identities—it is possible to make some broad generalisations about Australian travel writing in comparison to travel accounts that were written by authors of other nationalities. In this contested colonial space, Australian travellers re-positioned themselves in relation to other prominent imperial powers: the British, New Zealanders, German, French, Japanese and Americans.

The Oxford Book of Australian Travel Writing makes some claims about how Australian travel writing is distinct—namely, that it is distinguished by its obsession with cleanliness or a supposed 'casual seriousness'—but this risks oversimplification when considering the specific context of Australia's relationship with the Pacific.[73] Compared to the crowded urban cities of Europe and Asia, the small villages and towns of Pacific Islands did not commonly evoke comments about cleanliness or sanitation. Rather, tropical disease was a more pressing concern for Australians. Similarly, the notion of 'casual seriousness' in Pacific travel writing is also questionable. Although the Pacific was promoted as a relaxed and leisurely destination, Australian travellers were conscious of their precarious position as colonisers and colonial subjects abroad, with their accounts frequently

---

71   Warwick Anderson, 'Liberal Intellectuals as Pacific Supercargo: White Australian Masculinity and Racial Thought on the Boarder-Lands', *Australian Historical Studies* 46, no. 3 (2015): 425–39, doi.org/10.1080/1031461x.2015.1071417.
72   Kirkpatrick, *The Sea Coast of Bohemia*, 52.
73   Pesman, Walker and White, *The Oxford Book of Australian Travel Writing*, xv, xxiii.

appealing to British themes and sensibilities. British cultural values and literature strongly influenced the travel writing that was produced in the antipodes. The style of British travel writing in the Pacific specifically and in other locations more generally has been well studied. The bulk of theoretical scholarship on travel writing has focused on Anglophone European travel accounts since the sixteenth century. Holland and Huggan identified a 'cult of gentlemanliness in contemporary Anglophone travel writing'—a theme that was communicated to colonial readers in Australia and in the rest of the empire during the late nineteenth and early twentieth centuries through boyhood adventure tales, many of which that were set in the Pacific.[74] Colonial Australians thus formed notions of racial superiority and civilisation that were based on British literature, and many of their notions of the Pacific region were based on British representations. These notions and the stereotypical British gentleman were only gradually modified by Australian writers into the 'coming man' that typified distinctly Australian values.

Overt displays of Australian patriotism were rare in travel writing. In some cases, the Sydney school of writers for *The Bulletin* newspaper and the Victorian-based Australian Natives Association influenced authors and travellers, such as Louis Becke, Jack McLaren and George Meudell.[75] The 1917 diary of Australian sailor Chris Syvertsen while anchored in Suva aboard the HMAS *Fantome* is a rare example of a distinctively Australian 'voice'—one containing references to what he termed 'Australian Slanguage' and poems about what it meant to be Australian.[76] Patriotic statements that distinguished Australia from England were more commonly stimulated by the presence of foreign threats, such as reactions to French colonial presence in the New Hebrides and New Caledonia or the Japanese expansion in the North Pacific. In some cases, travellers criticised the British empire, as Eric Baume did in his description of Fiji as a 'typical smug British colony';[77] however, to advocate that Australia take the colonial mantle from Britain was usually a step too far. Therefore, travel accounts did not always mirror public opinion regarding Australia's

---

74   Holland and Huggan, *Tourists with Typewriters*, 6. See also Saxby, *A History of Australian Children's Literature* 1841–1941, 24; Pearson, *Rifled Sanctuaries*, 58; Brian V Street, *The Savage in Literature: Representations of "Primitive" Society in English Fiction, 1858–1920* (London: Routledge, 1975), doi.org/10.4324/9781315617275; Dixon, *Writing the Colonial Adventure*.
75   John Hirst, *The Australians: Insiders & Outsiders on the National Character since 1770* (Melbourne: Black Inc., 2010), 11–13; Pearson, *Rifled Sanctuaries*, 78.
76   Chris Syvertsen, Private Record, PR01438 (Canberra: Australian War Memorial, 1917–1918).
77   Eric Baume, *I Lived These Years* (Sydney: George G. Harrap & Co., 1941), 160.

colonial ambitions in newspapers and political discourse, presumably because travel could evoke an uncertainty about the young nation's ability to rule over others.

The benefit of being on the periphery of the empire was that travellers were less constrained by British etiquette and social norms. As one female author noted in a private letter in 1898, the view from the periphery could offer important truths for metropole readers:

> A little wholesome truth might shock 'em [the British public], but might it not prove bracing? ... If I could afford it, I would risk publishing all the indelicate facts—because they are full of teaching which is needed—but I can't afford it—and so must let off the good souls who, in my estimation, so require a tonic.[78]

In this way, Australian writers shared much with their New Zealander neighbours. In her study of trans-Tasman print culture, Helen Bones noted that:

> New Zealanders and Australians were able to use their colonial status as an advantage. There was a great deal of British interest in the 'colonial exotic', and British audiences were eager to read material on the subject.[79]

For this reason, she argued that scholars should consider trans-Tasman writers a collective rather than differentiate between Australians and New Zealanders.

However, there were also subtle differences between Australian and New Zealander travel writers. In his history of Fiji, Brij V Lal argued that during the interwar period, 'The New Zealanders thought of themselves as better, more refined representatives of colonial English culture, and the Australians were generally less respectful of the rituals and protocols of colonial life'.[80] This distinction was clearer in colonies like Fiji, where Australians and New Zealanders had equally competing interests, as opposed to other British colonies like Samoa or Papua and New Guinea, where one country possessed more influence than the other. The works of Lydia Wevers, Helen Bones, Frances Steel and Anna Johnston have begun

---

78 David, 'Letter to Mrs Scott, 1898'.
79 Bones, 'New Zealand and the Tasman Writing World', 138. See also Denoon, Mein-Smith and Wyndham, *A History of Australia, New Zealand and the Pacific*.
80 Brij V Lal, *Broken Waves: A History of the Fiji Islands in the Twentieth Century* (Honolulu: University of Hawai'i Press, 1992), 106.

to address the lack of research on New Zealand travel writing.[81] Their studies address how New Zealand was connected to the Pacific Islands, arguably in a way that was distinct from Australia's connection. According to Denoon, Mein-Smith and Wyndham, 'Since the opening of the Suez Canal it [New Zealand] looked in a different direction from Australia to overcome its remoteness, across the Pacific rather than through Suez to Britain'.[82] Although Australia was the commercial hub of the Pacific, it remained culturally distinct from it, while New Zealand embraced its Polynesian identity enthusiastically. Kerry Howe's discussion of the relationships between colonialists and Indigenous peoples in Australia and New Zealand identifies a more equitable relationship between the *Pakeha* (European) and the Maori population, in comparison to Australian settler relations with Indigenous Australians. This greatly influenced New Zealand perceptions of the Pacific Islands.[83]

This may explain why Maori would often feature in Australian travel accounts of the Pacific, while Aboriginal Australians were strangely absent. Although Aboriginal Australians were present in the travel accounts of the Australian continent, travellers rarely combined their continental travels with the Pacific Islands.[84] This may reflect the practicalities of travel, as overland voyages and sea voyages are largely separate ventures. It may also highlight the popular beliefs of racial hierarchies at the time, with Aboriginal Australians considered racially inferior to Pacific Islanders. Or perhaps writers were reluctant to compare the romanticised and exoticised Pacific Islands to the realities of the large and harsh Australian continent. This would explain why travellers were reluctant to reference any familiar Australian people or places in their Pacific travel accounts. Only in certain accounts of Papua and New Guinea did Australian writers compare the inhabitants to Aboriginal Australians, with the motivating factor likely being Australia's colonial responsibilities in the territory.

Similarities between Australian, New Zealander and British travel writing did not only reflect shared cultural ties; the travel writing was also shaped by the nature of British colonialism in the region. British colonialism in the Pacific was generally characterised by an emphasis on settlement

---

81 Wevers, *Country of Writing;* Bones, 'New Zealand and the Tasman Writing World'; Bones, 'Travel Writers and Traveling Writers in Australasia'; Katie Pickles and Catharine Coleborne, eds, *New Zealand's Empire* (Manchester: Manchester University Press, 2015).
82 Denoon, Mein-Smith and Wyndham, *A History of Australia, New Zealand and the Pacific*, 197.
83 See Howe, *Race Relations*.
84 See Robert Clarke, *Travel Writing from Black Australia: Utopia, Melancholia, and Aboriginality* (New York: Routledge, 2015), doi.org/10.4324/9781315851129.

and trade, as compared to other European colonial powers in the region (e.g. Germany and France) whose colonial systems have been portrayed as more accommodating than the British style of rule.

Germany's colonial reach extended to north-eastern New Guinea, Samoa and the Bismarck, Marshall, Caroline and Mariana Islands between 1884 and 1914, though its Pacific colonies were isolated and relatively insignificant compared to its African colonies. This meant that although German travel writing considered the Pacific Islands to be within a more global colonial project, Australian travel writers were much more focused on the Pacific as an important and immediate area of interest. Primarily focused on economic gains, the German colonies had a 'civilian tone' compared to other colonial powers in the region, with less military, official or missionary presence.[85] They have been characterised by Lal and Fortune as 'rudimentary compared to the practised colonial cultures of Britain and France', and were 'neither racist nor nationalistic'[86]—a key point of difference compared to what was described in Australian literature at the time. Although German and Australian travel writing both featured race as a prominent theme, Germans went one step further and imagined similarities between Polynesians and Germans; their writing was 'organised around tropes of empathy with the colonised', as argued by Russell Berman.[87] Such a notion signified that unlike its African colonies, Germany's colonial practices in the Pacific recognised indigenous models of governing.[88] This does not mean that German colonial rule was always benevolent. As Stewart Firth demonstrated in his history of German New Guinea, the territory's colonial rule could be erratic and harsh, and Australian writers were eager to portray the German trader as ungentlemanly.[89]

---

85   Sara Friedrichsmeyer, Sara Lennox and Susanne Zantop, eds, *The Imperialist Imagination: German Colonialism and Its Legacy* (An Arbor: University of Michigan Press, 1998), 11; Peter J Hempenstall, *Pacific Islanders under German Rule: A Study in the Meaning of Colonial Resistance* (Canberra: ANU Press, 2016), 22–3, doi.org/10.22459/piugr.06.2016.
86   Brij V Lal and Kate Fortune, eds, *The Pacific Islands: An Encyclopaedia* (Honolulu: University of Hawai'i Press, 2000), 236.
87   Berman termed this concept as 'salvage colonialism'; Russel A Berman, *Enlightenment or Empire: Colonial Discourse in German Culture* (London: University of Nebraska Press, 1998), 10.
88   Miriam Kahn and Sabine Wilke, 'Narrating Colonial Encounters: Germany in the Pacific Islands', *The Journal of Pacific History* 42, no. 3 (2007): 296, doi.org/10.1080/00223340701691975. See also Tracey Reimann-Dawe, 'German Travel Writing on Africa 1848–1914', in *German Colonialism and National Identity*, ed. Michael Perraudin and Jürgen Zimmerer (New York: Routledge, 2011), 21–32.
89   Stewart Firth, *New Guinea under the Germans* (Carlton: Melbourne University Press, 1982); Dirk HR Spennemann, '"Vell, I don't call dot very shentlemanly gonduck": The Portrayal of Germans as Ungentlemanly South Sea Traders in Louis Becke's Short Stories', *Pacific Asia Inquiry* 5, no. 1 (2014): 107–29.

French engagement in the Pacific region occurred on a greater scale and within a longer time frame than German engagement, with colonies created in eastern Polynesia, New Caledonia and the New Hebrides; however, its informal empire of traders and residents did not match the British network in size and scale. Matt Matsuda characterised French imperialism as being 'more fragmentary than comprehensive' and as focusing on alliance and accommodations rather than emphasising settlements and plantations as the British did.[90] For this reason, Australian travel writers offered more detailed descriptions of the economic and colonial processes at work than French writers, and they did not display the same degree of 'emotional sensibility' that Matsuda identified as a common feature of French texts. The influence of French explorers and writers was significant for Australians, with people like de Bougainville, Diderot, Loti and Gauguin enshrining Polynesia as a tropical paradise in the popular imagination. Of the French colonies, Australians were most concerned with the French colonial presence that was closest to Australia's shore (i.e. New Caledonia and the New Hebrides). In the New Hebrides, direct colonial competition with France signified that Australians often focused on the legal, religious and commercial conflicts between French and British citizens. The perceived French threat to Australians diminished after World War I, as did French interest in the territories. This indicated that French ambitions in the Pacific gradually yielded to indifference in the first half of the twentieth century, just as Australians assumed a more active and international interest in the region.

In contrast to Australian, German, French and British rule, the Japanese colonial system in the Pacific was heavily bureaucratic and authoritarian.[91] And yet, the development of Japanese literature regarding *Nanyo* (the South Seas) shared many similarities with Australian writing. Japan's official entry into the Pacific was dominated by its occupation of Micronesia during the interwar period—from when it was awarded all of Micronesia (except Guam) as a Class C mandated territory after World War I until the Pacific War in 1941. Japan produced a prolific number of writings about the Pacific during this time, as well as before the interwar

---

90 Matt Matsuda, *Empire of Love: Histories of France and the Pacific* (New York: Oxford University Press, 2005), 7.
91 Lal and Fortune, *The Pacific Islands*, 236–37; Mark R Peattie, *Nan'yo: The Rise and Fall of the Japanese in Micronesia, 1885–1945* (Honolulu: University of Hawai'i Press, 1988), 104.

period, of which several scholars have written about.⁹² The broad trends in Japanese literature share similarities with Australian themes: they began with fictional, romantic stereotypes of the tropics and savagery due to European–American influences in the late 1800s (*nanshin ron*), which were then followed by the development of Japan's own distinct and nationalistic prose that advocated expansion into the Pacific (*shosetsu*), which was then subsequently followed by a more empathetic shift in the interwar period that corresponded to the opening of shipping lanes and tourism.⁹³ Both Australia and Japan were relatively new nations and were keen to distinguish themselves from the 'old world', with their authors affirming the racial relationships between their nations and their colonial subjects (though the Japanese used ethnography in support of anti-Western sentiment to justify Japanese claims to the region).⁹⁴ Ryota Nishino's research on Japanese travel writers in the Pacific has revealed that, like Australians, Japanese travel writers were also keenly aware of their audience and publishers, and they frequently had ambiguous responses to meeting Pacific Islanders face to face.⁹⁵

Although Japan and Australia were both relatively new nations on the international scene, they rarely identified with one another. Conversely, the US was an emerging colonial power in the Pacific that Australians respected and sometimes even imitated. Scholars have thoroughly addressed the subject of the US's literary imaginations of the Islands, often in reference to American imperialism in the North Pacific and the

---

92 See Peattie, *Nan'yo*; David L Hanlon, *Upon a Stone Altar: A History of the Island of Pohnpei to 1890* (Honolulu: University of Hawai'i Press, 1988), doi.org/10.2307/j.ctvp2n4g9; Francis X Hezel, *Strangers in Their Own Land: A Century of Colonial Rule in the Caroline and Marshall Islands* (Honolulu: University of Hawai'i Press, 1995); Faye Yuan Kleeman, *Under an Imperial Sun: Japanese Colonial Literature of Taiwan and the South* (Honolulu: University of Hawai'i Press, 2003); Naoto Sudo, *Nanyo–Orientalism: Japanese Representations of the Pacific* (New York: Cambria Press, 2010); Michele M Mason and Helen JS Yee, *Reading Colonial Japan: Text, Context, Critique* (Stanford: Stanford University Press, 2012); Mark Alan Ombrello, 'Monstrous Projections and Paradisal Visions: Japanese Conceptualizations of the South Seas (*nan'yō*) as a Supernatural Space from Ancient Times to the Contemporary Period' (PhD thesis, University of Hawai'i, 2014); Robert Thomas Tierney, *Tropics of Savagery: The Culture of Japanese Empire in Comparative Frame* (Berkeley: University of California Press, 2010), doi.org/10.1525/california/9780520265783.001.0001.
93 Sudo, *Nanyo–Orientalism*, 5, 8.
94 Sudo, *Nanyo–Orientalism*, 5; Peattie, *Nanyo*, 91–5.
95 Ryota Nishino, 'Tales of Two Fijis: Early 1960s Japanese Travel Writing by Kanetaka Kaoru and Kita Morio', *Journal of Pacific History* 49, no. 4 (2014): 440–56, doi.org/10.1080/00223344.2014.974300; Nishino, 'The Self-Promotion of a Maverick Travel Writer', 1–13.

Caribbean.⁹⁶ Australians were influenced by American literature, and their work found popularity with American readers. This literary relationship preceded Australia's official diplomatic shift away from Britain and closer to the US after World War II. American and Australian perspectives of the Pacific shared many similarities. Both nations were keen to distinguish themselves from European colonial powers, and both considered the Pacific a space in which to enact their own imperial ambitions. Australians referred to this as a 'new imperialism', while Americans relied on the concepts of a 'Manifest Destiny' and 'America's Pacific Lake'. Although the US had already engaged in imperialism in other parts of the world, William Davis attested that the US's involvement in the Pacific was perceived to have been conducted in a discrete period that marked the country's transition into an empire.⁹⁷

Like Australia, the US's initial engagement in the Pacific region was marked by commercial ventures, and the travel writing that was produced reflected this accordingly. Rob Wilson argued that:

> Authors of national cultures (such as Melville, Twain, Henry Adams, Michener, P.F. Kluge, and Theroux) in prolific works of prose possessed these 'Happy Isles of Oceania' as innocent isolatos of their own democratic–commercial empire.⁹⁸

Americans were actively engaged in whaling, trade and plantation activities in the Pacific, with Hawai'i quickly becoming a global port of call. It was a frequent destination for Australian and American travellers. Although Hawai'i was notable among Australians for its hybridised cultures (both Asian and American) and its modern tourist developments, it was

---

96 For example, see William Davis, 'Pioneering the Pacific: Imagining Polynesia in United States Literature from 1820 to 1940' (PhD thesis, The Claremont Graduate University, 2002); Jeffrey Geiger, *Facing the Pacific: Polynesia and the U.S. Imperial Imagination* (Honolulu: University of Hawai'i Press, 2007); Paul Lyons, 'Pacific Scholarship, Literary Criticism, and Touristic Desire: The Specter of A. Grove Day', *Boundary* 24, no. 2 (1997): 47–78, doi.org/10.2307/303763; Paul Lyons, *American Pacificism: Oceania in the U.S. Imagination* (New York: Routledge, 2006); Christopher McBride, *The Colonizer Abroad: Island Representations in American Prose from Herman Melville to Jack London* (New York: Routledge, 2004), doi.org/10.4324/9780203494400; Rob Wilson, *Reimagining the American Pacific: From South Pacific to Bamboo Ridge and Beyond* (Durham: Duke University Press, 2000), doi.org/10.1215/9780822380979; Peter Hulme, 'The Silent Language of the Face: The Perception of Indigenous Difference in Travel Writing About the Caribbean', in *Perspectives on Travel Writing*, ed. Glenn Hooper and Tim Youngs (London: Routledge, 2004), 85–98; Christine Skwiot, *The Purposes of Paradise: U.S. Tourism and Empire in Cuba and Hawai'i* (Philadelphia: University of Pennsylvania Press, 2010), doi.org/10.9783/9780812200034.
97 Davis, 'Pioneering the Pacific'.
98 Wilson, *Reimagining the American Pacific*, 65.

represented in numerous ways in US literature—including as a luxurious and exotic holiday destination, as a hill from which the US radiated the benefits of civilisation to the Pacific, or as the ideal melting pot from which to model the nation.[99] Australia's own relationship with its colonial acquisitions in the Pacific was markedly different from the US in this respect.

Both US and Australian travel writing used the Pacific as a space for ideological and cultural debate, as well as a place in which the forbidden could be explored. This was crucial for the development of a national culture and identity in both nations. In some cases, American writers were opposed to the US's imperialist expansion in the Pacific.[100] Australian attitudes to American colonialism were much less critical, especially since the American empire was largely confined to the North Pacific—a region that Australians rarely visited (except for Hawai'i). Australians were instead more concerned about the islands closer to home and focused their colonial critiques on the British empire, with who they were most familiar. This distinguished Australian travel writers from their American counterparts for most of the early twentieth century.

Ultimately, Australian travellers were willing to adapt and incorporate different notions, themes and styles into their accounts; as such, a clearly defined Australian character is difficult to discern in the broad corpus of travel writing. The records that Australian travellers left behind highlight a more complex understanding of what it meant to be an 'Australian' in the late nineteenth and early twentieth centuries—an understanding that was influenced by notions of race, gender and class. Australia's position on the periphery allowed travellers to test the boundaries of what was acceptable in European society, and the Pacific Islands were the closest region in which this experiment could be engaged. These records thus illuminate how notions about the new Australian nation were formed in response to global encounters and interactions.

Shrouded in myth and mystery, the South Seas were an attractive notion in Australian and European imaginings, persisting throughout the nineteenth and early twentieth centuries. Australia's early maritime connections to the Pacific have often been overlooked in favour of a nationalist history

---

99   See Christine Skwiot, 'Itineraries of Empire: The Uses of US Tourism in Cuba and Hawai'i, 1898–1959' (PhD thesis, The State University of New Jersey, 2005); Skwiot, *The Purposes of Paradise*.
100 Geiger, *Facing the Pacific*, 13.

that focused on the continent rather than on the connections that spread outwards from it. Travel writing offers glimpses into how Australia was connected to the broader region and how the South Seas were a part of other regional and national spheres of influence. The political boundaries that divided islands and cultures could be as temporary and fluid as the travellers themselves; as such, travellers preferred more generalised terms to imagine the geographical region. Similarly, Australians were as diverse as the peoples that they encountered—and whether they considered themselves Australian, Britisher, colonial or Australasian, the experience of travel served only to magnify the ambiguities and uncertainties of identity. Some travellers returned confident and proud to be distinctively Australian citizens, while others could be unsettled from their initial convictions. This process of self-questioning began as soon as these travellers stepped onto the boat.

2

Steamships and Tourists

> Romance and adventure are inseparably bound up with our literature of these Islands, and we have almost got to think of them as mythical isles of beautiful imaginings, creations of the poetic brain of genius, only to be enjoyed in book or picture, like fairy tales of modern Arabian Nights. And yet, these beautiful scenes are very real, and very easy to reach for the fortunate residents of this great Southern Continent … Sydney is the starting point of the fleets of vessel which carry the flag of Commerce amongst the Southern Seas, and the advent of the modern mail steamer, with its charted route and regular timetable, has proved a real 'open sesame' for the everyday holiday makers, to scenes which before were only accessible to the fortunate ones of wealth and leisure.[1]

As suggested by this 1912 promotional brochure from Burns, Philp & Company (an Australian shipping business), the rise of the steamship made travel to the Pacific Islands more accessible to Australians. Offering safe, comfortable and exciting journeys through the Islands, steamships popularised certain routes throughout the Pacific. The expansion of steamship routes from the Australian continent to the Pacific in the late nineteenth century coincided with the growth of travel writing and public interest in the wider region. These steamship vessels did not only carry passengers and cargo; they were also loaded with symbolism, which was emblematic of modernity, mobility and nationalism. They relied on the routes that overlaid pre-existing imperial networks (and that occasionally subverted them), and their cargo supported island nodes in the 'webs

---

1   Burns, Philp & Company, Limited, *Picturesque Travel*, no. 2 (1912), 54.

of empire'.[2] Controlling these lines of communication offered steamships and the companies that owned them immense power that could shape Australian government policy as well as the Island destinations. Yet they were also precariously situated in a relationship that relied on government subsidies and approvals, and their business reflected colonial ambitions and desires. This was most clearly visible in the composition of the ships' crews who, by the twentieth century, were carefully chosen according to the immigration rules of the White Australia policy.

The ways in which this mode of transportation shaped Australian perceptions of the Pacific Islands is not yet fully understood. The most obvious influence that steamship companies exerted on the Australian public was through branded publications—countless holiday promotions and tourism ephemera that spread editorialised messages of leisure and pleasure in the Pacific. However, steamships also shaped the experience of travel in more subtle or unintentional ways. Within the confines of a ship, travellers were carefully guided towards particular expectations, and the islands that they saw with their own eyes were framed through a porthole. For travel writers, the arrival was the most anticipated and vividly described moment of the journey. But unlike the first encounters of Europeans on the beach, arrival by steamship was set to a predictable rhythm and pace, and the Island ports were ready and waiting.

It is unsurprising that the transformation of cargo ships into cruise liners could be credited as creating a particular kind of traveller, one often termed as the 'tourist'. In contrast to the lone, adventurous explorer or wealthy yachtsman of the past, the tourist was considered the modern voyager of the twentieth century. The increasing number of tourists in the 1920s and 1930s encouraged the development of a commercial industry in Australia and the Islands that catered to their increasingly conformist routes and responses. However, the popularity of the masses sat uneasily with some, particularly Australian travellers who had grown up reading pioneer legends of the Australian outback and romantic tales of South Sea vagabonds. These travellers desired to forge their own paths in Australia's unexplored backyard instead of following in the footsteps of their colonial predecessors. Travel writing highlights the uncertainties and ambiguities that characterised the early growth of steamships and tourism in the Pacific.

---

2   Ballantyne, *Webs of Empire*.

Steamships, Stopovers and Destinations

The first steamer in the Australian colonies travelled along the Parramatta River in 1831, though it was not until the 1840s that the invention of the screw propeller and metal hulls began to displace sailing ships. Sailing ships were still useful in the nineteenth century, in part because they were cheaper to build and run and because they were important in inter-island Pacific trade (as they did not require deep harbours or channels). Constrained by the wind and seasonal weather variations, prompt arrival at port was never guaranteed, though sailing ships did follow predictable paths in the Pacific to try and maximise efficiency. Several significant local and global events were needed to trigger the widespread use of the steamship in the Australian and Pacific colonies. This included a period during the Australian gold rush of the 1850s (which attracted steamers from the US), the construction of railways (e.g. in Panama from 1850 to 1855, in the US with the US transcontinental railway from 1861 to 1869 and within Australia from the mid-1850s), the extension of communication cables (including the Pacific Cable in 1902) and the opening of the Suez and Panama Canals (in 1869 and 1914). The opening of the canals was especially important for bringing Australians closer to the northern hemisphere. As Grimshaw noted in 1907: 'The opening of the Panama Canal route will bring the islands so much nearer to the great trading highways, that they [the New Hebrides] will become more important than they are at present, both from a strategic and a trading point of view'.[3] Indeed, steamships contributed to the gradual compression of time and space, which made Australians ever more conscious of their global citizenry. In doing so, these ships disrupted the established routes and ports of call in the Pacific, and their journeys were plotted on maps according to straighter and sharper lines.

Multiple services were provided to Australians travelling to, and through, the Pacific Islands by competing steamship companies—most notably by the Oceanic Steamship Company, Compagnie des Messageries Maritimes, Union Steamship Company, Burns, Philp & Company and the Australasian United Steam Navigation Company. Beginning as coastal services, these companies slowly expanded their fleets and routes into the Pacific, diversifying their operations to include passenger transportation, island trading stores and plantations so that they could remain profitable.

---

3   Beatrice Grimshaw, *From Fiji to the Cannibal Islands* (London: Eveleigh Nash, 1907), 177.

Winning lucrative government mail contracts in this competitive environment was important for maintaining long Pacific voyages, with the major mail routes running from Brisbane to Singapore (via the Torres Strait), from Sydney to Vancouver or San Francisco (via Fiji and Honolulu, or Rarotonga and Tahiti) and from Sydney to London (via the Cape or the Suez).[4] As the rise and fall of certain shipping companies in the Pacific has already been well documented in economic and business histories, only a brief summary of their major routes and achievements is provided below. Recent maritime histories have tried to address this myopia by emphasising themes of mobility and interconnectedness, but the prolific archival record of tourist promotions and company publications scattered throughout the region has yet to be studied in depth. Like travel writing, this subject area can potentially expand our understanding of the relationship between company, crew and traveller within colonial Pacific networks.[5]

The Oceanic Steamship Company began its operating services from the North American coast to Hawai'i from 1881, later establishing a regular route from San Francisco to Honolulu, Pago Pago, Suva and Sydney in conjunction with the Union Steamship Company. It was acquired by Matson Navigation Company in 1926—another American-owned company that had been competing in the Hawaiian route since 1882 and that continued Oceanic's trans-Pacific services until 1970.[6] In response to the growing passenger traffic to Hawai'i, Matson constructed some of the fastest and most luxurious ships to traverse the Pacific at the time. In 1927, the *Malolo* was the fastest ship in the Pacific, cruising at 22 knots. It was followed by the *Mariposa*, *Monterey* and *Lurline* between 1930 and 1932. The *Mariposa* and *Monterey* regularly conveyed Australians through the Pacific and were so popular that their names were re-used in subsequent

---

4   Kevin T Livingston, *The Wired Nation Continent: The Communication Revolution and Federating Australia* (Melbourne: Oxford University Press, 1996), 21.

5   For example, see Steel, *Oceania under Steam*; McCreery and McKenzie, 'The Australian Colonies in a Maritime World'. See also the special issue titled 'Crossing Over' in *Australian Historical Studies* 46, no. 3 (2015).

6   See Jacob Adler, 'The Oceanic Steamship Company: A Link in Claus Spreckels' Hawaiian Sugar Empire', *Pacific Historical Review* 29, no. 3 (1960): 257–69, doi.org/10.2307/3636164; Duncan O'Brien, *The White Ships: Matson Line to Hawai'i, New Zealand, Australia via Samoa, Fiji, 1927–1978* (Victoria: Pier 19 Media, 2008); John E Cushing, *Captain William Matson (1849–1917): From Handy Boy to Shipowner* (New York: Newcomen Society in North America, 1951); 'About Matson: History', Matson, www.matson.com/corporate/about_us/history.html; S Swiggum and M Kohli, 'The Fleets: Matson Line 1882–1980', The Ships List, www.theshipslist.com/ships/lines/matson.shtml.

liners until 1970. Matson was also responsible for the construction of the Moana Hotel in 1901 (the first hotel of its kind in Honolulu), followed by the Royal Hawaiian Hotel in 1927.

The Compagnie des Messageries Maritimes (MM) was a French steamship service founded in 1835. It began its services from Marseille to Melbourne, Sydney and then Noumea from 1882, transporting mail, passengers and cargo. From 1901, a smaller vessel named the *Pacifique* operated an inter-island route between Sydney, Noumea and the New Hebrides. From 1922, ships travelling via the Suez Canal terminated at Sydney, and a new Panama Canal route to Noumea added Papeete, Wellington and Suva to the list of stopovers. After the severe losses that followed World War II, MM's passenger fleet was rebuilt; however, it was eventually abandoned by 1972.

The Union Steamship Company (USSCo., or the Union Line) was a Dunedin-based coastal shipping company that was established in 1875. It ran a regular route from Auckland to Fiji from 1881, expanding to Melbourne in the following year and to Sydney by the end of the decade. USSCo. established cruises that were specifically aimed for tourists travelling from Auckland to Fiji, Samoa and Tonga in the 1880s. Its success, though limited until the late 1890s, was due to effective marketing and the construction of the passenger steamer, *Waikare*.[7] Services were then expanded, including an additional tour of the Cook Islands, Tahiti, Samoa and Tonga, as well as an extension of the Fiji–Tonga–Samoa circuit to the New Hebrides, New Caledonia, Norfolk Island and Sydney. In 1901, USSCo. acquired the Canadian–Australian Royal Mail Line—also known as the 'All-Red Route', because it used British-owned ships and only visited British territories (excepting Honolulu). This allowed USSCo. to deliver passengers from Sydney to Auckland, Suva, Honolulu, Victoria and Vancouver until 1953. In 1909, USSCo. redirected its service from Sydney to San Francisco via Rarotonga and Tahiti in response to the US's restrictions on trading between US coastal ports. This service lasted until 1936.

Burns, Philp & Company (BP) became the most prominent Australian shipping company in the Pacific in the early twentieth century. Originally a Queensland coastal shipping company, it expanded to the pearl-shelling

---

7   Frances Steel, 'An Ocean of Leisure: Early Cruise Tours of the Pacific in an Age of Empire', *Journal of Colonialism and Colonial History* 14, no. 2 (2013): 1–12, doi.org/10.1353/cch.2013.0019.

industry in northern Queensland in the 1880s. From its branch at Thursday Island, it extended its services across the Torres Strait to Port Moresby in 1883. Demand for shipping and commerce in the British protectorate was inconsistent, and BP's early ventures abroad were a struggle. Similarly, trips to the Solomon Islands and the New Hebrides were intermittent until 1896, when the purchase of two steamships allowed BP to offer a circuit from Sydney to British New Guinea, returning via the Solomon Islands, and a circuit from Sydney to the New Hebrides.[8] From 1902, BP operated a service to the Gilbert and Ellice Islands, gradually extending to the Marshall Islands, and transported phosphate from Ocean Island. In 1904, it established a six-weekly service from Sydney to Java and Singapore. BP diversified its commercial operations by purchasing land, operating plantations, opening trading stores, acting as an agent for other shipping companies and even issuing its own stamps and banknotes. Copra, phosphate and sugar were the company's major investments. The 1910s and 1920s were marked by an expansion of BP's inter-island trading networks, through its Suva-based offshoot, Burns, Philp (South Sea) Company.[9]

The Australasian United Steam Navigation Company (AUSN) initially disrupted BP's attempts to monopolise the entire Melanesian trade. AUSN was another Australian-owned shipping company that was formed in 1887 by the amalgamation of the Australasian Steam Navigation Company and the Queensland Steamship Company. By this time, routes between Australia and New Zealand, and between Sydney, Brisbane, Fiji and Noumea, had already become well established.[10] In cooperation with USSCo., the newly formed AUSN expanded its services to, and within, Fiji and the New Hebrides. After World War I, it gradually abandoned these services until it had completely withdrawn from Pacific trade by 1928. Careful to avoid conflict, BP operated copra trading in Fiji through a subsidiary company called Robbie, Kaad and Co., and then poached the government contract from AUSN in 1923 for an inter-island Fiji service. This was the first of many contracts that AUSN lost to BP.

---

8   Kenneth Buckley and Kris Klugman, *The History of Burns Philp: The Australian Company in the South Pacific* (Sydney: Burns, Philip & Co. Ltd, 1981), 68–71.
9   Kenneth Buckley and Kris Klugman, *The Australian Presence in the Pacific: Burns Philp, 1914–1946* (Sydney: Allen & Unwin, 1983), 108–24.
10 See Norman Lang McKellar, *From Derby Round to Burketown: The A.U.S.N. Story* (St Lucia: University of Queensland Press, 1977); Ronald Parsons, *A History of Australasian Steam Navigation Company and Australasian United Steam Navigation Co. Ltd* (Adelaide: publisher unknown, 1960).

Due to their size and the extent of their routes, these five companies had a significant and long-lasting influence on Australian travel to the Pacific, and they appeared more regularly in public discourses about the region. Of course, there were many other competitors who engaged in Pacific transportation. European liners dominated passenger traffic between Fremantle and Sydney until the late 1890s, when Asian companies such as Nippon Yusen Kaisha and the China Navigation Company began to undercut prices. The Singapore route was also crowded by German, Dutch and British shipping companies—including the German company Norddeutscher Lloyd; the Dutch-owned Koninklijke Paketvaart-Maatschappij; the British India Steam Navigation Company; and the British-owned Peninsular and Oriental Steam Navigation Company (P&O). Other smaller ships plied the Pacific waters, owned by trading companies such as Lever Brothers, W.R. Carpenter & Company and the Colonial Sugar Refinery, as well as other ships that were directed by Christian missions, such as the *John Williams* and *Southern Cross* fleets.

As shipping companies grew in size and strength, they became significant players in national and international geopolitics. Because the economic viability of routes was often determined by government subsidies and mail contracts, shipping companies actively lobbied governments and contributed to public debate. In the late nineteenth century, Pacific shipping had to negotiate with the Australian colonies of Queensland, New South Wales and Victoria, who competed to subsidise direct mail routes.[11] Other private organisations complicated this competitive situation, such as Christian missions or major export businesses in the Islands who also provided lucrative subsidies. Additionally, growing nationalistic sentiment in the Australian colonies concurrently resisted foreign influence and competition. Foreign vessels were regarded with suspicion, according to Frank Coffee's recollection of a Sydney journalist's impressions when the first passenger boat arrived from the US in the 1870s:

> Her entry into the trans-Pacific trade aroused jealousy in the breasts of many people, who thought that the new line would interfere with the P. & O. steamship service, and, furthermore, by bringing Australia into closer relationship with the wide-awake United States weaken the ties that bound the Colonies to Great Britain.[12]

---

11 McKellar, *From Derby Round to Burketown*, 194.
12 Frank Coffee, *Forty Years on the Pacific: The Lure of the Great Ocean; A Book of Reference for the Traveller and Pleasure for the Stay-at-Home* (Sydney: Oceanic, 1920), 6.

In this competitive colonial environment, the steamships themselves were bestowed with a symbolic status of national pride, which was evident in the naming of the vessels and in their routes of passage. The All-Red Route symbolised the imperial connections to which Australian and New Zealand shipping companies contributed. This route circumnavigated the globe and privileged British transportation and communication networks to connect the empire in the late nineteenth and early twentieth centuries.[13]

As the new Australian nation emerged in 1901, internal conflict was gradually replaced by a growing concern about external threats. Australians turned their attention to colonial rivalries in the Pacific, many of which shaped, and were shaped by, the routes of steamships. Frances Steel asserted that the mobility of steamships in the Pacific signified that they crossed multiple colonial spheres of influence and that their routes were 'highly politicised relationships'.[14] This competitiveness was particularly rigorous before World War I, when shipping monopolies had yet to form and when Australia was one of many colonial powers asserting themselves in the Pacific. Steamship companies thus had to negotiate political rivalries, sometimes acting as agents of an informal imperialism—or, at other times, challenging them. Melanesia was one of the first regions in which the new Australian federal government staked its claim. When French government subsidies of MM limited the efforts of BP and AUSN to expand to New Caledonia, the Australian federal government responded by subsidising Australian shipping to stabilise Australian and British interests in the nearby New Hebrides.[15]

Colonies and companies clung to each other when it was convenient, but loyalty was not absolute. In the case of New Caledonia, French colonial officials were willing to use Australian vessels when French shipping companies became indolent.[16] Shipping companies also formed alliances

---

13 Steel, *Oceania under Steam*, 36, 43. See also Frances Steel, 'Re-Routing Empire? Steam-Age Circulations and the Making of an Anglo Pacific c1850–90', *Australian Historical Studies* 46, no. 3 (2015): 356–73, doi.org/10.1080/1031461x.2015.1071416; Frances Steel, 'Lines Across the Sea: Trans-Pacific Passenger Shipping in the Age of Steam', in *The Routledge History of Western Empires*, ed. Robert Aldrich and Kirsten McKenzie (London: Routledge, 2013), 315–29, doi.org/10.4324/9781315879499.ch21; Frances Steel, 'Maritime Mobilities in Pacific History: Towards a Scholarship of Betweenness', in *Mobility in History: Themes in Transport: T2M Yearbook 2011*, ed. Gijs Mom et al. (Neuchatel: Editions Alphil, 2010), 199–204.
14 Steel, 'Maritime Mobilities in Pacific History'.
15 Steel, 'Maritime Mobilities in Pacific History', 31.
16 McKellar, *From Derby Round to Burketown*, 175.

among themselves, as was the case with several Australian companies in response to unionism. This in turn fostered public suspicion of large monopolies and their agendas in Australia, which can be evidenced in popular nicknames such as 'Bloody Pirates' (for BP) and 'Would Rob Christ' (for W.R. Carpenter & Company).[17]

Shipping companies also had to negotiate port regulations in the Pacific Islands and, in this way, European colonial powers could exercise a degree of control over shipping to protect their own interests. These regulations could entail significant ramifications for mobility and commerce in the Pacific. For example, in 1900, the US declared Honolulu a coastal port, prohibiting foreign ships from trading between Hawai'i and the US mainland. This forced foreign steamships to divert to Canada or to transfer passengers to American steamers at Honolulu. Concurrently in Australia, the *Navigation Act of Australia* (1912) impacted Australian shipping wages and the use of 'coloured' labour. A part of the White Australia policy, the *Navigation Act* was resisted by Australian shipping companies whose profits relied on cheap foreign labour. During the debate, BP lobbied to include Papua within Australia's coastal area. This bid failed and a clause was added to all government shipping contracts that prohibited foreign labourers on their ships from entering Sydney Harbour. This meant that foreign crews had to be unloaded from the ships at the last port of call before Australia and then retrieved on the next journey out.[18]

Excessive or restrictive government regulation of ports occasionally provoked resistance from shipping companies who defied international diplomatic protocols. One Australian case illustrates this situation. In 1904, BP publicly protested against being charged exorbitant fees for trading licences in the Marshall Islands, as German trading company Jaluit Gesellschaft protected its monopoly. Not only did BP actively generate public interest in the matter in the Australian press, it also pursued the German company to Europe for compensation, extending beyond diplomatic channels to publicise its cause in the British press and Parliament until the issue was resolved in 1906.[19] In 1920, BP still proudly boasted about its triumph against 'the Kaiser's government' in its company publication, *Picturesque Travel*. Although Australia may

---

17 Steel, *Oceania under Steam*, 37; McKellar, *From Derby Round to Burketown*, 147.
18 Buckley and Klugman, *The History of Burns Philp*, 235–41.
19 Buckley and Klugman, *The History of Burns Philp*, 149.

have been a relatively small player on the global stage at this time, it was actively concerned with establishing its presence in the Pacific arena, with shipping companies being crucial players in solidifying Australia's commercial Pacific empire.

In this contested and competitive environment, BP and USSCo. quickly recognised the potential of Pacific Island tourism for expanding their revenue in the Australian and New Zealand markets. BP's general manager, James Burns, possessed a strong flair for publicity and was ahead of his time in his aiming for the tourist trade.[20] The first tourist trip that BP offered was in 1884 aboard the *Elsea*, from Thursday Island to Port Moresby and back in seven to eight weeks. For £25, it provided that 'capital shooting and fishing is sure to be had, and intending passengers should therefore take rifles and fishing tackle'.[21] Subsequent trips that BP offered varied from an around-the-world trip commencing from Sydney, to a three-week trip for school teachers during the Christmas holidays. USSCo. was also eager to expand its New Zealand coastal tours to the Pacific, which it did in 1883 by offering a winter cruise from Auckland to Fiji. From 1884 to 1899, it offered several more round-trip tours—initially a circuit to Fiji, Samoa and Tonga, and then expanding to eastern Polynesia and Melanesia. USSCo. was innovative in its approach because it constructed a steamer, the SS *Waikare*, that was specifically designed for cruising. William Meeke Fehon's travel account in 1898 described how the 3,000-ton *Waikare* carried 160 passengers and that:

> The steamer was specially fitted with first-class accommodation only and she carried no cargo … no expense appears to have been spared in studying the most minute details for the comfort of the passengers.[22]

---

20 Buckley and Klugman, *The History of Burns Philp*, 53.
21 'Clipper Yacht Elsea, for New Guinea', *Sydney Morning Herald*, 29 September 1884, 1, nla.gov.au/nla.news-article28369242.
22 William Meeke Fehon, *Six Weeks' Excursion to the South Seas and Eastern Pacific Islands: Comprising Raratonga, Tahiti, Raiatea, Samoa and the Friendly Islands, by the New Steamer 'Waikare', 3,000 tons: (Union Steam Ship Company of N.Z., Ltd) from Sydney, 30th June, 1898* (Sydney: S.D. Townsend and Co. Printers, 1898), 1.

These early forays into tourist cruises were short lived and did not become economically viable until the interwar years. Indeed, they were only possible due to the size and profitability of BP's and USSCo.'s business operations, as the two had gradually incorporated smaller competitors in the region. For most shipping companies in the late nineteenth and early twentieth centuries, passenger travel to the Islands was an additional source of income, and travel schedules were second to the demands of cargo.

Despite the sluggish growth of tourism in the Pacific in the early twentieth century, BP and USSCo. are notable for their tourist publications. These were widely circulated in Australia and New Zealand and contributed to the development of the travel writing genre in both countries. In the same year that BP created its first tourist trip, it published and distributed 5,000 copies of a *Queensland Handbook of Information*, which was designed to publicise BP's shipping services. This was followed by a booklet, *British New Guinea*, in 1886 and a quarterly magazine, *Picturesque Travel*, in 1911. This magazine series (later renamed *BP Magazine)* initially printed 20,000 copies and offered readers a mix of educational travel accounts, corporate promotions and exciting illustrations. The front covers of *BP Magazine* tended to feature more global destinations and general travel themes than Pacific content; however, some of the earliest copies of *Picturesque Travel* featured Pacific icons (see Figure 5). Similarly, USSCo. tried to publicise its tours, publishing its first Pacific travel guide in 1895 (*A Cruise in the Islands*) and a periodical (*The Red Funnel*) from 1905 to 1909. Like BP, USSCo.'s 'descriptive booklets' relied on travel writers to disguise promotions within stories that blended fact and fiction. These minor publications initially relied on amateur writers and volunteers to contribute short pieces to an issue. However, as the tourism industry became more profitable, these publications became more sophisticated and specialised, with journalists, academics and freelance writers being paid for favourable articles of travel. Shipping companies funded the publication of reference books, guidebooks, histories and travelogues about the Pacific, as USSCo. did in 1914 when it published Beatrice Grimshaw's *Tours to the South Sea Islands, Tonga, Samoa, Fiji* (see Figure 6).

Figure 5: Burns, Philp & Company Publication.
Source: Front cover of Burns Philp & Company, Limited, *Picturesque Travel*, no. 3 (1913).

Figure 6: Rear Cover of a Union Steamship Company Publication.
Source: Beatrice Grimshaw, *Tours to the South Sea Islands, Tonga, Samoa, Fiji* (Dunedin: Union Steamship Company of New Zealand, 1914).

Figure 7: Translate Your Precious Holiday Moments into Pathescope Home Movies.
Source: *BP Magazine* 8, no. 1 (December 1935).

As camera and printing technology improved, more exciting and colourful illustrations took precedence over written text in the 1920s and 1930s. Travel magazines encouraged the practice of photographing one's Pacific travels by printing advertisements for the latest camera technology (see Figure 7). The messages that popular images and illustrations conveyed revisited the same stereotypes that travel writing had used since Europeans were first in the Pacific—many of which are discussed throughout this book in further detail. Norman and Ngaire Douglas suggested four 'fundamentals' of cruise imagery that are useful for considering these representations within the context of a growing commercial tourism industry: romance, luxury, exotica and nostalgia.[23] In a Pacific Island context, romance was typically symbolised by the alluring (often scantily dressed) female, while Melanesian men adorned with weapons or unusual dress provided the exotic element. Both figures were usually situated against a backdrop of coconut palms, mountainous islands or sandy beaches. Notions of luxury were conveyed with images of cruise ships or interiors, with the contrast against natural surroundings

---

23 Norman Douglas and Ngaire Douglas, *The Cruise Experience* (Frenchs Forest: Pearson Education, 2004), 156–74.

and supposedly primitive peoples used to amplify this message and invoke nostalgia. Images of children suggested a primitive innocence and playfulness. Promotional images about the Pacific could also be ambiguous and contradictory at times. In some company publications, cruising was marketed as superior to regular sea travel because it prioritised the interests of tourists and brought them to islands that lay outside the major trading routes, offering a more complete Pacific experience.[24] However, the idea of sailing in the Pacific was nostalgic and attractive, so it often appeared simultaneously alongside cruise ship images.

These early travel accounts and promotions may have presented the Pacific Islands as a region of endless opportunities and adventures, but the colonial reality was that travel was highly regulated and controlled. For travellers, this was most commonly expressed in their frustrations with quarantine and customs officials, who were either too slow or too strict. One visitor to Suva in 1911 wrote, 'The Doctor from the shore was very slow in making his appearance, and the steamer waited, drifting, in the harbor, much to the discontent of the passengers', and later complained about paying an 'Alien Tax' to land at Honolulu.[25] In 1916, George Taylor noted:

> Everyone's nerves were all askew, and by the time the medical officer came along to inspect, with his ferrety little eyes piercing through fierce bushy eyebrows, seeming to look into one's soul, one felt as if he had all the ills in the big medical dictionary.[26]

Those with their own private vessels fared no better, with one sailor complaining in 1927 that the 'red tape in Tahiti is awful'.[27]

Access was also a challenge. As the size of ships increased dramatically in the 1920s and 1930s to accommodate more passengers, the choice of port was limited to islands that had sufficient harbours to accommodate them, which were deep enough or possessed docks large enough. The tight scheduling of ships and the costly nature of layovers necessitated the

---

24 Steel, 'An Ocean of Leisure'. USSCo. also composed *Maoriland: Illustrated Handbook to New Zealand* (Melbourne: George Robertson & Co., 1884); *Trip to the South Sea Islands by Union Steam Ship Company's S.S. 'Waikare': July–August, 1898* (Dunedin: J. Wilkie & Co., 1898); and *The All-Red Route: The Scenic Route to London* (Union Steamship Company of New Zealand, n.d.). It also published Thomas Bracken, *The New Zealand Tourist* (Dunedin: Mackay, Bracken, 1879).
25 George Stanley Littlejohn, *Notes and Reflections 'on the road'* (Sydney: Swift Print, 1911), 13, 24.
26 George Augustine Taylor, *There!: A Pilgrimage of Pleasure* (Sydney: Building Limited, 1916), 42.
27 Albert William Pearse, *A Windjammer 'Prentice* (Sydney: John Andrews & Co., 1927), 7.

development of infrastructure in the Islands that catered for large numbers of travellers—such as refuelling facilities, quarantine and customs officials, shipping branches, stores, hotels, banks, cars, roads and reliable communication. The port towns of Honolulu and Suva were strategically positioned at the crossroads of multiple trans-Pacific routes and were the largest and most developed port towns of their day, which explains why they featured in more travel accounts than any other Island stopover.

The development of organised tourism as a commercial operation in Hawai'i began in the late 1890s, coinciding with the end of the Hawaiian monarchy. A group of US-backed businessmen and sugar planters forced Queen Liliuokalani to abdicate in 1893, and by 1898, Hawai'i was formally annexed by the US. This marked the culmination of more than 70 years of American influence in the Island group since missionaries first arrived in the 1820s, during which time US business became firmly entrenched in Hawaiian society. After the abdication, it was these wealthy elites who supported efforts to promote Hawai'i as a tourism destination, with the Hawai'i Promotion Committee being formed in 1903 (later renamed the Hawai'i Visitors Bureau). As Christine Skwiot argued, tourism in Hawai'i was a tool for legitimising and strengthening American colonial authority; it was initially used to attract permanent white settlers to Hawai'i and, after World War I, to provide for and entrench privileged white people within Hawai'i.[28] The growth of tourism in the Islands did not occur without indigenous resistance, as Noenoe K Silva uncovered in her analysis of Hawaiian-language newspapers (though Australian travellers rarely noticed this local tension).[29]

Advertisements framed Hawai'i as an extension of the US and as a gateway to the Orient. The natural features of the islands were initially promoted over the people, with only occasional generic images of alluring native women in tropical scenes.[30] It was only later in the 1920s that the iconic image of the 'hula girl' appeared—and by the 1930s, it had become firmly entrenched. Live hula performances became a key attraction and were

---

28   Skwiot, *The Purposes of Paradise*, 11; Christine Skwiot, 'Geneologies and Histories in Collision: Tourism and Colonial Contestations in Hawai'i, 1900–1930', in *Moving Subjects: Gender, Mobility and Intimacy in an Age of Global Empire*, ed. Tony Ballantyne and Antoinette Burton (Urbana: University of Illinois Press, 2009), 200.
29   Noenoe K Silva, *Aloha Betrayed: Native Hawaiian Resistance to American Colonialism* (London: Duke University Press, 2004), doi.org/10.1215/9780822386223.
30   Desmond, *Staging Tourism*, 6, 36. For more information regarding the beginnings of tourism in Hawai'i, see Dawn Duensing, *Hawai'i's Scenic Roads: Paving the Way for Tourism in the Island* (Honolulu: University of Hawai'i Press, 2015).

marketed to the growing number of tourists that flocked to Hawai'i in the 1930s. According to figures published in the first edition of the *Pacific Islands Yearbook* in 1932, Hawai'i received 44,452 tourists—almost half of whom stayed two days or more.[31] In traditional Hawaiian society, hula was one of several dances that performed important religious, social and political functions; however, many of these dances were suppressed to satisfy missionary sensibilities. Hula resurged again during King Kalakaua's reign in the late 1800s as a form of resistance and was then appropriated as a symbolic tourist attraction. Amy Ku'uleialoha Stillman characterised this cultural dance as being 'dis-membered then re-membered'.[32] Scholars have since critiqued the complex meanings and adaptations of the hula, which has been variously invoked as an authentic cultural marker, as a form of resistance against colonial rule and as a symbol of 'Hawaiianness'.[33] The iconography of the hula, and promotional material in general, overlooked the racial complexities of Hawai'i, which can be most vividly evidenced by how Hollywood appropriated and circulated images of the hula girl.

Most Australian travellers were unaware or unconcerned with these complex cultural symbols and racial hierarchies in Hawai'i. Rather, it was the American culture and the pace of development that they noted most often. Australians admired Honolulu for its luxury and modernity and frequently identified the port town as being part of the US rather than the Pacific. In 1909, one Australian observed that Honolulu was 'fast becoming completely Americanised'; by 1937, another traveller remarked that it was 'a typical American city'.[34] The construction of luxury hotels, beginning with the Moana Hotel in 1901, and the subsequent development of Waikiki beach contributed to this view of Honolulu. As Skwiot noted, *haole* (white residents) offered the tourist an opportunity 'to act out their fantasies of royalty and empire' in luxury resorts, with the indigenous Hawaiian featured only as a hula girl or beach boy.[35] The account of George Stanley Littlejohn, an Australian businessman who visited Suva and Honolulu en route to the US in 1909, is typical of many Australian

---

31 Robert William Robson, ed., *The Pacific Islands Yearbook*. 1st ed. (Sydney: Pacific Publications Ltd, 1932), 102.
32 Amy Ku'uleialoha Stillman, 'Re-Membering the History of the Hawaiian Hula', in *Cultural Memory: Reconfiguring History and Identity in the Postcolonial Pacific*, ed. Jeannette Mageo (Honolulu: University of Hawai'i Press, 2001), 187, doi.org/10.1515/9780824841874-011.
33 Desmond, *Staging Tourism*; Amy Ku'uleialoha Stillman, ed., *The Hula: A Revised Edition* (Honolulu: University of Hawai'i Press, 2011); Amy Ku'uleialoha Stillman, *Sacred Hula: The Historical hula ala apapa* (Honolulu: Bishop Museum Press, 1998).
34 Littlejohn, *Notes and Reflections 'on the road'*, 24; Baume, *I Lived These Years*, 168.
35 Skwiot, *The Purposes of Paradise*, 11.

travellers. Aged 47, Littlejohn was an experienced traveller and, having visited both islands three years previously, could make comparisons on the progress of development. He observed that, in Honolulu:

> Great improvements effected in the wharfage accommodation within the last five years, coal elevators have been erected, and large vessels can get good berths with plenty of wharf space and plenty of water under the keel … There is a good service of electric cars, electric light, and a telephone system. The streets are well cared for, and there is an adequate police corps … building is progressing rapidly … the hotels are excellent.[36]

Although travellers frequently admired Honolulu for its modern development, this sentiment came at the expense of Hawai'i's other Pacific qualities, including its local scenery, agriculture and indigenous inhabitants, who were often ignored in travel accounts. Very rarely did travellers identify the problems with the rapidly growing tourism industry in the Pacific Islands. Eric Baume, a traveller who visited Pago Pago in American Samoa, remarked that, like Hawai'i, Pago Pago had 'also trodden the Coney-phoney path'.[37]

The scale of the tourism industry in Suva was much smaller than that in Hawai'i, and historians have written much less about it.[38] In the same way that foreign businesses lobbied for Hawaiian tourism, the Fiji Visitors Bureau was established in 1923 by a group of businessmen known collectively as the White Settlement League. Its purpose was to encourage foreign investment and settlement in Fiji. Advertisements drew on similar stereotypes as those for Hawai'i (with generic scenery and alluring women), and efforts were made to construct adequate hotels and facilities for accommodating luxury liners. Indigenous Fijians were staged to pose for photographs at the wharf, but the bodily display never reached the same extent as the heavily commercialised hula in Hawai'i did.

---

36 Littlejohn, *Notes and Reflections 'on the road'*, 24.
37 Baume, *I Lived These Years*, 44.
38 For more on the Fiji Visitors Bureau, see RJ Scott, *The Development of Tourism in Fiji since 1923* (Suva: Fiji Visitors Bureau, 1970) and Nicholas Halter, 'Tourists Fraternising in Fiji in the 1930s', *Journal of Tourism History* 12, vol. 1 (2020): 27–47, doi.org/10.1080/1755182x.2019.1682688.

The annual colonial reports of Fiji provide some insight into the gradual development of tourism in the Pacific Islands. In Fiji, visitors increased from an estimated 3,000 in 1926 to 5,001 by 1938.[39] In 1926, the report proudly attributed the growth of tourism in Fiji to:

> Increased shipping facilities, the advertising which the Colony received at the Wembley and Dunedin exhibitions, the opening of a bowling green, and other increased facilities in Suva, and the issue of advertising matter by the shipping companies and the local tourist bureau.[40]

The reports also provided reasons for the fluctuations in tourist traffic. For example, in 1929, they recognised that tourism was 'hampered by the lack of good road communications and hotel or rest-house accommodation away from Suva' and that most Australians and New Zealanders travelled during the winter months.[41] These facts were well known by shipping companies who targeted Australian tours during the winter months. By 1937, the annual colonial reports' statistics were more detailed; they recorded 11 vessels that brought 6,426 visitors who were specifically engaged on tourist cruises, 13,923 travellers who were passing through Suva on other boats, and 1,328 people who were staying a week or longer.[42]

Fiji was in much closer proximity to Australia than to Hawai'i, and its British heritage meant that Australian travellers were more confident about conveying their final judgements. Compared to Hawai'i, Littlejohn found Fiji poorly developed, with 'plain roads' and 'no means of public conveyance other than a few hack carriages'.[43] Littlejohn was particularly scathing of the British rule in Fiji, arguing for an Australian or American takeover. Skwiot stated that such travel narratives 'presented bad hotels, inadequate infrastructure, and poor public health as proof that the government in power was incapable of moral or material progress'.[44] Littlejohn's disappointment starkly contrasts other opinions, such as those of William Allan, who

---

39 Great Britain Colonial Office, *Fiji: Annual General Report for the Year 1926* (London: H. M. S. O., 1927), 9; Great Britain Colonial Office, Foreign and Commonwealth Office and Ministry of Information, *Annual Report on the Social and Economic Progress on the People of Fiji, 1938* (London: H. M. S. O., 1938), 31.
40 Great Britain Colonial Office, *Fiji: Annual General Report for the Year 1926*, 9–10.
41 Great Britain Colonial Office, *Fiji: Annual General Report for the Year 1929* (London: H. M. S. O., 1929), 9–10.
42 Great Britain Colonial Office, Foreign and Commonwealth Office and Ministry of Information. *Annual Report on the Social and Economic Progress on the People of Fiji, 1937* (London: H. M. S. O., 1938), 33.
43 Littlejohn, *Notes and Reflections 'on the road'*, 13.
44 Skwiot, *The Purposes of Paradise*, 3.

enjoyed taking a 'stroll' through the shopping area and was impressed that Suva had two picture houses, which he noted was 'better than Australia'.[45] This inconsistency suggests that first impressions of Suva also depended on individual expectations, on what specific comparisons were being made and on personal allegiances to colonial governments.

Although Suva was not as developed, its status as the British colonial centre of the Pacific, and as a major copra and sugar producer, required that it meet the demands of high shipping traffic levels. As a 1916 AUSN handbook detailed:

> This wharf is soon to have a compeer in the great cement and rock structure, now in course of construction a short distance away. The cost is estimated at a quarter of a million.[46]

The handbook also advertised the convenience of 'palatial buildings', swimming baths, five hotels, 'several good boarding houses', a library, a museum, an Office of the Pacific Cable Board, New South Wales and New Zealand bank branches, a Chamber of Commerce, a hospital, two newspapers and 'several sporting and athletic clubs'. The most popular and well-known symbol of modernity in Suva was the Grand Pacific Hotel, which was constructed by USSCo. in 1914 to match the luxury and opulence that Hawaiian hotels promised. This hotel was described as 'Suva's Ritz' by Australian resident Betty Freeman, and it vastly improved on existing accommodation.[47] Beachcombers Edward Way Irwin and Ivan Goff described it as 'Suva's only hotel—the others were just pubs … This was indeed an occasion for Suva's aristocracy. Hardly any half-breeds were there. Government officials, well-to-do planters, and leading storekeepers'.[48]

Few other Pacific Islands matched Suva and Hawai'i's pace of development in the early twentieth century. This pace partly depended on shipping companies' routes, such as USSCo.'s routes through Samoa, Tonga and Tahiti, which brought increasing numbers of passengers to those shores. It also depended on location and geography—with New Caledonia's proximity to Australia rendering travel quick and affordable—and deep harbours that facilitated the berthing of larger ships. Security and local

---

45 William Allan, *Homeward Bound, from Australia to Scotland: Impressions by the Way* (Helensburgh: Helensbugh and Gareloch Times, 1915), 24.
46 William Lees, *Around the Coasts of Australia and Fiji Illustrated: A Handbook of Picturesque Travel and General Information for Passengers by Steamers of the Australasian United Steam Navigation Co. Ltd* (Brisbane: Robert McGregor & Coy Printers, 1916), 174, 177.
47 Betty Freeman, *Fiji—Memory Hold the Door* (Balgowlah: B. Freeman, 1996), 57.
48 Edward Way Irwin and Ivan Goff, *No Longer Innocent* (Sydney: Angus & Robertson, 1934), 97.

governance were important for encouraging or discouraging further travel. It was common for visitors to make observations regarding the local police, prisons, crime and the effectiveness of local governance. The location of certain 'attractions' was influential in luring more visitors. These attractions were distinctive natural or historical sites and required easy access. Journalist Julian Thomas alluded to this in his description of one of the New Hebrides groups: 'They have not, on Tanna, visitors sufficient to make it pay as a show place, a la Vesuvius'.[49]

Norfolk Island and Lord Howe Island are prime examples of how important these factors are, as Australians considered both Islands ideal tourist destinations. Both Islands benefited from their close proximity to the Australian coast and from their status as Australian territories. Alan John Villiers described Lord Howe Island as the 'Tourists' Paradise', particularly for 'holiday-makers from New South Wales'.[50] M Kathleen Woodburn, a traveller en route to the New Hebrides, also remarked when she passed by that visitors 'still felt within the pale of civilisation'.[51] In Norfolk Island, tourist handbooks sold the benefits of its 'tropical charm with the calm reasonableness of the temperate zones', as well as its natural scenery and isolation.[52] The main tourist attraction for Norfolk Island was its convict and Pitcairn Islander heritage. Of course, this was a sanitised version of a brutal past, with visitors searching for local ruins of prisons and hoping to meet an old Pitcairner. In 1886, one traveller described how 'an atmosphere of tears, and sighs, and curses hung around these pens', and over 50 years later, another traveller described the island as 'subdued by the aura of misery'.[53] The absence of Pacific Islanders on both Islands, except for those training at the Melanesian Mission station, did not damage the Islands' tourist appeal. Both were scenic stopovers en route to other Pacific Islands, where cross-cultural encounters were expected. Further development of Australian tourism in these Islands was hampered by their small resident populations; their limited economic resources; the difficulty of landing due to reefs and the absence of suitable harbours; and the steamship routes themselves, which determined whether visitors could stay a few hours or whether they had to wait a month for a returning boat.[54]

---

49 Thomas, *Cannibals and Convicts*, 281.
50 Alan John Villiers, *Cruise of the Conrad: A Journal of a Voyage Around the World, Undertaken and Carried Out in the Ship Joseph Conrad, 212 tons, in the years 1934, 1935 and 1936 by way of Good Hope, the South Seas, the East Indies and Cape Horn* (London: Hodder & Stoughton, 1937), 270.
51 M Kathleen Woodburn, *Backwash of Empire* (Melbourne: Georgian House, 1944), 23.
52 'The Charm of Norfolk Island', *The Pacific Islands Yearbook*, 1st ed, ed. Robert William Robson, (Sydney: Pacific Publications Ltd, 1932), 129.
53 Thomas, *Cannibals and Convicts*, 35; *Woodburn, Backwash of Empire*, 32.
54 Robson, *The Pacific Islands Yearbook*, 124.

Onboard Ship

Part of the popularity of steamship travel was the companies' offer of services that were safe, reliable, comfortable and affordable. Coffee reflected on this in his numerous trans-Pacific voyages:

> For the most part, the service has been comfortable and safe, and as fast as the remuneration warranted ... the rates were reasonable, and most of the time the seas were smooth—indeed, enjoyably so.[55]

Although steamship cruising did not reach its peak until the interwar period, by the 1880s and 1890s, steamships had begun to challenge the belief that sea travel was dangerous, boring and uncomfortable. For the first time, sea travel could be undertaken as a leisure activity rather than as a necessity, and large corporations saw the value of tourism as a separate venture rather than one to be tacked onto trade and cargo operations.[56] BP's magazine, *Picturesque Travel*, marketed its travel to the 'change-seeking tourist', or to those seeking a 'healthful holiday' away from the colder climates.[57]

An example of this is AUSN's 1916 handbook (see Figure 8), which provided 'Picturesque Travel and General Information' to 'those who desire rapidity of transit with high-class comfort'.[58] Like BP's and USSCo.'s publications, AUSN's illustrated handbook emphasised modern conveniences and luxury onboard ship, for 'a very moderate expense'. Its passenger ship, *Levuka*, was 'specially designed for this service'—it was 'lighted with electricity throughout' and catered for 100 first-class passengers and 50 second-class passengers, with '4000 cubic feet of refrigerated space'. Existing photographs showcase the luxurious interiors of the drawing rooms, smoking rooms and dining rooms, as well as passengers lying on deck chairs. The handbook was careful to militate against preconceptions of monotony, claiming 'at no time is the vessel more than a few days out of sight of land'.[59] It also suggested specific activities that passengers could do ashore—offering connecting services with the inter-island vessel, *Amra*, motor launches and motor cars, and providing detailed timings and costs. Ironically, the steamship's ability to collapse distance meant that it had become more closely connected to land than sail ships.[60] Described by historians as the 'Golden Age' of travel,

---

55 Coffee, *Forty Years on the Pacific*, 5.
56 Steel, 'An Ocean of Leisure'.
57 Burns, Philp & Company, Limited, *Picturesque Travel*, no. 1 (1911), 50.
58 Lees, *Around the Coasts of Australia and Fiji Illustrated*, 3.
59 Lees, *Around the Coasts of Australia and Fiji Illustrated*, 14, 161.
60 Steel, *Oceania under Steam*, 16.

the 1920s and 1930s witnessed the growth of publications emphasising the spaciousness, opulence and speed of travel.[61] By this time, AUSN and smaller companies were replaced by much larger liners owned by P&O and the Oceanic Steamship Company.

Figure 8: Australasian United Steam Navigation Co. Travel Guide.
Source: Front cover of William Lees, *Around the Coasts of Australia and Fiji Illustrated* (Brisbane: Robert McGregor & Co. Printers, 1916).

---

61 Douglas and Douglas, *The Cruise Experience*, 66.

Steamships changed the rhythms of mobility in the Pacific, shaping individual experiences of travel and arrival. As sociologist John Urry argued, rapid transportation can transform how passengers comprehend landscapes, as well as create new public spaces such as docks and restrict social activities to a specified timetable.[62] Young travel companions Irwin and Goff were excited to place themselves at the mercy of the machine:

> She was dead to time, remorselessly to time, ruthless and efficient. What knowledge, what organization, what perfection of machinery was required to bring that mass of steel to Suva wharf, to a pin-point in an ocean, arriving at the scheduled second! Pilot, captain, deckhands, greasers—all at their jobs. On shore, clerks, stevedores, carriers, customs men … It was all a huge machine of brains and flesh and steel, adjusted to the penny and the second. Into that machine, blindly, we must toss ourselves.[63]

The modern conveniences of the steamship were frequently contrasted to the primitivity of Islanders. Pictorially, the contrast of traditional canoes and steamships were common (see Figures 5 and 8). Steamships were objects of national and imperial pride, and one of the defining images of modernity.[64] They embodied the values of progressive Europe, with luxury interiors catering to wealthy travellers by the late nineteenth century. The emphasis on modern comfort and safety assured travellers that they would have a familiar refuge in a savage and exotic land. Of course, not all promises made in advertisements were fulfilled. Some customers, like Littlejohn, were impressed: 'This steamer is practically a floating hotel. There are many conveniences on board, including a barber's shop … and a laundry.'[65] Others, like writer Alan Durward Mickle, who travelled aboard the *Amra* in 1908, discovered:

> On the shipping plan in the office the two-berth cabin looked quite spacious, but shipping plans can be very deceptive, and this one was. We found that there was a space of about nine inches between the parallel bunks and that the bunks were extremely narrow … the first night on board was not exactly peaceful.[66]

---

62 John Urry, *Consuming Places* (New York: Routledge, 1995), 131.
63 Irwin and Goff, *No Longer Innocent*, 114.
64 Steel, *Oceania under Steam*, 26.
65 Littlejohn, *Notes and Reflections 'on the road'*, 18.
66 Alan Durward Mickle, *Of Many Things* (Sydney: Australian Publishing Co., 1941), 180–1.

Travelling through the Pacific by ship entailed close-quartered living for extended periods. Aboard the sailing ships that explored the Pacific, 'The essence of shipboard life was boundary maintenance', argued Greg Dening, which was no different to the cruise liners of the twentieth century.[67] Steamship passengers entered a microcosm of Western society onboard, with its own traditions, social etiquette and physical areas that were demarcated according to the fare paid. However, travel writing about the Pacific Islands reveals that travel was not only a luxury reserved for the wealthy. Although most Australian travellers belonged to the middle or upper classes, travel could be achieved via cheaper berths aboard sailing and cargo ships, as well as by working aboard vessels. In fact, travellers from the Australian colonies in the 1880s and 1890s were as likely to be opportunists seeking a better life in the nearby Islands as they were to be wealthy travellers. As larger iron hulls allowed for more room below deck, companies could offer two fares; by the interwar period, another fare was introduced between first and third class to serve a growing middle class. First-class passengers enjoyed grand saloons, while steerage class varied between small cabins or sleeping berths. Earlier steamships were hot and cramped, and passengers struggled in the tropical heat. Some steamships also catered specifically for female travellers by employing stewardesses and segregating certain areas on the ships. Crew members, many of whom were Islanders, were also segregated. Elinor Mordaunt, a 51-year-old Australian woman visiting New Caledonia in 1923, travelled aboard the *El Kantara* with 20 first-class passengers, an unspecified number in second class, cargo, French soldiers and an international crew that included a 'colored steward called Chocolat'.[68] This final comment was typical of the observations that attributed simplistic and racialist generalisations to Pacific Island labourers.

Several travellers described these social distinctions onboard and the gradual breakdown in conventions during travel. Irwin and Goff were eager to escape the 'cage of conventions' at home in Perth and described their adventures as beachcombers and stowaways in *No Longer Innocent* (1934). When they were caught sneaking aboard a USSCo. ship to Honolulu, they described their new-found fame among the passengers:

---

67 Greg Dening, *Islands and Beaches: Discourse on a Silent Land* (Honolulu: University of Hawaii Press, 1980), 158.
68 Mordaunt, *The Venture Book*, 11–14.

> We bore no stigma. We were, in fact, celebrities. Passengers ventured from the dim splendours of the first and second class to view the stowaways and to take photographs to thrill their friends at home. Among the steerage passengers our prestige was enormous.[69]

They offered one example of a woman who visited them from first class, and who was persuaded to travel steerage next time because she considered the people 'more interesting'. She continued, adding that 'third-class passengers aren't just holiday-makers or whisky-drinking business men. They're more human. They're poor people, and struggling, and courageous.'[70]

For some travellers, this mixing of people was an attraction. Thomas Allan McKay was a self-proclaimed 'plain British–Australian business man, wearing no political party labels, disowning all class prejudice', who gladly recalled how:

> On shipboard especially, thrown pell-mell into contact, one meets, to the confusion of many preconceived ideas, all sorts and conditions of men. They range from red-rag revolutionaries to artistically crusted Tories; from people whose mental horizons are rimmed by racehorses and film stars, to intellectuals copiously crammed with 'perilous stuff' that must out.[71]

Freeman also recalled how first-class travel was an opportunity to 'actually get to know' the famous and the successful.[72] For other travellers, certain class distinctions remained uncrossed: European refugees and Chinese immigrants travelling in steerage were 'reserved' and 'messed by themselves'.[73] For Eric Muspratt, who faced a sea voyage home after having worked for six months overseeing a copra plantation, steamships created an 'atmosphere of petty snobbery', and steamer passengers 'seemed to be offensively smart and smug and sleek-looking in their well-laundered white ducks'.[74] He blamed the missionaries and government officials for 'this constant sense of social distinctions'.

---

69   Irwin and Goff, *No Longer Innocent*, 134–5.
70   Irwin and Goff, *No Longer Innocent*, 135.
71   Thomas Allan McKay, *Seeing the World Twice 1926–1935* (Melbourne: Robertson & Mullens, 1936), vii–viii.
72   Freeman, *Fiji—Memory Hold the Door*, 77.
73   Freeman, *Fiji—Memory Hold the Door*, 78; Sydney Walter Powell, *Adventures of a Wanderer* (London: Jonathan Cape, 1928), 132.
74   Eric Muspratt, *My South Sea Island* (London: Martin Hopkinson Ltd, 1931), 21.

The liminality of sea travel—or 'cruise culture', as George M Foster describes it[75]—was the result of the confined spaces onboard, the nature of travel as a time of transition and uncertainty, and the shared interests of many travellers. These interests included a desire for leisure, the search for self-education and improvement, or a pilgrimage 'home' to Europe. As William Ramsay Smith, a traveller, noted in 1924, 'There must be something about shipboard life that changes one's ordinary standards regarding socially permissible or individual duty, or the practice of shore etiquette'.[76] Group activities also generated a sense of *communitas* onboard—or, as one traveller observed, passengers became 'a happy family'.[77] Such activities included deck games, common dining, reading and smoking rooms, lectures, regulated patterns of meal times and sightseeing departures. Deck games comprised 'racing, jumping, quoit-throwing, bull-board, drafts, chess, &c. Nearly £50 were subscribed and distributed in prizes during the voyage to America. Several games were specially arranged for ladies'.[78] This sense of community was even more acute in the smaller confines of yachts, as expressed by Ralph Stock at the conclusion of his voyage: 'Already, we were changed to each other's eye'.[79]

The most popular and widely practised communal ritual onboard cruise ships was reserved for crossing the equator, and it relegated all passengers to an equal social status of 'landlubbers' and 'polliwogs' (those who had never crossed the equator). Based on a seafaring tradition that began as a religious offering and then gradually became an initiation rite, crew members dressed as King Neptune and his court attendants.[80] Charles Henry Matters, a traveller, described the sight of Neptune and his wife: 'Enthroned in royal state, and mounted on a car, the sailors in line wheel them round and round the deck'.[81] Based on the notion that those who refused to pay Neptune a bribe of silver must be punished, Matters added that:

---

75   George M Foster, 'South Seas Cruise: A Case Study of a Short-Lived Society', *Annals of Tourism Research* 13, no. 2 (1986): 215–38.
76   William Ramsay Smith, *In Southern Seas: Wanderings of a Naturalist* (London: John Murray, 1924), 8.
77   Alfred Joseph, *A Bendigonian Abroad: Being Sketches of Travel Made During a Ten Months Tour Through Europe and America* (Melbourne: Reardon & Mitchell, n.d.), 249.
78   Charles Henry Matters, *From Golden Gate to Golden Horn, and Many Other World Wide Wanderings: Or 50,000 Miles of Travel over Sea and Land* (Adelaide: Vardon & Pritchard, 1892), 13.
79   Ralph Stock, *The Cruise of the Dream Ship* (London: William Heinemann, 1921), 238.
80   Keith P Richardson, 'Polliwogs and Shellbacks: An Analysis of the Equator Crossing Ritual', *Western Folklore* 36, no. 2 (1977): 155, doi.org/10.2307/1498967.
81   Matters, *From Golden Gate to Golden Horn*, 13.

> Several victims are selected. In quick time, with great pomp and ceremony, they are lathered and shaved in comic style, and suddenly doused in a salt-water pond, formed by a sail tied up at four corners.

This was an event of horseplay and fancy dress that became more elaborate as shipping companies sought to attract more passengers. It was also a convenient excuse to break the monotony of travel and appease any conflicts aboard.

Another important activity onboard centred on reading, writing and cultural discussion. Shipping companies emphasised the benefits of travel for education and self-development, which resonated with the European tradition of the grand tour. Consequently, Australians were avid readers prior to the journey, with guidebooks providing recommended reading lists for prospective travellers. Many ships were equipped with libraries that were well stocked with canonical Pacific literature. Woodburn noted how there was an adequate library even on the small, no-frills boat, *Morinda*, with Charles Nordhoff and James Norman Hall's trilogy of the HMS *Bounty* mutiny being the most popular title. In the library, the books 'worked overtime, having the advantage of local colour'.[82] Published travel accounts often provided their own reading recommendations, and it was common for authors to compare their own first impressions to those of previous writers. The books that were read onboard allowed travellers to process their journeys, shaping their expectations and equipping them with familiar literary tropes on which they could rely. Writing was also an important activity for passing the time, and for gaining a sense of progress at sea.[83] Diaries and letters served as both aide-memoires and as records to be sent home and shared among family and friends. Travellers would also discuss their experiences of travel with one another, and ships would sometimes organise lectures. In his *Notes of Travel* (1894), JC Hickson mentioned listening to the Reverend George Brown onboard as the ship returned to Auckland.[84]

---

82 Woodburn, *Backwash of Empire*, 14–15.
83 Andrew Hassam, *Sailing to Australia: Shipboard Diaries by Nineteenth-Century British Emigrants* (Manchester: Manchester University Press, 1994), 102.
84 JC Hickson, *Notes of Travel: From Pacific to Atlantic, with Description of the World's Fair at Chicago; Also Travels by Sea and Land round the World* (Parramatta: Fuller's Lightning Printing Works, 1894), 4.

Journeys and destinations could both play a major role in a traveller's expectations and impressions. For those transiting the Pacific from Australia to Europe, the Islands were described in little detail and were sidelined in favour of European settings. These travellers were almost in equal number to those for whom the Pacific Islands was their main destination. Pacific Island travellers were attracted to the Islands because of the isolation, the difficulty of access and a sense of the unknown and adventure, with their texts emphasising these characteristics accordingly. The most common complaints onboard ships were seasickness and bad weather, which could heighten an individual's experience when landing onshore. Wilfred Burchett, an experienced traveller and journalist, recollected a bout of terrible seasickness and vividly described smells such as the 'rancid smell of rotting copra' and the 'tantalising fragrance' of Tahiti; he likened his arrival on land to 'scurvy-ridden sailors from whaling fleets of old', with his experience of weariness and impatience shared by many others.[85] When taken to the extreme—such as in the case of Fred Rebell, who sailed by himself from Sydney to San Francisco—the experience of sickness and danger while travelling could stimulate a religious epiphany.[86] Reactions to the Islands could also be shaped by the direction of the journey, as Joseph explained:

> It may easily be understood that passengers who are returning home are far more difficult to satisfy than those who are leaving Australia on their holiday trip. The latter are full of anticipation and expectancy.[87]

Of course, the other passengers onboard could be important in a personal journey. Baume's case is an extreme but demonstrative example. Travelling with his parents to San Francisco, Baume recalled:

> The spectacle—amazing to my eleven-year-old eyes—of a missionary making violent physical love to one of the Rarotongan natives brought aboard the ship for the two days' run from Rarotonga to Tahiti.[88]

---

85 Wilfred Burchett, *Passport: An Autobiography* (Melbourne: Thomas Nelson, 1969), 101, 105.
86 Fred Rebell, *Escape to the Sea: The Adventures of Fred Rebell, who Sailed Single Handed in an Open Boat 9,000 Miles across the Pacific in Search of Happiness* (London: J. Murray, 1939).
87 Joseph, *A Bendigonian Abroad*, 249. See also Prue Ahrens, Lamont Lindstrom and Fiona Paisley, *Across the World with the Johnsons: Visual Culture and American Empire in the Twentieth Century* (Burlington: Ashgate Publishing Co., 2013), 37.
88 Baume, *I Lived These Years*, 34.

By mentioning it in his autobiography, it is clear that this event left an impression on him, and Baume's attitude to the Islands was marked by his dismay at the corruption of natural beauty by foreign influences. Mordaunt's experience of witnessing tension and conflict between crew members aboard small vessels was typical of Australian yachting narratives:

> These men have, indeed, been so long at sea that, apart from the usual taciturnity of sailors, they are acutely on one another's nerves, can scarcely bear the sight of one another.[89]

Sometimes, a traveller's first encounter with a Pacific Islander would occur onboard a ship, particularly on smaller sailing boats and traders but also occasionally on larger cruise vessels. For some travellers, especially before the 1900s, the stereotypes of lazy, incompetent or dangerous Islanders were confirmed. One Australian traveller, Richard Cheeseman, observed:

> His crew were composed of white officers and colored seamen, these latter continually deserting, so others have to be taken on wherever opportunity offers. They are good working fellows when well officered, but useless otherwise.[90]

Of all accounts, those of traders—specifically labour traders—offer the most detailed descriptions of Islander crews. 'The *force majeure* of circumstances was overcoming all my prejudices', remarked Thomas while aboard a recruiting ship in the New Hebrides in 1883.[91] The use of individual names in travel writing, as opposed to generic terms like 'native' or 'Tommy the Tongan', suggests that travellers sometimes had close and intimate personal contact onboard ship. Some Australians, like Joseph Hadfield Grundy, even made lifelong friends; he maintained an 18-year-long friendship with a 13-year-old boy from Suva named Tim.[92] These encounters were different from others because they occurred in a safer, more familiar environment than the beach, and because they shaped attitudes and expectations before the travellers had even arrived.

---

89   Mordaunt, *The Venture Book*, 131.
90   Richard Cheeseman, *The South Sea Islands: Notes of a Trip* (Brighton: publisher unknown, 1901), 2.
91   Thomas, *Cannibals and Convicts*, 164.
92   Joseph Hadfield Grundy, *A Month in New Zealand; A Trip to Fiji, Tonga and Samoa* (Adelaide: Hunkin, Ellis & King, 1931), 7.

First Impressions

The moment of first arrival was a significant event for many travellers, and it was commonly described in greater detail than the rest of the journey. As Mary Louise Pratt argued, 'Arrival scenes are a convention of almost every variety of travel writing and serve as particularly potent sites for framing relations of contact and setting the terms of its representation'.[93] This was a powerful and much-anticipated moment for travellers, when imagination met reality. Island arrivals were particularly potent, as the crossing from water, to sand and to land prompted shipboard visitors to 'explore and metaphorise the psychologies of arrival and departure more explicitly' than in continental settings.[94] Some aspects of the arrival experience resembled European exploration literature—travellers reported a spirit of friendship almost immediately, betraying a familiar 'European desire for amicable relations' and an assumption of indigenous consent, according to Vanessa Smith.[95] However, the arrival procedures for steamships in the late nineteenth and early twentieth centuries were significantly different from the beach crossings of explorers, missionaries and traders that preceded them. Travellers bypassed the 'in-between spaces' of the beach, a concept that Greg Dening has explored in depth, and moved directly from ship to port.[96] The chaos and confusion of the classic Polynesian arrival scene, in which Islanders paddled from the shore and swarmed ships, was replaced by a controlled and regulated process. The predictability of the steamship movement ensured that the experience of incomprehension when arriving at the harbour was not present.[97] This meant that Australian travellers did not describe the Islanders' bewilderment for all things 'civilised', nor did they observe a European fascination with all things 'native'. Rather, visitors focused on verifying their expectations and legitimising their experiences.

First arrival in the Pacific commenced with a period of observation rather than engagement, with the slow approach of the ship allowing passengers time to appraise the scene before encountering any inhabitants. As William

---

93   Pratt, *Imperial Eyes*, 77.
94   Vanessa Smith, 'Pitcairn's "Guilty Stock": The Island as Breeding Ground', in *Islands in History and Representation*, ed. Vanessa Smith and Rod Edmond (New York: Routledge, 2003), 116.
95   Vanessa Smith, *Intimate Strangers: Friendship, Exchange and Pacific Encounters* (New York: Cambridge University Press, 2010), 5.
96   Dening, *Islands and Beaches*, 159.
97   Dening, *Islands and Beaches*, 159. See also Pratt, *Imperial Eyes*, 35.

John Stephens remarked, 'Landing in Suva … is an adventure in itself. Long before we reached the harbor we began to see the islands'.[98] Although travellers unanimously agreed that the Islands possessed an 'indescribable beauty and charm', they nonetheless tried their best to describe the scenery in detail, focusing on vivid colours, pleasant fragrances and abundant vegetation that implied mystery, potential and natural perfection.[99] With a closer inspection of these islands, evidence of colonial settlement came into view. For example, Allan wrote:

> The dawn was quickly merging into daylight, and in the gathering brightness the coast line was losing much of its quondam vagueness. The brilliant green of the prolific tropical vegetation was assuming a richer tint, and the saw-edged configuration of the mountains, which slant upwards from the city … was becoming more plainly outlined … The city rose in irregular tiers from the water front, and the partiality for red and ochre, so much in evidence at Auckland, was found here also.[100]

Eric Leed's history of travel termed the first step in the arrival procedure as 'identification'—a step in which the traveller identified the place and the place identified the traveller.[101] Travellers would occasionally be aware that they were being watched, as was the case for Woodburn in the New Hebrides in 1944, when she wrote of 'the somewhat uncomfortably fly-under-the-microscope-ish conviction accompanying that feeling [of being watched]'.[102]

The visual consumption of the Islands may be evidence of a 'tourist gaze', one driven by literature and corporate promotions that encouraged an 'anticipation, especially through day-dreaming and fantasy, of intense pleasures'.[103] However, the prolific use of the term 'picturesque' more clearly highlights the increasing conformity of travellers in the Pacific. This label was indiscriminately applied to all aspects of the Pacific Islands—not only to the natural scenery but also to the people, artificial constructions, objects and even sounds and personal expressions. The 'picturesque' was universally accepted as conforming with 'standard pictorial representations of beauty' and was 'immediately compatible with all one's

---

98 William John Stephens, *Samoan Holidays* (Bendigo: Cambridge Press, 1935), 13.
99 John J Gay, *Through Other Lands* (Sydney: Edwards, Dunlop, 1931), 3.
100 Allan, *Homeward Bound*, 22.
101 Leed, *The Mind of The Traveler*, 85.
102 Woodburn, *Backwash of Empire*, 64.
103 Urry, *Consuming Places*, 132.

fond preconceptions', according to Malcolm Andrews.[104] Originating from the vocabulary of mid-eighteenth-century tourists travelling to the English countryside, the term developed as travellers appraised a scene according to the conventions of landscape painting and classical notions of beauty. The term's popularity was associated with the democratisation of travel and the rise of popular international tourism from the 1840s onwards.[105] Just as these tourists observed locations through the frame of a painting or a Claude glass, so too did travellers of the twentieth century when they observed the Pacific view of the Islands within specific frames (of the painting, of the camera lens or even of the ship itself). In his travel account, meteorologist Clement Lindley Wragge frequently referred to the scenery as a 'panorama' and as a 'tableau of tropic beauty', later exclaiming, 'What a picture for an artist does the wharf present!'[106]

Travellers to the Pacific Islands remained bound by European artistic conventions. Like those who idealised English rural landscapes, travellers to the Islands continued to use 'picturesque' to aestheticise nature and the natural human figure.[107] In chasing this ideal, the search for the picturesque usually involved a selective modification or improvement. In some cases, the realities of industrial development at the wharves were ignored in favour of conventional descriptions of natural scenery and vegetation. In other cases, features that were inconsistent with romantic ideals (e.g. Indian labourers or European convicts) were labelled 'unpicturesque'.[108]

Based on this artistic convention, travellers responded more positively to volcanic islands than to coral atolls. Volcanic islands offered scenery that was comparable to celebrated locations in Europe, and thus aligned with classical notions of aesthetic beauty. The dense, green and 'luxuriant' vegetation, as well as the 'rugged grandeur of its mountain peaks', were features that travellers identified and admired.[109] Aletta Lewis, a traveller, described this aesthetic preference as 'a consuming thirst for green'.[110]

---

104 Malcolm Andrews, *The Search for the Picturesque: Landscape Aesthetics and Tourism in Britain, 1760–1800* (Aldershot: Scolar, 1989), vii.
105 Urry, *Consuming Places*, 175.
106 Clement Lindley Wragge, *The Romance of the South Seas* (London: Chatto & Windus, 1906), 128, 165.
107 Smith, *Imagining the Pacific*, 64.
108 For example, see Robert Brummitt, *A Winter Holiday in Fiji* (Sydney: Methodist Book Depots, 1914), 45; Richard Reynell Bellamy, *Mixed Bliss in Melanesia* (London: John Long, 1934), 18.
109 Pearse, *A Windjammer 'Prentice*, 141.
110 Aletta Lewis, *They Call Them Savages* (London: Methuen & Co. Ltd, 1938), 6.

Wragge recalled Scotland when he visited Tahiti, noting that 'the frowning mountains, wreathing clouds along the steeps, and the gurgling burn of the Fautaua, all remind one of the Land of Burns'.[111] In comparison, coral atolls were small, low, flat and less fertile. Sydney Walter Powell observed, 'We called at several atolls, which do not need description, since all atolls are of the same character'.[112]

Mountains (and volcanoes) also offered promises of the unknown, of danger and of potential wealth. As one guidebook described, 'The purple hills … seem to speak of a mysterious life hidden in their vastnesses'.[113] Imposing mountain ranges and the potentially savage peoples that they contained conveyed to travellers a quality of greatness, power, chaos and monstrosity. Atolls and reefs presented their own dangers to foreign travellers—yet it was the mountains that inspired the 'picturesque' and the 'sublime'. Mordaunt's experience of navigating dangerous reefs was monotonous and marked only by atolls that were 'overhung by a thick cloud of mosquitoes'; in contrast, the first sight of Tahiti prompted her to 'tremble with excitement'.[114]

Coming ashore, travellers of the twentieth century encountered Islanders at the wharf rather than at the beach. This experience of contact was different from that of previous European explorers and traders, who rowed ashore in smaller, exposed boats to Islands whose settlements or people may not have been visible from the shoreline. Their accounts are marked by apprehension, as they carefully looked for signs of welcome or hostility. The beach landing was still used for Australian travellers who strayed from the main Islands or tourist routes, but the reception was usually more predictable and safer. The modern wharf was a new and vibrant public area at major steamship destinations, with 'Steamer Day' being a major event for Island residents as much as it was for the new arrivals. The crowds created a festive atmosphere for visitors, full of exotic sights, sounds and smells. Similar trends in observation can be found in various Australian accounts of Asia.[115] For example, Aletta Lewis observed: 'It was a happy intimate scene. Every one and everything

---

111 Wragge, *The Romance of the South Seas*, 232.
112 Sydney Walter Powell, 'Each to His Taste', Papers of Sydney Powell [circa 1920–1950], MS10012 (Canberra: National Library of Australia), 258.
113 Robson, *The Pacific Islands Yearbook*, 70.
114 Mordaunt, *The Venture Book*, 59.
115 Sobocinska, *Visiting the Neighbours*, 21.

seemed to belong in the circle of the sheltering arms [the mountains].'[116] An AUSN shipping guide described how 'the mixture of races is noticed on every side as one passes to the end of the wharf'.[117] Powell was struck by the 'brightness, lightness and cleanness' of dresses, while Allan was entertained by the 'curiously dressed, mahogany skinned Fijian wharf lumpers'; others described the white 'ducks' of European residents and the distinctive uniforms of indigenous police.[118]

The industrial nature of working wharves sometimes dampened travellers' expectations of arrival. Walter Gill, an overseer, recalled his disappointment in the 1910s when he did not see a single Fijian at Lautoka, only an 'iron and steel behemoth' that was the wharf and 'the dark phallus of a tall chimney'.[119] M Lloyd was disappointed by the 'very dirty wharfs and black labor' at Honolulu, and Powell was repelled by the settlement at Rarotonga because it was 'so prim, so British'.[120] Disembarking the ship could also be another source of disappointment, as local tour guides and opportunists took advantage of the new visitors. In Suva, Littlejohn described the 'crowds of evil-smelling men offering at high prices rubbishy mats, spears, cocoanuts, shells, coral, and fruit'.[121] However, such disdain for local people reflected his own racial views rather than reality. Receiving advice from onboard the ship, Ivan and Goff refused to have their bags handled by labourers at the wharf, instead sprinting away with their luggage and earning the scorn of the residents: 'All united in a strenuous jeer of disapproval … Even a group of palm-trees that had nodded a welcome to us as we entered Suva Bay seemed suddenly aloof'.[122]

Beyond the wharf, travellers wandered the town—and their evaluations can serve as judgements regarding the effectiveness of colonial rule. Visually pleasing architecture, neat and clean streets, and sculpted gardens impressed, while ramshackle and disorderly dwellings, poor roads and disagreeable people reflected poorly. However, the final judgement was reserved for the view from above, as travellers climbed to higher ground. Handbooks and travel guides directed travellers to specific lookouts,

---

116 Lewis, *They Call Them Savages*, 6.
117 Lees, *Around the Coasts of Australia and Fiji Illustrated*, 174.
118 Powell, *Adventures of a Wanderer*, 133; Allan, *Homeward Bound*, 22; Muspratt, *My South Sea Island*, 255; Gay, *Through Other Lands*, 4.
119 Walter Gill, *Turn North-East at the Tombstone* (Adelaide: Rigby, 1970), 24.
120 M Lloyd, *Wanderings in the Old World and the New* (Adelaide: Vardon & Pritchard, 1901), 6; Powell, *Adventures of a Wanderer*, 132.
121 Littlejohn, *Notes and Reflections 'on the road'*, 15.
122 Irwin and Goff, *No Longer Innocent*, 39.

promising 'magnificent views' and 'unforgettable' scenes, while presenting pictures of these panoramas as evidence.[123] Climbing bestowed the visitor the power to possess and evaluate the scene by becoming the 'monarch of all I survey', as phrased by Pratt.[124] The colonial gaze from above—and the subsequent naming, mapping, writing and knowing of the Island—expressed aesthetic control and ownership.[125] By allowing the traveller to observe and inscribe the Islands as miniature, this gaze also contributed to the nostalgic romanticisation of the Islands.[126]

Due to the constraints of shipping services, passengers had limited time to explore the surrounding areas, with both island economies and shipping companies responding by offering day trip packages and guides. AUSN's 1916 handbook was one of the earliest travel guides to formalise a set of routes and sights in Fiji that were already well used by visitors. It offered a selection of day trips by boat and car that would be 'very picturesque, and … full of interest to tourists', complete with details of costs, timings, possible hotels and transportation.[127] Subsequent publications chart the development of specific tourist sites and attractions in the Pacific Islands. These attractions originated from the collective travel patterns of Island visitors, with their accounts acting as markers that identified specific sites to subsequent travellers. As these sites were 'named', 'framed' and 'elevated' (a process termed 'site sacralisation' by sociologist Dean MacCannell), their status as tourist attractions became cemented and were reproduced in photographs, prints, guidebooks and shipping advertisements.[128] Tourist sites in the Pacific Islands included natural features, colonial settlements and historic locations or remains.

Natural formations were picturesque locations for picnics, as well as popular for their ability to generate a sense of wonder and awe among travellers. These formations included hilltop lookouts, volcanoes, waterfalls, caves, rivers, lakes, lagoons and reefs. Specifically, travellers frequented Pali Pass in Honolulu, Flagstaff Hill in Suva, the Rewa river in Fiji, the Mapu'a 'a Vaea blowholes of Tonga and the Papase'ea sliding

---

123 For example, see Robson, *The Pacific Islands Yearbook*, 70; Allen, *Stewart's Handbook of the Pacific Islands*, 85.
124 Pratt, *Imperial Eyes*, 200.
125 Rebecca Weaver-Hightower, *Empire Islands: Castaways, Cannibals, and Fantasies of Conquest* (Minneapolis: University of Minnesota Press, 2007), 15.
126 Susan Stewart, *On Longing: Narratives of the Miniature, the Gigantic, the Souvenir, the Collection* (Durham: Duke University Press, 1993), 66, doi.org/10.1215/9780822378563.
127 Lees, *Around the Coasts of Australia and Fiji Illustrated*, 186.
128 MacCannell, *The Tourist*, 41–5.

rocks of Samoa. Although easy access was important, some natural formations were attractive because they were relatively inaccessible, such as a journey up a river or ascending a volcano, which offered a sense of adventure, mystery and, afterwards, achievement. The 'Swallows' and 'Mariners' underwater caves in Tonga were popular attractions. Their sense of mystery was expressed by artist, Arnold Safroni-Middleton, who described the caves:

> Where the tourist doubtless enters to take a snap-shot of Nature's transcendent beauty of coral, flowers and ferns, little dreaming of the secret they held for the guile of men years ago.[129]

Colonial constructions were also important for assisting visitors in accessing nature, such as glass-bottomed boats and an aquarium in Hawai'i, the development of Waikiki beach, or the Botanical Gardens of Fiji. Although many Islands contained impressive natural formations, their isolation and lack of development were barriers to tourism. This entailed judgements from popular handbooks that warned, for example, 'To the ordinary tourist or globe-trotter the [Solomon Islands] Protectorate offers few attractions'.[130]

Structures of colonial settlement also attracted foreign visitors because of their familiarity and their curious local adaptations. The reputation of certain luxurious and opulent hotels rendered them popular attractions, especially the Moana and the Royal Hawaiian Hotels in Honolulu and the Grand Pacific Hotel in Suva. They were popular rest stops and refuges after a long day's travel, even for non-residents. Travellers visited government buildings, museums, public squares and marketplaces, of which the Coconut Square in New Caledonia was particularly entertaining. Churches and mission stations were also popular, as travellers admired the exotic architecture of chapels and enjoyed observing Pacific Islanders in an environment that was safe and controlled. Travellers were interested in local industry, visiting sugar mills, plantations, pearling stations and trading stores, usually under the guidance and protection of a European resident.

---

129 Arnold Safroni-Middleton, *Wine-Dark Seas and Tropic Skies: Reminiscences and a Romance of the South Seas* (London: Grant Richards, 1918), 137.
130 Allen, *Stewart's Handbook of the Pacific Islands*, 9.

Historic sites in the Pacific Islands were perhaps one of the earliest attractions for foreigners. The graves of martyred missionaries and 'brave' explorers were significant markers in the Islands that reminded European visitors of the turbulent history of first contact. Along with other ruins of abandoned dwellings, derelict prisons and shipwrecks, these images of decay were valued for their historical worth. Freeman's observation of an abandoned church in Fiji highlighted this: 'These hallowed ruins in a picturesque setting amongst palms and bures were evidence of religious fervour and grandiose plans thwarted by hurricanes and hard times'.[131] Some indigenous ruins were also popular. The sites of the Tongan trilithon and royal tombs were considered evidence of an ancient and superior civilisation, which highlighted a general European fascination with royalty. Many tourists prized the chance to meet living kings and queens of the Pacific Islands. Joseph tried to visit the Hawaiian queen, but was refused, and Henley observed that the Tongan queen shrinks from 'inquisitive passengers, sometimes of the globe-trotting American type, who, from mere motives of curiosity, wish to interview her on the monthly steamer day'.[132] Alleged sacrificial sites were also highly desired—the Fijian island of Bau being especially popular and well known, and described as the 'cannibal capital of the Pacific'. For Australian travellers, the Island was only distinguished by some graves and a sacrificial stone; however, their travel accounts described, in detail, an imagined scene of barbarity and horror.[133]

Australian fascination with these ruins can also be explained by the attraction of the 'sublime', which, like the term 'picturesque', originated in earlier accounts of travel in Europe. Distinct from the beautiful, the sublime was terrifying, reckless, powerful and vast. As described earlier, mountains symbolised this greatness and potential danger. Ruins were also prized as evidence of these past horrors.[134] Richard White has demonstrated a similar fascination with sites that have been made famous by convicts and bushrangers, motivated by a 'vulgar curiosity' and a subversive interest in the darker aspects of history that authorities were trying to suppress.[135]

---

131 Freeman, *Fiji—Memory Hold the Door*, 81.
132 Joseph, *A Bendigonian Abroad*, 253; Thomas Henley, *A Pacific Cruise: Musings and Opinions on Island Problems* (Sydney: John Sands, 1930), 40.
133 Lees, *Around the Coasts of Australia and Fiji Illustrated*, 182.
134 Andrews, *The Search for the Picturesque*, 43–4.
135 Richard White, 'The Subversive Tourist: How Tourism Re-Wrote Australian History' (Harold White Fellow Presentation, Canberra, National Library of Australia, 28 February 2012).

Robert Louis Stevenson's home in Samoa was a major attraction to tourists passing through the Pacific. In 1907, Grimshaw wrote that 'Apia and Stevenson's home have been written about and described by almost every tourist who ever passed through on the way to Sydney'.[136] Stevenson, who had settled in Samoa in 1889, was considered an authority on the Pacific, and his books were frequently quoted in Australian travel accounts. A select number of travel writers boasted of having met him, including Coffee, Muspratt and Safroni-Middleton. After his death in 1894, he was buried on Mount Vaea, which overlooked the village of Vailima. Both his house and his grave became well-known attractions, despite the difficult mountain climb required to reach them (the route uphill took roughly an hour). Travel accounts reveal that Stevenson was an inspirational writer, traveller and idealist. Rather than being criticised, Stevenson was admired for choosing to live as an exile in the Pacific Islands (as he was often described), and his internal struggle was romanticised. Visiting the tomb was described as a pilgrimage by many travellers, who revered both the grave and the experience of travel as sacred.[137] Stephens's detailed description of his visit to Vailima focused on the challenging climb and the view itself, rather than on Stevenson's grave. He wrote:

> The view is delightful; on either side we see the winding trail up the hillside, the vast pinnacles of sculptural rock, the most stupendous scenes of nature, its overpowering grandeur and its inexpressible beauty … Among the green hills and rich woods the memories which the peaceful country scenes call up are not of this world, or of its thoughts and hopes.[138]

The appeal of Vailima at the time was distinct from that of any other attraction that was based on the life of a famous European visitor. This was due to Stevenson having resided there permanently, as well as due to his literary fame. At other sites (e.g. Mariner's Cave in Tonga and Point Venus in Tahiti), the initial contact that marked them as historically important was momentary. Although the mutineers from the HMS *Bounty* resided in the Pacific, their home on Pitcairn Island was too remote to attract the same interest as Stevenson's home.

---

136 Beatrice Grimshaw, *In the Strange South Seas* (London: Hutchinson & Co., 1907), 303.
137 Harriet Winifred Ponder, *An Idler in the Islands* (Sydney: Cornstalk Publishing, 1924), 86; Henley, *A Pacific Cruise*, 78–9.
138 Stephens, *Samoan Holidays*, 64.

Conspicuous in its absence was the role of Pacific Islanders as a tourist attraction. Travellers did not often engage with Islanders face to face; the few times that they did, they had short interactions with taxi drivers, baggage handlers, waiters and housekeepers. Rarely were visitors left alone without the supervision of a European resident or guide. As John Wear Burton, a missionary, observed in Fiji in 1910:

> At present, Fiji is but little known to the tourist world; and when visitors do come, it is difficult and expensive to get beyond the European towns. Each year, however, is taking away these reproaches. The colony is gradually becoming known by reason of the 'All Red' [shipping] route.[139]

Travel advertisements and guidebooks encouraged visits to local villages, yet the observations made in individual travel accounts were usually glimpses from a motor car or from the porch of a resident's home. Australian travellers occasionally commented on the Islanders who worked as guides, though they were reported as being desperate or unreliable.[140] The village domain and its people rarely crossed into the town space, except at wharves and in local markets, where tourists could purchase curios, pose with a decorated warrior or watch a dance performance. Amateur video footage from 1927 depicted tourists standing next to a Fijian male at Suva wharf who was dressed as a warrior and brandishing a club.[141] Islanders in these instances were considered an attraction in a vague, non-individualised way, and travellers were usually careful to maintain space between themselves and the 'other'. Intermixing was thus limited and generally frowned upon. Pacific Islanders were equally cautious of transgressing the racial and cultural boundaries that were policed in the colonial-controlled urban centres. Intermixing was easier further away in the villages, as shown in Figure 9. This figure is an unusual photograph taken in 1935 of two Australian children in Samoan cultural dress.

---

139 John Wear Burton, *The Fiji of To-Day* (London: C.H. Kelly, 1910), 34.
140 Rebell, *Escape to the Sea*, 85; J Mayne Anderson, *What a Tourist Sees in the New Hebrides* (Sydney: W.C. Penfold & Co., 1915), 96.
141 *[Pacific Islands Leg of Boat Trip to U.S.; Sydney to Los Angeles by Boat]*.

AUSTRALIAN SAMOANS.

Australian by birth and Samoan in dress, two grandchildren of the author, Dorothy and Jack. Dorothy is arrayed in a bride's dress, made and presented to her by the girls of the Avoka School at Faleula. It is composed of tapa, or native cloth, and ornamented with hardened red

berries. She is crowned with a head-dress of human hair, taken from a Samoan chief's daughter from Salani, in the southern portion of the island. Jack is robed faa Samoa, and holds in his hands one of the many native weapons, which are not now used on their enemies, but are only displayed on ceremonial occasions.

Figure 9: Australian Samoans.
Source: Stephens, *Samoan Holidays*.

Fiji was a notable exception to this trend, as travellers frequently commented on visiting a local village. These village visits were so popular that they became increasingly structured and prearranged. Stock's experience of 'A Day with a South Sea Prince' (as he titled his chapter in 1913) was typical of travellers visiting Fiji at the time. Stock described visiting Bau Island and being hosted by a local chief, after which he swam, ate and participated in a kava ceremony. Stock was impressed by the well-educated chief, emphasising 'a mingled atmosphere of past and present, barbarism and culture, truly bewildering in its contrasts'. Like other travellers, Stock valued his visit to the village because it allowed him to witness what he imagined to be 'the real life of the Fijian people, lying hidden, but not dead, beneath the—as yet—thin veneer of civilization'.[142]

There are several factors that might explain why Fijian villages became popular attractions for Australian travellers. Debates about depopulation in the early twentieth century led many Australians to believe that certain races would become extinct in the Pacific, and government policies in Fiji at the time that were designed to ensure the protection of the indigenous Fijian population may have inadvertently encouraged the belief that Fiji was an exception to the rule. The success of these village visits may have also been due to Fiji's location on the major trans-Pacific routes and the economic benefits of good road access and tourism promotion that was encouraged by the local bureau and shipping companies. Additionally, the structure of Fijian villages as large, concentrated settlements (compared to other Islands, whose villages were more spread out) made accessibility and control much easier. Perhaps a deeper power dynamic underscored the popularity of the village, with Australians ultimately enjoying the reassurance of their white superiority abroad. This claim closely resembles a trend that Sobocinska identified in her study of Australian travellers to Asia. Australians at home may have felt inferior to the British, but in the Asia-Pacific region, they were considered Europeans and enjoyed a newfound status.[143]

---

142 Ralph Stock, *The Confessions of a Tenderfoot: Being a True and Unvarnished Account of His World-Wanderings* (London: Grant Richards Ltd, 1913), 164, 169.
143 Sobocinska, *Visiting the Neighbours*, 21.

Representing the Tourist

The expansion of steamship companies, promotions and infrastructure, as well as the creation of a particular set of routes and attractions, highlight the growth of a tourism industry. However, did Australians consider themselves to be tourists? How did they represent themselves? Australian travel writing challenges the notion that authors can be conveniently labelled as either 'tourist' or 'traveller'. This distinction emerged in the late eighteenth century, with the tourist becoming associated with conventional sightseeing and the traveller being regarded as superior for avoiding the 'beaten track'.[144] The works of Dean MacCannell and John Urry, who pioneered sociological studies of tourism, are often applied to reinforce this simplistic dichotomy; however, the dichotomy can be problematic when applied to the historical context of the Pacific Islands.[145] Compared to the well-developed tourism industries of Europe or North America, on which initial theories were based, tourism in the Pacific Islands was still in its infancy by the mid-twentieth century, and the supposed characteristics of the tourist were not always evident. MacCannell characterised the tourist as someone who searched for universal truths and authentic expressions of the world; however, this authentic–inauthentic dualism can be problematic in a Pacific context, especially when considering that travellers in the late nineteenth and early twentieth centuries exhibited little concern for discovering an 'authentic' Pacific culture. The diversity of the Pacific Islands was not reflected in the generic stereotypes of European imaginings, which signified the scarcity of the sites possessing the attraction that MacCannell had identified in his theory of site sacralisation. Those few sites that most Australians recognised, such as Stevenson's tomb or Pitcairn Island, were valued as relics of European colonialism rather than as objects that represented a specific 'islandness'. Travellers could better understand and define colonial sites rather than indigenous spaces due to their familiarity. Indeed, Justine Greenwood and Richard White suggested that travel writing relies on the tension between 'sameness and difference'.[146]

---

144 Buzard, *The Beaten Track*. For example, see also G Bell Brand, 'Off the Beaten Track', *BP Magazine* 1, no. 2 (1934): 69–71.
145 MacCannell, The Tourist, 1. John Urry, *The Tourist Gaze,* 2nd ed. (London: Sage, 2002), 137.
146 Justine Greenwood and Richard White, 'Australia: The World Different and the Same', in *Routledge Companion to Travel Writing*, ed. Carl Thompson (London: Routledge, 2016), 404–14.

For Urry, the tourist gaze was focused on the different and the unusual, rather than on the authentic. This may better explain the motives of Australian tourists. Urry situated tourists within the context of modernity and the democratisation of travel, which were represented by a growing middle class who could travel for leisure and who believed that it was necessary for self-improvement. However, it is important to note that it was not simply the educated middle classes who established a pattern of touristic consumption in Australia. Unlike Europe, the Pacific broadly attracted numerous classes and travellers. Urry's distinction between 'romantic' and 'collective' gazes is more applicable in a Pacific Island context, though it still risks simplifying travellers according to a clear binary. The romantic gaze was characterised by solitude and 'a personal, semi-spiritual relationship with the object of the gaze', while the collective gaze relied on the social atmosphere that was created by the collective members.[147] Although the concept of being a lone explorer in the Pacific was popular among travellers, solitude was not always preferable or possible, depending on the island destination. Additionally, unless one owned his or her own boat, it was difficult to travel unimpeded by the movements of the collective. Even on larger Islands, travellers who were eager to avoid the well-travelled path were unlikely to stray far beyond the urban centres or the coastlines. It was not until much later in the twentieth century that the paths of tourists and travellers diverged.

Instead, Australian travellers sought to use the 'tourist' as a figure from which they could distinguish themselves. Very few Australian travellers identified themselves as tourists, as it was a status that opposed the romantic and heroic notions of a Pacific explorer. Travel writers were conscious of the literary context in which they wrote; what mattered to readers and critics was the work's 'authenticity', a judgement that was based on 'their knowledge and assumptions about the writer and their familiarity with the locality being described'.[148] Since few Australian readers were knowledgeable about the Pacific Islands, how the writer presented him or herself was crucial. Jonathan Lamb expressed this in terms of self-preservation:

> The popularity of books of travels, growing to greater heights as the century advanced, must be explained, then, not in terms the truth they produced (for they were broadly regarded as lies) but in terms of their potent dramatization of the feelings incident to the preservation of the self.[149]

---

147 Urry, *The Tourist Gaze*, 137.
148 Bones, 'Travel Writers and Traveling Writers in Australasia', 80.
149 Lamb, *Preserving the Self in the South Seas*, 6.

For Australian travel writers, the figure of the tourist was a convenient character to which they could compare themselves to claim legitimacy. As John J Gay wrote in his introduction:

> This is a story of the world and its people, written by an Australian journalist and business man, while wandering leisurely over land and sea. It is not the fevered chronicle of the typical globe-trotter who … with smug complacency inflicts upon long-suffering humanity a medley of crude impressions, banal platitudes and 'cheap' criticisms mainly directed against his own country.[150]

Criticisms were variously directed at American, British and Australian tourists, or at steamship passengers in general. Tourists were disliked because they followed the routes prescribed by shipping companies. Paul McGuire warned travellers to Fiji that:

> One should avoid that pilgrim's progress favoured by the Indian taxi-drivers for tourists up past the hospital and by the asylum to the cemetery … the Fijian deserves to be seen in his own land.[151]

Tourists were also shunned for travelling en masse. Safroni-Middleton described them as 'swells from the Australian cities', while Alan John Marshall recalled with hyperbole that when 'some seventeen hundred tourists vomited on to the beach' at Espiritu Santo (in the New Hebrides), the noise 'caused the natives to flee in terror to the hills'.[152]

Tourists were frequently identified with consumption, as Lewis identified:

> They had gone ashore in noisy gangs to buy things and see things and take things with their kodaks—in short to do Samoa in the way passengers do places at which their ships so obligingly and, thank God, so temporarily put them down. I did not want to be one of them any longer.[153]

'Armed with guide-books and cameras and the totally unnecessary puggaree that the traveling Briton loves to deck himself withal', tourists were rejected for their reckless consumerism.[154] This included being identified

---

150 Gay, *Through Other Lands*.
151 McGuire, *Westward the Course*, 66.
152 Alan John Marshall, *The Black Musketeers: The Work and Adventures of a Scientist on a South Sea Island at War and in Peace* (London: William Heinemann, 1937), 128, 258.
153 Lewis, *They Call Them Savages*, 7.
154 Grimshaw, *From Fiji to the Cannibal Islands*, 24.

with the qualities of sloth, greed and arrogance. Mordaunt described one tourist boat that was 'fattened with Philistines', and Marshall described in detail a 'tourist invasion' that:

> Mistook the Residency for a sort of a club and immediately took charge, consuming the bewildered D. O.'s [district officer's] beer and wines with a speed that amazed even that worthy as he wandered about in a daze trying to guard his possessions.[155]

Freeman observed similar qualities in the American tourists that arrived in Suva:

> During this prohibition era in the United States, Suva was the first 'wet' port of call on the voyage south. Following visits to local pubs, American tourists bedecked in souvenir necklaces of shells and seeds regularly made spectacles of themselves. Tipping generously, they fell out of taxis, lipstick and hats awry and tripped up steps. Their loud voices, broad accents, two-tone shoes, horned-rimmed spectacles, bobby socks, scarlet lips and finger-nails shocked and astonished all races. At Suva fancy dress parties, the prize for the most original costume now went to the 'American Tourist'.[156]

Her comments should be read in the context in which she lived—as an Australian resident in Suva, whose father worked for the sugar refinery. Freeman was proud to emphasise Australia's British heritage and to maintain certain cultural values abroad.

In addition to excessively consuming alcohol and food, tourists were identified by their desire for souvenirs or 'curios'. Collecting curios was an important part of most travel experiences, serving a legitimising purpose when the tourists returned home. Souvenirs also display the 'romance of the contraband' and 'allow the tourist to appropriate, consume, and thereby "tame" the cultural other', as argued by Susan Stewart.[157] Residents were aware of the demand for souvenirs, as Alfred William Hill warned readers in 1927 to 'remember that the native Indian shopkeepers and hawkers are keenly alive to the gullibility of the tourist'.[158] Island residents were opportunistic and responded to these new demands,

---

155 Mordaunt, *The Venture Book*, 116; Marshall, *The Black Musketeers*, 258.
156 Freeman, *Fiji—Memory Hold the Door*, 57–8.
157 Stewart, *On Longing*, 135, 146.
158 Alfred William Hill, *A Cruise among Former Cannibal Islands, Fiji, Tonga, Samoa: A Glimpse at the Countries, People, Customs and Legends* (Adelaide: W.K. Thomas & Co., 1927), 11.

evidencing a process that MacCannell termed 'staged authenticity'.[159] Islanders became familiar with posing for photographs by the 1900s, and travellers described numerous items that were for sale—ranging from fans and skirts to weapons, 'cannibal forks' and human bones. These items changed over time in response to these visitors; 'Thus the tourist aesthetic ensures that the object is continually exoticised and estranged'.[160]

Stereotypes of the Pacific Islander as being childlike, innocent and gullible were proven false when tourists were forced to bargain with shrewd sellers. One traveller, J Mayne Anderson, advised that 'the tourist on the look out for curios had better remain at home, and make his selection from a city dealer'.[161] Some lamented that tourists were corrupting the natural primitivity of the Islanders—such as Julian Thomas, who predicted as early as 1888 that the Tannese descendants may:

> Be a race of guides, cheats, and liars, who will peddle to the personally conducted tourists of the period all the bones they can scrape together, as those of white men consumed inwardly by their cannibal ancestors.[162]

Alternatively, these instances can be regarded as evidence of Islander agency and European gullibility, as British government official Hugh Hastings Romilly did in 1886:

> Ignorance of native languages prevents these travellers from collecting information from native sources, and is often the cause of their mistakes. More than one 'old hand' has told me that the sight of the note-book in the Globe-trotter's hand prompted him to draw on his imagination to a rather immoral extent, and caused him to supply ready-made facts which would astonish no one so much as the natives themselves.[163]

His comments confirm that Islanders had responded to the demands of visitors well before the tourist masses of the twentieth century had arrived to 'corrupt' them.

---

159 MacCannell, *The Tourist*, 98–9.
160 Stewart, *On Longing*, 150.
161 Anderson, *What a Tourist Sees in the New Hebrides*, 97.
162 Thomas, *Cannibals and Convicts*, 281.
163 Hugh Hastings Romilly, *The Western Pacific and New Guinea: Notes on the Natives, Christian and Cannibal, with Some Account of the Old Labour Trade* (London: J. Murray,1886), 4.

As travel to the Pacific Islands became increasingly structured, commodified and standardised in the 1920s and 1930s, criticisms of the effects of tourism intensified and more Australians searched for alternative paths and more remote destinations. Despite their best attempts to distinguish themselves from common tourists, Australian travel writers repeated common descriptions and tropes; their texts also contributed to the popularisation of routes and locations that were once prized because they existed off the beaten track. Similarly, criticisms of colonial rule overlooked the role that colonialism played in facilitating Australian travel. The steamship itself was an important new mode of transportation for Australians, as well as a symbol of the modern industrialisation that was so rapidly transforming the Pacific Islands. This colonial reality conflicted with the idealised explorer image of the Pacific traveller, as well as that of the Pacific as an unexplored region awaiting discovery.

Australian travel accounts reveal that steamships were not simply a mode of transport that brought an increasing number of Australians to the Pacific Islands from the 1880s onwards. Rather, they played a crucial role in the growth of Australian travel writing and the popularity of Pacific tourism. Steamship companies promoted a powerful new image of the Pacific that specifically catered for the leisurely tourist, an image that filtered into Australian travel writing over time. Steamship companies, crews and passengers also shaped the experience of travel from the point of departure to the moment of initial arrival at the Islands. Steamships became temporary homes and refuges for travellers during a period of heightened emotion, uncertainty and acclimatisation. These liminal spaces influenced how Australians represented the Islands and affected how they positioned and re-positioned themselves. This is evident in their travel accounts, which dedicated more pages and space to documenting their expectations and first impressions than to any other part of the journey or aspect of the Islands. Although travel writers tried to present themselves as lone explorers, they often followed in the footsteps of others and relied on familiar tropes and themes to describe the foreign and the unknown.

3

Polynesian Promises

> For climate, for loveliness, and grandeur of scenery, for comparative freedom from disease, for the gentleness of its own people—now so pitifully few—and because it is under the control of the convivial French, Tahiti is the best tropic island in the world … I like Tahiti. I have always liked Tahiti. I do not know anyone who has been there twice who does not wish to return—some day, somehow. But I do not blind myself to what has happened on this fair island which was once near to Paradise—to what has happened, and is happening still.[1]

The promise of an exotic island paradise in the Pacific was hard to resist. For Australians disenchanted with their lives at home, weary of the constraints of their society or apprehensive of the winter season, the Pacific offered escape and reprieve, either temporary or permanent. Just as explorers had previously done, travellers of the late nineteenth and twentieth centuries re-inscribed the Pacific as a region in which fantasies could be enacted, freedom and prosperity could be sought and true happiness could be found. It was ultimately in the region of Polynesia that popular tropes of the exotic, erotic and utopian Pacific Island were most frequently located. These tropes reinforced the romanticised image of the Polynesian as being feminine, alluring and inviting, which contrasted the masculine and threatening image of the Melanesian 'savage'. Within Polynesia, Tahiti was upheld as the ideal and authentic tropical island and Tahitians as the preferred type of 'native'.

---

1 Alan John Villiers, *Cruise of the Conrad: A Journal of a Voyage around the World* (1937), 292.

Australian representations of Tahiti and Polynesia were based on an extensive corpus of European literature—both fiction and non-fiction—that employed romanticised stereotypes to categorise the region as superior and idyllic. The most powerful allegorical device was the female body, which was used to portray the Islands as being natural, fertile, abundant and inviting, and the Islanders as carefree, primordial, physical and impassioned. Ascribing feminine characteristics to unexplored territories in the Americas, the Orient and the Pacific reflected the masculine nature of travel and exploration, as well as legitimised European colonisation. The notion of the south Pacific was contrary to that of the European north, suggesting a region that was subject to physical impulses and in which the laws of nature were inverted.[2] Although much has been written about Polynesia from the perspective of the north, few historians have concentrated on observations made from the antipodes. Australians occupied a distinct position, as a colony of the north that was positioned in the south.

The geographic isolation of Tahiti and French Polynesia, as well as their enduring dominance in European literature and fantasy, contributed to a persistent Australian fascination with these Islands. Despite widespread awareness of the fragility and temporality of this paradise in the early twentieth century, Australians continued to employ romanticised stereotypes to describe this region. What is most surprising about Australian representations of Polynesia is that they remained relatively unchanged from 1880 to 1941. When compared to the accounts of Melanesian Islands, in which public opinion shifted in response to the region's changing political and economic developments, Australian accounts of Polynesia were unusually static. This is distinct from the colonial accounts of European and American travellers, which had changed over time. At the turn of the twentieth century, the colonial powers of the north were more invested in the eastern Pacific; they exerted greater influence over the region's societies compared to Australians, with French colonial claims to parts of this region limiting Australian mobility to the east. Although most Australians confirmed Polynesian stereotypes, travel writing can reveal traces of a more nuanced understanding of Australian notions of femininity, masculinity and sexuality in the Pacific Islands. This is evident in the accounts of the Australian idealists and escapists who pursued the utopian lifestyle in Tahiti and who described the limitations of the Polynesian ideal.

---

2   Patty O'Brien, *The Pacific Muse: Exotic Femininity and the Colonial Pacific* (Seattle: University of Washington Press, 2006), 37, 57.

Paradise Found

The reports of three European explorers—Samuel Wallis, Louis-Antoine de Bougainville and James Cook—were influential in marking Tahiti as a 'site of desire'.[3] Reaching Tahiti in 1767, 1768 and 1769, respectively, these explorers' accounts emphasised the beauty, sexual desire and desirability of the women whom they encountered; they drew on the European myths of Arcadia, paradise and utopia that had originated in classical antiquity and medieval Christianity.[4] Although the sexual practices of the Tahitian *Arioi* held sacred and cultural significance, they were interpreted by Europeans as being symbolic of social freedom or moral weakness.[5] These first reports of Tahiti, compounded by the arrival of Tahitians in Europe as early as 1769, generated public excitement and interest. Tahiti consequently became symbolic of the Pacific Islands as a whole in Europe's imaginings. As a 1932 handbook described:

> Ever since the exploration of the Society Islands by Cook, 150 years ago, writers and travellers have vied with each other in giving to tired humanity picturesque and delightful descriptions of the Society Islands; until Tahiti has come to be known, throughout the world, as the place of all others which most truly presents the beauty, charm and romance of the South Seas.[6]

In comparison, European visitors to Hawai'i encountered stricter rules that regulated sexual exchanges. Additionally, the nature of US commercial tourism development in Hawai'i in the 1900s ensured that the Island group was less mysterious than Tahiti and thus less desirable to Australian travellers.

The term 'Polynesia' was initially imbued with a sense of promise and potential. First coined by French geographer, Charles de Brosses, in 1756, it was used to encourage French expeditions in the Pacific, suggesting that the Pacific Ocean held 'a large number of islands rich in spiceries'.[7] However, it was not until the 1890s that the Pacific shifted from 'being

---

3 Margaret Jolly, 'Desire, Difference and Disease: Sexual and Venereal Exchanges on Cook's Voyages in the Pacific', in *Exchanges: Cross-Cultural Encounters in Australia and the Pacific*, ed. Ross Gibson (Sydney: Historic Houses Trust of New South Wales, 1996), 187.
4 O'Brien, *The Pacific Muse*, 61; Smith, *European Vision and the South Pacific*, 43.
5 Jolly, 'Desire, Difference and Disease', 197; Gavan Daws, *A Dream of Islands: Voyages of Self-Discovery in the South Seas* (New York: Norton, 1980), 8.
6 Robson, *The Pacific Islands Yearbook*, 309.
7 Tcherkezoff, 'A Long and Unfortunate Voyage', 179.

at the periphery of the imperial gaze to being at its centre', as argued by Patty O'Brien. In her history of exotic femininity in the Pacific, O'Brien emphasised the specific context in which the impressions of popular European travellers contributed to popular notions of the Polynesian idyll and how they made the female a central figure in both written narratives and visual forms. These European travellers included US writer Herman Melville, Scottish author Robert Louis Stevenson, French artist Paul Gauguin and French novelist Pierre Loti. Accounts of Polynesia at this time reflected modernist concerns with primitivism, nature and sexuality, which challenged conventional European notions of race and gender. Concurrently, feminist movements advocated for women's political and economic independence from men; 'in these social and political struggles, the female body was strongly contested ground'.[8] Although O'Brien highlights the broader racial and gendered dimensions of Polynesia's representations that were exhibited by colonial powers in the north, her analysis overlooks the specific historical context of Australian society and how it influenced popular tropes.

Arrival at Tahiti was highly anticipated by Australian travellers of the twentieth century, whose first glimpses of the Island confirmed that it was a natural paradise. As one 1920s handbook noted, 'Every traveller has extolled the beauty of Tahiti and the title "Paradise of the Pacific" is well bestowed'.[9] The Island (and its capital port, Papeete) inspired travellers with its mountain peaks and luxuriant vegetation, which were deemed to be the 'most beautiful and picturesque' and 'superbly beautiful' in comparison to others.[10] As Sydney Elliott Napier, a journalist, approached the Island in 1938, he wrote, 'And there, beyond, embowered in its scented groves, and bright against the dusky and contorted walls of triple-crowned Mont Diademe, we saw the roofs of queer, anomalous Papeete'.[11] Notably absent was any sense of danger or the sublime that was attributed to these mountains in Australian travel accounts. Other observations included the use of jewel metaphors to signify the Island's worth, such as 'pearl of the Pacific' and 'a perfect gem of an island'.[12] Such language was also frequently used to describe the Pacific Islands more generally (see Figure 10).

---

8   O'Brien, *The Pacific Muse*, 218.
9   Allen, *Stewart's Handbook of the Pacific Islands*, 293.
10 Allen, *Stewart's Handbook of the Pacific Islands*, 293; Villiers, *Cruise of the Conrad*, 286.
11 Sydney Elliott Napier, *Men and Cities: Being the Journeyings of a Journalist* (Sydney: Angus & Robertson, 1938), 14.
12 Gerald Stokely Doorly, *In the Wake* (London: Sampson Low Marston & Co., 1937), 175; Mabel M Stock, *The Log of a Woman Wanderer* (London: William Heinnemann, 1923), 143.

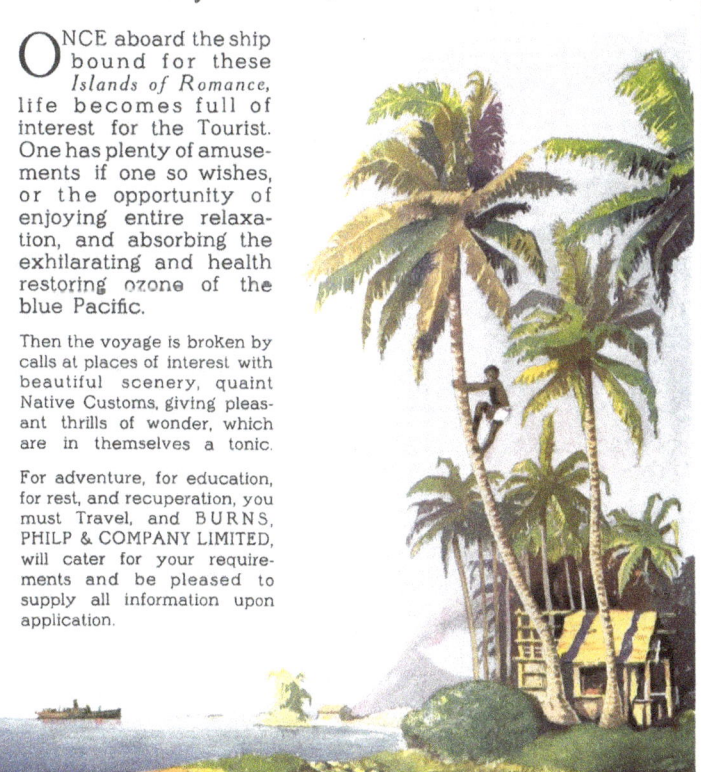

Figure 10: Pearls of the Pacific.
Source: *BP Magazine* 2, no. 1 (December 1929), 55.

Australians also attributed mystical and mythical qualities to Tahiti, with the Island acting as a blank canvas upon which imaginings and desires could be cast. Tahiti was frequently noted for its dream-like and supernatural qualities. Rather than following in the footsteps of other heroic explorers, Australians like Wilfred Burchett believed that they were visiting untouched territories: 'We had discovered what for us was an entirely new world'.[13] Eric Muspratt characterised the Island as 'a dramatic citadel of land', Sydney Powell claimed that 'it belongs to fairy-land: an earthly beauty purified of earth's grossness' and Arnold Safroni-Middleton imagined it as 'some celestial harbour of a world beyond the stars'.[14] These romantic visions were sometimes tinged with regret. This was the case for Alan Villiers, a sailor, who noted:

> The loveliness of the Tahitian hills, abrupt and grand, the summits of the high mountains often hidden in the clouds, as if the gods of Orohena dislike to look too long upon the Tahiti of today.[15]

First impressions of the scenery usually confirmed Tahiti's status as a primordial Garden of Eden—as a place protected by its isolation, 'where time melts like the mist upon the mountains'.[16] 'Each morning was like the morning of creation', wrote Sydney Walter Powell.[17] In addition, Christian allusions were frequent and not reserved for missionaries. The mountain ranges 'resembled some old chaos of unhewn creation' that was populated by 'the savage children of Adam and Eve', wrote Safroni-Middleton. Clement Lindley Wragge, a meteorologist, also labelled Tahiti as 'the Summer Isles of Eden' and described it as possessing 'a warm, soft atmosphere, sweet as Elysium'. Wealthy yachtsman, Harold Nossiter, was pleased to encounter 'Nature's gentlemen'. All these popular descriptions[18] of Eden reflected the influence of Christian missionaries who were well established in the eastern Pacific and whose conversion efforts had been more successful than those in Melanesia.

---

13   Burchett, *Passport*, 108.
14   Eric Muspratt, *Fire of Youth: The Story of Forty-Five Years Wandering* (London: Gerald Duckworth, 1948), 181; Arnold Safroni-Middleton, *South Sea Foam: The Romantic Adventures of a Modern Don Quixote in the Southern Seas* (London: Methuen & Co., 1919), 72; Powell, *Adventures of a Wanderer*, 171.
15   Villiers, *Cruise of the Conrad*, 292.
16   Mordaunt, *The Venture Book*, 68.
17   Powell, 'Each to His Taste', 266.
18   Safroni-Middleton, *South Sea Foam*, 73; Wragge, *The Romance of the South Seas*, 125; Harold Nossiter, *Southward Ho!* (London: Witherby, 1937), 123.

Allusions to Eden also rested on an assumption of Tahiti's natural abundance and fertility: 'It was truly a land of plenty, where those lucky sons of Adam who had found it could live as their forefather before he was sent packing'.[19] Following this logic, and encouraged by prolific descriptions of fruit and vegetation, Australians believed that Tahiti supported a carefree lifestyle for all its inhabitants (as opposed to only possessing suitable resources for European exploitation). This was most clearly demonstrated by the depiction of Tahiti and the Pacific Islands in general as 'lotus-eaters'—a reference to Homer's *Odyssey*, which described a mythical island in which the people ate lotus plants, a narcotic that instilled relaxation and apathy.[20] This idle existence was attractive to many Australians who sought a better life, as Powell noted:

> The lotus isles, these islands used to be called, and you can still see the name in steamer advertisements. You were supposed to spend your life under a tree waiting for the fruit to fall. This idea retains a strong appeal.[21]

Imagery of flowers and descriptions of their scents were popular literary devices in travel accounts. Flowers suggested beauty, femininity, fertility and love, while fragrances were effective metaphors for articulating the more mysterious and indefinable qualities of the tropical island. Flower 'leis' were popular tourist souvenirs in Hawai'i. In Tahiti, visitors commonly associated flowers with women and were aware that their adornment signified their availability.[22] Fragrances, be they of coconut oil, frangipanis or even 'the indefinable scent of dusky humanity', were often alluring and satisfying in the descriptions of Tahiti.[23] The HMS *Bounty* mutineers were frequently cited as a reminder of the potentially overpowering nature of this 'lure' and the attraction of forbidden pleasures. In contrast, Melanesia was rarely associated with flowers or fragrances; if it was, then it was usually associated with scents of stench and decay.

Utopian ideals were also applied to the Tahitian people. Observations about their appearance and behaviour informed (and were informed by) racial theories about the Polynesians and their place in the racial order of

---

19 Powell, 'Each to His Taste', 200.
20 Burchett, *Passport*, 109. See also John Archibald Fraser, *Gold Dish and Kava Bowl* (London: J.M. Dent & Sons, 1954), 174; Robert McMillan, *There and Back: Or Notes of a Voyage Round the World by 'Gossip'* (Sydney: William Brooks, 1903), 353.
21 Sydney Walter Powell, *A South Sea Diary* (London: V. Gollancz, 1942), 53.
22 Mordaunt, *The Venture Book*, 77.
23 Napier, *Men and Cities*, 18.

the Pacific. The term 'Polynesia', as it was used by Australian travellers in the 1900s to articulate physical, social and mental differences among Pacific Islanders, was defined in opposition to Melanesia. This racialised category was distinct from the original use of the term 'Polynesia', which was intended to describe a geographical region that comprised 'many islands'. Serge Tcherkezoff has demonstrated that the perceived dichotomy between dark- and light-skinned peoples was first noted in the Pacific in 1595 by Spanish explorers. Searching for the Solomon Islands, Pedro Fernández de Quirós's report emphasised the Marquesans' beauty and admired the naked women, observing that they appeared 'almost white' and that they did not practise cannibalism.[24] Following this first European–Polynesian exchange, a 'science of race' developed in the nineteenth century. It challenged Christian beliefs of a common humanity by proposing the concept that race was innate and absolute. Most Australian travellers of the twentieth century repeated many of the racial debates and theories of the previous 200 years, but in forms that were simplified, indiscriminate and inconsistent.

Few Australians challenged popular racial assumptions in their travel accounts. Labour recruiter William Twizell Wawn noted in 1893 that 'the true Polynesian' was superior to the 'Malay' and 'Papuan/Negrito' races (this included Aboriginal Australians and Melanesians).[25] Albert William Pearse, a tourist, admired the 'handsome' Polynesians because they were 'without a trace of the Melanesian or "nigger" type'.[26] This racial superiority was believed to be identifiable by a lighter skin colour, described as romantic shades of 'copper', 'brown' or 'mahogany'.[27] Journalist Paul McGuire even argued that Polynesians were 'basically Europoids' and that they descended from the West.[28] Polynesians were admired for their physical beauty—the men for their handsome, muscular physiques and the women for their graceful, beautiful forms.

---

24 Tcherkezoff, 'A Long and Unfortunate Voyage', 188–9.
25 William Twizell Wawn, *The South Sea Islanders and the Queensland Labour Trade: A Record of Voyages and Experiences in the Western Pacific, from 1875 to 1891*, ed. Peter Corris (Canberra: Australian National University Press, 1973), 7.
26 Pearse, *A Windjammer 'Prentice*, 133.
27 Louis Becke, *Notes from My South Sea Log* (London: T. Werner Laurie, 1905), 142; Allan, *Homeward Bound*, 22.
28 McGuire, *Westward the Course*, 46.

Polynesians were also believed to be morally superior. Compared to the 'inelegant and cruel Melanesians', Polynesians were 'kind and sympathetic', as argued by Safroni-Middleton.[29] Henry Tichborne admired 'their sterling qualities, their large hearts, their lovable natures, and their genial humours' and argued that 'no women of any colour or kind are more beautiful or tender-hearted than theirs, no men on earth more modest or brave'.[30] Wilfred Burchett further noted 'the noble, kindly character of the Tahitian people' and Muspratt, in admiration of their primitivism, wrote that 'the very soul of these people turned away from money and all modern values'.[31] An extensive history of Christian evangelism in the East encouraged this distinction between Polynesians and their 'heathen' Melanesian neighbours. Reverend John Burton argued that Polynesia contained 'loyal converts' and 'higher and more vigorous races' because the East was Christianised first.[32] Political organisation within the Islands (which was often more centralised than in Melanesia) and the existence of kings and queens in Hawai'i, Tahiti and Tonga also reinforced popular assumptions of Polynesian superiority.

Symbolic of this superiority was the Polynesian woman, a popular stereotype that was usually situated in Tahiti. The trope of the 'South Sea Maiden' or 'Pacific muse' possessed numerous appealing characteristics: she was pure, natural, fertile, beautiful, graceful, exotic, sexually alluring, compliant, passionate and available.[33] The Polynesian woman became a symbol of youth and purity in the same way that Australia's purity was represented by a young female figure.[34] This figure was consistently connected to nature, with imagery of ripening fruit and blooming flowers, descriptions of her oceanic characteristics and photographic images portraying her as naked or semi-naked. Her docile, passive and graceful nature, which served to justify colonial dominance, was balanced by her potential to be a seductress or femme fatale.[35] Tahitian women were believed to be especially skilled in the art of seduction. Nossiter observed that:

---

29 Safroni-Middleton, *Tropic Shadows*, 23.
30 Henry Tichborne, *Noqu Talanoa: Stories from the South Seas by Sundowner* (London: European Mail, 1896), vi; Henry Tichborne, *Rambles in Polynesia by Sundowner* (London: European Mail, 1897), 5.
31 Burchett, *Passport*, 107; Muspratt, *Fire of Youth*, 182.
32 John Wear Burton, *The Call of the Pacific* (London: Charles H. Kelly, 1914), 15.
33 O'Brien, *The Pacific Muse*, 3–5.
34 White, *Inventing Australia*, 120.
35 O'Brien, *The Pacific Muse*, 44.

> The charm of the women is hard to define. They possess a certain seductiveness helped by a femininity that women are losing today, and an assurance and experience of men, whom they well understand … There is a glamour about these women, for they had a reputation for beauty which seafarers have given them in the past.[36]

His reference to the loss of femininity also reflected wider concerns among some Australian men that European women were becoming more masculine, in light of the feminist movement for equal rights that had gained momentum worldwide.

An interesting exception to this stereotype was the Polynesian queen, a popular figure in the royal kingdoms of Tonga (Sālote Tupou III), Hawai'i (Lili'uokalani) and Tahiti (Pōmare IV). Most fantasised about the female monarchs, since face-to-face encounters were rare, with romantic notions of power and prestige replacing ideals of beauty and youth. Narratives that celebrated their status were 'usually linked to a nostalgia about their past romances and a lament about their faded beauty', as argued by Margaret Jolly.[37] Representations of the queens varied from exotic romanticisms (at 'once Helen of Troy and Cleopatra') to respectful admiration ('stood out above all of them in her dignity and serenity').[38] Whether admired for their innocent youth or royal wisdom, Polynesian women were portrayed in stark contrast to Melanesian women, who were usually represented as ugly, savage and undesirable 'beasts of burden'.[39] Similarly, although naked Polynesian men were depicted in active positions that often symbolised their 'virility and aggression as warriors', Melanesian masculinity was portrayed as a violent and sexual threat.[40] In some cases, such as in a 1933 advertisement in *BP Magazine* (see Figure 11), Polynesian ideals of a South Sea Maiden were transposed onto Melanesia in an attempt to lure tourists to the region.

---

36   Nossiter, *Southward Ho!*, 139.
37   Margaret Jolly, 'From Point Venus to Bali Ha'i: Eroticism and Exoticism in Representations of the Pacific', in *Sites of Desire, Economies of Pleasure: Sexualities in Asia and the Pacific*, ed. Lenore Manderson and Margaret Jolly (Chicago: University of Chicago Press, 1997), 108.
38   Safroni-Middleton, *Wine-Dark Seas and Tropic Skies*, 83–6; Mordaunt, *The Venture Book*, 180.
39   Anderson, *What a Tourist Sees in the New Hebrides*, 99.
40   Jolly, 'From Point Venus to Bali Ha'i', 119.

Figure 11: Cruise to the Solomon Islands.
Source: 'A Typical Portrayal of a South Sea Maiden in the Solomon Islands', *BP Magazine* 5, no. 2 (March 1933).

Interactions with Polynesian women were limited for many Australian travellers of the 1900s. In the Islands, the women were supposedly considered static and silent objects on which visitors could gaze, similar to how they had been in position as alluring photographic illustrations in travel accounts and advertisements. Dance performances presented an opportunity for Australians to remark about the local females; however, descriptions tended to emphasise the primitive and savage nature of dances rather than the seductive and sexual. Missionary influence had restricted more provocative dances, and Australian accounts suggest that the Hawaiian hula was not popular and well known until after World War II. The image of the Polynesian woman was gradually commodified and standardised by tourism advocates. Young travellers Edward Way Irwin and Ivan Goff recalled being beckoned to the Pacific by an Auckland billboard in the 1930s, showing a girl with 'gleaming brown skin', 'black curly hair' and 'warm eyes'.[41] Cinematic productions in the 1930s also distributed a Hollywood version of the Polynesian that blended Hawaiian characteristics, such as the lei and the hula dance, with European actors and fantasies. This became a powerful medium that normalised colonial stereotypes 'and their accompanying insidious ideas, attitudes and interactions', as argued by O'Brien.[42] Polynesian tropes even spread to inland Australia, where Indigenous women performers were provided with Pacific Island personas and names.[43]

Although this distinction between Polynesian and Melanesian was clearly articulated in Australian travel accounts, the differences between Islanders within these racial categories were less certain; they depended on traveller's personal sympathies. Every individual discovered his or her own paradise. For example, Hawai'i's location on major shipping routes and the development of a commercial tourism industry explains the large number of Australian impressions recorded about the region. Samoa was also a popular stopover, and Stevenson's legacy prompted further European fascination with the Island. Accounts of Fiji, which was situated between the eastern and western Pacific, sometimes stressed Polynesian attributes because they were more favourable. Other accounts of the Maori in New Zealand considered them to be the most advanced.

---

41   Irwin and Goff, *No Longer Innocent*, 31.
42   O'Brien, *The Pacific Muse*, 231. See also Sean Brawley and Chris Dixon, eds, *Hollywood's South Seas and the Pacific War: Searching for Dorothy Lamour* (New York: Palgrave Macmillan, 2012).
43   Kate Hunter, 'The Interracial Theatre of "Strip Tents" in Travelling Shows: Spaces of Sexual Desire in Southeastern Australia, 1930s–1950s', *Journal of New Zealand Studies*, no. 14 (2013): 54–66, doi.org/10.26686/jnzs.v0i14.1747.

Australians generally regarded Tahiti as the superior, ideal Polynesian island. This is partly due to the literary legacy of past explorers and to the more recent works of artists such as Gauguin, who inspired future travellers and influenced their style of writing. It was also due to the isolation of Tahiti, as well as its limited exchange with Australia, which allowed fantasies about these Islands to endure much longer than in other places. Apart from a brief pork trade with New South Wales from 1801 to 1826, transportation to Tahiti from Australia was limited, and communication was difficult due to the absence of a wireless telegraph until 1915.[44] Romanticised notions about Tahiti were perpetuated by the nature of French colonialism in the region, which overlooked narratives of conquest and conflict in French Polynesia in favour of a narrative that was based on love, alliance and devotion, as argued by Matt Matsuda.[45] Christian outreach in Polynesia encouraged a more sanitised representation of the region in comparison to the dangerous and 'savage' Melanesia. Australians were consequently convinced about the safety of these Islands.

Unlike Australian attitudes to the French territories of New Caledonia and the New Hebrides, Australians were not opposed to French colonial rule in Tahiti. Narratives about the natural abundance of Tahiti and French Polynesia did not allude to the possible exploitation of resources and wealth as had been done with Melanesia. In fact, Australian travellers often admired the influence of French culture in Tahiti, which was believed to have brought a particular refinement to the people: 'The French had a flair for gaiety that appeals to the Polynesian with his own happiness of heart'.[46] Australians acknowledged Tahiti's importance as a regional hub, but they recognised it as a region existing beyond Australian colonial desires. Ralph Stock noted that Tahiti was the 'metropolis of the southeastern Pacific Islands, just as Honolulu is of the northeastern'.[47] Consequently, Tahiti was enshrined as an exotic ideal because it was out of Australia's imperial reach.

---

44   Colin Walter Newbury, *Tahiti Nui: Change and Survival in French Polynesia, 1767–1945* (Honolulu: University of Hawai'i Press, 1980), 9.
45   Matsuda, *Empire of Love*, 7, 94.
46   Villiers, *Cruise of the Conrad*, 292.
47   Stock, *The Cruise of the Dream Ship*, 169.

'Too Good to Be True'

The expansion of shipping routes through Polynesia encouraged the marketing of the Islands as being an untouched paradise, while simultaneously making the region more available and vulnerable to Australian tourist traffic. Consequently, the imagined ideal was increasingly challenged by the colonial reality. USSCo.'s establishment of a regular steamship route to San Francisco via Rarotonga and Tahiti from 1909 to 1936 unlocked a new region that was once out of reach to Australian travellers. As Wragge noted in 1906, 'People don't know; they have no conception of the glories of Tahiti; the globe-trotter follows the beaten tracks, and leaves this fascinating spot out of his calculations'.[48] This growth in travel is evidenced by the number of travel accounts. Between 1880 and 1900, three colonial Australians described their experiences of travel to Tahiti. George Robertson Nicoll, Henry Tichborne and William Meeke Fehon were of similar ages and class, and their travel accounts emphasised similar themes of the alluring Polynesian maiden, of picturesque scenery and of adventures involving reefs, storms and cannibals. Between 1900 and 1918, seven Australians wrote nine accounts of Tahiti, and between 1919 and 1941, 14 travellers wrote 18 accounts. This growing body of travellers expressed their dissatisfaction with Tahiti, as it failed to meet their expectations of a pristine paradise. This was in part prompted by the effects of war (physical destruction caused by the German bombardment of Papeete in 1914) and a general disillusionment with the European world order. However, this dissatisfaction could also be attributed to a gradual weariness of exaggerated stereotypes and to the colonial influence of development and commerce within the Pacific. As Eric Muspratt noted, it was 'too good to be true and too good to last'.[49]

Evidence of colonial settlement in the port of Papeete frequently tarnished the natural paradise that Australians expected. Villiers advised those who sought 'wondrous scenery' to trek beyond the 'unlovely little town', regretfully noting that 'if it had been still a native island I should have loved it'.[50] Nossiter's reaction was mixed; he found Tahiti to be 'a land of glamour and false romance', and Papeete to be filled with

---

48 Wragge, *The Romance of the South Seas*, 247.
49 Muspratt, *Fire of Youth*, 182.
50 Villiers, *Cruise of the Conrad*, 292, 287.

'a conglomeration of artistic and unsightly buildings'.[51] He was also surprised by the strong Chinese presence, as was Napier, who wrote: 'What we found was a somewhat prosaic dusty little town, filled—or so it seemed to us—with Chinamen and bicycles'.[52] The town's residents were also unappealing and amoral, with the 'debauchery and drunkeness' shocking several Australians. Expectations of a carefree life were thus shattered by the reality of economic depression and corruption: 'There is the depression now; there had been, it was vaguely whispered, a financial scandal. Some of the leading citizens had been in jail.'[53]

In this environment, the Tahitian was considered corrupt and ignoble.[54] Stock found the Islanders to be 'a sad relic … of a once-superb race' and Muspratt noted that 'some strange quality dwelt here, a lonely forgotten spirit now dying in isolation in this modern world. Like Honolulu, only more so'.[55] Blame was generally attributed to contact with Europeans, though the specific causes were varied and speculative. Safroni-Middleton deemed missionary efforts to be futile, alleging that 'girls and boys made love to each other and eloped with the missionaries chasing after them', and that:

> The brave old chiefs … loved their old customs deep down in their heart … and cherished hopes that some day the gods would help them drive the white men into the sea.[56]

Others blamed the influence of traders and beachcombers for bringing disease, alcohol and misguided notions of progress. Upon reflection, Stock questioned the merits of his own 'civilisation': 'Perhaps—who knows?—these things are but another proof that we harbingers of progress were not intended to invade the sanctuary of the South Seas'.[57] Tourists were also held responsible, with Villiers remarking that 'the nasal tones of

---

51 Nossiter, *Southward Ho!*, 138.
52 Napier, *Men and Cities*, 21.
53 Arnold Safroni-Middleton, *Sailor and Beachcomber: Confessions of a Life at Sea, in Australia and amid the Islands of the Pacific* (London: Grant Richards, 1915), 149; Villiers, *Cruise of the Conrad*, 287, 292.
54 Ian Christopher Campbell, 'Savages Noble and Ignoble: The Preconceptions of Early European Voyagers in Polynesia', *Pacific Studies* 4, no. 1 (1980): 45–59; Ian Christopher Campbell, *'Gone Native' in Polynesia: Captivity Narratives and Experiences from the South Pacific* (Westport: Greenwood Press, 1998).
55 Stock, *The Cruise of the Dream Ship*, 174; Muspratt, *Fire of Youth*, 181.
56 Safroni-Middleton, *Sailor and Beachcomber*, 149–50.
57 Stock, *The Cruise of the Dream Ship*, 195; Safroni-Middleton, *Sailor and Beachcomber*, 149; Allen, *Stewart's Handbook of the Pacific Islands*, 293.

loud Americans being "free" offend an ear that strains for the loveliness of Polynesian speech' and Baume recounting the perspective of a female resident in 1913 who resented the 'Americanisation' of Tahiti and the 'bastardising' influence of Gauguin impersonators.[58] George Meudell also argued that the 'Isle of Dreams' had been 'spoilt by the tourists', and he predicted the future construction of large hotels and a casino.[59]

Some Australian travellers found faults with French colonialism, such as Nossiter, who regarded Tahiti as 'an island that Britain should never have allowed France to possess'.[60] However, this was a minority view, as French Polynesia was too distant from Australia to be of strategic interest. This attitude also reflected the reality of French rule in Tahiti, which allowed trade to be dominated by foreign enterprises and which had limited influence over the Island's development.[61] When Stock questioned a British resident, he replied that he preferred French rule because 'they leave you alone'. Stock likened the act of providing Australia and New Zealand with mandates to 'giving a kid something to play with. He's bound to break it'.[62] Conversely, Nossiter judged French rule to be inferior because it failed to acknowledge racial hierarchies:

> In justice to the British I must say they fall for native women less than do men of other nations, for the pride of race and caste is more strongly embedded in the British character and it is that aloofness from coloured races that makes the British the best colonizers. Not that the British despise the natives, far from that ... but the British simply do not mix with the natives, except, of course, in isolated cases ... A native or half-breed of good circumstances is treated by the French as an equal and for this reason they do not look upon the Frenchman as a superior being.[63]

Australians were surprised by Tahiti's racial diversity, with Safroni-Middleton observing a population of 'all kinds of half-castes'.[64] Specifically, Australians found the prevalence of Chinese people most surprising and disturbing. In 1911, when the number of French citizens in Papeete was 2,153, the Chinese numbered 975; by 1917, this number

---

58 Villiers, *Cruise of the Conrad*, 292; Baume, *I Lived These Years*, 43.
59 George Meudell, *The Pleasant Career of a Spendthrift* (London: Routledge, 1929), 145.
60 Nossiter, *Southward Ho!*, 130. See also Pearse, *A Windjammer 'Prentice*, 13.
61 Newbury, *Tahiti Nui*, 227, 315.
62 Stock, *The Cruise of the Dream Ship*, 193.
63 Nossiter, *Southward Ho!*, 139–40.
64 Safroni-Middleton, *Sailor and Beachcomber*, 148.

increased to 2,481.⁶⁵ The Chinese were economically well entrenched and freely intermarried with Polynesians. Pearse wrote, 'It is a pity that the Chinese and other races are interbreeding'.⁶⁶ Nossiter observed that the 'Chinaman' owned most of the businesses in Papeete, and that this threatened to 'dominate this land if his march is not stopped'. He argued that the desire for expensive European clothes drove Tahitian women to 'drift to the Chinaman', and thus that 'the pure Tahitian is doomed'.⁶⁷ Other nationalities resided in Tahiti, but it was the prominence of the Chinese nationality that challenged Australian notions of a racially pure and uncorrupted paradise.

Although Australians were disappointed by the supposedly corrupted Tahitian ideal, they continued to believe that a utopia could be found in the vicinity and sought more isolated Islands within French Polynesia and the Cook Island group. These Islands possessed the Polynesian traits that travellers desired: they were isolated enough to discourage tourists, yet reasonably accessible from the major stopovers of Tahiti and Rarotonga. For those with access to a small yacht or charter, the Marquesas Islands were 'extraordinarily beautiful', wrote Mabel Stock. Meudell recommended them to so-called 'real travellers'.⁶⁸ Rarotonga was also popular because it was relatively unknown and isolated. Nossiter argued, 'To me it is more beautiful than Tahiti and Bora Bora, whose charms are much exaggerated', with Pearse concluding that 'although Tahiti is supposed to be the loveliest island, I think Rarotonga is better'.⁶⁹ In Nossiter's case, British colonialism in Rarotonga provided a familiar reassurance. He remarked, 'What a contrast the Government of this island presents in comparison to the Marquesas and Society Islands!'⁷⁰

Utopian Dreaming

In addition to steamship tourists, for whom Tahiti was an exotic point of transit, were Australians who were attracted to the Pacific by the promise of a more permanent escape. For them, the alluring Pacific Islands were

---

65 Newbury, *Tahiti Nui*, 271.
66 Pearse, *A Windjammer 'Prentice*, 134.
67 Nossiter, *Southward Ho!*, 141.
68 Stock, *The Log of a Woman Wanderer*, 110; Meudell, *The Pleasant Career of a Spendthrift*, 145.
69 Nossiter, *Southward Ho!*, 160; Pearse, *A Windjammer 'Prentice*, 133.
70 Nossiter, *Southward Ho!*, 162.

more familiar than the harsh and uninviting Australian outback.[71] They were also isolated from the social conventions of civil society in Europe, the US and Australia. Although there were many Islands to choose from, and lucrative incentives to move to Melanesia, the more distant Islands of Polynesia proved to be a popular attraction, especially for a band of wanderers, vagabonds, artists and idealists. Their accounts distanced them from the fleeting observations of tourists and displayed a closer interaction with Islanders and a more earnest endeavour to embrace and understand Island life.

Part of the attraction of French Polynesia was the difficult voyage and the long distances to be traversed, which presented an irresistible challenge to those seeking the road less travelled. Pearse, Stock, Nossiter and Villiers described in detail the romance of sailing to their own schedule in the 1920s and 1930s, their accounts tinged with a nostalgia for the sailing culture that was being lost to the steamship. Sailing resisted the trend towards modernisation and, in doing so, was perceived to be closer to nature and to a more idyllic past, in the same way that Polynesia was. Images of sailing ships anchored in peaceful harbours were popular in travel accounts for this nostalgic purpose (see Figure 12). As Stock noted in his book, *Cruise of the Dream Ship:*

> You begin to see how the average sailor-man feels in 'polite society', and your heart goes out to him. 'How's the wind?' Ah, of course, it makes no difference to this smoke-belching machine that bears you at thirteen knots, and according to schedule towards civilization.[72]

The nostalgia felt for sailing symbolised the wider search for a more authentic way of life, one away from the constraints of modern urban society. This sentiment was prompted by a moral disillusionment that followed World War I, as well as by economic depressions, a growing urban middle class and cultural maturity in Australia in the 1920s and 1930s. This is evident in the targeted advertising of *BP Magazine*, which directly addressed 'the busy city man seeking a few weeks' respite for his tired brain from the hurry and bustle and strain of modern high pressure of commercial life', as well as the 'squatter' and the 'mining man'.[73]

---

71 Max Quanchi, 'Contrary Images: Photographing the New Pacific in *Walkabout* Magazine', *Journal of Australian Studies* 27, no. 79 (2003): 76, 78, doi.org/10.1080/14443050309387889.
72 Stock, *The Cruise of the Dream Ship*, 132.
73 Burns, Philp & Company, Limited, *BP Magazine* 1, no. 1 (December 1928): 9.

Memories of Moorea

An impression of an unforgettable night on this loveliest of Pacific Isles, one of the Society Isles, of which Tahiti is the best known

By ERIC RAMSDEN

FROM the Yacht Club in Papeete, where in the old days Prince Hinoi lounged, one can see Moorea, lovely Moorea, across the strait, silhouetted against the sunset. Nothing lovelier can possibly be imagined as the clouds flame behind the castellated pinnacles—every peak, every crag, famous in story and in song.

It seems like some enchanted island, something unreal, yet sufficiently close to touch—a fairy isle, maybe inhabited by a fairy people. Something fantastically weird that had arisen from the fastnesses of the sea; something, too, that would disappear just as mysteriously as it had reared heavenwards. I had seen Moorea in the early dawn as we steamed along her palm-fringed shore. The morning sun with his revealing fingers had clothed with green and gold and ochre each scintillating peak, and gently removed the wisps of mist ascending from the valleys, hundreds of feet below.

I had seen Moorea at sunset from Punauuia, on the western side of Tahiti. In the immediate foreground was the lagoon, mirroring a thousand delicate pastel shades, its surface occasionally rippled by the leaping of a fish. On the reef, past the golden Path of Tane that led into the heart of the sun, men were fishing—slim, bronzed figures etched against the amethyst outline of Moorea's rugged mountains. Away in the distance, too far to be heard, a launch, laden with tuna for the morrow's market in Papeete, "phut-phutted" its way back to harbour.

It was here that the coco-nut palms, feathery things of unforgettable grace, leapt down from the foothills to greet the sea. Along the shore a fire crackled, ready for the fish caught that

Figure 12: Memories of Moorea.

Source: Eric Ramsden, 'Memories of Moorea', *Walkabout* 1, no. 8 (1 June 1935): 11. Image courtesy of the Australian National Travel Association.

Reports of utopian settlements frequently appeared in Australian newspapers throughout the twentieth century, as they imagined an escape from life's hardships. Utopian experiments reached a high point in American, European and Australian literature in the 1890s. In Australia, drought, depression, labour unrest and socialist ideology drove this utopian dreaming.[74] Tropical islands were a popular location because they promised isolation from civilisation and its temptations, a natural abundance that fostered a carefree lifestyle and a pleasant climate that encouraged nakedness. 'There is a fascination in remoteness', as Beatrice Grimshaw argued.[75] Uninhabited islands, such as those along the Queensland coast, or islands that did not have indigenous inhabitants, such as Pitcairn, Norfolk and Lord Howe, were preferred.[76] However, the utopian dream had its faults, as one anonymous author warned:

> The 'comic-opera' simple life, as you may live it now in Tahiti, Bali, or Capri, is very much simpler than trying to discover Utopia on primitive islands. After all, it is very unpleasant to revert to the primitive. In theory it sounds all right, but so few can be nicely, and picturesquely, primitive. The search for the perfect island is really but part of the universal search for happiness.[77]

The isolation of French Polynesia made it a popular choice for both Americans and Australians. One famous attempt to travel to the region was by Ernest Darling (also known as the 'nature man'), who left the US to pursue a life close to nature in Tahiti in the 1900s.[78] According to a 1912 article in the *Daily Herald*, Darling lived 'on berries', was naked and discarded 'all the institutions of civilisation'. His existence was admired: 'The ideal wife, the ideal life, and ideal work are now awaiting any man who cares to follow the example of Mr John Darling'.[79] Australian couple, Mr and Mrs Briggs, also made a highly publicised attempt to establish an 'International Goodwill Settlement' at Nukuhiva, in the Marquesas Islands, in the 1930s. The media hype quickly disappeared when the couple's yacht failed to sail beyond the Bass Strait.[80]

---

74 Bill Metcalf, *From Utopian Dreaming to Communal Reality: Cooperative Lifestyles in Australia* (Sydney: UNSW Press, 1995), 18–19.
75 Grimshaw, *In the Strange South Seas*, 29.
76 For example, see 'A South Sea Utopia', *Wagga Wagga Advertiser*, 7 December 1901, 2, nla.gov.au/nla.news-article101857168.
77 'The Universal Need for "Escape"', *Sydney Morning Herald*, 16 October 1939, 4, nla.gov.au/nla.news-article17639412.
78 Ahrens, Lindstrom and Paisley, *Across the World with the Johnsons*, 30.
79 'An Ideal Wife', *Daily Herald*, 16 March 1912, 13, nla.gov.au/nla.news-article105221614.
80 'Modern Utopia Planned by Tasmanians', *Sunday Times*, 31 July 1938, 17, nla.gov.au/nla.news-article58987760.

Writers and artists formed the majority of the Australian travellers who attempted to live a utopian existence in Tahiti and Polynesia. Nine left behind detailed records of their experiences, which offered greater insight into their personal struggles than the short and observational tourist accounts. The remoteness of Tahiti offered these travellers the promises of escaping the 'repressiveness of civilised life' and of crossing conventional sexual, racial and gendered boundaries (as famous artists like Stevenson and Gauguin had tried to accomplish).[81] The experiences of Australian travellers often mirrored these artists, their romantic ideals and their disappointment with the reality of living in the Pacific. Arnold Safroni-Middleton and Sydney Walter Powell were two prolific writers whose works offer insights about this struggle.

Arnold Safroni-Middleton (1873–1950) was a writer, poet, musician, composer and self-styled vagabond who wandered Australia and the Pacific Islands during the late 1880s and 1890s. Following his early travels, he returned to England and became a successful writer, publishing five travel books: *Sailor and Beachcomber* (1915), *A Vagabond's Odyssey* (1916), *Wine-Dark Seas and Tropic Skies* (1918), *South Sea Foam* (1919) and the autobiography, *In the Green Leaf* (1950). His books were a collection of anecdotes, fictional tales and reminiscences that were often written in the style of a sailor's yarn and that were thematically dominated by a romantic nostalgia for a primitive paradise. He also wrote poetry and romance and mystery novels that contained Pacific settings.

Safroni-Middleton's experience was typical of those Australians who blended realism and the imaginary to create an exaggerated and romanticised account of the Pacific. He frequently admitted that his reminiscences were nostalgic and idealistic, describing one book as a 'frank autobiographical romance'.[82] What he failed to acknowledge in his texts was how World War I shaped his reminiscences as he wrote them in England. Claiming inspiration from his personal encounters with Stevenson and Joseph Conrad, Safroni-Middleton was a bohemian who cherished artistic expression and rejected the 'analytical conclusions' of science books.[83] He regarded Islander myths as 'poetic babblings of the children of nature' and ships' crews as 'true sea-poets'. His own memories, he argued, 'become tinged with that indefinable glamour, that something

---

81   Daws, *A Dream of Islands*, 256.
82   Safroni-Middleton, *Tropic Shadows*, 7.
83   Safroni-Middleton, *In the Green Leaf*, 72.

which men call poetry'.[84] The influence of sailors is evident in the style of his texts, which resembles a selection of yarns that is sometimes loosely organised in chronological order, but that also blends myths (both Islander and European), fictional tales and personal experience.

Safroni-Middleton was critical of the corruption that civilisation caused in the Pacific, which he described as 'immense vandalism'; he frequently alluded to an ancient lost empire, the 'past splendour of the South Sea Rome' or 'the never-to-be South Sea Empire'.[85] Of all the Islands, Samoa was where he spent most of his time, and he believed it was the ideal Polynesian paradise. Yet he also admired the old beachcombers and traders who he met in the Islands—'those old-time semi-embalmed sea-apostles of ancient "salt-junk"'—and the role that they played in his 'boyish contemplations over the great world of romance that I had thought existed beyond undiscovered seas'.[86]

Safroni-Middleton was well aware of stories involving interracial romance. He wrote that he often mixed with sailors and traders who drunkenly shared their stories of sexual exploits. He was also highly critical of the missionaries who he believed frequently 'succombed [sic]' to women while they wrote pious accounts at home.[87] Many of the women that Safroni-Middleton described conformed to the stereotypical alluring female:

> One of them, she is one of many, wears almost nothing, the curved, thick lips in her wide mouth murmur forth alluring Samoan speech. Her girth is enormous, and her brown bosom heaves with simulated professional passion, like a wave on the treacherous deep dark ocean of sensuality—whereon so often travelling men are shipwrecked. Her eyes are large, the pupils widely encircled with white, and warm with the sunlight gleam of downright wickedness; she has been taught her art in the vast university of experience with white men in the foremost ranks of civilisation's pioneer tramp.[88]

---

84   Safroni-Middleton, *South Sea Foam*, vii, 53.
85   Safroni-Middleton, *Tropic Shadows*, 13; Safroni-Middleton, *Wine-Dark Seas and Tropic Skies*, 81.
86   Safroni-Middleton, *In the Green Leaf*, 7, 74.
87   Safroni-Middleton, *In the Green Leaf*, 76.
88   Arnold Safroni-Middleton, *A Vagabond's Odyssey: Being Further Reminiscences of a Wandering Sailor, Troubadour in Many Lands* (London: Grant Richards, 1916), 59.

In his accounts, Safroni-Middleton portrayed Polynesian women as active seductresses and emphasised his own youthful innocence. He claimed that Samoan girls were 'born flirts' who 'longed for the romantic white youth'.[89] When staying with a sailor in Apia, Safroni-Middleton was supposedly seduced by the sailor's Samoan wife, who 'made violent love to me'.[90] In another encounter, a Samoan woman with whom he fell in love, Papoo, left him because the novelty of dating a white man had diminished.[91]

Safroni-Middleton's stories of romance also reveal the common racial prejudices of that time. He frequently noted 'all kinds of half-castes' who lived in the Islands during his travels and was critical of non-European races (e.g. Indian, Chinese and Malay). In Tahiti, he observed that:

> The varied offspring of men from many lands, the half-caste children of white traders, Chinese mongrels, Polynesian niggers, descendants of wandering, adventurous viciousness, mixed up with the outcasts of civilisation, and more often than quite enough the puny offspring of touring American and German missionaries, and English too.[92]

In another text, he criticised foreign sailors who left children behind so that they could return to their families in Europe.[93] Although this suggests that Safroni-Middleton perceived this as the irresponsible corruption of Tahitian racial purity, his fictional and actual romances encouraged interracial liaisons. Like most fictional romances that are set in the Pacific, Safroni-Middleton represented the mixed-race woman as desirable ('she was the most English-looking South Sea Island girl I ever saw') and described the ideal life as being married to a 'native' woman.[94] This desire for the 'half-caste' was amplified in Tahiti, which was considered 'a country where the colour line is indefinite, where West comes nearer to meeting East than possibly in any other part of the world'.[95] Few acknowledged the reality, as M Kathleen Woodburn did in 1944, that 'the life of the half-caste is a continual internal war'.[96]

---

89   Safroni-Middleton, *A Vagabond's Oddyssey*, 79.
90   Safroni-Middleton, *Sailor and Beachcomber*, 142.
91   Safroni-Middleton, *Sailor and Beachcomber*, 67.
92   Safroni-Middleton, *Sailor and Beachcomber*, 57.
93   Safroni-Middleton, *Sailor and Beachcomber*, 118.
94   Safroni-Middleton, *Sailor and Beachcomber*, 217.
95   This was according to a book review of Sydney Walter Powell's novel, *Tetua*: 'The Book World: Reviews', *The Mercury*, 30 October 1926, 15, nla.gov.au/nla.news-article29464188.
96   Woodburn, *Backwash of Empire*, 107.

In practice, Safroni-Middleton failed to maintain a permanent relationship or a relationship that was at least more than a sexual exchange. He offered many reasons—such as women being unwilling or unable to leave, his own preference to remain a wanderer or having love stolen by another, as had happened in the case of a Maori woman that he had desired (Hine-e-moa). Instead, Safroni-Middleton seemed to have found happiness only in imagined relationships. These fantasies permeated his travel accounts, such as in the *Wine-Dark Seas and Tropic Skies*: a large portion of the book was dedicated to the fictional tragedy of Waylao, a 16-year-old girl of mixed Marquesan and European ancestry. Safroni-Middleton coveted Waylao, who was portrayed as 'the dusky heroine of a romantic South Sea novel', though she was never within reach, much like in his other romances. The incomplete nature of these encounters highlights the problematic nature of Safroni-Middleton's 'reminiscences' and the reluctance to transgress the boundaries of European convention beyond a fictional and imagined space. This response was shared by other travellers and readers who preferred fictional romances to reality. For example, Michael Sturma argued that popular notions of the HMS *Bounty* mutineers tended to focus on the idyllic nature of their love affairs with Tahitian women; these notions overlooked the realities of married life once the men had settled on Pitcairn Island and the inevitable conflicts that arose between sailors and their Islander wives.[97]

Sydney Walter Powell (1878–1952), like Safroni-Middleton, was also a wanderer and writer, as well as more vocally Australian. Best known for his descriptions of World War I, Powell's fiction and poetry about South Africa and the Pacific Islands have been overlooked. Born in England and raised in South Africa, Powell then moved to Australia to work various jobs there before joining the artillery. His posting to Thursday Island sparked his interest in the Pacific Islands, and he began writing for *The Bulletin*. He visited Tahiti before serving in World War I, which became the subject of his two published travel accounts, *Adventures of a Wanderer* (1928) and *A South Sea Diary* (1942), and the subject of an unpublished autobiography, *Each to His Taste*. Each text provides a different perspective of Powell's journey to Tahiti from New Zealand in 1908 and his short residence there, followed by his return trip in 1916 to the Tuamotu Group in French Polynesia. Despite adamantly stating in his introduction to

---

97   Michael Sturma, *South Sea Maidens: Western Fantasy and Sexual Politics in the South Pacific* (Westport: Greenwood Press, 2002), 52.

Adventures of a Wanderer that 'this book is not fiction', 'never inventing nor falsifying', his second and third texts contain inconsistent dates, reasons for leaving and his relationships with women in Europe and Tahiti.

Powell's experience as a writer shaped his journey and the subsequent texts that he wrote. Like Safroni-Middleton, he also drew inspiration from Robert Louis Stevenson, observing at Rarotonga 'the sight of which from the sea answered perfectly to the descriptions of South Sea writers. I felt that Stevenson's lyricism was justified'.[98] *A South Sea Diary* was not intended to be a diary 'in the literal sense', Powell wrote, and it is unclear whether sections were written after the time of his travel, which could explain certain inconsistencies in the content of each text.[99] He also explicitly described the difficulties that he faced in finding work as a writer, his change in perspective over time and the writing technique itself. In regard to the importance of using active dialogue in text, he wrote:

> Treat a thing as completely past and the indistinctiveness of the past begins to descend on it; the dissolution of the past has already commenced. Hold it in the present … it preserves the present's vividness. And no record is worth a damn that is not vivid. It is the one essential virtue of a diary, which lives in the day-to-day present.[100]

Powell was initially 'exultant' about being in a foreign environment and considered Tahiti 'the land of my dreams'.[101] He gradually realised that the Tahitian ideal that he expected to experience was to be found outside busy Papeete. He preferred to reside in the village, which he considered a more authentic way of life: 'I don't care for merely visiting places: I want intimacy or nothing. I hate tourism of any sort.'[102] At times, his life appears ideal—especially in his second text, in which he describes purchasing a coconut plantation in a Tahitian rural village, building a house, establishing himself in the community and falling in love. He wrote, 'I have never been anywhere where my instincts had such freedom, my diversity so much satisfaction, where I felt so much a harmony'.[103] This freedom was also espoused by the Tahitians themselves, whom he admired for their sense of equality and respect. However, he was also disappointed

---

98 Powell, *Adventures of a Wanderer*, 132.
99 Powell, *A South Sea Diary*, 7.
100 Powell, *A South Sea Diary*, 62.
101 Powell, *Adventures of a Wanderer*, 134.
102 Powell, *A South Sea Diary*, 47.
103 Powell, *A South Sea Diary*, 40.

with colonial influence. He observed 'the corrupting power of money on a primitive people', referring to 'illusions' of paradise, and ultimately moved to the outer Tuamotu group because Tahiti was too 'sophisticated and Europeanised'.[104] Contracting elephantiasis was another blow to his utopian dreams.

Powell's travel accounts were less prone to fictional embellishments than Safroni-Middleton's. This was acknowledged in an Australian book review, which commended his knowledge as being 'of a more intimate and familiar kind'.[105] His intimate relationship with a Tahitian woman offered insights into the practicalities of interracial romance and into what was permissible in society at the time. Inconsistencies in the details between the three accounts, most notably the omission of his Tahitian wife, Tehiva, in his first and last works, cast some doubt regarding the accuracy of his recollections. The reason for omitting Tehiva is unclear—perhaps it was due to Powell's changing readerships, as the first book was published in 1928 and the second in 1942, when attitudes to cross-cultural romance may have been more conciliatory. The final work was an unpublished manuscript and may have been intended as an authoritative biography rather than as a work for public consumption (so Tehiva may have thus been a fictional character).

As an Island resident, Powell provided more detailed observations about Islander women and their roles and responsibilities within the family and in society. He provided them with a greater agency than other authors did, noting how during his residence as a guest of a chief in Tahiti, he observed the wife and housemaids talking to the chief freely, treating him 'with respect but without servility'.[106] He realised that their notion of modesty was different, though 'his [Tahitians'] sense of it is strong enough to make him charge us with immodesty'.[107] He distinguished his relationship as being different from other interracial romances, noting that an association with foreign sailors was of the utmost degradation and that although many girls went to Papeete in search of men, it was for better social prospects rather than for pleasure. Prostitution was not desirable.[108]

---

104 Powell, *A South Sea Diary*, 33, 81; Powell, 'Each to His Taste', 188.
105 'Books in Brief', *The West Australian*, 25 August 1928, 5, nla.gov.au/nla.news-article32218170.
106 Powell, *Adventures of a Wanderer*, 147.
107 Powell, *Adventures of a Wanderer*, 167.
108 Powell, *A South Sea Diary*, 24, 28.

Powell's description of marriage in Tahiti departed from conventional narratives of interracial romance. He wrote that his attraction to Tehiva was primarily based on her personality rather than her appearance and that she was not a 'craving of the hour', nor 'an appetite to be indulged and done with'. Similarly, Tehiva was serious, and her affection was not easily offered: 'I knew that she was no *hulahula* girl, and I had learned that girls in Tahiti are not to be got for the mere asking'.[109] He elaborated further on the morality of women:

> In Tahiti the moral code may be called easy, but this gives a latitude of choice which makes a girl more particular than she could otherwise afford to be. And the girls of Tahiti have quite pronounced tastes … for I had learned a little already of Tahitian psychology.[110]

This idea was reinforced by his visit to Rarotonga, a place that he considered inferior due to the regulations that prohibited mixed marriage: 'As a result, there was far more promiscuity here than in Tahiti and relations between white and brown were furtive instead of frank'.[111] In *South Sea Diary*, he described his daily life of living in a bamboo-thatched hut, with a native oven, selling just enough copra to cover his living costs. Powell and Tehiva's relationship appeared to be equal, with Powell writing that work was shared equally between them, that 'no man is above cooking the dinner' and that Tehiva's 'natural intelligence' was as high as his.[112]

Powell's adaptation to Tahitian life had its limitations. In some cases, he refused to eat without cutlery: 'My European blood revolted at doing this habitually'.[113] When meeting an elderly English resident whose marriage had failed (named Tioti or George), Powell reflected on his own marriage. He much preferred his informal partnership with Tehiva, criticising the formal marriage arrangements that were required in Europe. He also noted the limitations of having children in the Islands:

> I am intelligent enough to see that the children of a Tahitian mother must be Tahitian, unless the father has exceptional strength of character … I think that every marriage of this kind

---

109 Powell, *A South Sea Diary*, 15.
110 Powell, *A South Sea Diary*, 15.
111 Powell, *A South Sea Diary*, 66.
112 Powell, *A South Sea Diary*, 13–14.
113 Powell, *A South Sea Diary*, 18.

> where there are children must be a disappointment, even in those rare cases where the dominating character of the father has left its indelible stamp, for it is never so strong as he would wish it be.[114]

Occasional references suggest that Powell's relationships were not always functioning smoothly either. In his first account, he admitted that one relationship in Tahiti had already failed and that, after trying to relocate to the Tuamotu group as a trader, he realised 'the extent of my ignorance of her', when Tehiva was opposed to being away from her home for too long.[115]

In contrast to Safroni-Middleton, a self-styled vagabond who was reluctant to settle in one spot, Powell was opposed to the temporary tourist, as well as eager to make a new permanent life in Tahiti. His works demonstrate empathy for the people and a deeper understanding and appreciation of their culture and traditions (e.g. his comparison of adoption in Europe and Tahiti). His relationship with Tehiva was crucial to this appreciation, as he had explained in his concluding chapter of *South Sea Diary*; he had ultimately decided to leave the Island after her death. It was also a relationship that could never be shared with another European woman:

> I would not live here with a European woman; she alone would be enough to separate me from the life in which I now participate; having no natural link with the people, we should become a foreign body; and I would not live here under such conditions. Unless you are merged in the life about you, you cannot realise your own life. You must yield yourself up unconditionally in order to possess yourself.[116]

Many other travellers shared Powell's aversion to white women in the Pacific Islands. Not only does this reflect the tensions between European male and female travellers abroad, but it also highlights the overwhelming dominance of masculine narratives of the Pacific in Australian travel writing, along with the frequently silent, or discreet, female voice.

---

114 Powell, *A South Sea Diary*, 49.
115 Powell, *A South Sea Diary*, 74.
116 Powell, *A South Sea Diary*, 54.

'Damned Civilised Women'

Travelling to the region was a male-dominated activity at this time, which was encouraged by the remoteness and perceived savagery of the Islands and by the rudimentary berths provided for females aboard ships until the 1920s. Female travellers frequently encountered social resistance or hostility in their acceptance onboard.[117] They were criticised for spoiling the romanticised ideal, as one male artist in Tahiti exclaimed: 'You damned civilized women oughtn't to be allowed in the place, spoiling everything!'[118] Women were also considered vulnerable and were criticised by both men and other women for travelling unaccompanied. Mabel Stock, a British traveller, argued that the Pacific Islands were 'too uncivilised and out of the world for a young girl to be happy in'.[119] The works of Claudia Knapman and Angela Woollacott have drawn attention to a broad spectrum of Pacific Island representations that have been authored by Australian women. They range from representations that reinforced the masculine colonial gaze to those that advocated for a modern Australian woman and a more nuanced depiction of Pacific women.[120] Studies of public figures, Annette Kellerman and Osa Johnson, who travelled the Pacific in the early twentieth century, have revealed how both women used their bodies to transgress gender and race boundaries. An Australian actress and aquatic performer, Kellerman was ambiguously portrayed as exotic and foreign, while Johnson, an American documentary filmmaker, presented herself as both a Pacific explorer and a devoted wife and mother. This flexibility allowed both women to express 'the values of freedom, emancipation, and non-conformity', which were consistent with the 'Modern Girl' of the 1920–1950s.[121] Like Kellerman and Johnson, female travel writers were aware of the social conventions that they were expected to fulfil, not only while they were travelling but also in the accounts that they wrote.

---

117 Margaret Jolly, 'Colonizing Women: The Maternal Body and Empire', in *Feminism and the Politics of Difference*, ed. Sneja Marina Gunew and Anna Yeatman (New York: Routledge, 1994), 106, doi.org/10.4324/9780429039010-7.
118 As reported by Elinor Mordaunt in Mordaunt, *The Venture Book*, 108.
119 Stock, *The Log of a Woman Wanderer*, 144.
120 Claudia Knapman, *White Women in Fiji 1835–1930: The Ruin of Empire?* (Sydney: Allen & Unwin, 1986), 6; Claudia Knapman, 'Western Women's Travel Writing About the Pacific Islands', *Pacific Studies* 20, no. 2 (1997): 31–51; Woollacott, '"All This Is the Empire, I Told Myself"'; Woollacott, *To Try Her Fortune in London*; Angela Woollacott, *Race and the Modern Exotic: Three 'Australian' Women on Global Display* (Clayton: Monash University Publishing, 2011).
121 Ahrens, Lindstrom and Paisley, *Across the World with the Johnsons*, 94–5; Woollacott, *Race and the Modern Exotic*, 39.

Laura Olcelli's study of Australian–Italian travel writing suggests that this ambiguous position of women reflects a tension between the 'old' and 'new world'.[122] European men popularly regarded women as being the 'ruin of empires' because they were perceived to incite sexual jealousy and racial hostility within the Pacific Islands.[123] Elinor Mordaunt, a professional Australian travel writer, was keenly aware of her delicate position during her travels in the Pacific. She simultaneously rallied against the 'altogether mistaken ideas people have about the women of the Victorian age!' and cautiously observed that 'manners are, like morals, the merest matter of latitude and longitude'.[124] Her travel accounts, among others, illustrate how women were adept at presenting ambiguous and diverse personas to serve a wide-ranging audience.

Mordaunt was one of only 15 Australian women who wrote about their Pacific travels between 1880 and 1941, and she was second in fame only to Grimshaw. This group of Australian women was drawn from diverse social and economic backgrounds: six were tourists, two were professional writers, three were a painter, war nurse and delegate for the Institute of Pacific Relations, and three accompanied their husbands.[125] Born in England, Elinor Mordaunt lived with her newborn son, Godfrey, in Melbourne from 1903 to 1909, after a failed marriage. Fiercely independent, she refused offers of help and scraped together a living on her earnings from sewing, painting, decorating and briefly editing a women's monthly magazine. In 1909, she and her son left for England, and she continued writing to support herself. She published over 40 volumes of mainly novels and short stories. Following an around-the-world trip for the London *Daily Mail* in 1923 at the age of 51, she finally earned a reputation as a travel writer, publishing *The Venture Book* and *The Further Venture Book* in 1926, as well as the autobiography, *Sinabada*, in 1937.

---

122 Olcelli, *Questions of Authority*.
123 Knapman, *White Women in Fiji*, 6; Knapman, 'Western Women's Travel Writing About the Pacific Islands'.
124 Mordaunt, *The Venture Book*, 195.
125 This group includes Florence Bond, Hannah Chewings, Alice Combes, May Cook, Caroline David, Beatrice Grimshaw, Doris Hayball, A Jamieson, Rosa Kirkcaldie, Aletta Lewis, Janet Mitchell, Elinor Mordaunt, Harriet Ponder, Betty Freeman and M Kathleen Woodburn. Out of these women, three wrote diaries and three followed their scientist, missionary and overseer husbands. Other well-known Australian females who travelled the Pacific include the missionaries Florence Coombe and Florence Young, actress Annette Kellerman and editor Judy Tudor.

Mordaunt was as enamoured with Tahiti as Safroni-Middleton and Powell were, writing that it had excelled all her expectations. Dreaming and writing from the veranda of a boarding house in Papeete, Mordaunt used conventional tropes of natural beauty, childlike innocence, timelessness and a carefree life to describe Tahiti. 'Love and langour' were 'the keynote to Tahiti', she argued.[126] Islander women were part of this ideal, and her observations resonated with the romanticised images of the 'half-caste': 'a tall, deep-breasted creature with great dark eyes swimming with passion, love, and melancholy'.[127] Although Mordaunt admired several male chiefs that she had encountered, they were not portrayed as alluring or sexual (nor were any other European men). This may have been due to her mature age and the social conventions that regulated the relationships between white women and Islander men. Jolly also identified this trend in the work of Grimshaw, whom she argued had adopted the white male gaze, had eroticised and exoticised females and rarely had objectified men.[128]

As a white woman, Mordaunt was privileged to access some of the Island customs that were reserved for male guests. She also witnessed the domestic spaces within villages and the women who inhabited them, was allowed to drink kava, had titles bestowed upon her and was hosted by various chiefs.[129] During one such occasion, she reflected on her ambiguous status as a white woman:

> He [the chief] is very polite to me, very punctilious about helping me first, but I wonder what he really thinks about civilized women, for even his own wife never eats with him.[130]

Similarly, painter Aletta Lewis recognised the confusion that she had created for the Samoan community with whom she stayed as they debated what rank and status she would occupy, being unmarried, white and female. However, gender could also be advantageous. In Mordaunt's case, she could have close interactions with women, bathe or sleep in areas that were prohibited to men and help with domestic duties and other activities, such as making *tapa*.[131] She often recorded her conversations with women, an act that distinguished her accounts from other male perspectives that rarely mentioned women, except for their physical appearance.

---

126 Mordaunt, *The Venture Book*, 78.
127 Mordaunt, *The Venture Book*, 75.
128 Jolly, 'From Point Venus to Bali Ha'i', 110.
129 Mordaunt, *The Venture Book*, 189; Elinor Mordaunt, *Sinabada* (London: Michael Joseph, 1937), 246.
130 Mordaunt, *The Venture Book*, 281.
131 Mordaunt, *The Venture Book*, 97, 189.

Mordaunt's insights into domestic life in the Pacific Islands resonate with other Australian female travellers—many of whom had closer access to Islander women and their families and who wrote more detailed descriptions of them. Caroline David accompanied her husband on a coral-boring expedition to Funafuti in 1897 and made extensive observations of daily life in the village, with her chapters titled 'food and cooking' and 'clothes and plants' and the inclusion of English translations of local myths. Like Mordaunt, David was independent and critical of what she perceived to be the poor treatment of women in the Islands, noting that women did most of the work in the village and making nuanced observations about the behaviour of females.[132] Although she still used colonial rhetoric to describe the people, she became very attached to the village, adopting a 'native mother', Tufaina, and 'native daughter', Naina.[133]

Similarly, Helen Cato described her domestic responsibilities as a missionary's wife: teaching, cooking, gardening, cleaning and offering medical advice. Writing in 1947, her account reflects the changing gender values of the time:

> A woman's place, we are told, is in the kitchen. It is not surprising that this particular kitchen window, so situated, is like a peephole upon life. It commands a grandstand view of many little dramas played out in Richmond from day to day, dramas of which the *marama* (lady) is the only witness.[134]

For Woodburn, who also wrote in the 1940s, living in the Islands made her grateful for the relative freedom that she possessed in Australia:

> Erromanga [sic] is a man's world into which the vexed question of woman's suffrage has not as yet entered. They are the heavy draught workers, and apparently content to remain so. Children, clothes, gardens, drudgery of all kinds, that is the woman's share.[135]

In some cases, women fulfilled the traditional gender role that was expected of them. Although representing herself as independent of her husband, Caroline David published her account under the name 'Mrs Edgeworth David'. This was not an unusual convention at the time. Jolly has demonstrated how women were not simply victims of male myths, but

---

132 Mrs Edgeworth David, *Funafuti, or, Three Months on a Coral Island: An Unscientific Account of a Scientific Expedition* (London: John Murray, 1899), 35–6.
133 Edgeworth David, *Funafuti*, 133.
134 Helen D Cato, *The House on the Hill* (Melbourne: Book Depot, 1947), 15.
135 Woodburn, *Backwash of Empire*, 153.

how they also contributed to male myths, naming Grimshaw as one who entrenched gender roles.[136] Betty Freeman, who grew up on a Colonial Sugar Refinery plantation in Fiji in the 1920s, described the part that her mother played in maintaining social etiquette and British customs. She organised social outings and activities with the European residents and passed down her knowledge of good manners to her daughter:

> A successful hostess needed discretion when arranging bridging tables. Standard of play had to be considered and it was crucial to know whether a coolness existed or worse, if any two were daggers drawn. Homemade delicacies … were nibbled all the afternoon but alcoholic refreshment never offered before sundown.[137]

Penny Russell argued that maintaining these protocols was important when living in a foreign environment and that the task usually fell to women.[138]

Representing herself as an adventurer and social outcast in her books, Mordaunt was opposed in principle to the 'people who go to the same English seaside resort every summer of their lives'.[139] She considered herself a recluse ('there is nothing on earth that I desire so little as human companionship'), yet headstrong and willing to confront anyone who offended her, no matter their status.[140] She also chose the path less travelled, preferring to travel by trading schooner rather than by liner, to live in boarding houses and to traverse up river in canoes and inland on horseback. Her account resonates with other famous Pacific adventurers, such as Australian Grimshaw and American Osa Johnson. Like these women, Mordaunt projected her ambivalent identity as a woman who challenged gender conventions, as well as one who yet maintained a sense of decorum. For example, she was careful to avoid bathing naked or publicly undressing, and she was conscious of transgressing Victorian sensibilities in the Pacific:

> I wonder what on earth the other guests would think of me if they could see me now, without shoes or stockings, my wet hair dripping down my back. Or if they could have seen me eating pork and chicken with my fingers.[141]

---

136 Jolly, 'From Point Venus to Bali Ha'i', 108.
137 Freeman, *Fiji—Memory Hold the Door*, 43.
138 Russell, *Savage or Civilised?*, 212.
139 Mordaunt, *The Venture Book*, v.
140 Mordaunt, *The Venture Book*, 20.
141 Mordaunt, *The Venture Book*, 186.

Figure 13: How a Lady Travels on Ocean Island.
Source: Thomas J McMahon, *Pacific Islands Illustrated* (Sydney: McCarron, Stewart and Co., 1910). Image courtesy of the Barr Smith Library, the University of Adelaide.

Images of women abroad compounded this ambiguity. Because female authors were conscious of not offending the sensibilities of readers at home, they rarely appeared in their own photographs and focused instead on the ethnographic subject. The practicalities of female travel in the Pacific were often left to the readers' imaginations. When women did appear in photographs, they were dressed and positioned in a manner that was appropriate to Victorian values (see Figure 13).

In her account, Mordaunt expressed the challenge of 'one's own quick readaptation' during travel and the 'difficulty there is in preserving any kind of fixed standard'.[142] She encountered other Europeans on the way that she considered amoral and corrupted in contrast to the hospitable Islanders and began to question her own identity, 'wondering if this was, indeed, I'.[143] Throughout the text, her self-identification is unclear and, at times, contradicted Victorian principles and societal constraints; however, she also compared herself to other English travellers and referred to England as home. Lewis also recorded a similar experience, although her youthful account highlighted a willingness to abandon her European

---

142 Mordaunt, *The Venture Book*, ix.
143 Mordaunt, *The Venture Book*, xii.

qualities completely. Lewis lived in American Samoa for eight months in 1929 as a painter, first in Tutuila and later on some of the outlying Islands of the Manua Group. During this time, she passionately embraced Islander culture, rejecting the tourist trade and American society in Pago Pago that made her feel 'caged in'.[144] Her artwork that was published in her travel account reinforced her admiration of the Samoans and her disapproval of foreign tourism. She appears to have been sincere in her admiration of Samoans and in her willingness to be a part of the community: 'I had come to respect him so sincerely that I had quite forgotten the division that lay between his experiences and mine, and his race and mine'.[145] However, despite her best attempts, her self-understanding remained ambivalent, and she wrote that 'the Samoan and the *palagi* [European] attitudes were at war inside me, and I felt oddly traitorous to both'.[146]

The ambivalent identities that were expressed by Mordaunt and Lewis resonate with other studies of female travellers in the Pacific that emphasised the diverse experiences of women abroad. Although not every account challenged European gender conventions and Polynesian stereotypes, it is important to consider these sources within the context of an overwhelmingly masculine narrative of the Pacific Islands. As an isolated and remote region far from the Australian mainland, Polynesia was a suitable location for Australian travellers to negotiate and transgress the social, racial, sexual and gendered expectations of European 'civilisation'. Not only did this geographical distance encourage Australian visions of a paradise or utopia, it also contributed to the perpetuation of standardised tropes that described these imagined isles. Australian perceptions of Polynesia (and specifically of Tahiti) closely resembled conventional European narratives of the region. However, unlike other regions in the Pacific, Polynesia remained largely unchanged within the broader Australian imagination. Despite a growing awareness of the fragility of this Polynesian paradise, popular stereotypes persisted in Australian travel writing in the late nineteenth and early twentieth centuries. Australians continued to travel to Tahiti in search of Polynesian promises, ignoring the travel accounts that repeatedly expressed the travellers' disappointment when they faced the realities of colonial impact.

---

144 Lewis, *They Call Them Savages*, 76.
145 Lewis, *They Call Them Savages*, 109.
146 Lewis, *They Call Them Savages*, 252.

The experiences of travellers like Safroni-Middleton and Powell highlight the difficulties that Australians encountered when trying to satisfy their idyllic visions of Polynesia. These few travellers who attempted to escape the constraints of civilisation permanently recorded their struggle of reconciling their expectations with reality. These travellers also represented the dominant masculine narrative that shaped Australian perceptions of the Pacific Islands. A more careful reading of the often-understated female voice in Australian travel writing can offer a more nuanced perspective of Australian notions of gender roles and relationships in the Pacific Islands.

4
Degrees of Savagery

> I didn't believe all these stories of barbarity and savagery. I had heard similar stories of the cannibals of the Gulf of Papua, and I had found those same cannibals rather good chaps in the main … I considered the inhabitants of the Solomons maligned at least in part. And I was mistaken. I was to learn that there were degrees of savagery, that the word was after all a relative term.[1]

Like their European and US counterparts, Australian travellers were fascinated with the possibility of encountering the 'savage' in the Pacific Islands. Australian knowledge of the Pacific Islands in the early twentieth century was significantly influenced by the discourse of the savage, which remained a persistent and dominant literary trope since the appearance of first European explorer accounts. The dualism of the 'noble' and 'ignoble' savage became a popular image in Australian travel writing, one that became distorted, conflated and contested over time. Australians were exposed to the savage in multiple forms—it was a convenient and ambiguous figure in children's literature, newspaper reports, mission and government propaganda, films, photography, tourism and travel accounts that were used to entertain, educate and justify. Australian notions of the savage were also underpinned by an increasingly racialised scientific discourse that informed notions about white racial superiority and a distinctively 'Melanesian' savagery.

Travel to the Pacific Islands provided Australians with an opportunity to come face to face with the savage of their imaginations. In doing so, some Australian travellers wrote specific and localised accounts that

---

1   Jack McLaren, *My Odyssey* (London: Jonathan Cape, 1923), 213.

adapted, or departed from, the conventional stereotypes of the Islander savage. Jack McLaren's quotation above is one example of this, as he was a popular writer and experienced traveller who sometimes confirmed these racialised and essentialised stereotypes; however, he also perceived 'degrees of savagery' within the region. A closer analysis of travel writing, contextualised within the historical relationship of Australia's engagement with the Pacific Islands, highlights a more nuanced and diverse range of travellers' perceptions.

Australian representations of the savage in travel writing often emphasised one or more of the following characteristics: the bestial, infantile, primordial and cannibal. Popular notions of the bestial savage were encouraged by the Queensland labour trade in the late nineteenth century. This trope was gradually eroded by persistent missionary influence in Australia from the 1900s that emphasised the childlike qualities of the savage. By the 1920s and 1930s, Australians were more familiar with the Pacific Islands, and the growing tourist trade had paradoxically both exoticised and standardised Islander savagery. Tourists lamented the loss of the primitive and natural savage due to modern developments and colonial influence in the Pacific. However, the most persistent fascination by far was with Pacific Island cannibalism, despite this practice's abandonment by the early twentieth century.

Whether bestial, infantile, primordial or cannibal, Pacific Islanders were characterised as different from, or opposed to, those who observed and described them. Marianna Torgovnick's work on the notion of 'primitive' is important here, and equally applicable to the concept of savagery. She argued that primitive societies were places in which Europeans could project their feelings about the present and test ideas for the future, so the value and nature of the primitive thus reflected the concerns of the time.[2] Like in European and American literature, Australian travel writing was underscored by a tension that existed between the rhetoric of control and the rhetoric of desire, which were often expressed simultaneously. European notions of the primitive or the savage may have been generic, but the contexts in which individual Australians observed Pacific Islanders were not; the distinctive Australian contribution to this composite image has yet to be fully explored. Bestiality may have dominated initial concerns in the colonial Australian imagination, but some travel writing has evidenced

---

2   Marianna Torgovnick, *Gone Primitive: Savage Intellects, Modern Lives* (Chicago: University of Chicago Press, 1990), 244.

a gradual softening of Australian attitudes towards the savage in the 1920s and 1930s, despite the persistent and racialised rhetoric found in fictional literature, newspapers and political debate. Conventional representations of the violent and bestial savage were eroded by several factors, such as a growing number of Australian travellers to the region; greater Australian interest in, and engagement with, the Pacific; and popular messages advocated by missions, governments and tourists for protecting and preserving the savage. This is evident in the accounts of Australian travellers who expressed a weariness regarding the fictional trope of the savage, as well as a more discerning attitude towards representations of the Pacific Islands.

Savage or Civilised?

The term 'savage' was originally used to refer to a wild and untamed forest—deriving from the French term *sauvage*, which in turn was derived from the Latin *silva*. However, it was not until the sixteenth century that 'savage' was used to describe 'a wild person'. By the 1880s, descriptions of the savage environment and people in the Pacific Islands tended to be formulaic and predictable, with travellers increasingly reproducing stereotypical descriptions. This was a process of confirming one's expectations, of validating and authenticating one's travel and, often, of writing for a commercial market that demanded adventure and excitement. Terms such as 'cannibal', 'headhunter', 'primitive' and 'native' were used interchangeably to denote savagery, and travellers tended to label all Islanders with these generic markers rather than identify individuals by their specific names. 'Savage' was an ambiguous, versatile and value-laden term. Although it was commonly used in Australia during the nineteenth and twentieth centuries to describe Aboriginal Australians and Pacific Islanders, it was also applied to convicts, drunkards, politicians, vagrants and people living in remote rural areas.[3] For foreign travellers to the Australian colonies, Australia's penal origins marked the nation as 'a place where only savage natives, degraded whites and economic opportunists could thrive'.[4]

---

3   Russell, *Savage or Civilised?*, 3.
4   Anna Johnston, 'Writing the Southern Cross: Religious Travel Writing in Nineteenth-Century Australasia', in *Travel Writing in the Nineteenth Century: Filling the Blank Spaces*, ed. Tim Youngs (London: Anthem Press, 2006), 205, doi.org/10.7135/upo9781843317692.012.

Rather than delineating a specific set of individual characteristics and behaviours, the term 'savage' defined people according to what they lacked. For European explorers who were confronted by human difference abroad, their descriptions of the savage 'other' were informed by their own notions of European civilisation.[5] The 'noble savage' had appeared in European thought well before Europeans reached the Pacific; it was a neoclassical ideal of primitivism often attributed to Jean-Jacques Rousseau. The noble savage was distinguished by his or her innocence, primitivity and a simple life that was lived close to nature. Uncorrupted by civilisation, the noble savage embodied a critique of European decadence.[6] The ideal of the noble savage influenced many of the eighteenth-century French and British explorers in the Pacific Islands who described an Arcadian paradise. Developing out of Christian mission outreach in the Pacific in the early 1800s, the 'ignoble savage' was a stereotype used to present Islanders negatively. Emphasising nakedness, savage dances, warring and idol worship, missionaries used the ignoble savage to justify their conversion efforts. Subsequent violent confrontations between Europeans and Islanders confirmed this trend.[7] The killing of Captain James Cook in Hawai'i was an early symbolic marker of Island savagery that resounded with Australians who regarded Cook as a national hero.

The development of science served to confirm and explain the savagery of Islanders, as well as their supposed depopulation. This influenced later Australian travel writing, which incorporated Enlightenment notions of progress and biological theories of race. During the eighteenth century, the purpose of scientifically studying non-European peoples was framed in terms of better understanding the civilised self and the origins of civilised 'man', rather than for learning about how other societies functioned. In scientific and philosophical European thought, 'savage' was a term used to denote a certain level in a developmental sequence. Enlightenment philosophers often speculated that societies progressed through stages of increasing development, in which agriculture and commerce set civilised people apart from the savages. In this process, human beings

---

5   Thomas, *Colonialism's Culture*, 71; Gananath Obeyesekere, *Cannibal Talk: The Man-Eating Myth and Human Sacrifice in the South Seas* (Berkeley: University of California Press, 2005), 184.
6   Smith, *European Vision and the South Pacific*, 318; Kerry R Howe, 'The Fate of the Savage in Pacific Historiography', *New Zealand Journal of History* 11, no. 2 (1977): 137.
7   Smith, *European Vision and the South Pacific*, 317.

progressed from savagery (hunting) to barbarism (nomadic pastoralism) to civilisation (agriculture and commerce). However, used in this way, 'savage' was initially a neutral term rather than a derogatory label.[8]

These notions of progress gradually became entangled with a biological conception of race. Increasingly racialised scientific thought explained the savage state as being caused by innate racial deficiencies rather than by environmental stimuli. For Australian travel writers of the twentieth century, who absorbed and applied these scientific theories, the savage was considered an inferior racial type in comparison to the civilised white race. Due to these hardened racial classifications, the region of Melanesia was widely perceived to be more savage than Polynesia or Micronesia. Racial assumptions about the Islanders' physical and psychological characteristics supported the entrenched stereotypes of Melanesian savagery that early European explorers in the Pacific had articulated. Dumont D'Urville, a French explorer, observed that the Melanesian 'condition' was 'always close to barbarity'.[9] In general, the difficulty of accessing the Melanesian Islands combined with their relatively late contact with Europeans, as compared to Polynesia, signified that Melanesia was a region of unknown possibilities and 'an openly imagined reality'.[10]

Although the general savagery of Melanesians was assumed knowledge to most Australian travellers in the twentieth century, the savagery of particular peoples within Melanesia was highly contested. Media reporting was partly responsible for this, as it encouraged caricatures such as 'Tommy Tanna', a figure that was based on the Melanesian labour recruit who worked in Queensland sugar plantations.[11] Savage reputations were also fostered by certain violent encounters with Europeans, some of which were highly publicised and fixed in Australian public memory. The Islands of Malekula in the New Hebrides and Malaita in the Solomon

---

8   Ronald L Meek, *Social Science and the Ignoble Savage* (Cambridge: Cambridge University Press, 1976), 5; Russell, *Savage or Civilised?*, 31; Russell McGregor, *Imagined Destinies: Aboriginal Australians and the Doomed Race Theory, 1880–1939* (Carlton: Melbourne University Press, 1997), 31; Bronwen Douglas, 'Climate to Crania: Science and the Racialization of Human Difference', in *Foreign Bodies: Oceania and the Science of Race 1750–1940*, ed. Bronwen Douglas and Chris Ballard (Canberra: ANU E Press, 2008), 35, doi.org/10.22459/fb.11.2008.02.
9   Dumont D'Urville, in Tcherkezoff, 'A Long and Unfortunate Voyage', 176.
10 Tracey Banivanua-Mar, *Violence and Colonial Dialogue: The Australian-Pacific Indentured Labor Trade* (Honolulu: University of Hawai'i Press, 2007), 22, doi.org/10.1515/9780824865467.
11 For example, see 'Tommy Tanna's Present Position', *Worker*, 1 June 1901, 4, nla.gov.au/nla.news-article70830894; 'Tommy Tanna', *The Clipper*, 28 December 1901, 8, nla.gov.au/nla.news-article 83085521.

Islands were frequently identified as the most savage in the 1900s due to their history of violence with labour traders, missionaries and government officials. For example, in the case of Malaita, violent encounters with labour recruiters were highly publicised (e.g. the attack on the *Young Dick* in 1886) and the murder of Resident Commissioner William Bell in 1927 sparked outrage within Australia, prompting the immediate dispatch of an Australian warship.[12] Denoting an island or island group as savage also functioned as a justification for colonialism, distinguishing the successes of certain mission societies, businesses or governments in comparison to others.

Given the pervasiveness of the racialised stereotypes of savagery that saturated media coverage, popular fiction, public debate and official government policies, it is unsurprising that the existence of the Melanesian savage was often assumed. Science offered a powerful authority to those who applied the labels of 'savage' and 'civilised'. Travellers may have been influenced by these standardised and distorted images, but once they began travelling, they constructed their own notions of the savage by selecting particular characteristics to describe. Bernard Smith identified this trend in the writers and travellers of the 1800s who combined elements of the noble and ignoble savage, as well as elements of the civilised European, to forge a 'romantic savage'. He argued that travellers used this blended version of the savage to reflect on the future of the Pacific and to frame both savage and civilised within a discourse of progress.[13] Australians of the twentieth century similarly blended savage and civilised attributes as they saw fit. This was especially important for those who sought to justify their own roles in the Pacific Islands (for reasons evangelical, commercial or colonial), which was often expressed with the intention of bringing 'civilisation to the savages'.

---

12   See Peter Corris, 'Passage, Port and Plantation: A History of Solomon Islands Labour Migration, 1870–1914' (PhD thesis, The Australian National University, 1970), 130; Roger M Keesing and Peter Corris, eds, *Lightning Meets the West Wind: The Malaita Massacre* (Melbourne: Oxford University Press, 1980); Roger M Keesing, 'The Young Dick Attack: Oral and Documentary History on the Colonial Frontier', *Ethnohistory* 33, no. 3 (1986): 268–92, doi.org/10.2307/481815; Wilfred Fowler, 'The Young Dick', *Queensland Heritage* 2, no. 1 (1969): 23–5.
13   Smith, *European Vision and the South Pacific*, 326, 331. See also Campbell, 'Savages Noble and Ignoble'.

Although some could use the savage trope to reinforce colonial authority, it was also shaped and reformed by travellers who were sincere about trying to understand other peoples. As Smith argued, the development of the romantic savage:

> Was grounded upon a longer and better acquaintanceship with primitive peoples. Faulty as knowledge still was, the conception of the romantic savage was a genuine effort on the part of the European imagination to make contact with the personal life of primitive peoples.[14]

Similarly, Pacific travel in the twentieth century offered individuals the opportunity to test the merits of Australian civilisation in a purportedly savage and foreign environment. In doing so, they blended different discourses and representations of the savage according to their individual experiences, which were spatially and temporally specific. These representations contributed to a growing body of Australian knowledge about the Pacific Islands, and the voices of Australian travellers increasingly challenged European-based theories and assumptions.

Expectations of Bestiality

For the colonial Australians who embarked on a Pacific voyage in the 1880s and 1890s, the experiences of Queensland labour recruiters significantly shaped their expectations of the Melanesian savage. From 1869 to 1904, approximately 60,819 Pacific Islanders were brought to Queensland to work on sugar cane plantations.[15] Most of the 10,000 recruits who remained in Australia in 1901 were repatriated between 1904 and 1906 under the provisions of the *Pacific Island Labourers Act* (1901) (though many descendants of these labourers presently live in Australia today). Queensland recruiting vessels visited the Torres Strait Islands, the New Hebrides (including the Banks and Santa Cruz Islands), the Solomon Islands and, later, Papua and New Guinea. The inhabitants of these Islands were indiscriminately termed 'Kanakas' (a term derived from the Hawaiian language), and the trade was often called 'blackbirding'. The demand for cheap labour initially motivated colonial Australians and other colonies or nations to recruit in Melanesia from the 1860s, a process

---

14   Smith, *European Vision and the South Pacific*, 326.
15   Deryck Scarr, 'Introduction', in *A Cruize in a Queensland Labour Vessel to the South Seas*, ed. William E Giles (Canberra: Australian National University Press, 1970), 2.

that Clive Moore has discussed in detail.[16] Considerable opposition in colonial Australia eventually ended the trade, due to humanitarian grounds and fears that Pacific Islander labourers threatened the living standards of white workers. For both those who favoured and opposed the trade, the savage was a key figure in the debate. In regard to Australian travel writing about the Pacific Islands, notions about the bestial nature of the savage arose most clearly from the debates about the Queensland labour trade.

Limited surviving firsthand accounts of the Queensland labour trade that were written by colonial Australians exist. Five accounts were published by ship captain William Wawn, recruiter and trader John Cromar, government agents John Gaggin and Douglas Rannie, and traveller William Giles.[17] Journalists John Stanley James, Joseph Melvin and George Morrison followed labour-recruiting ships and published accounts in newspapers.[18] In addition, 26 surviving journals organised by Queensland recruiters and government agents exist. These witnesses described the prevalence of public hostility that was directed towards recruiting and increasingly strict government regulation. Giles, a curious traveller who accompanied the recruiting ship *Bobtail Nag* to the New Hebrides in 1877, described the public tension in the Australian colonies:

> The Queensland Press at this time, was constantly publishing Articles on the so-called slave trade. Several furious letters had lately been published by Correspondents denouncing the

---

16   Clive Moore, ed., *The Forgotten People: A History of the Australian South Sea Island Community* (Sydney: Australian Broadcasting Commission, 1979); Clive Moore, *Kanaka: A History of Melanesian Mackay* (Port Moresby: University of Papua New Guinea Press, 1985); Clive Moore, 'Pacific Islanders in Nineteenth Century Queensland', in *Labour in the South Pacific*, ed. Clive Moore, Jacqueline Leckie and Doug Munro (Townsville: James Cook University of Northern Queensland, 1990), 144–7; Clive Moore, 'The Counterculture of Survival: Melanesians in the Mackay District of Queensland, 1865–1906', in *Plantation Workers: Resistance and Accommodation*, ed. Brij V Lal, Doug Munro and Edward D Beechert (Honolulu: University of Hawai'i Press, 1993), 69–99.

17   Wawn, *The South Sea Islanders*; Cromar, *Jock of the Islands*; John Gaggin, *Among the Man-Eaters* (London: T. Fisher Unwin, 1900); Douglas Rannie, *My Adventures among South Sea Cannibals: An Account of the Experiences and Adventures of a Government Official among the Natives of Oceania* (London: Seeley, Service & Co., 1912); Giles, *A Cruize in a Queensland Labour Vessel to the South Seas*.

18   James published his voyage aboard the recruiting vessel *Lizzie* in the *Argus* from 27 August 1883 to 9 February 1884, as well as in his travelogue, *Cannibals and Convicts*, under the pseudonym 'Julian Thomas'; Joseph Melvin published 'Our Representative—The Kanaka Labour Traffic' in the *Argus* from 5 to 19 December 1892. See also Joseph Dalgarno Melvin, *The Cruise of the Helena: A Labour-Recruiting Voyage to the Solomon Islands*, ed. Peter Corris (Melbourne: Hawthorn Press, 1977). George 'Chinese' Morrison published 'A Cruise in a Queensland Slaver' in *The Leader* from 21 October to 9 December 1882, and an anonymous diary was published under the title 'Diary of a Recruiting Voyage' in the *Brisbane Courier* between 25 October 1884 and 19 February 1885.

Trade, as scan[d]alous, iniquitous, and a disgrace to our Colony. Of course on the other hand, Articles had appeared in its defence stating that without its continuance the important sugar industry along the Coast country would entirely fail.[19]

Facing this hostility and scrutiny, some recruiters and government officials aimed to set the record straight in their own accounts.

One example was Wawn, whose description of his recruiting voyages in *The South Sea Islanders and the Queensland Labour Trade* (1893) was the most widely read firsthand account of the trade. His book was commonly cited by subsequent Australian travellers to the New Hebrides and the Solomon Islands. Mark Twain even devoted an entire chapter to discussing Wawn's book and to criticising the labour trade in *Following the Equator* (1897).[20] Born in England in 1837, Wawn trained as a mariner and moved to Australia in 1867. He worked as a labour recruiter for Queensland and Fiji for 20 years, during which time he encountered all the typical troubles of a labour trade recruiter. Wawn's book was primarily intended to counter the growing antagonism towards recruiters in the Australian colonies—which included scathing attacks on what he alleged to be inexperienced and corrupt colonial Australian authorities (including government agents onboard), overregulation, propaganda, misinformation and an 'unsophisticated', gullible public who believed fanciful stories about recruiters.[21] In the book, he also refuted multiple accusations of kidnapping, murder and theft and contested his debarment from the labour trade for three years.

Wawn was one of many proponents of the labour trade who defended their work as heroic and considered their intentions noble, often by contrasting the bestial nature of the savage to the civilised colonial Australian trader and planter. Wawn dedicated his book 'to the sugar planters of Queensland, to those bold pioneers, to those good men and true'.[22] This heroic theme resonated with popular fictional literature of the nineteenth century that juxtaposed the savage Islander and the civilised Englishman. Children's fiction further entrenched stereotypes of the savage by narratively pitting courageous, gentle and chivalrous English gentlemen against cruel and

---

19 Giles, *A Cruize in a Queensland Labour Vessel*, 34.
20 Mark Twain, *Following the Equator: A Journey around the World* (Hartford: American Publishing Company, 1897), 53.
21 Wawn, *The South Sea Islanders*, 359.
22 Wawn, *The South Sea Islanders*, xlvi.

barbaric Pacific Islanders. Just as these formulaic fictions cultivated British ideals of civilisation, masculinity and racial superiority, so too did tales of the labour trade convey a romanticised view of pioneering Australian colonials.[23]

In contrast, the 14 unpublished manuscripts written by recruiters and government agents are distinguished by the absence of hyperbole and common savage characterisations that are typically mentioned in published accounts (though seven men were involved in malpractice).[24] Few recruiters or government agents went ashore or spent a long time living with Pacific Islanders. Instead, their daily logs reflect the monotony of labour recruiting, containing short descriptions of weather, the number of recruits, illnesses and ship maintenance. When they did describe Islanders, it was their humanity that quite often surprised them. Christopher Mills wrote in his journal:

> Everyone reports them as treacherous and unfit to be trusted, I find them the reverse—but I make a practice, and trust I always shall, of treating them as human beings, hence the difference.[25]

Although the reality of Island encounters might have contradicted the savage stereotype, the temptation to exaggerate and dramatise was strong. It is difficult to determine whether authors succumbed to this temptation deliberately, or whether they unconsciously romanticised the savage to meet their expectations (and those of the readers). Giles claimed he was inspired to join a recruiting ship by the imagined savage that he expected to encounter:

> The noble savage arrayed in mantle of scalps, fastened with human hair, and dyed in blood, disposed in graceful festoons around his manly form; leaning on his long spear tipped with human bone, and thoughtfully masticating a succulent morsel of his last victim, as he anxiously gazed on the approaching ship, and considered how many meals her crew would provide for himself and his cannibal brethren.[26]

---

23 Street, *The Savage in Literature*, 55.
24 As described by Scarr in Giles, *A Cruize in a Queensland Labour Vessel*, 17.
25 Christopher Mills, 'Briefs and Associated Papers in Cases Involving Pacific Islanders', in Crown Solicitor's Office, Series ID 12102, Item ID 7876 (Queensland: Queensland State Archives, 1884).
26 Giles, *A Cruize in a Queensland Labour Vessel*, 36.

Although his expectations were not met, he still found reasons to criticise their allegedly 'intolerable perfume' and 'unclassically shaped nose'.[27] Similarly, despite Rannie's opposition to the labour trade (he was motivated to be a government agent because he considered the labour trade 'most diabolical, and a disgrace to civilisation'),[28] his book conformed to stereotypical accounts of cannibals and savages. Titled *My Adventures Among South Sea Cannibals*, it was published 19 years after the event in 1912. Pictured alongside the recruiting crew in Figure 14, Rannie interspersed his account with reproduced images that were obtained from John Watt Beattie. Rannie frequently used hyperbole in his account, most likely to entertain and shock readers. In one instance, he recalled his first encounter with Islanders, in which he witnessed a canoe with the bleeding head of a woman on the prow upon arrival in the Solomon Islands.[29]

Figure 14: The Author, Recruiter, Captain, and Boat's Crew of Natives.
Source: Rannie, *My Adventures among South Sea Cannibals*, 238.

---

27 Giles, *A Cruize in a Queensland Labour Vessel*, 36.
28 Rannie, *My Adventures among South Sea Cannibals*, 17.
29 Rannie, *My Adventures among South Sea Cannibals*, 26.

Figure 15: Front Cover of a Book in 'The Vagabond' series published by *The Australian*.
Source: John Stanley James, *South Sea Massacres* (Sydney: The Australian, 1881).

Without photographic proof, some writers and publishers relied on hand-drawn illustrations to embellish their accounts. The cover of Thomas's publication in 1881, titled *South Sea Massacres*, is one such example (see Figure 15). It was dedicated to the 'memories of the murdered white men' in the Pacific.

Australians purported to have observed various degrees of bestiality in the Pacific, ranging from the animalistic to the grotesque and monstrous. Savages were commonly situated within a foreboding dark environment— Gaggin's impression of the Solomon Islands as 'a very black diamond indeed' and Joseph Melvin's description of their 'low type of features, the savagery of which was exaggerated by black teeth, stained by the chewing of betelnut', typically used darkness as a metaphor for savagery and evil to describe both the landscape and the people.[30]

Islanders were often likened to animals, which encouraged the fantasy that one could observe savagery. In some cases, physical similarities were imagined: Wawn described Islanders as 'excited monkeys', Ralph Stock observed 'lizard men' and Henry Tichborne expected Islanders to have tails.[31] Alternatively, savages were attributed animalistic temperaments and were regarded as unpredictable, wild and possessing a 'treacherous, cowardly and savage disposition'.[32] These extreme and exaggerated representations were not accurate and reflected popular misconceptions within the Australian colonies at the time.

When travellers met Islanders who appeared physically the same as them, they were frequently ascribed grotesque features. The 'grotesque' was a hybrid form of human and monster, and depending on the traveller, either end of the spectrum could be emphasised.[33] The grotesque was part of a performance for John Gibson Paton, a Presbyterian missionary: 'The more grotesque and savage-looking, the higher the art!'[34] For Charles Stuart Ross, another Presbyterian minister, the 'occasional grotesqueness' of Fijians could be tolerated in 1909; however, he distanced himself from the local dancing, which he found 'too grotesquely wild and

---

30 Melvin, *The Cruise of the Helena*, 4; Gaggin, *Among the Man-Eaters*, 43.
31 Wawn, *The South Sea Islanders*, 237; Stock, *The Cruise of the Dream Ship*, 188; Tichborne, *Rambles in Polynesia by Sundowner*, 91.
32 Gaggin, *Among the Man-Eaters*, 237; Giles, *A Cruize in a Queensland Labour Vessel*, 39.
33 Dixon, *Writing the Colonial Adventure*, 64.
34 John Gibson Paton, *Thirty Years with South Sea Cannibals: Autobiography of John G. Paton*, ed. James Paton (Chicago: Moody Press, 1964), 40.

barbaric'.[35] Descriptions of grotesque body mutilations (e.g. head binding, teeth removal, piercings and scarification) were exaggerated and embellished to generate an image of a corrupted and deformed race. Gaggin once claimed to witness a chief suddenly grab his young daughter and knock out her teeth with stones, supposedly so he could purchase a pig. By offering no explanation for the ritual, nor one for the cultural significance of the practice, Gaggin suggested that the people were exploitative and vicious.[36] Similarly, Rannie's remark that it was common for Islanders to carry a basket containing human heads to trade for tobacco is unlikely due to other accounts documenting Islander resistance to selling human skulls.[37]

By portraying Islanders as monsters, Australians created an image that was devoid of any humanity and that extended beyond the grotesque. Monsters embodied savagery and represented a break away from the Christian notion of a great chain of being. Margaret Hodgen argued that after Columbus's voyages of discovery, the human monsters and wild men of the Middle Ages were transferred to representations of the savage, contributing to the conception of the savage as not fully human.[38] Similarly, Australian travel narratives throughout the early twentieth century reaffirmed beliefs that the Islands were populated by giants, pygmies and other monsters. When travellers encountered humans rather than monsters in the Pacific, they created monstrous personas for the Islanders instead. These included descriptions of traditional ceremonies that involved monstrous masks and pagan idols, threatening war dances, shrieking and chanting to the beat of drums, and human sacrifices (all activities that were typically performed at night). Arnold Safroni-Middleton, an artist, stood in a forest 'as fierce, stalwart savage men and women danced around a monstrous wooden idol'.[39] Similarly, Gaggin wrote that 'hideous masks are worn in their secret Masonic rites'.[40] Gananath Obeyesekere argued that the inability to find monsters in the real world had one notable exception—anthropophagy.[41]

---

35 Charles Stuart Ross, *Fiji and the Western Pacific* (Victoria: H. Thacker, 1909), 67, 209.
36 Gaggin, *Among the Man-Eaters*, 104.
37 Rannie, *My Adventures among South Sea Cannibals*, 51. For examples of resistance, see Gaggin, *Among the Man-Eaters*, 162; Woodburn, *Backwash of Empire*, 188; and Gunga, *Narrative of a Trip from Maryborough to New Caledonia* (Maryborough: publisher unknown, 1878), 13.
38 Margaret T Hodgen, *Early Anthropology in the Sixteenth and Seventeenth Centuries* (Philadelphia: University of Pennsylvania Press, 1964), 18; Weaver-Hightower, *Empire Islands*, 152.
39 Safroni-Middleton, *Wine-Dark Seas and Tropic Skies*, 30.
40 Gaggin, *Among the Man-Eaters*, 105.
41 Obeyesekere, *Cannibal Talk*, 14.

Cannibalism was the most commonly identified marker of bestiality and, in some cases (e.g. in Gaggin's account), every Islander was labelled either as a perpetrator or as a victim of cannibalism.

As European contact with Melanesians increased over time, images of mythical beasts and monsters were gradually eroded. Incidents of violent encounters between labour recruiters and Melanesians also decreased, as Islanders were becoming more familiar with white traders. With significantly less evidence of Melanesian savagery in the 1880s and 1890s, colonial Australian travel accounts emphasised the savage potential of Islanders instead, suggesting that they were prone to animal instincts and unpredictable emotions. These notions were encouraged by labour recruiters who were wary of experiencing ambush and treachery while they recruited, often referencing violent encounters in the past as proof. This was evident in the tendency of recruiting accounts to preface their descriptions of each Island with a summary of European deaths. For example, Rannie's account of Ambrym Island began with 'Belbin and Heath were shot with rifles, Craig was done to death with thirteen spear wounds in his body, while Booth and Bowen were both poisoned'.[42] Colonial Australian newspapers also reported incidents of violence and cases of European deaths in the Islands in a sensationalised and exaggerated manner; they described Islander resistance with hyperboles such as 'massacre', 'butchery' and 'vengeance' and framed Europeans as innocent victims who were only trying to bring civilisation to ruthless savages. Newspapers memorialised the fallen and maintained a historical memory of Islander violence towards white people long after the events had occurred.[43] Consequently, notions of Melanesian unpredictability persisted well into the twentieth century, as demonstrated by McLaren's impression:

> I could never be sure of them, for they were possessed of instincts at which I could only vaguely guess and over which they had no control. At all times they were liable to give expression to certain queer impulses which were their age-old heritage, and causelessly murder the stranger in their midst—to regret it deeply afterwards no doubt.[44]

---

42 Rannie, *My Adventures among South Sea Cannibals*, 16.
43 Keesing and Corris, *Lightning Meets the West Wind*, 154.
44 McLaren, *My Odyssey*, 68.

The supposedly unpredictable temperament of the savage resonated with scientific theories positing that some races were incapable of, or possessed a limited capacity for, reason and judgement. Supporters of labour recruiting framed savagery within a discourse of justice, contrasting a 'British sense of justice' with the treachery and betrayal of Islanders.[45] They justified the labour trade by claiming that it could help civilise the Melanesian savages by bringing them into contact with Australian civilisation. Wawn argued:

> At 16 he is a man, with all his savage habits rooted in him. When middle-aged he cannot be altered, except for the worse. Take him away from savagery as a child, and you can make him what you like.[46]

Despite labour recruiters' attempts to portray themselves as being fair and just, they struggled to counter the growing public antagonism that was directed towards them and their practices. Wawn described himself as innocent and just when compared to the Islanders who he encountered. He offered a 'curious example of the South Sea Islander's sense of justice', in which he was held accountable for the physical harm done to an Islander who had accidentally injured himself with a rifle.[47] Similarly, Melvin questioned whether the recruits understood the benefits of civilisation:

> Did they realise that they were about to pass from civilisation back into savagedom—from the care of parental Government back to the lawless tyranny of island life; from bread, meat, and etceteras in abundance to a scramble for native food; from peace to war; from a country where toil is rewarded and protected to one where might only is right?[48]

The injustice of the system was self-evident for opponents of the labour trade, and it was the colonial Australian recruiters and planters who were regarded as savages. The claims made by these planters and pastoralists that Islander labour was docile, dependable and beneficial to all parties involved were eroding away in the 1880s, as evidence of high numbers of fatalities on Queensland plantations surfaced (as high as 8.5 per cent in 1878).[49] Newspaper coverage of public trials involving members of the labour

---

45 Rannie, *My Adventures among South Sea Cannibals*, 61.
46 Wawn, *The South Sea Islanders*, 76.
47 Wawn, *The South Sea Islanders*, 239.
48 Melvin, *The Cruise of the Helena*, 13.
49 Scarr, 'Introduction', 25.

trade kept colonial Australians well informed about the misdemeanours of both sides; it also prolonged Australian awareness of, and interest in, Pacific Island incidents. Churches in the Australian colonies were vocal opponents objecting to the labour trade in principle and in response to the potential loss of their Island congregations to recruiting ships. Paton was influential and effective in mobilising support against the so-called 'slave trade'. The mission's call was eventually answered by a Royal Commission in 1885, which concluded that the labour trade was 'one long record of deceit, cruel treachery, deliberate kidnapping and cold-blooded murder'.[50]

However, opponents to the labour trade also emphasised Melanesian savagery and portrayed Islander recruits as a threat to a white Australian civilisation. This was a powerful message, delivered at a time when the colonies were debating whether to federate and create a new Australian nation at the turn of the century. A growing number of white working-class Australians felt threatened by a perceived arrival of cheap foreign workers and supported the push for government regulations that restricted non-white labour. The Queensland labour trade thus formed part of the discourse of a national White Australia policy. In this debate, the discourse of civilisation was appropriated to argue for better working conditions. In the first session of the Federal Parliament, Liberal politician HB Higgins expressed this sentiment when he argued: 'We do not want men beside us who are not as exacting in their demands on civilisation as ourselves'.[51] By emphasising the savage nature of Islanders, opponents to the labour trade generated fears that Islanders could not be contained within Australian plantations, let alone be trained, educated and civilised. Travellers such as Giles were susceptible to these racialised distortions, which led him to the conclusion that 'it is almost, if not quite a hopeless attempt, to ever civilize them in the true meaning of the word'.[52]

The threat posed by the Melanesian savage was made worse by the claim that these Islanders would adopt the vices of civilisation while they worked in Australia. Raymond Evans, Kay Saunders and Kathryn Cronin have revealed that the working-class opinion became 'positively rabid' as Australians feared the barbarous activities of Islanders, whom they believed

---

50 'General News: The Labour Trade', *The Queenslander*, 9 May 1885, 753, nla.gov.au/nla.news-article19797950.
51 *Australian Parliamentary Debates, House of Representatives*, 5077. See also Marilyn Lake and Henry Reynolds, *Drawing the Global Colour Line: White Men's Countries and the Question of Racial Equality* (Carlton: Melbourne University Press, 2008).
52 Giles, *A Cruize in a Queensland Labour Vessel*, 69.

would become addicted to alcohol, gambling, opium and sexual desire.[53] James criticised the missionary attempts to Christianise the recruits as also being ineffective: 'The Kanaka, during his three years' service in either of the labour fields, only learns the name of God as a curse'.[54] Australians drew different conclusions about the danger that Queensland recruits posed. Some dismissed them as 'pseudo-Europeans' who would abandon their civilised habits once home, while others suspected that they could potentially become more dangerous because they were overly familiar with Europeans.[55] This sentiment was expressed by Beatrice Grimshaw, who observed Melanesian labour recruits when they returned to their Islands:

> With Tommy Tanna of Queensland—full of civilisation's vices, sharper and more knowing than his fellows, yet a savage to the tips of his fingers—joins in the conservative party of the island, the older chiefs, who hate the white man and all his doings, and the younger and more savage savages, who are beginning to take alarm at the increasing power of the missions ... Backed up by the Queenslander Tannese, they are beginning to talk in an unpleasantly significant way. The Queensland labourer has, after all, learned something during his foreign travels; and the cry that he is now spreading about the island is: Tanna for the Tannese!ature[56]

As an experienced professional writer who was often contracted by businesses and the government, Grimshaw's observation signalled her support for advancing Australian sub-imperialism in the region.

Representations of Melanesian savagery circulated during the Queensland labour trade and continued to influence Australian travellers in the 1920s and 1930s. Australians were familiar with the labour trade's history, although with a romanticised version of it, due to certain works such as Thomas Dunbabin's popular history, *Slavers of the South Seas* (1935). Dunbabin acknowledged not only the brutality of the trade but also its popularity with Australian audiences: 'Blackbirding was as full of horrors, of brutalities, of tragedies as was the African slave-trade—and fuller of romance, of heroism, and of self-sacrifice'.[57] Blackbirders regularly

---

53 Raymond Evans, Kay Saunders and Kathryn Cronin, *Race Relations in Colonial Queensland: A History of Exclusion, Exploitation and Extermination* (St Lucia: University of Queensland Press, 1988), 165, 208, 222.
54 Thomas, *Cannibals and Convicts*, 153.
55 John Henry Macartney Abbott, *The South Seas (Melanesia)* (London: Adam and Charles Black, 1908), 30.
56 Grimshaw, *From Fiji to the Cannibal Islands*, 318.
57 Thomas Dunbabin, *Slavers of the South Seas* (Sydney: Angus & Robertson, 1935), v.

featured as protagonists in fictional Pacific tales, simultaneously scorned and admired as being villainous and heroic (e.g. Louis Becke's descriptions of American recruiter Bully Hayes). Although the labour trade entrenched stereotypes of the bestial savage, it also remained an example of white Australian savagery and brutality. As Dunbabin explained:

> Not all the faults were on one side. They never are in this world. The natives of many islands were treacherous, murderous, brutal savages … But at least the savages were defending their own country and their own freedom, and living according to the only laws they knew. They were not sinning against the light, as were too many of the white savages who came to abuse, kidnap, and murder them.[58]

Australian travellers did not forget the exploitation of the blackbirding trade in the Pacific later in the twentieth century. When visiting Erromango Island in the New Hebrides in the 1930s, M Kathleen Woodburn lamented the damage that labour recruiters had caused to Islanders' prosperity, as well as the damage caused by the earlier sandalwood trade.[59] The significance of the labour trade to Australian commerce and development in the late nineteenth century ensured that subsequent Australian travellers were influenced by a collective historical memory of this colonial exchange.

'Children of God'

The infantile nature of the savage was another literary trope and colonial fantasy evidenced in Australian travel writing. Plantation overseer, Eric Muspratt, wrote in 1931: 'My first impression of them was as big, brown children, and this I finally decided was as near to the truth of their essential difference as one could get'.[60] Though various individuals and groups used the trope to justify their colonial exploits and reinforce the racial inferiority of the savage, it was an image that was actively and widely propagated by Christian missionaries. Their message of salvation for the 'children of God' in the Pacific Islands was sustained and influential in Australia; it was distributed in literature, churches, Sunday schools and

---

58 Dunbabin, *Slavers of the South Seas*, xiii–xiv.
59 Woodburn, *Backwash of Empire*, 90.
60 Muspratt, *My South Sea Island*, 35.

public arenas. Missionaries' portrayal of the Islander as being infantile in the early twentieth century represented a significant departure from the traditional message that emphasised the ignoble savage.

European missionaries were initially responsible for devising the figure of the ignoble savage to justify their conversion of a heathen Islander population as part of their expansion throughout the region from the late eighteenth century. The London Missionary Society (LMS) was the first to establish missions in the Pacific Islands at Tahiti, Tonga and the Marquesas Islands in 1797. It was followed by missionaries from Europe, New Zealand and Australia who spread westwards from Polynesia, and missions from the US that spread through Micronesia from Hawai'i. Early missionaries were convinced of the utter depravity of Islanders, witnessing practices of infanticide, human sacrifice, cannibalism, homosexuality, widow strangling and idolatry.[61] By emphasising (and dramatising) the former bestial savagery of Islanders, missionaries created a 'narrative of conversion' that emphasised the successes of transforming Islanders to 'an elevated and purified Christian state'.[62] Mission texts tended to memorialise and romanticise the 'martyrdom' of pioneering missionaries at the hands of brutal savages. Australian readers were repeatedly reminded about the murders of missionaries John Williams (1839), George Gordon (1861) and John Patteson (1871) not only in texts but also in the names of ships and institutions.[63] In response to the deaths of white missionaries, future expeditions were led by trained Indigenous pastors, who were more successful in entering hostile and isolated communities (and more expendable, in the eyes of Europeans).

For colonial Australians who grew up from the late nineteenth century, Melanesia rather than Polynesia was the most immediate site of conversion for pioneer missionaries. Christianity did not reach Fiji until 1835, and it slowly spread north through Melanesia, reaching Papua and New Guinea in the 1870s. Due to the great distance from Europe, Australia was a major source of supplies and support for missionaries in the Pacific. Australians were conventionally religious, carrying with them the religious affiliations of Europe across to their new homeland. Census data from 1911 reveal that Christians comprised 95.9 per cent of the population. The Church of England was the largest denomination (38.4%), followed by Roman

---

61 Niel Gunson, *Messengers of Grace: Evangelical Missionaries in the South Seas, 1797–1860* (Melbourne: Oxford University Press, 1978), 185.
62 Thomas, *Colonialism's Culture*, 126.
63 Gunson, *Messengers of Grace*, 4.

Catholics (20.7%), Presbyterians (12.5%) and Methodists (12.3%).[64] By 1947, Presbyterians outnumbered Catholics. The Presbyterian influence was particularly strong in Victoria, while a Catholic presence was more predominant in Sydney. Australian congregations offered funding, supplies and human resources to mission societies from Europe and New Zealand (specifically, to the LMS and Anglican Melanesian Mission) and to those at home (e.g. the Australasian Wesleyan Methodist Missionary Society and the South Sea Evangelical Mission). In this highly competitive environment, missionaries were justifying their efforts against those of other missionaries as often as they were against Pacific Islanders.

Possessing a more thorough knowledge of the Pacific than the average Australian (as well as a vast network of receptive congregations at home), missionaries held considerable influence over Australian perceptions of the region. Missionaries were prolific writers and published numerous texts for different audiences and purposes. Most mission texts (e.g. church newsletters and magazines, missionary biographies and memoirs, children's textbooks) conformed to a narrative of conversion that justified mission work in the region, and they asked for further assistance. Many biographies of individual missionaries were popular due to their tales of pioneering heroism among savage peoples. Missionaries were also amateur ethnographers and anthropologists, with their observations circulating within academic circles in Australia and Europe. Notable Australian missionaries in this category include Lorimer Fison and George Brown.[65] In addition to the prolific missionary publications that were circulated to promote and evangelise, there were also private accounts of travellers who were closely associated with mission work, such as the wives of Pacific missionaries and those travelling aboard mission ships like the *John Williams* and the *Southern Cross*. There were also publications such as *The Southern Cross Log*, which more closely resembled travel writing and contained first impressions of the Pacific Islands from a collection of authors that included laypersons and Islanders.[66]

---

64 '2112.0—Census of the Commonwealth of Australia, 1911: Volume II Part VI—Religions', Australian Bureau of Statistics, last modified 11 November 2013, www.abs.gov.au/AUSSTATS/abs@.nsf/DetailsPage/2112.01911.
65 Helen Bethea Gardner, *Gathering for God: George Brown in Oceania* (Dunedin: Otago, 2006); Christine Weir, '"White Man's Burden", "White Man's Privilege": Christian Humanism and Racial Determinism in Oceania 1890–1930', in *Foreign Bodies: Oceania and the Science of Race 1750–1940*, ed. Bronwen Douglas and Chris Ballard (Canberra: ANU E Press, 2008), 286, doi.org/10.22459/fb.11.2008.08.
66 Cecil Wilson, *The Wake of the Southern Cross: Work and Adventures in the South Seas* (London: John Murray, 1932)

Missionaries were also leading figures in Australian public debate, with their publications used to lobby for specific topical issues. Methodist minister John Wear Burton exposed the abuses of Indian indentured labour in Fiji in his book, *The Fiji of To-Day* (1910). This was followed by his children's reference book, *The Call of the Pacific* (1914). He also commanded leading positions in the Methodist Church of Australasia and was editor of *The Missionary Review* for 23 years. John Gibson Paton was also well known in Australia, but mostly for his fundraising efforts rather than his mission work in the Pacific. He motivated popular opinions in Australia regarding the Melanesian labour trade and advocated for a religious conviction of national destiny and duty.[67] His son, Frank Paton, followed in his father's footsteps, publicising mission work and leading an Australian campaign to end the Anglo-French condominium in the New Hebrides in 1923.[68]

Christine Weir argued that missionary activity was changing from the 1900s to the 1920s, 'From the exuberance of the era of early conversions to the routine work of educating and guiding converts—less glamorous and more frustrating than pioneer work'.[69] Corresponding with this shift was an emphasis on the childlike qualities of Pacific Islanders in mission propaganda. This encouraged the domestication of the savage and the welcoming of the native 'child' into the missionary family.[70] In her study of Protestant Sunday school literature, Weir identified a general trend towards a more child-oriented subject matter in the early twentieth century; the trend shifted away from evoking pity for Pacific children towards encouraging identification with them.[71]

In many mission texts of the early twentieth century, the childlike nature of the Islanders was a central tenet of their description; it emphasised their ability to be 'saved' from primitive savagery. In 1914, Burton wrote:

> We must remember, right through our study, that it is childhood with which we have to deal, and we must orient our minds accordingly. It will be child-vices—black as they have been; child-

---

67   John Garrett, *To Live among the Stars: Christian Origins in Oceania* (Suva: World Council of Churches, 1982), 177.
68   Niel Gunson, 'Paton, Francis Hume Lyall (Frank) (1870–1938)', *Australian Dictionary of Biography*, adb.anu.edu.au/biography/paton-francis-hume-lyall-frank-7976.
69   Weir, '"White Man's Burden", "White Man's Privilege"', 286.
70   Edmond, *Representing the South Pacific*, 117.
71   Christine Weir, '"Deeply Interested in These Children Whom You Have Not Seen": The Protestant Sunday School View of the Pacific, 1900–1940', *The Journal of Pacific History* 48, no. 1 (2013): 2, doi.org/10.1080/00223344.2012.758921.

faces—though old and wrinkled; child-minds—though cunning and treacherous; and child-virtues—neither deep nor strong, which will occupy our attention.[72]

It was an effective theme for signalling the essential humanity of the savage, and for rebutting evolutionary theories that the primitive races lacked the capacity to progress. However, this message was not universally applied. As Weir demonstrated, different missionaries negotiated between their firsthand experiences of Islanders and the broader global debates about race and racial hierarchies.[73] On one side of the spectrum, childlike Islanders were presented in a positive light that emphasised their innocence, honesty and trusting nature. Missionary wife Helen Cato conveyed this image in several light-hearted anecdotes that described incidents of Islander misunderstanding or over-enthusiasm. In a chapter titled 'Cumbered with Much Serving', Cato described the process of teaching Fijians not to wipe the floor with a tea towel or not to clean the oven while a cake was cooking.[74] Yet, acknowledgement of a common humanity was often tempered by certain accounts that affirmed the racial assumptions of inferiority and that applied scientific categories. This was the case with Fison, who was notably racialist for a missionary and who cautioned that childlike savages left unsupervised could return to former uncivilised behaviours:

> Lord Avebury … was right in saying … that savages 'unite the character of childhood with the passions and strength of men'. There is, on the outside of their character, much of the simplicity and even something of the amiability of childhood; and these traits may be all, or nearly all, that comes under the notice of those who have the opportunities for no more than superficial observation … the testimony of competent observers, who have been enabled to look below the surface, is unanimous to the effect that beneath this simple and childlike exterior there is too often a horror of cruelty and filth.[75]

The representation of missionaries as adult parents and Islanders as children in photographs and texts simultaneously depicted this negotiation between the realities of mission life and the ideologies of

---

72   Burton, *The Call of the Pacific*, 3.
73   Weir, '"White Man's Burden", "White Man's Privilege"', 287–8.
74   Cato, *The House on the Hill*, 25–31.
75   Lorimer Fison, *Tales from Old Fiji* (London: Alexander Moring Ltd: The De la More Press, 1904), xiii.

white superiority and colonial rule. Nicholas Thomas described this representation as reconciling the contradictory colonial objectives of hierarchising and incorporating.[76] The trope of the family re-inscribed missionaries' paternal authority, legitimised their work and implied the potential to civilise, educate and mould Islanders, bringing them from a proto-social condition to Christian salvation. The infantilising of Islanders created a people in miniature, 'A perfect interior world capable of being entirely possessed and manipulated'.[77] Emphasising paternal dominance was also a response to sceptics and critics who questioned the benefits of Christianity in the Pacific Islands. Missionaries were facing increasing scrutiny as Pacific Islands became more accessible and conflicts with traders, planters and other missionaries or colonial officials became more common.[78] By stressing the potential for Islanders to revert to savagery, missionaries justified their continued presence in the Pacific to maintain civilised standards.

The trope of the family also reflected the structure of mission stations in the Pacific, as missionaries (and their wives) created spaces in which Islanders could be incorporated into Christian living. Islanders were instructed not only in religious training but also in 'the whole field of practical, recreational and spiritual living'.[79] This is indicated in the journals of missionary wives Helen Cato and Mary Cook, who described teaching numerous domestic skills, Christian doctrine, language, health and hygiene. They also nursed the sick, farmed, attended local ceremonies and travelled to other villages. Their focus on children partly reflects the nature of their work, as missionaries identified children as being more susceptible to conversion, as well as being potential vehicles of evangelisation. Regardless of whether missionaries had greater exposure to children or adults, they formed close attachments with the converts, which they understood in familial terms. Cato, who stated that 'with about two hundred young people daily on the station we are our own village', fondly recalled celebrations at the end of the school year.[80] Similarly, in 1906, Cook found it difficult to leave the mission at Naduri, Fiji:

---

76 Thomas, *Colonialism's Culture*, 128–9.
77 Ballard, 'Collecting Pygmies', 130.
78 Street, *The Savage in Literature*, 64–5.
79 Thomas, *Colonialism's Culture*, 140.
80 Cato, *The House on the Hill*, 2.

> Tears were on many faces, and my own eyes were not dry … It was most affecting … Joeli was weeping copiously, and watched until the last glimpse had faded from his sight. Poor little chap, he is leaving country, friends, and all, to go with us. It is nice to have a 'Nasoso' face to look at, he is a link with the past.[81]

These personal experiences, though using language that reinforced the trope of the family and its paternalistic connotations, demonstrated that Australian missionaries were often informed by the basic principle of Christian humanism, which guided their work in the Pacific.

Australian travellers repeated mission representations of the infantile savage, with varying emphasis on the positive and negative implications. J Mayne Anderson, a tourist, believed in 1915 that the 'primitive children of the soil' were still governed by old savage laws in the New Hebrides, while McLaren perceived in 1923 that 'many [Papuans] were too uncivilized to tell lies … they were not given to subterfuge or deceit'.[82] Australian travellers regularly encountered missionaries in the field, describing their encounters onboard ships, at official functions and during escorted day trips to mission stations to observe schools and church services. In 1894, JC Hickson wrote:

> The Rev. and Mrs Newall, of the London Missionary Society, who were returning to Samoa, gave an address [on the ship] on the habits, customs and superstitions, of the natives of Samoa.[83]

Although travellers often admired the evident progress in Pacific mission stations, they were sometimes disappointed that their exotic expectations were not met. For example, Grimshaw observed:

> It is very gratifying, from a moral point of view, to see the clean, tidy, school-attending, prosaically peaceful folk that have replaced the original savage; but to the traveller, original savages are a good deal more interesting.[84]

---

81 May Cook, *Fijian Diary 1904–1906: A Young Australian Woman's Account of Village life in Fiji*, ed. Leigh Cook (Victoria: PenFolk Pub., 1996), 120. Cook does not specify why Joeli had accompanied them to Australia.
82 Anderson, *What a Tourist Sees in the New Hebrides*, 46; McLaren, *My Odyssey*, 67.
83 Hickson, *Notes of Travel*, 5.
84 Grimshaw, *From Fiji to the Cannibal Islands*, 330.

Children were often convenient photographic subjects and served to reinforce notions of Pacific innocence. However, images and captions could be easily constructed or manipulated to hint at savage pasts or potentials.

The mission's shifting emphasis away from the bestial nature of the savage to an infantile one also links to a wider public and political debate about civilisation during the interwar period. Christine Weir argued that 'an international discourse of Christian humanism' informed debates about Australia's responsibilities in the Pacific following World War I—particularly in relation to its acquisition of the League of Nations Mandate for New Guinea, which was officially described as a 'sacred trust of civilisation'. Although missionaries did not completely abandon their racialist assumptions, they 'reframed them in the language of obligation', as argued by Weir.[85] Burton's call that 'we must still bear the White Man's Burden' was rooted in the popular belief that 'the source of the European's success in the Pacific has been our moral and intellectual superiority'.[86] Frank Paton described this as 'a national duty' and 'the white man's privilege'.[87] This call to action resonated with many Australians who believed in the ultimate superiority of white Australia over the brown Pacific. Missionaries were influential in lobbying Australian governments to take action, both in New Guinea policies and in stressing a general national obligation to halt rampant depopulation in the Pacific. This likely influenced Australia's domestic policies as well; Warwick Anderson's history of white Australia highlighted a similar shift in the official perceptions of Aboriginal Australians in the 1930s.[88]

Although the White Australia policy may have officially implemented notions of racial exclusivity in Australia, not all travellers believed that the Pacific Islanders were utterly depraved savages. This was partly due to the missions that engaged Australians through a literature that maintained a delicate balance between science and salvation—and one that emphasised a common humanity while confronting 'darkness without Christianity'.[89] The depiction of the infantile Islander was central to their message and bolstered their petitions for the civilised taking responsibility of the savage.

---

85   Weir, '"White Man's Burden", "White Man's Privilege"', 298.
86   Burton, *The Fiji of To-Day*, 173, 265.
87   Frank Hume Lyall Paton, *The Kingdom in the Pacific* (London: United Council for Missionary Education, 1912), 35.
88   Warwick Anderson, *The Cultivation of Whiteness: Science, Health and Racial Destiny in Australia* (Carlton: Melbourne University Press, 2002), 206.
89   Weir, '"Deeply Interested in These Children Whom You Have Not Seen"', 14.

Primordial Promises

The accounts of missionaries and blackbirders, among other travellers, paved the way for an increasing number of Australian tourists who travelled on tourist cruises around Papua, New Guinea, the Solomon Islands and the New Hebrides in the 1920s and 1930s. As BP expanded its routes, it effectively marketed Melanesia as being a primitive paradise; the company offered the safety and comfort of a luxury steamer, and the region offered the potential for a dangerous and savage encounter. Descriptions of the primitive were marked by a certain ambiguity, in which moderate notions of the wild Islander savage were balanced against idyllic promises of natural and primordial beauty. Australian travel accounts conveyed a desire to imitate adventurous expeditions into unknown lands, along with the travellers' cautiousness to not be completely immersed in savagery for fear of their own safety or of losing their civilisation. This notion of the primitive life was personified and exemplified by the beachcomber, who was simultaneously admired and vilified for completely rejecting the civilised world.

Australian travellers in the 1930s re-inscribed the primitivism of the eighteenth century, idealising the primitive as a simpler and more natural state of human being. Brian Street argued that this evoked a long tradition in European literature, in which 'life nearer to nature is more virtuous and "real" than in the superficial urban environment that man creates for himself'.[90] Travellers searching for authenticity found it in what they perceived to be the primitive and natural aspects of the Melanesian savage, rather than in the bestial images that dominated nineteenth-century representations. This is consistent with studies of tourism, which suggest that tourists attribute authenticity to primitive societies and that they constantly exoticise and distort them.[91] McLaren searched for the 'Real Wild' in the 1900s because he regarded civilisation 'with scorn'; he was also critical of city life because 'people seemed unreal-artificial like' and because they were 'denied the spice of existence'.[92] For South Australian tourist Hannah Chewings, the exotic and the savage were shaped by her Christian worldview:

---

90 Street, *The Savage in Literature*, 120–1.
91 MacCannell, *The Tourist*, 91; Stewart, *On Longing*, 150.
92 McLaren, *My Odyssey*, 11, 41, 66.

> Though some were heavily burdened with barbaric jewellery, hundreds were as bare as our first parents in the Garden of Eden before the sense of sin caused them to blush and the constant use of clothes turned them white.[93]

Similarly, Dickinson identified the Islands with a freedom 'from conventions, worry, trouble and drudgery' and attributed the 'lure' of the Islands to 'a link with our long ago, primitive freedom'.[94]

The act of marking a territory or people as primitive could also serve to justify colonialism as progress or redemption. Although Polynesia was more accessible, increased instances of European contact had tarnished the romanticised ideal, and travellers had to subsequently travel further abroad to find the unknown and the unexplored. This was the case for Burton, who lamented:

> The ruthless hand of Commerce has not yet touched the wild grandeur of the mountains, nor its breath dulled the vivid greens of the vegetation ... Yet he [the traveller] cannot help admitting that he is somewhat disappointed that the town is so English and civilized in appearance ... What a pity there is so much civilization.[95]

Although Aboriginal Australians were popularly and racially regarded as the most primitive of people, most Australian travellers separated their descriptions of the Pacific and of the Australian primitive. This may be due to Australians believing that the two races were unrelated, or perhaps it suggests that Melanesian primitivity was considered preferable in light of its association with generalised and exotic Pacific stereotypes. This may have also reflected official government policies that prioritised the administration of Papua and New Guinea over Aboriginal Australians and that considered the Aboriginal Australian race doomed to extinction.

Primordiality was closely associated with the natural and the physical, so Australian travellers thus frequently admired the physique of Islanders and their closeness to nature. Tourists would frequently comment on the strength and form of males. William Stephens remarked in 1935 that

---

93 Hannah Chewings, *Amongst Tropical Islands, or, Notes and Observations Made during a Visit of the S.S. 'Moresby' in 1899, to New Guinea, New Britain and the Solomon Islands* (Adelaide: publisher unknown, 1900), 30.
94 Joseph HC Dickinson, *A Trader in the Savage Solomons: A Record of Romance and Adventure* (London: H.F. & G. Witherby, 1927), 206.
95 Burton, *The Fiji of To-Day*, 74, 76–7.

'the native Fijian is a handsome man, broad shouldered and slim hipped. He clothes himself in sleeveless shirts that permit his muscles full play'.[96] Anderson also admired New Hebrideans and had regarded them as the 'ideal natives, tall, muscular, broad, brown, shining-skinned people'.[97] Other forms of admiration drew attention to Islanders' 'copper-' or 'bronze-' coloured skin, their dress and, in the case of females, the floral decorations symbolising their closeness to nature. The natural abundance of the environment and the skill with which Islanders utilised local materials were also considered evidence of their close connection with nature. Although Polynesians were more frequently idealised and admired, Melanesians were not exempt from the regard of travellers. While in the New Hebrides in the 1930s, scientific researcher Alan John Marshall wrote, 'I was delighted at the opportunity to witness the spontaneous revellings of these unspoiled children of nature'.[98]

Australian travel accounts were sometimes marked by a sense of nostalgia or regret that the primeval world was disappearing. Pacific Islanders were romanticised as primitive peoples who originated from an idyllic past—which was sometimes specified as the Garden of Eden, a Golden Age or a utopia. In the 1930s, some Australian travellers displayed an increasing concern that the purity and innocence of the Pacific Islands were threatened by the spread of civilisation (and its vices). Living in Erromango, Woodburn predicted that air travel would 'destroy the charm of simplicity'.[99] This fear was exaggerated by the perception of widespread population decline in the Pacific. Artist Arnold Safroni-Middleton lamented that:

> Islands that twenty years ago had populations numbering many thousand, to-day have a scattered population of a hundred or so … We have weighted ourselves with the thick armour of civilization … Nevertheless, we are the old savages, the Dark Ages, in a double sense, dreaming that we are the children of the Golden Age![100]

In Melanesia, where areas were still isolated and unexplored, Australian travellers believed they could chase the authentic primitive. In 1923, Elinor Mordaunt fondly recalled her time in the Trobriand Islands and in New Guinea:

---

96 Stephens, *Samoan Holidays*, 14.
97 Anderson, *What a Tourist Sees in the New Hebrides*, 38.
98 Marshall, *The Black Musketeers*, 88.
99 Woodburn, *Backwash of Empire*, 20.
100 Safroni-Middleton, *South Sea Foam*, ix, xii.

> It delighted me to 'go bush' like Adam, to 'go walking in canoe'. I loved to have my tent pitched on the hard pinkish-cream sands on the very edge of the sea; listen to the patter of small waves, the swish of palm leaves far overhead, the cry of the flying foxes.[101]

Savagery (even cannibalism) could be tolerated and justified when chasing the authentic because it was primordial and natural.

Travellers who idealised the ancient in the Pacific Islands had to reconcile their romantic expectations with a scientific discourse—one arguing that Islanders lacked brain development, which meant that they consequently lacked any sense of history or memory. The influence of this discourse is evident in the numerous travel accounts in which Australians referred to phrenology, attempted to collect skulls or alluded to an Islander's inability to have complex thoughts. Naturalist William Ramsay Smith employed this scientific logic in 1924, when he wrote:

> He [the Pacific Islander] has none, in fact, of the complex passions which make the chief wear and tear of civilised life. His conscience is a very primitive affair, being no more than a sense of right attaching to the beliefs and customs of his tribe ... He obeys his tribal conscience, as the animal obeys its instincts, without feeling any temptation to violate it.[102]

McLaren was more sympathetic in his judgement of the Solomon Islander native, whose 'brain reacted to impulses foreign to European understanding'.[103] By marking the other as primitive, travel writing reinforced popular assumptions of the savage's animal instincts and infantile mentality.

It was in this setting, surrounded by the primitive and natural, that the notion of the beachcomber excited the Australian imagination. Although beachcombing was no longer common by the twentieth century, the archetypal beachcomber of the nineteenth century was a persistent and romanticised figure in Australian literature. Like blackbirders, beachcombers were simultaneously admired for their carefree lifestyle and scorned for corrupting Islanders, or for becoming corrupted by them. They were precariously positioned on the border between the savage and the civilised. Edmund Banfield was a popular beachcomber in Australia in

---

101 Mordaunt, *Sinabada*, 251.
102 Smith, *In Southern Seas*, 56.
103 McLaren, *My Odyssey*, 234.

the 1900s who produced multiple books about his self-imposed isolation with his wife on Dunk Island, off the coast of north Queensland. Living on an uninhabited island, Banfield enjoyed an idyllic island lifestyle, without having to manage cross-cultural exchange. He described the romanticism of beachcombing as so:

> The Beachcomber of tradition parades his coral islet bare-footed, bullying guileless natives out of their copra, coconut and pearl shell; his chief diet, turtle and turtle eggs and fish; his drink, rum or coconut milk—the latter only when the former is impossible. When a wreck happens he becomes a potentate in pyjamas, and with his dusky wives, dressed in bright vestiture, fares sumptuously … A whack on his hardened head from the club of a jealous native is the time-honoured fate of the typical Beachcomber.[104]

This popular trope was usually male and advocated for exploitation and conquest (both sexual and physical). For Safroni-Middleton, beachcombers were 'humanity in its most blessed state' because they were the outcasts of a dysfunctional European society—a 'postage-like stamp collection of men who had once been recognised as genuine currency by governments, but had long since gone through the post and had become valuable and rare'.[105]

Those Australians who were disenchanted with social conditions or restrictions in Australia favourably regarded the white residents of the Pacific Islands, who were perceived to lead carefree, happy and profitable lives. Articles that promoted economic development in the region encouraged the notion that wealth could be easily found in the Pacific Islands. The travel accounts of self-styled beachcombers and vagabonds encouraged the notion that travellers could start anew and occupy a position of power within the community, as they could not do at home. Muspratt 'felt like a king' when he worked on a coconut plantation in the Solomon Islands for six months:

> I loved their savage, untrammeled ways, their wild, abandoned zest, simple and unspoilt as a child's. I shed all the reserves and artificialities of civilization as easily as I shed my clothes. The only remaining difference was that I dominated and dispensed justice unswervingly.[106]

---

104 Edmund James Banfield, *The Confessions of a Beachcomber* (London: T.F. Unwin, 1908), 57.
105 Safroni-Middleton, *Wine-Dark Seas and Tropic Skies*, 14, 61.
106 Muspratt, *My South Sea Island*, 64.

Although Australians were inspired by beachcombers, the romanticism was tempered with a concern about 'going native'—a phrase suggesting that one could become uncivilised and degraded. Travellers were only willing to ignore the social conventions and norms of Australian (and British) society to a certain extent, fearing that they could be consumed by the alleged 'red, raw, primeval barbarity' of the Pacific Islands.[107] Aside from the cautionary tales found in children's literature, the mutiny onboard the HMS *Bounty* in 1789 was the most frequently cited example of the temptations of the Pacific Islands, as well as of the limits to abandoning civilisation and its values. Rather than fearing the corrupting influence of savage Islanders, most accounts exhibited a fear of prolonged exposure to a savage and/or tropical environment.[108]

Penny Russell has demonstrated how Australians defined social position and etiquette at home to ease the discomforts of social mobility.[109] Just as early migrants to Australia feared that civil society would be lost to a savage wilderness, so too did Australians visiting the Pacific feel vulnerable about being far away from familiar, civilised surroundings. As they travelled through a 'primitive Pacific', Australians reflected on the origins of humanity, on the merits of their own civilisation and on the constraints of modernity. This was particularly significant in the 1920s and 1930s, when representations of the Pacific Islands were shaped by rapid growth in the travel and tourism industries, a surge in Australian publishing and cinema and a renewed emphasis on cultural vitality and self-reliance within the nation.[110]

Consistently Cannibal

A constant feature of almost every travel account, imagined or otherwise, was cannibalism—the most popular and best-known form of savagery. It was simultaneously infantile, primordial and bestial, flagged by blackbirders, missionaries and tourists alike. It was the ultimate marker of savagery and monstrosity, with accounts of cannibalism being in high demand in Europe: 'Cannibalism is what the English reading public relished. It was their definition of the savage.'[111] Although the prevalence

---

107 McLaren, *My Odyssey*, 212.
108 Banivanua-Mar, *Violence and Colonial Dialogue*, 34.
109 Russell, *Savage or Civilised?*, 3.
110 White, *Inventing Australia*, 148.
111 Obeyesekere, *Cannibal Talk*, 28.

of the Melanesian cannibal discourse appears throughout Australian travel writing from 1880 to 1941, it is not 'chronologically or temporally defiant', as Tracy Banivanua-Mar argued.[112] Rather, the cannibal was tested, manipulated and, at times, rejected by Australian travellers. The different Australian representations of the cannibal correspond with the 'degrees of savagery' that were previously observed by Pacific travellers.

Australians were like most Europeans in regard to their fascination with cannibalism. Gananath Obeyesekere and William Arens have written extensively on anthropophagy (the actual consumption of human flesh) and the origins of the European fantasy of cannibalism.[113] Scientific theory and language, childhood fantasy, sailors' yarns and mission propaganda intertwined and fed a stereotype of the cannibal that 'gained authorisation through its exoticism and conformity and longevity over time'.[114] It was this mix of content that shaped travellers' expectations of their Pacific journeys; travellers were affected to the extent that finding evidence of cannibalism was crucial in satisfying one's desire for the exotic and validating one's journey. This is evident in the growth of a vibrant tourist market of postcards, travel narratives, exhibits and curios from the early twentieth century, some of which still exist today.

Most Australian travellers 'aspired to meet real cannibalistic savages' from the 1880s.[115] By the twentieth century, firsthand encounters with cannibalism were rare. Rather than a feared reality, the cannibal of the early twentieth century was an attraction and a symbol of past savagery. This figure 'was represented as a normalised, systemic, and casual practice of the everyday, and as constantly observable through every sensory perception', as argued by Banivanua-Mar.[116] For travellers who sought validation, physical proof of cannibalism was essential (e.g. skulls, bones, weapons and burial or sacrificial sites), regardless of the reactions of the locals. In 1924, Smith admired human teeth necklaces at a museum in Noumea and took a tooth, tapa cloth and a skull with him.[117] Woodburn, a temporary resident of Erromango and an aspiring anthropologist,

---

112 Banivanua-Mar, *Violence and Colonial Dialogue*, 24.
113 Obeyesekere, *Cannibal Talk*; William Arens, *The Man-Eating Myth: Anthropology & Anthropophagy* (New York: Oxford University Press, 1979).
114 Banivanua-Mar, *Violence and Colonial Dialogue*, 22.
115 Safroni-Middleton, *In the Green Leaf*, 123.
116 Tracey Banivanua-Mar, 'Cannibalism and Colonialism: Charting Colonies and Frontiers in Nineteenth-Century Fiji', *Comparative Studies in Society and History* 52, no. 2 (2010): 264, doi.org/10.1017/s0010417510000046.
117 Smith, *In Southern Seas*, 20.

searched a burial cave to acquire a skull, noting (yet ignoring) that 'every one was very serious. It was obviously a momentous occasion'.[118] Journalist Wilfred Burchett visited 'Konienne Island' in New Caledonia in 1941 and reported the discovery of 'relics of a cannibal feast', despite his local guide's explanation to the contrary.[119] Whether out of scientific curiosity or touristic desire, the search for 'curios' was paramount to many Australian travellers—and the Islanders responded to the demand. In 1897, Henry Tichborne noted an opportunistic market for curios developing:

> The phenomenal relic which is popularly treasured in Fiji. 'Baker's fork' they call it. This is the fork with which the body of poor Mr. Baker was eaten[.] I have myself seen about two hundred and fifty … Everybody has it. The traveller to Fiji is invariably sold the real 'Baker's fork'. I bought one myself once for half a dollar, but the burst of laughter which greeted me when I produced it at any hotel in Levuka made me ponder, and I was glad soon to abandon the treasure.[120]

Cannibalism was thus appropriated by Islanders as often as it was envisaged by foreigners.

The souvenir can be regarded as a trace of an authentic experience. Susan Stewart argued that it can be a sign of a traveller's survival and that it allows the tourist 'to appropriate, consume, and thereby "tame" the cultural other'.[121] When physical evidence could not be found, it was invented. Islanders were often ascribed cannibalistic tendencies, with authors citing historical record or hearsay as proof. After arriving at Malekula in 1933, businessman Joseph Hadfield Grundy made a suspect claim that 'two months before we arrived there had been a murder and the victims had been eaten … it is probable 10 other murders will be done'.[122] When offered food, Gaggin cautiously 'had a good look before the pig was cut up, to satisfy [himself] it was … not a baked boy or girl'.[123] Such ludicrous remarks were likely written to shock and entertain readers. If the food was not suspected, then it was the smells and sounds that

---

118 Woodburn, *Backwash of Empire*, 191.
119 Wilfred Burchett, *Pacific Treasure Island: New Caledonia; Voyage through its Land and Wealth, the Story of its People and Past* (Melbourne: F.W. Cheshire, 1941), 48.
120 Tichborne, *Noqu Talanoa*, 40.
121 Stewart, *On Longing*, 146.
122 Joseph Hadfield Grundy, *The New Hebrides Group of Islands* (Adelaide: Hunkin, Ellis & King, 1933), 7.
123 Gaggin, *Among the Man-Eaters*, 58.

suggested cannibalism. In Santa Cruz, journalist John Henry Macartney Abbott described 'a sour, offensive, depressing smell' that emanated from the people.[124] Savage drums and dancing satisfied Gaggin's curiosity, who described 'three hundred wild cannibals, of all ages, sizes, and sexes, innocent of clothes, dancing in the half gloom of a great cavern'.[125] As the link between anthropophagy and imagined cannibalism became more tenuous, the cannibal archetype became distorted and romanticised over time. Photographic proof of cannibalism was unlikely, so photographs were staged with willing bodies and props. In many instances, benign images were transformed into savage depictions by mentioning 'cannibal' in the caption. The cannibal could even be alluring and feminine. Albert Stewart Meek's 1913 travel account included in its frontispiece a photograph of a woman with the caption 'a cannibal belle'.[126]

To meet an ex-cannibal was the ultimate achievement, and Australians frequently expressed admiration rather than disgust at the thought. Elinor Mordaunt recalled that 'the Chief of Fishermen of Human Beings' said that he did not like eating human flesh, and Dickinson fondly remembered Taki, 'an old genial historic cannibal and headhunter chief … a truly grand old man'.[127] A similar impression was recorded by Norman H Hardy (see Figure 16), who toured Melanesia from 1895 to 1897. His vivid paintings first appeared in a London publication titled *The Savage South Seas* in 1907 and became so popular that they were reproduced in Australian compendiums by JHM Abbott (*The South Seas [Melanesia]*, 1908) and Frank Fox (*Oceania*, 1911).[128] Rather than a feared reality, the cannibal of the 1910s and 1920s was 'picturesque, polite, and gentle-seeming'—it was a nostalgic symbol of a savage past that always hinted at the potential to revert to former behaviours.[129] Some Australians rejected the prevailing perception of cannibalism as an uncontrollable addiction or an 'intense love of human flesh'.[130] They lamented the loss of a primitive custom in the face of European corruption and recognised the ceremonial significance of the practice. In 1924, Winifred Ponder drew attention to 'wildly impossible yarns' to prove that cannibalism was a primitive custom

---

124 Abbott, *The South Seas (Melanesia)*, 80.
125 Gaggin, *Among the Man-Eaters*, 134.
126 Albert Stewart Meek, *A Naturalist in Cannibal Land*, ed. Frank Fox (London: T.F. Unwin, 1913).
127 Mordaunt, *The Venture Book*, 210; Dickinson, *A Trader in the Savage Solomons*, 203.
128 Max Quanchi, 'Norman H. Hardy: Book Illustrator and Artist', *The Journal of Pacific History* 49, no. 2 (2014): 214–33, doi.org/10.1080/00223344.2014.906298.
129 Frank Fox, *Oceania* (London: Black, 1911), 33.
130 Burton, *The Fiji of To-Day*, 104.

rather than a heinous crime, while Frank Fox concluded in 1911 'that the horrors were but a slight and inconsiderable feature of Fijian life until the arrival of the white man'.[131]

Figure 16: Old Cannibal Chief of the Island of Aoba, New Hebrides.
Source: Illustration by Norman H Hardy in Fox, Oceania, 49.

---

131 Fox, *Oceania*, 31; Ponder, *An Idler in the Islands*, 39.

Cannibal attributes were not only restricted to Pacific Islanders. Young travellers Edward Way Irwin and Ivan Goff ascribed cannibal traits onto white visitors when they described the passengers of the cruise ship *Aorangi* as having 'cannibal faces, feasting themselves on us'.[132] Similarly, travellers to New Caledonia often attributed cannibal behaviours to French convicts. Others sought to test the merits of 'going native' by identifying with the savage. As Obeyesekere and Arens have demonstrated, the roots of European fascination with cannibalism lie not only in depictions of the other but in the potential for the civilised to also turn to cannibalism. For this reason, Safroni-Middleton actively searched for a village in the 'Rewa cannibal district' in Fiji and proudly announced to his readers that 'I became a savage of the first degree'.[133]

As Safroni-Middleton alluded, cannibalism (and thus savagery) was perceived to occur in degrees, depending on particular Islands and regions. Such labels were tied to a colonial frontier that was always shifting, as argued by Obeyesekere.[134] The racial label of Melanesia as being the most savage region in the Pacific implied that it was also the most cannibalistic. British naval captain Cyprian Bridge wrote in 1918 that 'to the unscientific eye of people like myself it seemed that there were three distinct races and many mixtures'. He identified Melanesians as being 'woolly-haired negroes' and noted that 'except where they have been brought into close and long contact with white men, especially missionaries, they are all cannibals'.[135] Wawn was more specific in identifying the racial component, which encouraged the belief that the further west one travelled, the more savage one would become: 'Solomon Islanders have more Papuan blood, therefore excel the New Hebridean in cannibalism and bloodthirstiness'.[136] The Islands of Polynesia were not commonly attributed cannibal features, even though the ritual had been practised by Marquesas Islanders and Maori. This fact may have been forgotten in Australia by the twentieth century, or it might have been overshadowed by descriptions of Melanesian savagery. Some travellers to Polynesia explicitly denied any trace of cannibalism, such as Clement Lindley Wragge in 1906: 'There appears to be no proof that the Tahitians were ever actually cannibals'.[137]

---

132 Irwin and Goff, *No Longer Innocent*, 145.
133 Safroni-Middleton, *Tropic Shadows*, 17.
134 Obeyesekere, *Cannibal Talk*, 150.
135 Cyprian Bridge, *Some Recollections* (London: J. Murray, 1918), 232.
136 Wawn, *The South Sea Islanders*, 240.
137 Wragge, *The Romance of the South Seas*, 286.

Literature of the early twentieth century generally placed Solomon Islanders in a more savage position than those from the New Hebrides. Fox's 1911 reference guide stated that 'the Solomon Islanders have been always the most notorious cannibals of the Pacific, and undoubtedly certain of their religious rites demanded that human flesh should be eaten'.[138] Australians particularly associated the Solomon Islands with head hunting, a practice that had been exaggerated in travel accounts of the nineteenth century. Labour recruiters who found recruiting increasingly more difficult in the New Hebrides turned to the Solomon Islands after the 1880s and, as violent encounters inevitably ensued, the group featured more strongly in the public's imagination.[139] In contrast, accusations of cannibalism directed at Aboriginal Australians had dissipated by the twentieth century, despite their perceived primitivity. This was expressed much later in 1953 by Australian travel writer, Colin Simpson:

> The eating of human flesh was not practised by the Australian native to the extent that it was by the South Sea Islander. The term 'cannibalism' is usually taken to mean gorging on human flesh, and with relish; and that seems a valid description of the cannibalism of the Melanesian *indigenes* of New Caledonia, who appear to have regarded man-meat much as we regard the Sunday joint. Not all cannibalism is the same in purpose.[140]

Such tongue-in-cheek comparisons were used as literary devices to entertain rather than to reflect any serious consideration of the similarities and differences that existed between indigenous cultures.

In the Melanesian group, Fiji was an outlier. Situated simultaneously between Melanesia and Polynesia—geographically, racially and ideologically—Fiji was considered a 'special case' by Australian travellers. It was not considered as savage as the 'wicked cannibal groups' in the Solomon Islands and the New Hebrides, as marked by Grimshaw in 1907, but neither did it have 'the nameless dreamy charm of the Eastern Islands'.[141] McLaren similarly noted, 'I went to Fiji as a tourist, a man of leisure, intent on comparing the Civilized Wild [Fiji] with the Palaeolothic

---

138 Fox, *Oceania*, 38.
139 Corris, 'Passage, Port and Plantation', 1–2.
140 Colin Simpson, *Adam in Ochre: Inside Aboriginal Australia* (New York: Frederick A. Praeger, 1953), 203.
141 Grimshaw, *From Fiji to the Cannibal Islands*, 7.

Wild [sic] of my roamings'.[142] Fiji's development as a key stopover and major industrial centre in the Pacific rendered it a well-travelled and modern destination.

The island of Bau in Fiji was frequently acknowledged as being the traditional centre, or 'the shrine of cannibalism'. Mordaunt described the Island in 1926:

> This is by far the most romance-haunted spot—the spot which almost speaks, and groans in speaking, of what is past—in all the islands. It is the center of all that was dreadful in the wild days of old Fiji; the home of kings and chiefs, the shrine of cannibalism. Mbau [Bau] the beautiful, Mbau the terrible.[143]

Bau rose to prominence in the mid-1830s and became Fiji's seat of power under its chief, Ratu Seru Epenisa Cakobau, until Fiji's cession to Britain in 1874. Cakobau became a legend among European and Australian tourists; his personality was exaggerated to describe a ruthless former cannibal who converted to Christianity. Bau became a site for historic tourism, with steamer tourists frequently making day trips to the Rewa River and Bau, where they could visit the graves of pioneer missionaries, see Cakobau's memorial and the 'relics of heathen Fiji', and reflect on the victory of Christian civilisation over cannibalism.[144] Christian missions had been effectively promoting the success of their work by emphasising the miraculous transformation of Fiji from its cannibal past. As John Gibson Paton noted:

> Thus died a man who had been a cannibal chief, but by the grace of God and the love of Jesus has been changed, transfigured into a character of light and beauty.[145]

In contrast to the highly publicised savagery of pre-cession Fiji, the popular image of Fiji in the early twentieth century was increasingly sanitised and romanticised, with its reputation as 'the Cannibal Isle' receding.

An analysis of Australian representations of cannibalism in the Pacific Islands from 1880 to 1941 can offer insights into how Australians perceived themselves and their Pacific neighbours over time. Initially symbolising

---

142 McLaren, *My Odyssey*, 247.
143 Mordaunt, *The Venture Book*, 199–200.
144 Brummitt, *A Winter Holiday in Fiji*, 115–18.
145 Paton, *Thirty Years with South Sea Cannibals*, 108.

the brutality and inhumanity of the ignoble savage, the cannibal of the late nineteenth century was perceived as a threat to Australian civilised values, despite the dependence of domestic agricultural production on cheap Melanesian labour. By the first two decades of the twentieth century, Australian missionaries changed their propaganda to encourage an identification with the childlike savage; they wished to emphasise their common humanity and potential salvation rather than a heathen past. This shift suggests a softening of racial attitudes and assumptions towards Pacific Islanders, particularly after World War I, as well as a greater concern for Australia's obligations to the Pacific. In the 1920s and 1930s, Pacific tourism had fostered a romanticised and sanitised version of the primitive ex-cannibal savage. Although this image became increasingly standardised, the growth of travel to the region encouraged more diverse representations of Pacific Islanders.

The Melanesian savage was a complex and ambiguous figure, formulated and reformulated by the entanglement of scientific discourse, racial theory, childhood fiction, Christian promotion, political propaganda, tourist guides and traditional European fantasies. Although this complexity became simplified, standardised and stereotyped in the popular imagination of Australians over time, some strands of Australian travel writing also highlighted a more discerning and nuanced collection of responses to the savage–civilised dichotomy. Some journeys reaffirmed individual preconceptions, while others found it difficult to reconcile the savage of the imagination with reality. In 1937, Marshall frequently referred to the Islanders whom he met as savages, yet he was unsatisfied with his own 'civilisation':

> Our generation are indeed a curious people … so ultra-modern, yet so hopelessly backward and ignorant of most of the things that matter … The people of the future will regard us as barbarians, much in the same manner as we regard our ancestors. And if not for a hundred other things, it will be for the appalling way we have treated and are treating the primitive races whose territories we have taken.[146]

---

146 Marshall, *The Black Musketeers*, 239.

In 1924, Smith reflected that 'we are as much the slaves of habit and the creatures of convention as they are, only we assume that our habits are good and our conventions are virtuous'.[147] In the concluding chapter of her 1944 travel account, Woodburn asked the reader: 'What right have we to interfere with the individual's freedom of thought and action?'[148]

These dissenting voices may have been a minority in Australian travel writing, but they signalled a gradual shift away from traditional notions of the bestial savage. They also contributed to the erosion of racialist assumptions regarding Islander inferiority in the 1920s and 1930s. This reflected a broader shift in the public attitudes of post–World War I, one in which attention was directed towards the Pacific Islands and Australia's role as a colonial power in the region. The increase in Australian travel to Melanesia at this time facilitated more face-to-face human encounters between Australians and Pacific Islanders, and it highlighted a weariness regarding the conventional savage trope, which had been an overused and exaggerated stereotype since first European contact with the Pacific.

---

147 Smith, *In Southern Seas*, 57.
148 Woodburn, *Backwash of Empire*, 219.

5

In Search of a Profitable Pacific

I join the Australian Argonauts in their search for the land of the golden cocoa-nut. They are the genuine article all right—hard-handed anxious-faced men—shearers, mechanics, miners, farmers, prospectors, out-back men, and a few born wanderers never happy unless they are on the move ... They very often got a spear through them, and they invariably had a bad time but they saw the world. A lot of these settlers were like walk-about blacks and if a new venture were started at the North Pole they would be off to it.[1]

Commissioned by an Australian shipping company to report on a newly established settlement scheme to the New Hebrides in 1902, Paterson—a poet and journalist—used extracts from his diary in an unpublished radio script for the Australian Broadcasting Commission. More commonly known by his pseudonym, Banjo, Paterson's reflections on the voyage of a group of prospective settlers from Sydney to the New Hebrides are often overlooked in light of his contribution to rural Australia and bush mythology. His brief visit to the Pacific offers a momentary glimpse into the diverse range of motives that underscored Australian travel, as well as shaped how the Islands were perceived. Australians were not the only travellers in the Pacific motivated by commercial success, but their travel writing played a significant role in encouraging Australian

---

1   This quotation was taken from a radio transcript; Andrew Barton Paterson, 'The Pioneers', Talks—AB Paterson, Australian Broadcasting Commission (Sydney: ABC, 1935) (series no. SP 1558/2, 629, National Archives of Australia), 2.

investment and public interest during a crucial time in the new nation's growth. Situated at the periphery of an empire at the turn of the century, Australia was poised to take advantage of the economic opportunities that other colonial powers were unwilling or unable to grasp. Opportunistic workers were at the forefront of Australia's expansion into the neighbouring regions. As literary figures, these workers became emblematic of Australian nationalism, progress and development abroad. To what extent did these workers, and the travel accounts that described them, contribute to the dominant narrative of the Pacific Islands as a lucrative location for Australian commercial enterprise?

The enterprising Australian worker visited the Pacific Islands in search of opportunities for economic and social betterment, well before others arrived to travel for leisure. The masculine and heroic figure of the intrepid trader, prospector, overseer or farmer was the most frequent type of colonial Australian traveller in the nineteenth century. It was not until after World War I that tourists began to outnumber them. Accounts written by these workers were distinct from those written by leisure travellers. Simultaneously caught between two worlds, these workers often occupied the position of mediator in European–Islander relationships. Their close encounters and day-to-day observations of the Islands differentiated their accounts from the shallow, touristic impressions of the region and its peoples. Often self-motivated, their descriptions were distinctive from the biases that missionary and government records were subject to. Of course, their accounts were not always honest or accurate, but their close experiences with Pacific Islanders legitimised their authority as Pacific experts in Australia. This authority underscored the popularity of accounts that were written by these opportunists-cum-writers when they returned home.

Commerce historically motivated initial contacts between colonial Australians and the Pacific. Traders and seamen were among the first to pioneer new routes to, and create relationships with, the Pacific Islands in the nineteenth century. These economic ventures exploited, and often exhausted, certain Pacific Island resources—such as whales, seals, pearls, meat, sandalwood, copra, *bêche-de-mer* and other seafood, fruits, sugar, gold and even people (see Figure 17). As Australian economic enterprises expanded in Melanesia, larger companies consolidated small-scale operations and increased their profits by monopolising inter-island trade, as well as the production of copra, sugar, gold and phosphate. For this reason, Thompson argued that 'Australia's informal economic empire was dominant in Fiji, the Solomon Islands and the Gilbert and Ellice Islands'.[2] Nickel exports from New Caledonia were also valuable to Australia, but they were controlled by the French. Firms with significant Australian capital or ownership included:

- Sydney-based traders, Burns, Philp and Company and W. R. Carpenter and Company
- Fiji-based traders, Morris Hedstrom
- Sydney-based copra firms, On Chong and Lever Brothers (who owned plantations in the Solomon Islands)
- Colonial Sugar Refinery (CSR) in Fiji, which was headquartered in Melbourne
- Australian-owned Emperor Gold Mining Company and Loloma Gold Mines in Fiji
- Melbourne-based Pacific Islands Company (later known as the Pacific Phosphate Company), which mined Banaba and Nauru for phosphate.

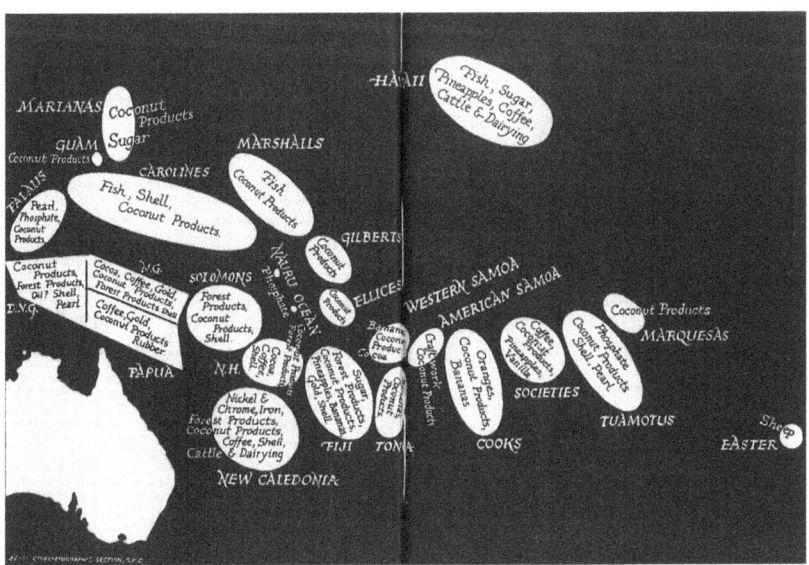

Figure 17: Products of the Pacific Islands.
Source: Australian Army Education Service, *The Pacific Islands* (Melbourne: Army Education Service, 1942), 10–11.

---

2   Thompson, *Australia and the Pacific Islands in the Twentieth Century*, 30–1.

Many of these businesses played an essential role in encouraging Australian notions of empire, whether by lobbying governments or by publishing propaganda. Only in Papua and New Guinea were Australian imperial ambitions realised, and these two territories subsequently became valuable sources of gold, rubber and copra.[3]

Popular notions of Pacific commerce in travel writing can be traced chronologically from their starting point in the late nineteenth century, when notions of the masculine and heroic colonial Australian worker began to emerge. These notions continued into the twentieth century, when the Australian worker was appropriated as a promotional tool for the economic exploitation of the region. This imagined ideal did not match the lived experiences of those Australians who worked in the Islands in the early twentieth century. One of the first authoritative writers about the Pacific who came from the Australian colonies was Louis Becke. He played an influential role in understanding the nineteenth-century's romanticisation of the life of a European working in the Pacific. Becke's representation of the trader and planter formed the groundwork for a body of travel literature in the twentieth century that imagined the Pacific as a region full of economic potential for Australian enterprise.

Louis Becke, the Archetypal Australian Trader

Louis Becke was the most famous travel writer of the late nineteenth century in colonial Australia. His significant contributions as a writer and as an expert on the Pacific have been acknowledged in the biographies compiled about him, as well as in various literature studies.[4] Born in 1855 in Port Macquarie, New South Wales, George Lewis Becke first encountered the Pacific when he travelled to San Francisco with his brother at the age of 14. Two years later, he stowed away on the *Rotumah*, bound for Samoa, where he worked as a bookkeeper in a local trading store. Over 20 years, Becke worked throughout the Pacific; he was a supercargo (representative of a vessel's owner) in the North Pacific, a resident trader in the Gilbert Islands

---

3   Nelson, *Black, White and Gold*, 11–12.
4   Arthur Grove Day, *Louis Becke* (Melbourne: Hill of Content, 1967); Henry Evans Maude, 'Review Article: Louis Becke: The Traders' Historian', *The Journal of Pacific History* 2, no. 1 (1967): 225–7, doi.org/10.1080/00223346708572118; Thomas and Eves, *Bad Colonists*; Dixon, *Writing the Colonial Adventure*; Sturma, *South Sea Maidens*.

and a performer of various short-term jobs in New Britain, the Marshall Islands and New Caledonia. Unable to find regular work in 1892, Becke turned to writing. He found employment with the Sydney-based periodical *The Bulletin*, with his first story appearing in 1893. In 1894, Becke's first collection of stories was published under the title *By Reef and Palm*, which launched him into the spotlight. Becke subsequently gained local and international commercial success and published a further 34 books and numerous articles in newspapers and magazines, earning the reputation of 'Rudyard Kipling of the Pacific'.[5] Although others tried to emulate his success, Becke's international popularity and his influence on Australian notions of the Pacific region were exceptional.

Becke's literary success has been attributed to his firsthand knowledge of the Pacific as much as to his writing style. The lived experiences of traders and seamen inspired fictional tales of adventure for children and adults, many proliferating from England and English authors in the late nineteenth century.[6] Although Becke's subject matter conformed to other English adventure fiction (i.e. pitting courageous white men against 'savage' people), his work also represented a departure from the romanticism and moral justifications of previous English literature. This proved to be popular among the colonial Australian audiences who welcomed the 'authentic' realism of his stories (which he based on actual experiences).[7] In England, he was considered an authority on the South Seas, with his main publisher, T. Fisher Unwin, producing multiple editions for the British and colonial markets. As Helen Bones has demonstrated, a healthy market for the 'colonial exotic' existed at the time.[8] Many of Becke's stories were published as collections of short and unconnected tales, similar to sailors' yarns, with a narration that was abrupt, intense and dramatic. Although his tales were often fictional, Henry Evans Maude, Nicholas Thomas and Richard Eves have highlighted the historical experiences of Becke's life that had underscored many of his stories.[9]

Becke's style of writing was nurtured and influenced by Jules Francois Archibald, the editor of *The Bulletin*. It both reflected and contributed to a new literary culture that was growing in Sydney from the 1890s. Under

---
5 Day, *Louis Becke*, 63.
6 Dixon, *Writing the Colonial Adventure*, 185. See also Saxby, *A History of Australian Children's Literature*.
7 Dixon, *Writing the Colonial Adventure*, 180.
8 Bones, 'Travel Writers and Traveling Writers in Australasia', 83.
9 Maude, 'Review Article: Louis Becke: The Traders' Historian', 226; Thomas and Eves, *Bad Colonists*.

Archibald's leadership, *The Bulletin* encouraged new Australian authors from the Australian colonies, rather than relying on overseas articles. It also fostered a patriotic, protectionist, masculine and racist literature.[10] From its first issue until the early 1960s, 'Australia for the White Man' was written on its masthead. *The Bulletin* editors preferred realism over romance, with the latter being considered 'foreign, unmanly and unsuited to expressing radical, egalitarian and nationalistic ideas', as argued by Robert Dixon.[11] *The Bulletin*'s popularity ensured that its notions about the Pacific were widely circulated. By 1900, its circulation was already 80,000. Its success continued until a decline after World War I.[12] Despite being regarded as the 'bushman's bible', it did publish articles about the Pacific Islands, with many of its contributors also writing Pacific fictions and travelogues elsewhere (e.g. Ion Idriess, Vance Palmer, Dale Collins, Lewis Lett, Albert Dorrington and Norman Lindsay).

The Bulletin's content incorporated and encouraged popular notions about Australian masculinity and national character that had been developing from the 1880s. Marilyn Lake identified *The Bulletin* as a domain in which the 'gender wars' of the 1890s were enacted; she drew further attention to the magazine's 'masculinist' representations of the iconic Australian 'bushman' and the response garnered from feminist social reform campaigners.[13] In this environment, Australian literature overwhelmingly presented the nation as young, pure and innocent. In the figure of the 'coming man', it idealised a people who were superior to the British stock, shaped by the Australian climate and proven in sports and war. This coming man displayed 'independence, manliness, a fondness for sport, egalitarianism, a dislike of mental effort, self-confidence, a certain disrespect for authority'.[14] He was embodied by the lifesaver and the noble worker—and, later, by the soldier or 'digger'. In a similar way that the Australian bush was regarded as shaping the coming man, so too could the tropics be a proving ground for the Australian character.

---

10 Denoon, 'Re-Membering Australasia: A Repressed Memory', 298.
11 Dixon, *Writing the Colonial Adventure*, 184.
12 Garry Wotherspoon, 'The Bulletin', *Dictionary of Sydney*, dictionaryofsydney.org/entry/the_bulletin.
13 Marilyn Lake, 'Historical Reconsiderations IV: The Politics of Respectability: Identifying the Masculinist Context', *Historical Studies* 22, no. 86 (1986): 116–31, doi.org/10.1080/10314618608595739.
14 White, *Inventing Australia*, 77, 117.

Becke's writing conformed to these masculine ideals, often presenting European traders, prospectors, planters and sailors as protagonists. Whether villainous or heroic, Becke's characters were men of action rather than romantics, and women often appeared only as love interests in formulaic interracial dramas.[15] This representation acquired greater significance in the parts of the Pacific in which colonial Australians were actively involved (e.g. Papua and New Guinea). Historian Nigel Krauth wrote that Becke:

> Established the pattern of the New Guinea colonial short story: its superficially tough male characters, its dangerously enervating female characters, its constant theme of white survival, its avoidance of the ethics of that survival in practice, its description of an environment devoid of divine assistance, and its blood-bespattered adventure drama.[16]

Becke's tales frequently focused on the trader, often through his alter ego, Tom Denison, and in the popular tales of villainous American labour trader, 'Bully' Hayes. Due to their transient nature, traders lent themselves to fictional tales, allowing writers to situate them in various exotic locations that contained different actors and new adventures. They were distinct from the nineteenth-century beachcomber, who had completely abandoned 'civilisation', or the government official and missionary, who were constrained by specific regulations and expectations pertaining to their jobs. Rather, Becke focused on the enterprising Australian pioneer— the trader, miner, farmer and businessman—who traversed and acquired the Pacific region. This predominantly male figure was heroic and noble, portrayed in literature as adventurous, ambitious and grappling with the dilemma of maintaining civilised standards in a savage environment. Becke described this figure as:

> Generally a rough character—a runaway from some Australian or American whaler, or a wandering Ishmael who, for reasons of his own, preferred living among the intractable, bawling, and poverty-stricken people of the equatorial Pacific to dreaming away his days in the monotonously happy valleys of the Society and Marquesas Groups.[17]

---

15   Day, *Louis Becke*, 144.
16   Krauth, *The New Guinea Experience in Literature*, 87.
17   Louis Becke, *By Reef and Palm* (Sydney: Angus & Robertson, 1955), 98.

Becke's tales often characterised traders as protagonists due to the dramatic tension that was achieved by focusing on their struggle to negotiate between two cultures. As one of Becke's fictional characters said:

> Had I gone back to Sydney, where would I be now?—a mate, I suppose, on some deep-sea ship, earning £12 or £14 a month. Another year or two like this and I could go back a made man ... No, I'll stay here: 'Kapeni Paranili' [his island name] will always be a big man in the Paumotus [Tuamotus], but Fred Brantley would be nobody in Sydney.[18]

As such, they were popular protagonists for interracial romances (*By Reef and Palm* was a collection of entirely interracial romances published in 1894, to great acclaim) or for stories in which they crossed from civilisation to savagery. Like previous European literature about interracial romances, the possibility of an interracial relationship was alluring, yet ultimately forbidden. These fictional romances thus rarely offered positive outcomes. However, this focus on romance influenced popular imaginings of Australians who lived in the Pacific. Paterson wrote:

> Everyone recalled Louis Becke's sketches of traders, languid, cultivated men of leisure, whose talk was mostly about square gin, and whose occupation was mostly fighting over the affections of brown maidens.[19]

Becke's trading tales contributed to a popular perception of Europeans who lived and worked in the Pacific Islands. This romanticised image of the trader, planter or overseer infiltrated everyday travel accounts about the Pacific Islands, as tourists were keen to meet a Becke-like trader or plantation owner face to face. Even before they arrived at the Islands, travellers encountered traders on ships and at ports on their way to the Pacific. In 1921, Ralph Stock described how several traders crowded the ships at Norfolk Island as they returned from the New Hebrides.[20] In light of the tourism industry that was commencing in the Islands, companies would organise day trips to local missions and plantations. White residents, either looking forward to good company or hoping to gain some financial benefit, welcomed visitors and offered tours around their properties. Marshall described this process in detail:

---

18   Becke, *By Reef and Palm*, 174–5.
19   Andrew Barton Paterson, 'The New Hebrides: The New Pilgrims' Progress', *Sydney Morning Herald*, 26 July 1902, 12, nla.gov.au/nla.news-article14471684.
20   Stock, *The Cruise of the Dream Ship*, 141.

> Throughout the South Seas you'll find them; little kingdoms wedged between a green wilderness … you will see a central group of buildings near the beach, flanked by an ordered forest of perhaps a hundred thousand coconut-palms … If it is steamer-time, when most visitors arrive, your most vivid impressions will be a harassed figure in soiled white … Sail in on any other day in the month and you will be met by a hardy individual in shirt-sleeves and a battered helmet, whose hospitality is as boundless as his capacity for conversation. He will suggest a drink and lead you to a shady thatched kiosk, and after lunch, if you are interested, will take you around the plantation.[21]

Marshall's observations were typical of those found in Australian travel accounts, which generally described residents as hardy workers (often emphasised by their alcoholism). Although occasionally criticised for succumbing to 'uncivilised' temptations, the resident European was mostly respected by visitors for his hospitality and resilience.[22]

Travellers also regularly admired the life of a plantation overseer. These men appeared wealthy and successful, possessing large, spacious houses, 'picturesque' grounds, well-behaved servants and employees, and an abundance of resources. Marshall observed that 'the planter, perhaps a white storekeeper, and usually a half-caste overseer, constitute an oligarchy which rules the coconut kingdom and its hundred-odd coloured labourers'.[23] The lives of plantation overseers were regarded as being carefree and unburdened. As Julian Thomas noted, 'From the point of view of a cane-bottomed chair and a full tumbler, a planter's life in the New Hebrides was one to be envied'.[24]

This romantic image of the life of a European or Australian resident in the Islands became increasingly irrelevant by the twentieth century. By his own admission, Becke's trading fantasies in the Pacific were nostalgic. He reminisced that the nineteenth-century 'wave-punchers' were different from the new steamers that 'exploited' the Islands for trade.[25] Not only had transportation routes and trade goods changed but so too had the Islands. Popular tales of lone pioneering individuals living among supposedly savage and dangerous Islanders may have resonated with the experiences

---

21 Marshall, *The Black Musketeers*, 281.
22 Marshall, *The Black Musketeers*, 289.
23 Marshall, *The Black Musketeers*, 283.
24 Thomas, *Cannibals and Convicts*, 222.
25 Becke, *By Reef and Palm*, 97.

of colonial Australian sandalwood and labour traders of the nineteenth century; however, by the 1900s, Islanders and Australian visitors were more familiar with one another. Although instances of violent encounters were less frequent, Australian travellers continued to imagine the trader, planter, overseer or miner as heroic and successful in the twentieth century. This was partly due to the persistence of conventional European notions of the Pacific's economic potential—a concept that was encouraged by Australian governments and businesses who wished to promote investment and expand commerce in the region.

Economic Potential in the Pacific

Becke's exciting tales of trading adventures linked to a wider narrative that had traditionally imagined the Pacific Islands as a region of unknown riches and prosperity. These idealistic descriptions were persistent from the 1880s to the 1940s and were indiscriminately applied to all the Pacific Islands. This trope was underscored by a European literary tradition of imagining the Pacific as an idyllic paradise, in which Australians' unfamiliarity with many of the Islands assisted with the perpetuation of this image. Travellers such as Henry Tichborne, who 'began to dream of new El Dorados', exaggerated the potential rewards that were hidden within the Islands and encouraged expectations of finding paradise, gold or other treasures that had yet to be tapped.[26] In addition to descriptions of gold mining and pearl diving, travel accounts often included vivid imagery of jewels and gold to describe the Pacific Islands. In 1900, Ernest Osborne described an atoll of the Gilbert Islands as a 'gemlike idyll', and in 1927, Arnold Safroni-Middleton observed that the mountains of Fiji 'have become storied windows of nameless crimson hues and burnished gold'.[27] This imagery also hinted at travellers' subconscious desires to possess these rich Islands, as Elinor Mordaunt did in 1926, when she described the Islands:

> All in the little, small as a jewel, so that it seems as though one were able to take it up in the hollows of one's two hands, feel the warmth of it, turning it, catching the glow upon it as upon a jewel.[28]

---

26   Tichborne, *Rambles in Polynesia by Sundowner*, 74.
27   Ernest Osborne, *Through the Atolls of the Line* (Five Dock: publisher unknown, 1900); Safroni-Middleton, *Tropic Shadows*, 20.
28   Mordaunt, *The Venture Book*, 328.

As well as the direct allusions to gold and other minerals, Australian travellers noted the abundance and fertility of the land—with its propensity for fruit and vegetation, the richness of the soil and the value of the goods that could be garnered. JB Nicoll, a tourist on a cruise through the Solomon Islands in 1902, was relieved 'to see the signs of cultivation and clearing after looking at so much virgin forest'.[29] In 1909, Presbyterian minister Charles Stuart Ross noted that Fiji possessed 'a large area of wonderfully fertile soil that is hardly equalled … [which] have been yielding annually crops of cane, cotton, maize, tobacco and other products without manure and without apparent impoverishment'.[30] In 1920, businessman Frank Coffee wrote about the Solomon Islands, stating that:

> All trade is done with Australia. With copra and other products exported, and merchandise imported, the amount runs to hundreds of thousands of value a year, and the war has not made any appreciable difference.[31]

These observations emphasised the development of business and industry in the Islands in the 1900s, as well as reinforced Australian perceptions of the Pacific Islands as being ready for taking. Aside from the obvious descriptions of natural resources, travellers also commented on the suitability of the tropical climate for Europeans and on the utility of Islanders as labourers. These issues were highly contested in Australian travel accounts because conventional stereotypes of the inherently lazy or savage Islander—as well as popular fears of the potentially dangerous tropical environment—contradicted efforts to promote business and settlement in the Islands. The labour issue also informed debates about the supposed indigenous depopulation of the Pacific.

Other travel publications also focused on economics and trade as a major feature of the Pacific Islands. This reflected the growing interest of Australian businesses, investors and governments in the potential resources of the Pacific Islands in the early 1900s. Travel guides such as the *Pacific Islands Yearbook* provided detailed economic overviews that listed imports and exports figures for each Island group, as well as current market prices and tariffs. The first edition in 1932 included an article by the editor, Robert William Robson, who described the 'opportunities for new settlers

---

29   JB Nicoll, 'A Cruise through Some of the Pacific Islands in 1902 by Mr and Mrs J. B. Nicoll', *The Life and Adventures of George Robertson Nicoll, 1824–1890*, MS 3292 (Canberra: National Library of Australia, 1902), 24.
30   Ross, *Fiji and the Western Pacific*, 289.
31   Coffee, *Forty Years on the Pacific*, 111.

in the Pacific'; he noted that the Pacific Islands were 'enormously rich in natural resources' and were awaiting 'men of pluck, vision, determination and moderate capital'.[32] Shipping and trading companies also published their own travel ephemera and regularly commissioned travel writers to compose favourable articles. As part of BP's successful expansion from its Australian coastal operation into Pacific trade and shipping, its quarterly magazine, *BP Magazine*, began to encourage tourism while simultaneously promoting itself as an informative and educative magazine. In its earliest editions during the 1910s, *Picturesque Travel* characterised the Pacific Islands as a primitive holiday destination, marketing the resident trader or planter as an exotic attraction to potential tourists. For example, a 1914 issue advertised a guided 'walk through the Government plantations' and 'a round of visits' to the local rubber and coconut plantations in the Solomon Islands'.[33] *BP Magazine* later began publishing articles specifically about trade in the Pacific, explaining particular industries and the goods and wealth that they produced. Articles had titles such as 'Coconuts and Copra', 'Pearl Shelling in the Torres Strait' and 'Phosphate Island'.[34] Efforts to promote the company's trading operations by showing examples of industry and labour in the Pacific were mediated by images of idyllic relaxation and natural landscapes that advertised its tourist cruises.

BP's rapid expansion in the Pacific ensured that it became a powerful and influential Australian company by the 1900s. Historian Judith A Bennett noted that 'to a world largely ignorant of island conditions the semi-monthly steamer was a continued source of information. It became the [Solomon Islands] protectorate's unofficial publicity agent in Australia'.[35] The company's political influence was widely acknowledged by Australians at the time. Paterson described one of its founders, James Burns, 'as near to an Empire builder as we ever saw in these parts' and noted that:

> Anywhere that there was a risk to be run and money to be made you would see the flag of James Burns. If he had been dealing in diamonds instead of copra and bananas, he might have been another Cecil Rhodes's understudy.[36]

---

32   Robson, *The Pacific Islands Yearbook*, 9.
33   Burns, Philp & Company, Limited, *Picturesque Travel*, no. 4 (1914), 40, 42.
34   BC Criswick, 'Coconuts and Copra', *BP Magazine* 1, no.4 (September 1929): 44; JL Adams, 'Pearl Shelling in the Torres Strait', *BP Magazine* 2, no. 2 (March 1930): 48; Taupo, 'Phosphate Island', *BP Magazine* 11, no. 4 (September 1939): 2.
35   Judith A Bennett, *Wealth of the Solomons: A History of a Pacific Archipelago, 1800–1978* (Honolulu: University of Hawai'i Press, 1987), 126–7.
36   Andrew Barton Paterson, 'Banjo Paterson Ends His Story: Political Giants and "Pilgrim Fathers"', *Sydney Morning Herald*, 4 March 1939, 21, nla.gov.au/nla.news-article17573640.

BP's periodicals were one part of a diverse strategy to justify and extend the company's reach throughout the Pacific Islands. Although scholars may presently debate the merits of these commercial publications as examples of travel writing, their popularity among a broad readership meant that they influenced subsequent travel accounts by reinforcing particular themes.

Other Australian periodicals concerned with the Pacific Islands devoted much of their content to issues of trade and commerce. The *Pacific Islands Monthly* from 1930 to 1945 included 148 general articles on agriculture, 74 on commerce and 205 on the economy, not including those articles about trade in specific Islands.[37] A similar focus can be observed in *Walkabout*, a monthly geographic magazine that was published by the Australian National Travel Association from 1934.[38] *Walkabout*'s interest in primary industries and rural development in remote Australia and the Pacific is evidenced by many articles that stressed the region's 'beckoning potential'. They informed readers about the lives of Island residents and the processes involved in certain industries.[39] Articles about coconut plantations were most common, but titles also included 'The Story of Nauru', 'Vanua-Lava and its Sulphur', 'Life on a Coco-Nut Plantation', 'Tuamotu Archipelago: Amongst the Pearl Divers', 'The Coco-Nut Tree', 'Cannibals and Talkies' (about a plantation owner), 'The Tricolour in the South Seas' (about French mining) and 'Fiji Gold'.[40] These were all positive portrayals of life as a trader or planter, as William C Groves noted: 'What a wonderful life these plantation chaps have. I'd give the world to exchange places with that chap we met to-day.'[41]

Although these examples may reflect the visibility of Australian business and settlement in the Pacific by the 1930s, a brief survey of earlier periodicals with Pacific content suggests that Australian readers were

---

37 Margaret Woodhouse and Robert Langdon, *Pacific Islands Monthly Cumulative Index: Volumes 1 to 15 [August, 1930 to July, 1945]* (Sydney: Pacific Publications, 1968). Most of these articles discussed the copra trade.
38 Quanchi, 'Contrary Images', 78.
39 Johnston and Rolls, *Travelling Home, Walkabout Magazine*, 105.
40 William J Dakin, 'The Story of Nauru', *Walkabout* 1, no. 5 (March 1935): 32–6; DS Askew, 'Vanua-Lava and its Sulphur', *Walkabout* (April 1935): 26–7; William C Groves, 'Life on a Coco-Nut Plantation', *Walkabout* (May 1935): 33–6; Mordecai Baruch, 'Tuamotu Archipelago: Amongst the Pearl Divers', *Walkabout* (January 1936): 45–7; Gerard Dillon, 'The Coco-Nut Tree', *Walkabout* (June 1937): 27–8; Winston H Burchett, 'Cannibals and Talkies', *Walkabout* (October 1938): 41–4; Basil Hall, 'The Tricolour in the South Seas', *Walkabout* (December 1939): 17–20; FI Ryan, 'Fiji Gold', *Walkabout* (August 1940): 15–18.
41 Groves, 'Life on a Coco-nut Plantation', 33.

interested in trade and commerce in the Islands much earlier. *The Lone Hand* (1907–1921), a sister publication of *The Bulletin*, published 22 articles about the Pacific Islands, 10 of which were about trade. This included articles such as 'Fiji Sugar Plantation', 'On a Fijian Cocoanut Plantation', 'Ocean Island and the Phosphate Industry', 'Australia and the Nauru Phosphate Deal' and 'Trading in the South Seas'.[42] Additionally, the *Sea, Land and Air* magazine—which focused mainly on transportation technology between 1919 and 1923—published 27 articles with Pacific Island topics, and six focused on trade or economics. Titles include 'Nauru Island', 'Isles of Pearl and Gold', 'Copra: A Gigantic Tropical Industry', 'Waters of Adventure' and 'Cocoanut Industry in the South Pacific: Its Growth and Possibilities'.[43] This reflects a broader and popular interest in Pacific trade, as well as a patriotic view of Australia's ability to garner these resources. Some magazines emphasised this economic potential as part of a nationalistic message that advocated for Australian development, progress and empire.[44]

Although these general observations may have overwhelmingly presented the Pacific Islands as a region of wealth and prosperity, it is also important to consider the specific historical contexts in which individual observations were made. The attraction of economic prosperity in the Pacific fluctuated in accordance with periods of economic strife in Australia and the Pacific (e.g. the Great Depression). Edward Way Irwin and Ivan Goff left lucrative jobs in Perth in the 1930s to search for adventure; instead, they found depression and unemployment in Fiji. They described struggling to find jobs in Suva, pawning their belongings and raiding the pantry of the boarding house in which they stayed. In their travel account, they wrote: 'Half of Suva was waiting for something to turn up—and so was half the world, it seemed'.[45] John Archibald Fraser, a gold prospector in Fiji, described fluctuations in the number of gold prospectors coming from Australia once news of a new discovery was released. Between 1933

---

42 'Fiji Sugar Plantation', *Lone Hand* (February 1909): 455; Ralph Stock, 'On a Fijian Cocoanut Plantation', *Lone Hand* (March 1912): 349; 'Ocean Island and the Phosphate Industry', *Lone Hand* (November 1912): 42; 'Australia and the Nauru Phosphate Deal', *Lone Hand* (August 1920): 37; Captain Strasburg, 'Trading in the South Seas', *Lone Hand* (November 1918): 508.
43 Thomas J McMahon, 'Nauru Island', *Sea, Land and Air* 1, no. 11 (February 1919): 656–60; Frank Reid, 'Isles of Pearl and Gold', *Sea, Land and Air* 3, no. 36 (March 1921): 759–61; Kat McDowell, 'Copra: A Gigantic Tropical Industry', *Sea, Land and Air* 4, no. 38 (May 1921): 97–101; Frank Reid, 'Waters of Adventure', *Sea, Land and Air* 4, no. 39 (June 1921): 179–81; Thomas J McMahon, 'Cocoanut Industry in the South Pacific: Its Growth and Possibilities', *Sea, Land and Air* 4, no. 47 (February 1922): 813–6.
44 White, *Inventing Australia*, 115.
45 Irwin and Goff, *No Longer Innocent*, 93.

and 1935, Fraser observed the sudden revival of Australian interest in prospecting, noting that 'most of the people we met in Fiji at that time were more or less infected with gold-fever'.[46] Fluctuations in the global economy could also affect Pacific Island economies, such as the fall in copra prices during the 1930s Depression and the general decline in Island trade during the interwar years.[47]

Fiji's proximity to Australia, its British colonial status and its location as a key stopover destination in the Pacific entailed that Australians frequently encountered Australian enterprises there. CSR represented the largest Australian economic interest in the Pacific Islands in 1883, and by 1901, it had invested over £2 million in Fiji.[48] Most of Fiji's imports came from Australia, mostly from New South Wales, prompting the Bank of New South Wales to open branches in Fiji. Australian companies were also invested in the Fiji copra trade and in the gold mining industry for a time. Beatrice Grimshaw's *From Fiji to the Cannibal Islands* directly addressed Fiji's economic potential in 1907. In Fiji, she claimed:

> Withal, there were tens of thousands of acres all over the islands unused and unoccupied; white settlers and planters seldom or never came to try their luck, and the resources of this, the richest of all the rich Pacific archipelagoes, were not one-hundredth part developed.[49]

She later asked, 'Why should these great wastes of grass lie idle?' Such comments intentionally overlooked the prosperous indigenous population who lived on the land and further strengthened colonial claims to own and exploit it. This travel account was one of Grimshaw's many texts that blended personal narrative and commercial advice, as she was frequently commissioned by shipping companies and the Australian government to publish materials that emphasised the potential for economic development and the suitability for white settlement. She published eight prospectus pamphlets, as well as three travel accounts and fictional romances that were 'based on the endeavours of the new planter-settlers and the pioneering fortune-seekers'.[50] Grimshaw did not disguise these ulterior motives from her readers. In her other travelogue, *In the Strange South Seas,* she wrote:

---

46 Fraser, *Gold Dish and Kava Bowl*, 155.
47 Bennett, *Wealth of the Solomons*, 218; Thompson, *Australia and the Pacific Islands in the Twentieth Century*, 94.
48 Thompson, *Australian Imperialism in the Pacific*, 164.
49 Grimshaw, *From Fiji to the Cannibal Islands*, 31.
50 Krauth, *The New Guinea Experience in Literature*, 4. See also Hugh Laracy, 'Beatrice Grimshaw (1870–1953): Pride and Prejudice in Papua', in *Watriama and Co: Further Pacific Islands Portraits* (Canberra: ANU E Press, 2013), doi.org/10.22459/WC.10.2013.

> To find out, as far as possible, what were the prospects for settlers in some of the principal Pacific groups, was the main object of my journey to the Islands. It had always seemed to me that the practical side of Pacific life received singularly little attention, in most books of travel.[51]

Grimshaw was not alone in publishing commercial agendas within travel narratives. Albert Fuller Ellis—an Australian-born prospector who published an account of the phosphate industry in Ocean Island and Nauru at this time—also blatantly emphasised the wealth that could be found in these Islands, which were valuable assets to Australian agriculture and business.[52] The colonial names for Banaba and Nauru belied the devastating environmental damage that was done to the Islands as a result of extensive phosphate mining operations headed by the British-owned Pacific Islands Company (later the Pacific Phosphate Company). These companies employed Australian workers, were headquartered in Australia and exported valuable quantities of phosphate for Australian agricultural use as fertiliser.[53] Both Islands were far from the Australian coast and were relatively small; they were thus rarely visited by Australian travellers, other than those employed by the mining company. These few descriptions of these Islands that featured in Australian literature usually focused on the benefits of mining, such as Thomas McMahon's article on Nauru in the *Penny Pictorial*, titled 'Lets-all-be-thankful Island'.[54] As a journalist and freelance photographer, Thomas McMahon also contributed to a photograph series on the phosphate islands in *The Queenslander* in the same year. Historian Max Quanchi argued that McMahon's career illustrated 'the importance of photography in constructing a colonial and hegemonic representation' of the Pacific.[55]

Ellis's mixture of personal recollections and business history in two books overlooked the exploitation of the Islands' resources, as well as romanticised the role of the prospector:

---

51 Grimshaw, *In the Strange South Seas*, 51.
52 Albert Fuller Ellis, *Ocean Island and Nauru: Their Story* (Sydney: Angus & Robertson, 1935); Albert Fuller Ellis, *Adventuring in Coral Seas* (Sydney: Angus & Robertson, 1936).
53 Thompson, *Australia and the Pacific Islands in the Twentieth Century*, 30, 83, 93.
54 Thomas McMahon, 'Lets-All-Be-Thankful Island', *Penny Pictorial* (September 1919).
55 Max Quanchi, 'Thomas McMahon: Photography as Propaganda in the Pacific Islands', *History of Photography* 21, no. 1 (2015): 42–53, doi.org/10.1080/03087298.1997.10443716; Max Quanchi, 'To the Islands: Photographs of Tropical Colonies in The Queenslander' (paper, 18th Pacific History Association Conference, University of South Pacific, Suva, 2008), 4.

> Prospecting for phosphate gets into the blood … for does it not bring one into close touch with lonely islands, frequently uninhabited, with their possibility of all sorts of discoveries and mysteries?[56]

In doing so, Ellis portrayed the Islanders as primitive and isolated and framed the mining operations as an adventurous endeavour that benefited all those involved. He argued that this was a process in which the Islanders were complicit, as well as one that they found agreeable; he noted that they were 'eager to come into closer touch with civilisation'.[57] Ellis emphasised the development that the mining created—which included the construction of buildings, schools, hospitals, sewers and water storage, as well as the provision of medicine, teachers, missionaries and governance. Consequently, 'it seemed as if a magic wand had been waved, transforming an enforced idle community into an industrious one'.[58] Ellis conveniently ignored the disputes between Australian administrators and Nauruans, as well as the devastating effects of the mining that ultimately stripped 90 per cent of the Islands' surfaces by the time it ceased operating in the 1980s.[59]

The British protectorate of the Solomon Islands was also profitable, its commerce being entirely with Sydney in 1904 and 1905.[60] The copra trade was its most lucrative asset, with many Sydney or Brisbane-based companies invested in planting and trading operations there (most notably Lever Pacific Plantations and subsidiary companies of BP). This development of plantations in the Solomon Islands peaked between 1905 and 1913, with the popular idea of profits being made in the Island group encouraged by books and newspaper articles at the time. Bennett highlighted one full-page spread in the Sydney newspaper, *The Sun*, on 6 August 1910, titled 'The Wealth of the Solomons', which typified the promotions that encouraged Australian investment.[61] The island-hopping schedule of shipping services to the Island group offered travellers opportunities to visit plantations and farmlands, where they would often repeat the narrative of economic prosperity. Coffee was one such traveller, who observed in 1920 that:

---

56 Ellis, *Ocean Island and Nauru*, 51.
57 Ellis, *Ocean Island and Nauru*, 58.
58 Ellis, *Ocean Island and Nauru*, 62.
59 Thompson, *Australia and the Pacific Islands in the Twentieth Century*, 93.
60 Thompson, *Australia and the Pacific Islands in the Twentieth Century*, 28–9.
61 Bennett, *Wealth of the Solomons*, 138.

> In the last twenty years the development has been marvellous ... There are many thousands of acres being developed into well laid-out, well managed cocoanut plantations, some in the first stages, and others already come to fruitful and profitable stages.[62]

Such impressions could meaningfully influence audiences at home, especially when they were published with frequency, and their messages were reinforced with images. Quanchi identified one instance involving a series of articles and 60 photographs that were published in the regional newspaper, *The Queenslander*, in 1917–18 that renewed Australian interest in sub-imperialism in the Solomon Islands.[63]

Although Australian investment and industry in the New Hebrides were not as extensive as it was in the Solomon Islands or Fiji, Australian governments and businesses made considerable efforts to entrench the narrative of economic development there to contest French influence in the Island group. This narrative supported the economic subsidies and settlement schemes for Australians that were launched in response to widespread public opposition to the shared Anglo-French colonial rule from 1887. In the New Hebrides, fertile land and favourable economic conditions were advertised to attract potential settlement; this was part of a broader scheme to bolster British and Australian resident numbers in the Island group. The Australasian New Hebrides Company (ANHC), in which BP had a controlling share, was one company that pushed this narrative from 1889 until its collapse in 1897. In a propaganda pamphlet, it argued that:

> Copra, coffee, ramiefibre, tea, spices and tropical fruits will be the principal produce, and in raising these a great exchange market for Australian produce and merchandise is opened up. The rich volcanic soil will grow almost every tropical product.[64]

The nationalistic tone of these pamphlets reflected the Australian public debate regarding the annexation of the New Hebrides at the time; evidence of this argument can be also be noted in ordinary travel accounts. For example, Thomas's account in 1886 used the natural resources of the

---

62 Coffee, *Forty Years on the Pacific*, 108.
63 Max Quanchi, 'Jewel of the Pacific and Planter's Paradise: The Visual Argument for Australian Sub-Imperialism in the Solomon Islands', *The Journal of Pacific History* 39, no. 1 (2004): 43–58, doi.org/10.1080/00223340410001684840.
64 Australasian New Hebrides Company, *Australia and the New Hebrides* (Sydney: Australasian New Hebrides Company, 1899), 6.

Islands as a justification for their annexation: 'If this were a sample of the soil of the New Hebrides, and if it would last, and not become impoverished, the islands were certainly worth annexing.'[65]

Popular notions of a prosperous settler's life in the New Hebrides continued into the early 1900s. BP attempted another settlement scheme in 1902, when Paterson was invited to accompany the settlers and report on their progress.[66] His account romanticised these men and their journey, which he termed the 'Pilgrims' Progress' in his series for the *Sydney Morning Herald* in July 1902. He described them as 'bona-fide settlers, hard-handed, anxious faced men: they all have a little capital to lose, and they feel the responsibility of their undertaking very keenly'.[67] He returned to Sydney confident that:

> Anything that could be done by a middle-aged Frenchman with a slightly protuberant outline could surely be done by these hard-handed men who had milked cows and shorn sheep and watched over travelling mobs of cattle on the dry stages of the outback.[68]

Paterson's account was not the only one that issued a challenge to enterprising Australian readers. Grimshaw also described 'a veritable gold-mine of copra' in Tanna; although she was concerned about local political instability, she framed this volatility as a challenge to entice readers into action:

> These are the things that mere schoolboys of the British race can do, when you take them away from the grandmammas and aunts at home, and turn them loose in the wilderness to shift for themselves.[69]

Accounts that described the resilience of the Australian trader or planter acquired particular significance in the New Hebrides, where opponents to French rule represented the trader or planter as an innocent victim who was subject to 'one of the most inefficient and unfair systems of government in the civilised world'.[70] However, they also fuelled a broader theme of the 'pioneer planter', who colonised and pacified the Pacific Islands in general.[71]

---

65   Thomas, *Cannibals and Convicts*, 180.
66   Buckley and Klugman, *The History of Burns Philp*, 101.
67   Andrew Barton Paterson, 'The New Hebrides: Voyage of the Pilgrims', *Sydney Morning Herald*, 1 July 1902, 5, nla.gov.au/nla.news-article14468684.
68   Paterson, *The Land of Adventure*.
69   Grimshaw, *From Fiji to the Cannibal Islands*, 312, 198.
70   Marshall, *The Black Musketeers*, 284.
71   Bennett, *Wealth of the Solomons*, 109.

Ultimately, tariffs, British restrictions of labour recruiting, and settlers' lack of capital contributed to the failure of these early settlement schemes. By the 1910s, the French both outnumbered and out-traded the British and Australians. According to Australian resident (and government spy), Wilson le Couteur, there were approximately two French residents to every one English resident in the New Hebrides in 1908.[72] Australian and French allegiance to the Allied cause in World War I also prompted a decline in Australian interest in the New Hebrides. Although public hysteria about the New Hebrides eventually dissipated, some travellers continued to describe the Island group's economic potential in the 1920s and 1930s. With the 'promise to yield handsomely in the near future', Coffee argued, 'The New Hebrides are truly a paradise for planters, and only await a different form of government to make them a desirable place to settle in'.[73] Whether in Fiji, Nauru, Banaba, the Solomon Islands or the New Hebrides, the alluring myth of Pacific Island riches and resources continued to resonate among Australians, despite the increasingly harsh economic realities of Pacific commerce and trade.

Confronting the Realities of Australian Enterprise

Although the bulk of Australian travel writing presented a romantic view of Australian enterprise in the Pacific, some travellers acknowledged the difficulties that workers faced. For example, in 1886, Thomas noted that disease, fear of death and fluctuating copra prices were factors that made a copra trader's life difficult.[74] In 1915, J Mayne Anderson's voyage to the New Hebrides left him with the impression that 'altogether here, as in most countries, the lot of the man on the land is not entirely free from care'.[75] In 1937, Marshall further observed that 'prolonged isolation and monotony have extraordinary effects upon some men'.[76] Unlike the lone pioneers of nineteenth-century trading tales, commercial development in the region by the twentieth century entailed that individual workers faced more competition, regulation and public scrutiny than ever before.[77]

---

72 Wilson le Couteur, 'The New Hebrides: Old Order and New: French Strides Forward', *Sydney Morning Herald*, 29 August 1908, 8, nla.gov.au/nla.news-article15021313.
73 Coffee, *Forty Years on the Pacific*, 106.
74 Thomas, *Cannibals and Convicts*, 245.
75 Anderson, *What a Tourist Sees in the New Hebrides*, 51.
76 Marshall, *The Black Musketeers*, 291.
77 Bennett, *Wealth of the Solomons*, 220.

Close encounters with these Australian workers in the Islands usually stimulated a more realistic portrayal of their characters in travel writing. Not all traders and planters were necessarily heroic, as the Pacific attracted those with criminal backgrounds or opportunists who were broke or desperate.[78] Many workers could appear quite ordinary, as Caroline David observed when meeting an Australian trader in Funafuti in 1897:

> He was not the sort of man that we expected the trader to be: he was neither a low-down ruffian, nor a romantic, adorable scamp, like some novelists' creations; he was just a normal, decent fellow.[79]

In his close encounters with the 'farmers, prospectors, labourers, bushmen, and tradesmen' who participated in a settlement scheme in the New Hebrides, Paterson noted that these men were 'well seasoned to the world's affairs' and that they were very discerning:

> They are decidedly cool-headed men, very unwilling to believe anything till they see it. They seem to have had hard experiences in their lives, and they take all the statements with a grain of salt. They hold a sort of Parliament in the fore-hatch each day, and talk over the maps and pamphlets they have got; also they cross-examine the missionaries who are on board … the French settlers question also troubles their minds a good deal, as they think the French will resent their coming.[80]

These people were uninterested in romantic notions of defending the Australian nation, wrote Paterson; he further noted that 'they want money now, not glory here-after'.

Although some travellers questioned the popular stereotypes underlying these heroic figures, it was the travel accounts of Australians who worked in the Pacific Islands that offered the clearest insights. These Australians possessed 'an astonishing knowledge of the most intimate affairs of his neighbours for several islands around'.[81] Four accounts are illustrative here—two by traders (John Ernest Philp and Joseph HC Dickinson), one by a gold prospector (John Archibald Fraser) and one by a plantation overseer (Walter Gill). These accounts demonstrated the difficulties of commerce that were experienced in the Pacific, despite the popular

---

78 Bennett, *Wealth of the Solomons*, 58.
79 Edgeworth David, *Funafuti*, 131.
80 Paterson, 'The New Hebrides: Voyage of the Pilgrims', 5.
81 Marshall, *The Black Musketeers*, 289.

romanticising of a life of freedom and wealth. Although it can be argued that some of these writers were residents, it is also true that their visits were temporary and that their accounts described the experience of travel within the Islands. As such, they are considered part of the broad and ambiguous category of travel writing.

Philp's unpublished log recorded his daily life as a roving trader in the Solomon Islands during the 1910s. Philp had worked as a railway surveyor in Tasmania before leaving his wife and family in 1912 to be a copra trader and labour recruiter in the Solomon Islands for two years.[82] He arrived in the Pacific eight years after the labour trade in Queensland had been terminated. Philp would thus have been aware of the heroic and villainous representations of labour recruiters during the fierce public debate about the Queensland labour trade in the late nineteenth century.

Philp's account of his travels through the Solomon Islands was marked by a certain mundanity that was distinct from published accounts. Although he read other popular travel accounts (including those of Grimshaw and Becke), his own account contained short and simple observations that consisted of little embellishment or personal reflection. In fact, he was critical of the popular accounts of amateurs who drifted through the Islands. He called US author Jack London's description of the Solomon Islands a 'piffle', noting that it was 'reckoned a huge joke' by the residents.[83] He also crossed the paths of several other travel writers, including those of Martin and Osa Johnson (US authors and filmmakers), that of Clifford Collinson (British author) and those of Muspratt and Dickinson (Australian workers). Philp's log has since been used to highlight the exaggerations and inaccuracies that are contained within these travel accounts.[84]

Philp's experience of the Solomon Islands was generally positive, diverging from the conventional notions of hostile and savage Melanesians. Apart from some difficulties that he experienced when trading with locals whom he described as 'cheeky' or 'hard bargainers', Philp himself rarely experienced violence (noting that his recruits were 'all very jolly').[85] Though he recalled many past events of conflict at each Island that he

---

82 John Ernest Philp, *A Solomons Sojourn: J. E. Philp's Log of the Makira, 1912–1913*, ed. Richard Allen Herr and E Anne Rood (Hobart: Tasmanian Historical Research Association, 1978).
83 Philp, *A Solomons Sojourn*, 112.
84 As described by Richard Allen Herr and E. Anne Rood in Philp, *A Solomons Sojourn*, 15.
85 Philp, *A Solomons Sojourn*, 42, 88, 93.

visited, the Islanders and Europeans were more familiar with one another by 1912. His prosperous time in the Islands was not always shared by the resident traders and plantation overseers whom he visited, including Dick Richardson, Frank B Rigby and Dickinson. His interactions with them demonstrate that Europeans were vulnerable to violence, illness and commercial strife. As Bennett's history of the Solomon Islands revealed, European residents were susceptible to local politics, to competition with other traders, planters or prospectors, and to conflict with other resident Europeans (especially missionaries). These European residents were also constrained by government regulations; they were often beholden to their investors or to employers in Australia. Fluctuating trade prices and shifts in supply and demand, both in Australia and in the Islands, could have had devastating effects as well.[86]

Dickinson's account, like Philp's, also stressed the hardships that he faced as a resident trader, planter and labour recruiter in the Solomon Islands in the 1910s and 1920s. Typical of many peripatetic workers in the Pacific Islands, Dickinson regularly travelled between Australia and various Islands, so it is difficult to assess whether his account should be counted as travel writing. Although his *A Trader in the Savage Solomons* (1927) was a more exciting and exaggerated account that was published for a wider audience, he framed the account as a response to the negative depictions of traders:

> There are missionaries, authors and American movie artists, who present to civilization a given type of white man who serves them as an asset for the collection of dollars. The South Sea trader is generally made to lend the colour. We see or hear of him exploiting the natives, and committing all kinds of villainy. Native girls are his pet diversion. A blackguard of the deepest dye. You may even see him knocked down on the movies by an admirable hero, and just in the nick of time.[87]

Dickinson argued instead that 'the trader in everyday life is the least able to defend himself'.[88] His experience stressed the vulnerability of the white trader and of his role as a mediator in the Islands, in which he often deftly negotiated with potentially hostile Islanders. He was aware of the conflicts between Europeans and Islanders, as well as the internal tribal

---

86   Bennett, *Wealth of the Solomons*, 46–54.
87   Dickinson, *A Trader in the Savage Solomons*, 80.
88   Dickinson, *A Trader in the Savage Solomons*, 81.

feuds. In one example from March 1909, he described the process of negotiating a truce during a Malaitan war council to prevent a revenge attack on a corrupt German resident. He also described encounters with local residents, noting that the most common struggles that they faced were debt and misunderstandings with Islanders.[89]

Although Dickinson may have presented his work as an authentic depiction of life in the Pacific Islands, his impressions are distinct from those of Philp's because he often portrayed himself as heroic. This was most clearly demonstrated when he described the Union Jack that flew above the British governor's residence in the capital, Tulagi:

> It floats high above the tree-tops in a little-known, savage land; for it signifies protection over its people, along with the advance-guard of pioneers, and those which follow them ... Beneath its shadow the pioneer and settler knows that there should be one of the Empire's representatives, who, traditions have taught them, will reflect what the flag stands for, and who, when they are in need, will extend assistance, sympathy and encouragement.[90]

Perhaps this patriotic emphasis explains why Dickinson did not mention any quarrels with British officials or missionaries—in fact, he had praised them. His heroism was further supported by his observations of Pacific Islanders, which repeated the usual stereotypes of Melanesian savagery.

Fraser's travel impressions while prospecting for gold offers a more nuanced account of Fijians and of Australian mining endeavours in Fiji during the 1930s. Born in Victoria, Fraser was an experienced miner who visited Fiji twice as a gold prospector. He first travelled to Tavua for nine months in 1933, then again with his brother in 1935, during which time he travelled extensively around Viti Levu. Gold was discovered in Viti Levu in 1932, and by 1935, there were 22 gold mining companies in Fiji, most of which were financed in Australia; this included the two most dominant companies, Emperor Gold Mining Company and Loloma Gold Mines.[91] After a year in Fiji, Fraser prospected in Guadalcanal in the Solomon Islands, but returned to Australia unsuccessful. Following his death in World War II, his manuscript was published posthumously in 1954 under the title *Gold Dish and Kava Bowl*. Fraser's account offers

---

89 Dickinson, *A Trader in the Savage Solomons*, 111, 118.
90 Dickinson, *A Trader in the Savage Solomons*, 29–30.
91 Thompson, *Australia and the Pacific Islands in the Twentieth Century*, 20–1.

insights about the practices of prospecting, the constant disappointment that miners experienced, the struggles of living and working with little financial support, the isolation that was felt, the conflict among miners that was experienced and the fervour that drove many inexperienced Australians and New Zealanders to try their luck. He wrote:

> Gold-seeking in these scattered island-groups had its difficulties. Their distance from main centres of industry, the rugged and jungle nature of the country, the tropical climate with its scorching heat and drenching rains, and the prevalence of malaria and other tropical diseases all combined to make the search for gold a costly and hazardous enterprise.[92]

Despite these difficulties, Fraser enjoyed living abroad and the opportunity for intimate encounters with Islanders. When he was not prospecting at work, Fraser was actively travelling to local villages, exploring along the coast and in the mountains and conversing with his Islander workers:

> There was also a language to be learned, and a happy and likeable race of people to become better acquainted with, who still retained enough loyalty to their old traditions to make them intensely interesting.[93]

He maintained good relations with the 'boys' who worked for him and considered them excellent craftsmen and workers, 'kindly, courteous, patient, and good-tempered'. Contrary to many accounts of allegedly lazy and indolent workers, Fraser described them as hard working, even competing among themselves to determine who could lift the heaviest load.[94]

Fraser also travelled through inland Fiji and gained a more thorough understanding of indigenous Fijians than most tourists did. In doing so, he sympathised with the plight of the Fijian:

> I think that a white man coming to know the Fijian well might sometimes feel, as Kipling's soldier did about brown-skinned brother: 'You're a better man than I am, Gunga Din!'[95]

---

92 Fraser, *Gold Dish and Kava Bowl*, 239.
93 Fraser, *Gold Dish and Kava Bowl*, 93.
94 Fraser, *Gold Dish and Kava Bowl*, 81–2, 97.
95 Fraser, *Gold Dish and Kava Bowl*, 131.

He noted that ownership of land was often a cause of Islander dissension, though he also conceded that it was a difficult job for government surveyors to resolve. His admiration of Fijian villages contrasted his distaste for the urban environment of Suva. Specifically, he was critical of ignorant Australian tourists there. On one occasion, he observed a Methodist ship from Australia that unloaded 400 passengers to celebrate the Church's centenary, who consumed the village's entire stock of food in the process.[96] His reflection on whether any tourists ever send the photos that they take back to the Islands was unusual for his time.[97] Fraser's sensitive account of Fiji and his overall harmonious experience with the Islanders contradicted popular tales of Australian miners who battled hostile tribes in the Pacific, as well as romantic notions of Australians finding untold riches in the Islands.

Idealistic preconceptions of commerce in the region overlooked the violence and abuse of Pacific labourers that frequently occurred under the supervision of white planters and overseers. Many of the plantations were in remote rural areas, where such abuses could be carefully hidden from plain view, and few travellers could stay long enough to observe the relationships between white supervisors and their local subordinates. This explains why Australian travel writing offers few details about certain operations, such as those of CSR, a vast organisation that employed many Australians to work in Fiji. Instead, historians like Michael Moynagh have used company archives to understand how CSR 'demanded of their subordinates hard work, honesty and, above all, dedication to the company', with Brij V Lal illuminating how the exploitative policies of CSR affected the lives of Indian indentured labourers in Fiji.[98] The account of Walter Gill, who worked as an overseer from 1915 to 1926, draws attention to the difficulty that Australian employees experienced in satisfying the demands of their employers and in maintaining control over a local labour force in the Islands. Published in 1970 with the benefit of hindsight and a more progressive readership, Gill's recollections of sexual liaisons, abuse and physical violence are useful for considering the issues that were omitted or disguised in travel accounts, as well as the difficulties that Australians experienced in negotiating and justifying colonial relationships abroad.

---

96   Fraser, *Gold Dish and Kava Bowl*, 213.
97   Fraser, *Gold Dish and Kava Bowl*, 68.
98   Michael Moynagh, *Brown or White?: A History of the Fiji Sugar Industry, 1873–1973* (Canberra: Pacific Research Monograph, The Australian National University, 1981), 28; Lal, *Broken Waves*.

Gill recalled that his experiences were very challenging; he had significant responsibilities and struggled to maintain an obedient and efficient Indian labour force that had been imported by the British to work on Fiji's sugar plantations from 1879 to 1916. In his early 20s, Gill was young, naive and unaware of the complex racial and religious divisions that existed among the workers. He held a disparaging view of most of the workers, describing them as 'feral unpredictables', 'apes' and 'cramped maggots in cell-like hutments'; he often felt isolated and vulnerable as the lone white man among them, noting, 'I lived in their jungle as one of them'.[99] Incidences of violence were common, such as one fight in which Gill disarmed a worker who threatened him with a knife. Moynagh has shown that:

> Growers saw the overseer as a man who acted arbitrarily, who demanded of them work which they were reluctant to perform, and who used brute force at times to ensure that his orders were carried out.[100]

Additionally, Gill described the numerous instances of suicide, murder, sexual abuse, prostitution, disease, drunkenness and a constant power struggle between 'sirdars' (Indian supervisors) and European overseers.

Gill also documented his struggle to satisfy the demands of CSR and to implement his required role in a business with which he had begun to disagree fundamentally. Gill increasingly felt alienated from the company and other Europeans, writing that 'among my own countrymen I had made few friends; a pattern which was to remain constant over the years'.[101] This disillusionment, compounded by the close relationships he developed with some of his employees, forced Gill to reconsider the merits of indentured labour:

> If we, the overseers and sirdars caught up in the rotten system of indenture servitude fathered by Big Business on that most fecund of whores, cheap Asiatic labour, had managed to survive in the tooth-and-claw jungle of the cane game, it was only by out-animalizing the horde of near-human apes in our charge.[102]

---

99 Gill, *Turn North-East at the Tombstone*, 38.
100 Moynagh, *Brown or White?*, 130.
101 Gill, *Turn North-East at the Tombstone*, 32.
102 Gill, *Turn North-East at the Tombstone*, 65.

It is unclear whether this reflects the pressures of the working environment at the time or a more conciliatory attitude that was made in hindsight to defend his actions. Nonetheless, Gill's account draws attention to the darker and exploitative side of Australian commercial enterprise in the Pacific, which conventional travel writing has avoided.

Travel writing by 'enterprising' Australian workers in the Pacific must be carefully examined for what it omits—notably these workers' relationship with women. Sexual liaisons between European men and local women (including Islanders and other non-Europeans) were notable only for their omission from most Australian travel accounts, likely because it was a subject of impropriety. Images of the Pacific often separated the white men from Pacific women, and it was unusual for travellers to publish photographs of intimate interracial mixing. British traveller Richard Reynell Bellamy believed that progressive French attitudes to 'sex and other veiled subjects' were superior to the British 'hush-hush attitude'.[103] Although intimate encounters between Australian workers and Islanders were rarely recorded, it is important to understand that 'sex, commerce and labour are inextricably connected in these networks of exchange'.[104] Travellers' observations of 'half-castes' and venereal diseases in the Pacific also highlight the prevalence of these sexual encounters.

Although tourists visiting the Islands imagined sexual transgressions, these intimate encounters tended to be more common among long-term residents than temporary visitors. This was due to the nature of employment in the Islands, as traders, planters and overseers were in regular contact with local females. This is reflected in the numerous descriptions of the trader or planter and his 'native wife'.[105] Sydney Walter Powell was surprised when he met a couple in the Tuamotus and realised that she 'was not the shrinking half-wild creature commonly presented in South Sea stories as "the trader's wife"'.[106] In fact, popular fictional tales of traders in the Pacific did not always employ 'native' women as tools to reinforce traditional gender roles. Such ambiguities and contradictions have even been found in the works of Becke.[107]

---

103 Bellamy, *Mixed Bliss in Melanesia*, 118.
104 Dixon, *Writing the Colonial Adventure*, 185.
105 Gunga, *Narrative of a Trip from Maryborough to New Caledonia*, 18; Osborne, *Through the Atolls of the Line*, 9; Irwin and Goff, *No Longer Innocent*, 47.
106 Powell, *Adventures of a Wanderer*, 232.
107 Sturma, *South Sea Maidens*, 110–11; Thomas and Eves, *Bad Colonists*, 144.

The marriage of European workers and residents to non-Europeans in the Islands was generally not frowned upon in Australian travel writing because the life of a trader or planter was acknowledged as lonely and 'to take a white wife there is also almost impracticable'.[108] However, bringing wives to Australia could create complications, as Joseph Hadfield Grundy observed when he met a 35-year-old trader who married a 'native woman', but who remained in the New Hebrides because she 'could not live in Australia being as Asiatic'.[109] These interracial relationships were not always sustainable, nor were husbands or wives necessarily expected to be lifelong partners. Dickinson fell in love with one woman, Tora-kene, but soon abandoned her in response to threats from other Islanders.[110] Becke married Nelea Tikena in Kiribati in 1881, but did not bring her to Australia, and then remarried soon after returning home.[111] Safroni-Middleton noted in 1915 that it was common for both European men and Islander women to have multiple partners.[112] These instances reveal the complexities of cross-cultural encounters that unsettled the simplified stereotype of the Australian male worker in the Pacific Islands. They also highlight the vulnerabilities of the supposedly heroic trader, planter, overseer and prospector as he tried to navigate the expectations and moral codes of two different worlds.

Due to its close proximity to the Pacific, Australian commercial enterprise in the region played a significant role in the new nation's development. For the well-established colonial powers of France, Germany and Great Britain, commercial activities in the Pacific were regarded as being within the context of much larger global networks; as such, the Pacific Islands were often marginalised or overlooked. Economic ventures were often small in scale, and short lived, with the distance from Europe reducing profit margins, making communication difficult and discouraging prospective settlers. For colonial Australians in the late nineteenth century, the Pacific was closer and more lucrative. It is thus unsurprising that opportunistic travellers who sought employment or fortune preceded the holiday-makers and tourists. Pacific commerce was so important to the Australian colonies that those who made the journey became trusted sources of information. The literary legacy of Louis Becke is a testament

---

108 Grundy, *The New Hebrides Group of Islands*, 6.
109 Grundy, *The New Hebrides Group of Islands*, 6.
110 Dickinson, *A Trader in the Savage Solomons*, 80.
111 Sturma, *South Sea Maidens*, 112.
112 Safroni-Middleton, *Sailor and Beachcomber*, 150.

to this; his distinct representations of the trader or planter in the Pacific formed the foundation for a broader imagining of the Pacific as a region of economic potential that was privileged for Australians. The archetype of the European trader was modified into the figure of the enterprising Australian in the early twentieth century. This individual reflected the nationalistic, masculine and racial ideals that existed within Australian society at the time. He also served as a convenient tool for promoting commercial development in the Pacific. Australian governments and businesses used travel writers and travel literature to encourage investment and public interest in the region by framing the Islands as available and rich in natural resources. In doing so, they portrayed Australia as an emerging centre of the region.

Closely analysing the firsthand accounts of these Australian travellers who sought economic prosperity in the Islands reveals that reality rarely met expectations and that the enterprising Australian was often vulnerable and unsuccessful rather than heroic. Nonetheless, the promise of a profitable Pacific remained consistent throughout the early twentieth century. Although readers of the interwar period grew weary of the market's saturation with predictable travel literature, the lived experiences of Australian workers in the Pacific continued to be considered a sign of authenticity. They privileged their accounts above the momentary observations of the steamer tourist. For audiences living abroad, stories of Australian enterprise in the Pacific continued to satisfy a market for the 'colonial exotic', as well as provide information about rapidly changing economic developments in the region. In times of economic hardship or instability, these stories offered hope to Australian readers.

6

Conflict, Convicts and the Condominium

> Everyone knows that 'La Nouvelle', as it is popularly called, is a French penal settlement, and thereby hangs a tale.[1]

> It was September 1905. The Anglo-French Convention, so Australians hoped, would get to work on the New Hebridean question almost immediately … Altogether, the New Hebrides were providing much food for talk and guesswork. It was an odd fact, under the circumstances, that no one really knew anything to speak of about the place.[2]

The French colonial presence in New Caledonia and the New Hebrides meant that Australian representations of these two Island groups would be distinct from any other Pacific Islands. In contrast to French Polynesia and Tahiti—which were represented as ideal, romantic and remote destinations—New Caledonia and the New Hebrides were widely perceived as posing an imminent threat to mainland Australia in the late nineteenth and early twentieth centuries. Australian travel accounts of these Islands were markedly different from those of British and French literature because they reflected national anxieties and fears that were felt about French colonial rule from 1880 to 1914. As suggested by the two quotations at the beginning of this chapter, provided by two Australian travellers in 1906 and 1907, respectively, Australians were preoccupied with French convicts in New Caledonia and in the joint Anglo-French

---
1 Wragge, *The Romance of the South Seas*, 3.
2 Grimshaw, *From Fiji to the Cannibal Islands*, 166.

political system in the New Hebrides. Although public interest in these Island groups peaked in the late nineteenth century, travel accounts continued to remind Australians of the French colonial legacy in the Pacific until World War I.

Australian representations of New Caledonia and the New Hebrides were marked by three main themes: conflict, convicts and the condominium. These themes were not mutually exclusive; rather, they overlapped and reappeared in the travel accounts of colonial Australians from the late nineteenth century and in the accounts of Australian nationals from the early twentieth century. Since the 1870s, colonial Australians were aware that New Caledonia and the New Hebrides were more closely tied by steamship routes—not only in the physical sense but also politically, economically and culturally. As such, colonial Australian observations of conflict between French settlers and Islanders in New Caledonia in the nineteenth century reflected greater concerns about the legitimacy of French colonial rule in the New Hebrides. Convicts were another persistent theme in New Caledonia, but how they were portrayed shifted from a perceived threat in the nineteenth century to a historical attraction in the twentieth century. This reflected New Caledonia's increasing popularity as a tourist destination for Australians by the early 1900s. Although convicts and conflict were clearly associated with New Caledonia, travellers' descriptions of the New Hebrides were more ambiguous. Their reactions to the joint Anglo-French condominium were characterised by confusion and uncertainty due to the diverse nature of the Island group, as well as the unresolved nature of the agreement. These sentiments existed despite the increasing number of travellers to the region and the widespread publicity of the expansion of French interests in New Caledonia and the New Hebrides. Since Australian interest in these Islands had significantly diminished by World War I, Australian travel accounts offer the most significant insights into the period from the 1870s to the 1910s. They are presented here in a loosely chronological order, commencing with French colonial rule in New Caledonia, then its rule in the New Hebrides and concludes with a discussion of tourism development in Noumea in the early 1900s.

Conflict and Convicts in New Caledonia

Situated only 1,500 km east of the Australian coast, New Caledonia was of great public interest to the Australian colonies in the mid to late nineteenth century. However, limited travel writing about it before 1900 exists. Of the 19 accounts that have described travels to New Caledonia, three were published between 1880 and 1899, nine between 1900 and 1914 and seven between 1915 and 1941. Although New Caledonia may not have been the preferred holiday destination at this time, it had sustained contact with colonial Australians from the 1840s. This was mostly done in the form of the sandalwood and *bêche-de-mer* traders, LMS and Marist missionaries.[3] Colonial Australians also travelled to New Caledonia as labour traders, though New Caledonia was a site for deploying rather than recruiting labour. The systematic recruiting of labour for New Caledonia began in 1865 to help develop the colony, with most of these recruits drawn from the New Hebrides, Solomon Islands and Gilbert Islands. Some indigenous people from New Caledonia travelled as ships' crews, with Loyalty Islanders possessing a positive reputation among Europeans as seamen.[4] The mining industry's development encouraged the continuation of the labour trade to extend beyond the 1940s, as well as to support British and Australian prospectors and entrepreneurs (though the scale of settlement was limited).

It was not until the 1880s that a regular steamship service brought more colonial Australians into contact with New Caledonia. From 1882 onwards, French-owned MM operated a service between Sydney and New Caledonia's main port, Noumea. This was followed by a service provided by AUSN from 1887. Noumea was often a layover port on the journey to the New Hebrides, stimulating comparisons in colonial Australian travel accounts between the two Island groups. Few travellers went beyond the mainland (Grand Terre) to visit nearby Islands such as the Loyalty Islands or the Isle of Pines.

---

3   Dorothy Shineberg, *They Came For Sandalwood: A Study of the Sandalwood Trade in the South-West Pacific, 1830–1865* (Melbourne: Melbourne University Press, 1967); Dorothy Shineberg, *The People Trade: Pacific Island Laborers and New Caledonia, 1865–1930* (Honolulu: University of Hawai'i Press, 1999), 11–12, doi.org/10.1515/9780824864910.
4   For examples, see Thomas, *Cannibals and Convicts*, 147; Wragge, *The Romance of the South Seas*, 33.

Since its annexation in 1853, the French occupation of New Caledonia was widely perceived within the Australian colonies as a potential strategic threat to the Australian mainland—which was a view encouraged by sensationalised and speculative media reports. This concern was exacerbated by the commencement of penal resettlement to the French territory in May 1864; it fostered further antagonism in the Australian colonies, which fed into the growing federation movement from the 1880s. Alexis Bergantz's historical study of French-ness in Australia identified the important role that New Caledonia played in the development of a national consciousness in the Australian colonies—a point, he argued, that has been overlooked in favour of other imperial rivalries.[5] Public record reveals that New Caledonia was a popular issue of debate at the time, as journalist Frank Fox noted in 1911: 'One result of the existence of this French penal settlement in New Caledonia was to hasten the growth of Australian Federal sentiment'.[6] The popularity of invasion narratives in the late nineteenth century also encouraged the idea that New Caledonia could be used as a staging ground for invasion.[7] The hostile public response was distinct from the benign reactions to the establishment of other French colonies—including those to the annexation of Tahiti in 1880, followed by those to the Gambier, Austral and Tuamotu groups in 1881 and to the creation of protectorates over Wallis and Futuna in 1886. Not only was French Polynesia beyond the Australian colonies' sphere of interest, it was also not as developed nor as highly populated by the French.

Colonial Australians' travel writing about New Caledonia in the 1880s and 1890s is marked by a general theme of conflict that reflected greater concerns. Conflict was often predicted, and occasionally observed, between several parties: the Australian colonies, the French and British governments, French colonial administrators, missionaries, convicts and the indigenous people. Travellers frequently and interchangeably used the Hawaiian term 'kanaka' and the New Caledonian term 'kanak' to describe the indigenous people. Australian journalist John Stanley James wrote extensively about his travels in New Caledonia in the 1870s and 1880s. His commentary offers glimpses into the colonial Australian perceptions that were prevalent in the public sphere during this time.

---

5   Alexis Bergantz, 'French Connection: The Culture and Politics of Frenchness in Australia, 1890–1914' (PhD thesis, The Australian National University, 2015), 56.
6   Fox, *Oceania*, 17.
7   Bergantz, 'French Connection', 63.

Born in England in 1843, James moved to Australia in 1875 when he became moneyless due to wandering across Europe and the US as a self-styled 'vagabond' and journalist. He began working for the *Melbourne Punch*, then for the *Argus* in 1876, writing under the pseudonyms of 'Julian Thomas' and 'the Vagabond'. James's popularity peaked at the end of 1876, partly due to a public fascination with his anonymity, as well as the resonance that his subject matter had with the colonial Australian middle class.[8] James made several trips to the Pacific Islands, which were sponsored by local newspapers, including a trip in 1878 to report on indigenous rebellions against French colonial rule in New Caledonia. His observations were widely circulated in newspapers and in his own publications, such as the travelogue *Cannibals and Convicts* (1886). Consequently, James's impressions of the Pacific Islands were a mix of journalistic reporting and personal narrative. James's travelogue was unillustrated, most likely due to the limitations of photographic technology at the time. However, he was visually represented inside the cover among a series of key protagonists in Pacific politics at the time.

In his self-published materials, James described himself as a journalist 'first and foremost', proudly claiming to be the only reporter to visit New Caledonia and the New Hebrides in 1886. He alleged that he was one of:

> That noble army of Special Correspondents who, taking their lives in their hands, amidst battle, murder, and sudden death, provide[d] not only news, but solid information, for the breakfast-tables of the world.[9]

Although James professed a desire to be impartial, he often had to negotiate the demands of his sponsors, choosing at times to oppose the popular views among specific editors and readerships. This included criticising British rule in Fiji in 1880 and defending the methods of Australian recruiters in the New Hebrides. His biographer, Michael Cannon, described his views as being 'liberal, conservative, free trade and anti-church'.[10] James's popularity and authority entailed that his reports were influential in informing colonial Australians about New Caledonia at

---

8   Michael Cannon, 'Introduction', in *The Vagabond Papers*, ed. Michael Cannon (Melbourne: Hyland House, 1983), 5. In previous chapters, I have referred to James by his own chosen pseudonym. However, in this chapter, I will refer to him as 'James' in the text and by his chosen pseudonym in the footnote.
9   Thomas, *Cannibals and Convicts*, vii.
10 Cannon, 'Introduction', 5.

a time when public interest in the group peaked. His role was particularly significant, given the limited number of existing travel accounts on the topic of New Caledonia in the late nineteenth century.

James detailed his travels to New Caledonia in 1878 and 1883 in *Cannibals and Convicts,* parts of which were published in the *Australasian* and *Melbourne Argus.* He had also mentioned his travels to Fiji, the New Hebrides and New Guinea, with a conclusion that described his views regarding Australian Federation and colonialism in the Pacific. Sailing on the *Gunga* from Sydney on 20 July 1878, James made the following remark after arriving in Noumea: 'New Caledonia is a land of the gum-tree and the convict; but there its similarity to early Australia ceases'.[11] His account was typical of many subsequent travel accounts that immediately characterised the Island as a penal settlement. His remarks noting the Island's geographical proximity to Australia, its resources (he identified mining as valuable) and its history of contact with Europeans were also repeated in other colonial Australian accounts. These observations not only informed but subtly conveyed a sense of conflict and antagonism between the French and the Australian colonies. For example, a school textbook in 1888 educated colonial Australians about Captain Cook's discovery of New Caledonia in September 1774 and about the 'unjust' nature of French annexation on 24 September 1853, which was similar to James's assertion of Great Britain's claim by 'right of discovery'.[12] Although James felt no open hostility after arriving (noting the helpful assistance that the French authorities offered to him), a certain tension was evident. He reported that his telegrams home were suppressed by the French, who restricted him from publishing his accounts until his return.

When James arrived in 1878, the tension between French settlers (who had arrived in growing numbers since annexation) and the Kanaks (whose land they had alienated) exploded, led by a significant chief named Atai. Historians have since revealed that European representations of this conflict that occurred between French colonial masters and Kanak resistance were not accurate. Rather, political alliances in New Caledonia

---

11   Thomas, *Cannibals and Convicts*, 46.
12   William Wilkins, *Australasia: A Descriptive and Pictorial Account of the Australian and New Zealand Colonies, Tasmania and the Adjacent Lands* (London: Blackie & Son, 1888), 236; Thomas, *Cannibals and Convicts*, 47.

were much more complex.¹³ For audiences in the Australian continent who were curious about their colonial neighbours, the 1878 rebellion was but one of a series of well-publicised conflicts since 1856 that was oversimplified in the press as a struggle between French civilisation and Melanesian savagery.

In general, James provided a damning account of French colonial rule during his visit to New Caledonia. Sent to report on the so-called 'native insurrection' in New Caledonia, James arrived one month after the French governor, Jean Baptiste Léon Olry, announced the outbreak of war. His first impressions of Noumea described French residents and officials, but Kanaks were not visible in the capital, despite numbering 60,000, as estimated by James.¹⁴ He was transported from Noumea with French soldiers to one of four fronts at Bouloupari. Over several months, James studied 'how France treats a native population', which involved observing French military tactics, accompanying patrols, visiting local villages of both French settlers and Kanaks and meeting Kanak chiefs and French military commanders.

James portrayed the ongoing conflict as a bloody battle 'with over 200 [French] massacred in one week'—with even more deadly reprisals by the French and evidence of casualties on both sides.¹⁵ In his reporting of the revolt, James noted the French side's poor military tactics and lack of knowledge of the interior. This assessment was accurate, given that French settlement and exploration of the northern inland areas were limited before the conflict.¹⁶ He was also critical of the brutality and unprofessionalism that French forces displayed, describing how French soldiers destroyed houses and crops and killed people indiscriminately and without trial: '"Man, woman, and child must be exterminated," was the cry of most of the gallant soldiers of France … It seemed to me that nearly

---

13   See Bronwen Douglas, 'Conflict and Alliance in a Colonial Context', *The Journal of Pacific History* 15, no. 1 (1980): 21–51; Bronwen Douglas, 'Winning and Losing? Reflections on the War of 1878–79 in New Caledonia', *The Journal of Pacific History* 26, no. 2 (1991): 213–33, doi.org/10.1080/00223349108572664; Bronwen Douglas, 'Fighting as Savagery and Romance: New Caledonia Past and Present', in *Reflections on Violence in Melanesia*, ed. Sinclair Dinnen and Allison Ley (Leichhardt: Hawkins Press, 2000), 53–64; Linda Latham, 'Revolt Re-Examined: The 1878 Insurrection in New Caledonia', *The Journal of Pacific History* 10, no. 3 (1975): 48–63, doi.org/10.1080/00223347508572278; Adrian Muckle, *Specters of Violence in a Colonial Context: New Caledonia, 1917* (Honolulu: University of Hawai'i Press, 2012).
14   Thomas, *Cannibals and Convicts*, 42.
15   Thomas, *Cannibals and Convicts*, 48.
16   Douglas, 'Conflict and Alliance', 41.

everyone in Noumea was mad'.[17] In one case at Teremba, James described the death of five Kanaks, including a 13-year-old boy, by firing squad without trial for the alleged murder of an ex-convict. James described the trial and subsequent execution of the men as 'an act illogical, unjust, and useless in its results [which] … to my dying day they will haunt me'.[18] These observations, which highlighted the brutality of French colonial rule, were repeated by a colonial Australian mining prospector who wrote under the pseudonym 'Gunga'. He witnessed 'frightful heart-rending scenes' during the 1878 rebellion and blamed the French in the conclusion to his travel account: 'If I was asked what brought about the revolt I should say ill treatment, unfair treatment, unjust treatment of the natives, by the Government and by the settlers themselves'.[19]

James' representation of the Kanaks was more ambiguous; he sympathised with those who supported the French and portrayed the others as conventional savages and cannibals. By admiring the physical characteristics of the Kanaks whom he met in French-controlled camps and villages, James contrasted them to the savage behaviours of the French settlers and soldiers. When travelling inland with Kanak guides who were assisting the French, James described them as a 'picturesque sight', and when meeting some chiefs at a French camp, he remarked:

> Naked and not ashamed, their supple, lithe, well-proportioned figures were beautiful to look upon. I have seen many a dusky warrior, whose form would have served the Grecian sculptor of old as a model for Apollo.[20]

However, other descriptions of beheadings, ambushes and people whom he claimed were 'as ugly a "nigger" as you could find in the world' betrayed James's deeply held conservative and racist views of Pacific Islanders being inferior.[21] Although he acknowledged the confusion of guerrilla warfare in the New Caledonian theatre, his observations of Melanesian fighting tactics being cowardly and primitive were consistent with other European descriptions. Bronwen Douglas and Adrian Muckle have since demonstrated the soundness of guerrilla tactics that the Kanaks used to resist French rule.[22]

---

17 Thomas, *Cannibals and Convicts*, 79.
18 Thomas, *Cannibals and Convicts*, 89–93.
19 Gunga, *Narrative of a Trip from Maryborough to New Caledonia*, 5.
20 Thomas, *Cannibals and Convicts*, 105, 197.
21 Thomas, *Cannibals and Convicts*, 21, 25.
22 Douglas, 'Conflict and Alliance'; Muckle, *Specters of Violence*.

Although news of the 1878 insurrection was highly publicised in the Australian colonies and contributed to notions of Melanesian savagery and French incompetence, a more serious threat was perceived in the convicts who were sent to New Caledonia. Colonial Australians had been opposed to the transportation of French convicts since the first convoy of 248 *bagnards* arrived in 1864. However, the expansion of the penal colony to accommodate convicted reoffenders reignited opposition in the 1880s. These criminals were especially feared in the Australian colonies, with James having described the recidivist as 'an outlaw of society, the scum which floats on the surface of civilisation'.[23] James highlighted the danger that the *bagnards* and recidivists posed by attributing them characteristics that were usually used for Melanesians: 'Thinking of the combined convict and cannibal Pierre, I was forced to the conclusion that New Caledonia sheltered a large number of most objectionable neighbours to Australia'.[24] James argued that convicts in such close proximity to the Australian continent would be considered a threat for two reasons:

> Here, on the island of [Île] Nou, one reflected that the danger to Australia was not only in the escape of the convicts (and scores have escaped and landed on our shores), but in the use to which they might be put in time of war … It may be said that France would hardly arm her convicts against Australia; but all is fair in love and war.[25]

Sensationalised press reports inflamed these concerns, with reports on escaped convicts reaching the Australian mainland and suggestions that the New Hebrides could become another penal settlement.

Realistically, the French threat to Australian security was overstated. Although several prisoners did escape to the Australian mainland, most who reached the shore had already served their terms or had been pardoned. Robert Aldrich argued that few, if any, posed any real threat to the Australian colonies.[26] Migration was even encouraged by ambiguous French laws regarding emancipists. These *libérés,* who were unpopular in New Caledonia and who struggled to find employment, were allowed to leave New Caledonia, provided that they did not return to France and

---

23 Thomas, *Cannibals and Convicts*, 144.
24 Thomas, *Cannibals and Convicts*, 113.
25 Thomas, *Cannibals and Convicts*, 120–1.
26 Robert Aldrich, *The French Presence in the South Pacific, 1842–1940* (Basingstoke: Palgrave Macmillan, 1990), 225.

that they returned to the colony only after three years.[27] Additionally, the number of French-born residents in the Australian colonies was relatively small, and their European background allowed them to assimilate within the community easily. Therefore, they did not constitute a threat as much as other more populous and non-white ethnic groups were perceived to.[28]

Due to James's travels, extensive publications and public reputation, he became an influential observer of New Caledonian affairs. His criticisms of French colonial expansion in the Pacific reflected broader colonial Australian public sentiment in the 1880s and 1890s. By drawing on conventional notions of Melanesian savagery and contributing to public hysteria regarding escaped convicts, James attacked the legitimacy of French colonial rule in New Caledonia. His observations, along with the subsequent impressions of Australian travellers, formed part of a more urgent argument that opposed French annexation of the New Hebrides. Further reading of travel writing that pertains to New Caledonia, whose French ownership was largely uncontested, should be reinterpreted in light of these broader concerns about the New Hebrides and their unresolved political status.

Contesting French Rule in the New Hebrides

Like New Caledonia, Australian travel writing about the New Hebrides was limited due to the nature of steamship routes. Consequently, the small number of reports available does not accurately reflect the high level of public anxiety felt in regard to this Island group. Four travel accounts about the New Hebrides were published between 1880 and 1899, seven between 1900 and 1914 and six from 1915 to 1941. Regular steamship routes to the New Hebrides were provided by BP from 1896 and by MM from 1901 to service the growing number of white settlers. Unlike New Caledonia, the New Hebrides were further away and contained more islands. Even in 1908, BP employee Wilson le Couteur described the monotonous journey of BP's inter-island steamer, *Tambo*, which anchored

---

27   Isabelle Merle, 'The Trials and Tribulations of the Emancipists: The Consequences of Penal Colonisation in New Caledonia 1864–1920', in *France Abroad: Indochina, New Caledonia, Wallis and Futuna, Mayotte: Papers Presented at the Tenth George Rude Seminar*, ed. Robert Aldrich and Isabelle Merle (Sydney: University of Sydney, 1997), 42.
28   Aldrich, *The French Presence in the South Pacific*, 199.

103 times over 33 days in the New Hebrides.[29] One tourist, Joseph Hadfield Grundy, declined a round trip of the Island group because the vessel *Induna* was 'not a floating palace', being 'infested with rats, mice and cockroaches'.[30]

Colonial Australians were familiar with these Islands due to the labour trade that recruited Islanders from the New Hebrides for Queensland's sugar plantations from the 1860s. This trade was strongly opposed by the Presbyterian Church, which was most powerful in Victoria. Led by Reverend John Gibson Paton in the late nineteenth century, the Presbyterians mobilised opposition to the labour trade in Melanesia and to that of French colonial ambitions in the New Hebrides, engaging public debate in both the Australian colonies and England. Presbyterians found support among some colonial Australian traders and farmers in the New Hebrides, as well as from the *Argus* and the *Age*, to push for annexation in the 1870s and 1880s. They also took advantage of the fear that the New Caledonian penal settlement would be expanded to the New Hebrides.[31] Ultimately, the Australian colonies and the British government were reluctant to bear the cost of extending the empire or possibly aggravating other colonial powers.

Several events in the 1880s contributed to a popular perception of British antipathy towards the region, as well as strengthened calls for Australian annexation and imperialism in the Pacific. This included the unopposed German annexation of north-eastern New Guinea in 1884 and the diplomatic crisis involving the New Hebrides in 1886. This crisis was precipitated by Britain's decision not to accept the 1883 proposal for French annexation of the New Hebrides in exchange for another Pacific Island, Rapa, and an agreement by the French to stop sending convicts to New Caledonia.[32] Presbyterian minister Charles Stuart Ross described the French response as openly hostile:

> In September 1886 … the French Republic, thirsting for Colonial expansion, having exhausted the resources for diplomacy to acquire possession of the New Hebrides, made a bold stroke for annexation by landing a body of troops at Havannah

---

29 Wilson le Couteur, 'The New Hebrides. Development at Vila. Copra and Cotton. Aneityum Depopulated', *Sydney Morning Herald*, 1 September 1908, 10, nla.gov.au/nla.news-article15021942.
30 Grundy, *The New Hebrides Group of Islands*, 7.
31 Thompson, *Australian Imperialism in the Pacific*, 44–5.
32 Aldrich, *The French Presence in the South Pacific*, 229.

> Harbour, with the purpose of seizing by force a tract of land the proprietary right to which was in dispute between certain French and British settlers … a temporary agreement was arrived … And Mr. Thurston [Acting British High Commissioner], who knew the value of the Islands to the Australian Commonwealth, and keenly watched every movement that aimed to alienate them from British influence and control, addressed a strong protest on the subject to the Victorian premier.[33]

Consequently, a joint Anglo-French naval commission was created in 1887. This event was widely remembered and repeated by subsequent travellers to the New Hebrides. James went as far as to publish a petition to the Queen, signed by the chiefs of Tanna, and to criticise the inaction of England:

> Great Britain should give a proof of their desire to aid us. We called out loudly against the German acquisition of territory near our shores. We still call out loudly against the further extension of the French possessions in the Western Pacific.[34]

Due to these colonial tensions, Luke Trainor argued that Australian interest in the Pacific reached its peak at this time, which is evident in newspaper coverage and regular public demonstrations.[35]

In response, the Australian colonies began subsidising shipping services by USSCo. and AUSN from Sydney and Melbourne to the New Hebrides. They also supported the formation of the ANHC in 1889, of which BP was a major investor. This was a joint venture created by several companies, prominent businessmen and politicians who considered settlement a key to gaining a foothold in the New Hebrides.[36] BP and ANHC consistently lobbied for the support of British and Australian interests in the New Hebrides, including shipping subsidies on which they relied. A brochure printed by the ANHC argued that these subsidies were vital for supporting 'flourishing Australian interests' in the group and for protecting it from 'jealous foreign powers'—specifically, the French 'menace to Australian peace and progress'.[37] Businesses promoted the New Hebrides as

---

33   Ross, *Fiji and the Western Pacific*, 169.
34   Thomas, *Cannibals and Convicts*, 406.
35   Trainor, *British Imperialism and Australian Nationalism*, 18.
36   Roger C Thompson, 'Commerce, Christianity and Colonialism: The Australasian New Hebrides Company 1883–1897', *The Journal of Pacific History* 6, no. 1 (1971): 25, doi.org/10.1080/00223347 108572181.
37   Australasian New Hebrides Company, *Australia and the New Hebrides*, 2–3.

a commercial haven that awaited the heroic Australian trader or planter. This self-promotion was particularly important during the 1890s, when public interest in the New Hebrides began to wane despite the continued efforts of the Presbyterian Church and the Victorian government to push for annexation.[38]

Although the ANHC ultimately collapsed in 1897, BP continued its commercial ventures in the region. It positioned itself as a national institution and encouraged nationalistic narratives about the New Hebrides in the twentieth century. The effect of this promotion is evident in Beatrice Grimshaw's 1905 newspaper article in the *Sydney Morning Herald*:

> To the outsider coming from far-away Britain, it seems as though France and Burns, Philp were politely disputing the ownership of the New Hebrides, rather than France and Australia. Burns, Philp is the general providence of the islands—rebelled against at times, as general providence and managers usually are; told flatly that it does not give value for its subsidy; that its freights must be lowered; that it does not do this, and ought not to do the other; but, nevertheless, clung to by the British element as its useful and true, though faulty, ally.[39]

It is unclear whether Grimshaw's remarks were part of a paid promotion, but Kenneth Buckley and Kris Klugman's history of BP suggests that the company was generally considered the Australian government's representative in the New Hebrides by the early 1900s.[40]

The turn of the century prompted renewed public debate about the New Hebrides. The newly federated nation of Australia responded by continuing official efforts to subvert French interests in the New Hebrides, including economic subsidies and even sending a spy. Wilson le Couteur was Australia's first official spy, travelling under the guise of a BP employee in the New Hebrides for three months in 1901. His report was released anonymously in the *Age*.[41] Although the ANHC settlement schemes of the 1890s had collapsed, negotiations regarding the naval commission reignited notions about Australian annexation, until an

---

38 Thompson, *Australian Imperialism in the Pacific*, 140.
39 Beatrice Grimshaw, 'Life in the New Hebrides', *Sydney Morning Herald*, 25 November 1905, 6, nla.gov.au/nla.news-article14734425.
40 Buckley and Klugman, *The History of Burns Philp*, 105–6.
41 Thompson, *Australian Imperialism in the Pacific*, 167.

Anglo-French condominium was agreed upon in 1906. Once signed, the agreement ended any possibility of Australia totally acquiring the group. Concurrently, the number of visitors to the Island group increased significantly—many of whom were attracted by the tourist cruises that were offered—and produced more travel writing in the process.

Most travellers knew the origins of the condominium at this time, with many of the accounts that were written between 1900 and 1914 offering a historical overview or commentary on the history of France's disputed claim to the New Hebrides. In 1915, self-described tourist J Mayne Anderson remarked that 'having recently read [Edward] Jacomb's book and various newspaper reports on the much vexed condominium questions, we were naturally curious to reach Vila'.[42] In 1901, while on a seven-week cruise, Richard Cheeseman described his trip as 'enjoyable and instructive'.[43] It confirmed his belief in Australia's claim to the Island group:

> Australia has, in the short interval of 50 years, become a power to be reckoned with, a voice that commands attention, and were we 50 years farther on, any dispute about who should possess the New Hebrides would not remain unsettled for long.[44]

Grimshaw's account in 1907 was more alarmist, warning her Australian readers that:

> For us, it means that the loss of our rights would place a hornet's nest belonging to a foreign power at the gates of our most important, and least effectively defended, colony [Papua].[45]

Grimshaw lobbied strongly for British rule in the New Hebrides, citing the success of the nation's colonial record in the Solomon Islands.

However, obtaining evidence of the merits or faults of the condominium was much more difficult in the capital of Vila. Apart from the novelty of Vila's combined French and British influence, visitors' accounts resemble those of other Islands. They admired the harbour and panoramic views from higher ground and described the colonial buildings and layout of the town. In Anderson's case, he expressed his reluctance to make any comment about the condominium at all in 1915, noting that:

---

42   Anderson, *What a Tourist Sees in the New Hebrides*, 9.
43   Cheeseman, *The South Sea Islands*, 17.
44   Cheeseman, *The South Sea Islands*, 6.
45   Grimshaw, *From Fiji to the Cannibal Islands*, 177–8.

> A few tourists are let go on a long-suffering island people, who have their hospitality returned by criticism of their method of government. A bad feeling is created on one side or other, and certainly no good results in any case.[46]

Such an ambivalent stance may have reflected the political sensitivity of the issue at a time when Australia was France's ally in World War I. Although Australians were generally critical of French rule, their accounts were also ambiguous about whether Britain, Australia or a combination of both governments should be the replacement.[47]

If evidence of the condominium's workings was elusive in the capital, then travellers searched for it during the numerous short stops of the inter-island steamer. Anderson's account revealed that by 1915, locals were catering to the tourist trade. He noted that the villages were cleaned in anticipation of the steamer's arrival and that Islanders sold curios, acted as guides and were familiar with being photographed.[48] A common element of the tourist experience was an encounter with a white resident who would usually act as a guide on the Island. This is evident in the details that travel accounts used to describe these encounters, often giving a voice to residents' complaints about the condominium. Anderson's meetings highlight the diverse encounters that travellers could have with Europeans in the New Hebrides: he met several missionaries and visited the Presbyterian missionary training college; he met an Australian sheep farmer and visited cotton, rubber and timber plantations; and he met scientific researchers, dining with New Zealand academic Professor Macmillan Brown and travelling with an ethnology student. Australian travellers were as likely to meet French residents as they were to meet British people, with these encounters not necessarily being hostile as expected.

Given the highly publicised settlement schemes and promotions that emphasised the natural resources of the New Hebrides, many Australians were eager to find a trader when they arrived. They were also eager to form their own judgement regarding the success or failure of commerce in the Island group. Visitors' descriptions tend to reflect the day-to-day difficulties of adapting to the condominium, rather than the heroic or patriotic overtones of BP propaganda. Importantly, travellers were often

---

46 Anderson, *What a Tourist Sees in the New Hebrides*, 29.
47 Grimshaw, *From Fiji to the Cannibal Islands*, 181.
48 Anderson, *What a Tourist Sees in the New Hebrides*, 102.

unsure where residents' loyalties lay; even during the politically charged context of the 1880s, James described meeting several residents who preferred French rule.[49] Grimshaw also observed that:

> The English or Australian settler often finds his way a hard one, unless need or greed drives him to discard his nationality, and take out French papers of naturalisation ... Their flag [the Union Jack] is an expensive luxury, but they stick to it—generally.[50]

BP's commercial influence did not always benefit European planters and traders in the Islands, as the nickname 'Bloody Pirates' suggested. Grundy observed this attitude during his voyage:

> Traders don't seem to mind whether the island is owned by the French or English. It is amusing to watch the effect on any Burns Philp people of a suggestion that the Germans should have the islands![51]

This suggests that despite the nationalistic rhetoric, traders and planters were just as concerned with profit as they were the major trading and shipping companies.

Australian travellers frequently reported that British restrictions on the trading of firearms and alcohol in the New Hebrides offered an unfair advantage to French traders and residents. For some Australians, such as Grundy, this was represented as a moral policy that distinguished British rule as superior: 'In trading with the natives the French sell them firearms, ammunition and drink, but the English know well these things are not for their good and refuse them'.[52] However, many residents found this economically detrimental to their own existence, with firearms being particularly useful as items of exchange for acquiring land. Fox's reference guide informed readers that:

> There is general dissatisfaction with the New Hebrides arrangement. It is said that the British trader is not allowed fair play in competition with the French, and the British government takes no interest in the affairs of its subjects.[53]

---

49 Thomas, *Cannibals and Convicts*, 184, 193.
50 Grimshaw, *From Fiji to the Cannibal Islands*, 182.
51 Grundy, *The New Hebrides Group of Islands*, 4.
52 Grundy, *The New Hebrides Group of Islands*, 3.
53 Fox, *Oceania*, 36.

6. CONFLICT, CONVICTS AND THE CONDOMINIUM

Others preferred the New Hebrides to the Solomon Islands precisely because British regulations could be avoided.

Visiting steamships also created opportunities for residents to bring their grievances to the attention of Australian travellers. In their travel accounts, these visitors observed that local opposition to British labour restrictions was one major issue. The Pacific Islanders' Protection Acts (passed in 1872 and 1875) prohibited the transport of an Islander for employment aboard an unlicensed British vessel. These acts were designed to protect the welfare of the Islanders and were applied to inter-island trading within the New Hebrides; however, it was not illegal for British settlers to employ labourers if they had been recruited by non-British ships, so many residents purchased Islanders from French ships.[54] The French use of imported Asian labour was also resented by British and Australian residents. Le Couteur remarked that 'the Javanese are much discussed in the group as the favoured labour to introduce'; he criticised the 'repatriated kanaka from Queensland' for driving labour prices high.[55] By the 1940s, this opposition had decreased, as shown in M Kathleen Woodburn's account. It identified the French system of indenture in the New Hebrides as superior. She described the 'Tonkinese' labourers as 'numerous, orderly, clean, squat, muscular, Mongolian types', and argued that British plantations 'languish[ed]' because they were 'prohibited from importing the superior coolie labour from the East'.[56]

The rule of law was also frequently appraised by both residents and travellers. Edward Jacomb's book, *France and England in the New Hebrides* (1914), was widely read and cited in travel accounts. As a British barrister in Vila, Jacomb's criticisms of the condominium (particularly of the joint court) resonated with Australians. Their travel accounts cited incidents that demonstrated the confusing and inconsistent nature of the court system. As zoologist Alan John Marshall explained in 1937:

> There is a Gilbertian court of justice maintaining both a French and British judge, with the presiding judge and prosecutor neutral and nominally of Spanish nationality. French residents are subject to French law; Britons to British.[57]

---

54 Buckley and Klugman, *The History of Burns Philp*, 61.
55 Le Couteur, 'The New Hebrides. Old Order and New', 8.
56 Woodburn, *Backwash of Empire*, 76, 285.
57 Marshall, *The Black Musketeers*, 285.

The dual system could also be used to an individual's advantage, as a pamphlet for the ANHC argued in 1899:

> An employee of the French New Hebrides Co., gave the British man-of-war the information that an Australian settler expected these fire-arms from Sydney, and he actually used the British man-of-war to serve his own ends, and force Australian settlers to buy their fire-arms, &c., from his French Co.[58]

Policing in the New Hebrides was difficult, with a common complaint being that Europeans were unable to maintain law and order among the Islander population. Rather than articulating the reasons why policing was difficult—particularly the legal ambiguities, limited resources and difficult geography—many Australians simply reported residents' anger towards perceived British inaction. James recounted one trader's observation that the French would defend the lives and properties of European settlers while the British would not.[59] Government agent John Gaggin recalled a similar case when explaining why other nations had established a 'footing in the Western Pacific'. He recalled the swift, official reprisal for the murder of a German trader in Malekula: 'These nations protect their individual subjects—if they deserve it. *The English do not.* There is the reason in a nutshell.'[60]

As well as incorporating popular nationalist and commercial narratives about the New Hebrides, travellers also appropriated the moral tone of mission propaganda; they critically evaluated the role of the missions in the Island group. Australian missions were actively proselytising in the New Hebrides and were crucial for stimulating public debate about the Pacific Islands in Australia. Of these missions, the Presbyterian Church in Victoria was the most vigilant overseer of French abuses in the New Hebrides in the late nineteenth century. It continued to watch over the Island group after public interest had dissipated in the 1910s. John Gibson Paton's son, Frank, continued his father's efforts as a leading figure in the church at this time, though his attitude to the labour trade and French influence in the Pacific was more moderate. He published several books and pamphlets, and in 1923, he led a public campaign in Australia to end the condominium. Although they did not achieve the desired outcome, the Presbyterians did have some success; they supplied

---

58 Australasian New Hebrides Company, *Australia and the New Hebrides*, 5.
59 Thomas, *Cannibals and Convicts*, 182.
60 Gaggin, *Among the Man-Eaters*, 116.

evidence to British authorities, which was used in negotiations during the Anglo-French conference of 1914.[61] Their strength lay not only with their influence in Australian politics but also in their sustained publishing work that brought news from missions to Australia with regularity and that maintained a clear and consistent message.

Mission accounts of the New Hebrides were generally influenced by the competitive nature of French and British missions in the Pacific Islands. This conflict was observed by travellers like Frank Coffee, who argued that there was 'more friction' between missions in the New Hebrides than in any other group.[62] In the race to convert souls, British Protestants had reached the Pacific over 40 years before French Catholics had. In the New Hebrides, specifically, Protestants had firmly established themselves since the first LMS ministers had arrived in the late 1830s. They were followed by the Presbyterians and the Anglican Melanesian Mission, who sent European pastors, as well as Islander preachers, who were responsible for rapidly evangelising the region. By the 1880s, the Presbyterian Church was influential in the southern New Hebrides and the Melanesian Mission in the north.[63] In contrast, the French Catholic missions (namely the Marists) had limited success in the Island group, failing to establish a base in 1848 and again in 1886. Instead, Sydney was the initial headquarters for the French Marist missions in the Pacific. Although the Catholics were dominant in New Caledonia, it was not until the 1900s that they made some headway in the New Hebrides, eventually increasing to a third of the Island group's population. The success of the Catholic missions in New Caledonia and the New Hebrides depended on support from the French government.[64] The fact that Presbyterian and Catholic missions drew on congregations throughout Australia for financial and moral support further complicated matters politically. While the Presbyterian Church in Victoria actively lobbied against the French, Catholic communities in Sydney supported the French missions in the Pacific. However, the religious affiliations of individual Australians did not always align with his or her commercial or political motivations.

---

61 David Hilliard, *God's Gentlemen: A History of the Melanesian Mission, 1849–1942* (St Lucia: University of Queensland Press, 1978), 240.
62 Coffee, *Forty Years on the Pacific*, 104.
63 Garrett, *To Live Among the Stars*, 294. See also David Hilliard, 'The South Sea Evangelical Mission in the Solomon Islands: The Foundation Years', *The Journal of Pacific History* 4, no. 1 (1969): 41–64, doi.org/10.1080/00223346908572145; Clive Moore, 'Peter Abu'ofa and the Founding of the South Sea Evangelical Mission in the Solomon Islands, 1894–1904', *The Journal of Pacific History* 48, no. 1 (2013): 23–42, doi.org/10.1080/00223344.2012.756162.
64 Aldrich, *The French Presence in the South Pacific*, 36–8.

In official Australian mission accounts, the condominium was portrayed as being a threat to missionaries' ability to civilise and Christianise, which they often framed within a nationalistic discourse. Missionaries were represented as champions of Australia, of traders and of Islanders, similar to the way that BP had branded itself to serve its own ends. Frank Paton's *Glimpses of the New Hebrides* is one such example. Describing his visit to the Island group in 1913 for a Presbyterian Synod meeting, Paton praised the work of the missions and described the problems that were associated with the condominium arrangement. When visiting the court to watch a trial, he was critical of the hostile French judge:

> Judge Colonna was a keen-looking Frenchman—the author of the famous anti-missionary speech that called forth strong but vain protests against his elevation to a seat on the Joint Court Bench. His appointment is regarded on the British side as an absolute scandal, yet the British Government felt utterly helpless to prevent it.[65]

Paton also provided a summary of the Synod's report, which stressed the mission's struggle against French opposition:

> The attitude of the French continues to be hostile. Their opposition to the work of the Mission, their policy of encouragement of heathenism, and the active interference with native Christians, constitute one of our most serious difficulties, and militates against the progress of the Gospel throughout the Group wherever French influence is felt. It is not only with regard to Mission work that difficulty is felt, but the general welfare of the New Hebrides is imperilled.[66]

Like many other mission accounts, Paton positioned missionaries as guardians of justice for British subjects and framed the condominium as a threat to British Christian morals. Using the example of an imprisoned Islander pastor, Paton portrayed French rule as a 'brutal oppression and cynical injustice', and then called for the restoration of 'justice and mercy'.[67]

---

65   Frank Hume Lyall Paton, *Glimpses of the New Hebrides* (Melbourne: Foreign Missions Committee, Presbyterian Church of Victoria, 1913), 15.
66   Paton, *Glimpses of the New Hebrides*, 47.
67   Paton, *Glimpses of the New Hebrides*, 93–4.

Resonating with calls for British or Australian rule that would restore order and 'civilise the savage', other travellers repeated Paton's moralising tone. Government agent Douglas Rannie portrayed the New Hebrides in a 'wild, uncivilised state', with 'many fearful acts of lawlessness' occurring 'under the influence of liquor, and the smell of gunpowder'.[68] The supposed degradation and depopulation of Pacific Islanders were also used to prove the failure of the condominium. In Grimshaw's perspective, the 'utter barbarism' that she observed among the Islanders served to strengthen her argument for strong British rule in the New Hebrides:

> At present, the islands are in the most uncomfortable and unsettled state it is possible to conceive. There is no other place in the world where an uncivilised coloured race is to be found in an entirely self-ruling condition, owning no real master, and not even 'protected' by any of the great Powers.[69]

Due to the temporary nature of their visits, Australian travellers to the New Hebrides rarely observed the nuances of conflicts between Christian denominations and between individual missionaries, government officials and traders. Missionaries were entangled in complex networks of exchange in the Islands—and they were not always directly opposed to traders and commerce. Rather, they relied on shipping for the transportation of goods and competed with one another in offering shipping subsidies. Co-lobbying proved effective when mission and business interests were aligned, as was demonstrated when Presbyterian missionaries passed a resolution in 1890 that opposed British restrictions on inter-island labour recruits.[70] Missionaries also supported new arrivals from Australia by acting as guides for tourists or by helping settlers adjust to their location, as Presbyterian missionaries had done for the Australian settlers who joined the BP settler scheme in 1902.[71] Similarly, traders and planters also helped new missionaries adjust to their environs. In light of these complex relationships, many travellers were uncertain whether missionaries were responsible for assisting or for hampering the development of the Islanders and local businesses, or for the functioning of the condominium. Travel impressions were glancing, and in their reflective

---

68 Douglas Rannie, *Notes on the New Hebrides* (Brisbane: Royal Geographical Society of Australasia, 1890), 9, 28.
69 Grimshaw, *From Fiji to the Cannibal Islands*, 178.
70 Buckley and Klugman, *The History of Burns Philp*, 62.
71 Buckley and Klugman, *The History of Burns Philp*, 101.

narratives, Australians tended to prefer the stereotype of missionaries as being saints or sinners. Marshall remarked on this practice in 1937, while in the New Hebrides:

> It is customary to condemn the missionary. Every tropic traveller has met individuals who find a perverted type of pleasure in destructively, often maliciously, criticizing missionaries and their work. Both whites and natives in tropical regions are inveterate gossips and the unfortunate missionary runs the full gauntlet.[72]

Rather than clarifying the workings of the condominium in the New Hebrides, Australian travel writing generally contributed to confusion and speculation about what was commonly termed the 'pandemonium'. By 1914, Australian public interest in the New Hebrides decreased as French settlement and commerce outpaced Australian and British efforts, along with the advent of World War I, which shifted attention away from the French towards German aggressors instead. Although support for, and interest in, the New Hebrides' annexation continued to surface in the following decades, public hostility directed towards French dominance in the group was not as fierce as before.[73] In light of this general atmosphere of confusion, Australian travel writers were just as likely to direct their criticism at British apathy as they were to French imperial designs. For many who advocated the moral duty of the Empire, British inaction had proven to be the most difficult to reconcile. Grimshaw used a metaphor of a runaway horse to describe the situation and to stress the need for strong leadership in the region:

> And I wished, most earnestly, that I could see the strong hand of Great Britain or her Colonies grasp the bridle of this wretched country, as unfit to be left to its own guidance as any runaway horse, and pull it firmly and determinedly into the road of civilisation and law-abiding peace.[74]

Others, like John Henry Macartney Abbott, were more ambiguous:

> Here, in the very essentials of the process of civilization, we find influences brought to bear upon the native that are utterly unlike, if not to a certain degree hostile to, one another. It would be strange if some small amount of chaos did not manifest itself in these earlier stages.[75]

---

72 Marshall, *The Black Musketeers*, 310.
73 Thompson, *Australian Imperialism in the Pacific*, 198.
74 Grimshaw, *From Fiji to the Cannibal Islands*, 305.
75 Abbott, *The South Seas (Melanesia)*, 29.

Although the New Hebrides may have been considered unstable and residing in a period of transition in the early twentieth century, travel writing about New Caledonia by contrast highlights the Island's transformation into a tourist destination.

From Detractions to Attractions in New Caledonia

As opposed to the accounts of the late nineteenth century that criticised French colonial rule and penal settlement in New Caledonia, travellers of the twentieth century increasingly identified the Island group as a tourist destination that was considered exotic, safe, close to home and cheap. New Caledonia's main attractions were commonly identified as its convict heritage and the exoticness of its French culture. Dying of asthma in Melbourne in 1896, one year before the end of penal settlement in New Caledonia, James's concerns for the threat that the colony posed to the Australian mainland were no longer shared by travellers of the 1900s. Meteorologist Clement Lindley Wragge was typical of these new visitors. He was one of five Australians identified in this study who wrote travel accounts of New Caledonia that were published between 1900 and 1914. An additional seven travel accounts were written by Australians from 1914 to 1941. Of these writers, Wragge travelled the most extensively through New Caledonia, and he wrote down his impressions in the greatest detail.

Born in England in 1852, Wragge ran away from home as a teenager, with his travels bringing him to Australia in 1874. Appointed to the surveyor-general's department in South Australia in 1876, he married a year later and studied meteorology. In 1878, Wragge travelled to Britain for three years to establish weather observatories. After returning to Australia in 1883, he continued to establish meteorological stations across the country, so he could try and predict and observe weather patterns. During this time, Wragge helped found the Royal Meteorological Society of Australia and was appointed Chief Meteorologist for Queensland (1887). He resigned from his Australian post and moved to Dunedin, New Zealand, in 1903, where he published his travelogue, gave lecture tours and raised a family until his death in 1922.

Wragge's travelogue, *The Romance of the South Seas*, was based on his travels to New Caledonia in c. 1893 to establish a meteorological observatory, which coincided with the connection of the Noumea–Queensland cable.

This allowed for the expansion of Wragge's meteorological observation and research network. As such, his impressions straddle two decades before and after the Australian Federation. Although he was travelling as part of a scientific mission, Wragge explicitly chose to not write as 'some cold official or scientist'.[76] In fact, the second part of his book about Tahiti was styled as a travel guide. He was also loyal to 'our Empire', referring to England as 'home'. However, Wragge did adopt some Australian customs, frequently referencing Australian places and idioms and often wishing that Australia had annexed New Caledonia for itself. He concluded his journey with the statement: 'Farewell, New Caledonia! … we wish you could join the Commonwealth of a free Australia!'[77] Although Wragge was loyal to British concerns, he was sympathetic to the French colonisers, describing them as 'a grand and noble people' who were supportive of his scientific mission. Wragge was also much kinder than James in his assessment of the French and of their attitudes towards Kanaks, noting that 'we agree with them in all but the treatment of prisoners'.[78] Unsurprisingly, not everyone shared this opinion: writing in 1901, Cheeseman focused on the potential danger that the French still posed, describing a harbour that could fit an entire French fleet, with forts and sentries everywhere, as well as hostile officials who scrutinised his every move.[79]

From the beginning, Wragge's fascination was focused on convicts. He called New Caledonia 'the Prison of the Pacific' and wrote that 'the convict element' was 'very strong', which was similar to James's observations 20 years before.[80] Like other travellers, Wragge was aware of New Caledonia's past before arriving in Noumea, noting in his introduction that:

> We knew full well of those miserable *escapés* who braved the seas and sharks in open boats, with parched throats and skeleton frames, just to reach fair Queensland—only to be interned there as suspects and undesirable vagrants.[81]

In 1903, George Phillips also empathised with escaped convicts, whom he argued 'merely sought Australia as a stepping stone for the purpose. Poor fellows! … These men are not all bad'.[82] These empathetic comments

---

76 Wragge, *The Romance of the South Seas*, 10.
77 Wragge, *The Romance of the South Seas*, 113–14.
78 Wragge, *The Romance of the South Seas*, 35–6.
79 Cheeseman, *The South Sea Islands*, 4.
80 Wragge, *The Romance of the South Seas*, 20; Thomas, *Cannibals and Convicts*, 117.
81 Wragge, *The Romance of the South Seas*, 4.
82 George Phillips, *Notes on a Visit to New Caledonia* (Brisbane: Brisbane Telegraph, 1903), 10.

suggest that popular colonial Australian attitudes of the previous two decades had shifted away from negative and threatening representations, especially since the transportation of convicts had ceased in 1897.

After arriving at Noumea, ships would pass Île Nou, the small island at the entrance to the harbour, where the main prison was located. 'That terrible islet of misery and degradation' wrote Wragge, when he recalled observing the convicts through his binoculars.[83] From this initial reminder, travellers would then encounter convicts in the port and town. The chance of meeting a convict was high, with convicts and emancipists outnumbering free settlers until the early 1900s. In 1897, 22,315 convicts had been transported to New Caledonia, and by 1902, emancipists comprised 50 per cent of the Island's white population.[84] Wragge observed 'a gang of doomed *condamnés*' building new wharves as soon as he arrived, and Phillips was fascinated that prisoners who worked on the roads were only lightly guarded and unshackled.[85] Of even greater interest to travellers was the idea that ex-convicts could be hidden within the population, as Wragge had described his surprise when he met two *libérés* in Noumea who were disguised as a French gentleman and a priest.[86]

The most famous attraction in Noumea was the Place des Cocotiers (Coconut Square), with its chief attraction being the convict band that played there. Wragge described the weekly concerts as 'sublime'; he was impressed by their 'God-like' harmony and 'chords of Love', but his applause was quelled by French authorities who did not think his appreciation was appropriate.[87] New South Wales politician John Charles Lucas Fitzpatrick was more entertained by the 'bizarre' group of people intermixing in the square, in close proximity with the criminals on stage:

> I can promise you a scene, which, of its kind, cannot perhaps be equalled in any part of the world. Here come the white-uniformed bandsmen, escorted by their officer ... loud-laughing groups of buxom Loyalty Island girls ... natives of both sexes, from the New Hebrides ... a few, only a few New Caledonians ... Solomon Islanders, and in fact, representatives of every group in the South Pacific.[88]

---

83   Wragge, *The Romance of the South Seas*, 15.
84   Merle, 'The Trials and Tribulations of the Emancipists', 40.
85   Wragge, *The Romance of the South Seas*, 113–14; Phillips, *Notes on a Visit to New Caledonia*, 9.
86   Wragge, *The Romance of the South Seas*, 39–40.
87   Wragge, *The Romance of the South Seas*, 24–5.
88   John Charles Lucas Fitzpatrick, *Notes on a Trip to New Caledonia and Fiji* (Windsor: Hawkesbury Herald, 1908), 42–3.

Wragge, like other Australian travellers, repeated the popular myth that the band's conductor reportedly had killed his wife's lover and had fed her his heart for breakfast.[89] This legend highlights the transfer of popular Melanesian tropes onto the convict population, as well as the beginnings of a tourist industry in New Caledonia.

For tourists who were searching for convicts, the prison on Île Nou was most easily accessible from Noumea by boat; it was more well known than any other camps. The prison on Île des Pins (Isle of Pines) was also infamous, but it was more difficult to access and had closed in 1890. With permission from the Minister of Penitentiaries, Wragge visited Île Nou and described it as a 'place of utter doom and the blankest despair', likening it to a 'living hell', in which 'the clanking of chains resounds from yonder, the agonies of the condemned seem wafted on the air'.[90] Wragge witnessed an execution with the 'ghastly' guillotine, visiting the prison cells and the cemetery and watching the labour gangs at work. Alarmed, he wrote that 'the French penal system is demoralizing. It does not bring out the best in man. *Au contraire,* it degrades him and makes him worse'.[91] His experience of Île Nou was similar to James's experience 20 years before. James had also visited the prisoners, including a 19-year-old boy who was sentenced to death for trying to escape—a sentence that the author judged to be 'a hard lot'.[92]

Wragge's experience of Île Nou was repeated during his visits to a prison in Bourail and in Camp Brun. He explored the prisons in depth, taking notes on the male and female quarters, conducting interviews with officials, missionaries and prisoners, and making detailed descriptions of the prisoners' living conditions:

> All the others appear utterly dejected and heart-broken, living but yet dead, hoping in very hope gone for that rest that should lead *not* to hell fire, but to eternal progress.[93]

---

89   Wragge, *The Romance of the South Seas*, 25; George Wirth, *Round the World with a Circus: Memories of Trials, Triumphs and Tribulations* (Melbourne: Troedel & Cooper, 1925), 39; Matsuda, *Empire of Love*, 113.
90   Wragge, *The Romance of the South Seas*, 90, 92.
91   Wragge, *The Romance of the South Seas*, 94.
92   Thomas, *Cannibals and Convicts*, 119.
93   Wragge, *The Romance of the South Seas*, 63.

Figure 18: Canaques Are After Them.
Source: Wragge, *The Romance of the South Seas*, 81.

He took several photographs of the prisons, which he used to illustrate his book, along with ethnographic portraits of Kanak men (see Figure 18; the men in this image likely worked in the prison). Although Wragge's account of the harshness of French rule shared similarities with James's earlier reports, his view was not shared by all travellers of the early 1900s. Phillips's views challenged the notion that the French prison life was horrible and credited the penal system with producing fine public works.[94] Other travellers did not encounter the realities of imprisonment face to face because the system was already in the process of dismantlement.

Wragge's empathy with the local convicts may have been motivated by his witnessing of the cruelty of the penal system firsthand. In fact, he explicitly stated that the 'subsequent experience during residence and travel in the island did but tend to strengthen a sympathy in their favour, as will duly appear'.[95] However, his response may also signpost a broader Australian colonial sympathy with French prisoners, based on a shared convict heritage. Peter Kirkpatrick argued that the Australian Bohemian community in Sydney embraced French customs and habits because it was an alternative to conservative British values, with notions about France as 'the land of revolution and democratic hope' resonating with their political ideology.[96] This can be evidenced in certain newspaper articles, such as the one in the *Sydney Morning Herald* in 1888, which described escaped French convicts as 'bushrangers'.[97]

Although French convicts prompted numerous empathetic and hostile responses in Australian society, it was a particular group known as the *communards* who generated a generally positive public response. The *communards* were 7,000 political prisoners who were transported to New Caledonia in 1872 for their role in the 'Paris Commune', which revolted against the French government in 1871. The close proximity of these political prisoners was initially a concern of Australian authorities due to the revolutionary ideas that they represented. However, the potential threat diminished over time, especially after they were pardoned in 1879.[98] As Bergantz revealed, the Australian media frequently downplayed the crimes of the *communards*, with the aim of distancing colonists from their own convict pasts and distinguishing them from the recidivist who was portrayed as the true criminal. When convenient,

---

94 Phillips, *Notes on a Visit to New Caledonia*, 2.
95 Wragge, *The Romance of the South Seas*, 17.
96 Kirkpatrick, *The Sea Coast of Bohemia*, 32.
97 'Escaped Convicts in New Caledonia', *Sydney Morning Herald*, 27 November 1888, 4, nla.gov.au/nla.news-article13704947.
98 Aldrich, *The French Presence in the South Pacific*, 225.

communards were alternatively used as scapegoats or as heroes for political purposes in Australia.⁹⁹ As one writer explained in a fictional piece in *The Clipper* in 1905:

> The word 'communard' has two different meanings. According to some he is a social leper, who despises everything good and revels in all things evil … But there are those who suffered from their connection with the Commune of 1871 … who were fighting for a principle, and who were proud to die in the cause of freedom and justice.¹⁰⁰

One *communard*, French journalist Henri Rochefort, was notable in this public debate, having escaped to Australia in 1874. He was widely portrayed as a hero in the Australian press and by James, long after the *communards* were released.¹⁰¹ Even in the 1900s, travellers to New Caledonia were aware of the *communard* story. Their imprisonment and release had become symbolic of the heroism and resilience of French convicts. In 1941, Australian journalist Wilfred Burchett still referenced the *communard* legacy: 'The Communards in New Caledonia … have helped to establish a new tradition of liberty and tolerance'.¹⁰²

The *communard* story was part of a larger narrative of emancipation that fascinated Australian travellers. Just as Australians had 'grown up' from their convict origins, so too were *libérés* commencing their own new lives. Empathising with the 'poor *libéré* who has atoned for his sins', Wragge noted:

> With us it is not so. A man convicted; well! He atones and pays for his mistake, be it twenty years and may rise again. But to climb under French jurisdiction to a once-held position in free society is practically impossible.¹⁰³

This is consistent with the romanticisation of the *libéré* as being the 'archetypal vagabond' in early colonial literature—a figure that remained a preoccupation for free residents of New Caledonia until the 1920s.¹⁰⁴

---

99 Bergantz, 'French Connection', 77–85.
100 J Sinclair Tayler, 'The Isle of Submarines: A South Sea Terror', *The Clipper*, 14 October 1905, 4.
101 For example, see 'A Famous Communard: The Adventurous Career of Louise Michel', *The Mercury*, 27 March 1905, 7; 'Personalities: Henri Rochefort', *Windsor and Richmond Gazette*, 24 August 1889, 12; Thomas, *Cannibals and Convicts*, 127.
102 Burchett, *Pacific Treasure Island*, 122.
103 Wragge, *The Romance of the South Seas*, 36–7.
104 Muckle, *Specters of Violence*, 7.

Consequently, Australian visitors were eager to seek them out. William Ramsay Smith was one such traveller who, in 1924, photographed two *libérés* living in a cave.[105]

Another element contributing to the Australian fascination with French convicts was their growing popularity as a tourist attraction. This included the prison buildings and the convicts themselves. Wragge's account suggests that he was motivated by a subversive desire to visit the prisons. An avid collector, Wragge took unusual souvenirs from the prisons, including the wings of a bird that a prison guard had killed in a solitary confinement cell and the stuffing from a woman's prison mattress. Despite recording the horrors of the prison system, including documenting an execution in gruesome detail, Wragge appeared not to be heavily affected by the scenes that he had witnessed. Returning to his hotel after visiting the prison, he casually remarked, 'Ah well! Such is an experience of human life'.[106] His behaviour may reflect a broader trend of 'dark tourism' that involves visiting sites associated with death and tragedy.[107] It also resonates with the behaviour of Australian tourists who visited prisons in Australia in the early twentieth century. As Richard White demonstrated, these tourists were eager to visit historic convict sites such as Port Arthur, and even re-enacted scenes of torture or execution. This was despite, or perhaps in reaction to, official efforts to restrict access to these sites due to shame regarding Australia's convict past and the denial of its convict ancestry.[108]

The convict element remained a lucrative attraction in the 1920s and 1930s, despite the cessation of convict transportation to New Caledonia in 1897 and the closure of penal settlements there by 1922. The sense of danger or violence had disappeared, yet tourists still recounted second-hand stories and reported hearsay about past prisoners and brutality. Although the Coconut Square's convict band was disbanded, a group still played there and attracted a large crowd by 1941, with Burchett observing that 'a treasure-house of interesting characters whose stories, pieced together, would compile a voluminous and colourful history'.[109] Burchett sought out and paid ex-convicts for interviews, many of whom were poor or homeless:

---

105 Smith, *In Southern Seas*, 19.
106 Wragge, *The Romance of the South Seas*, 70, 96.
107 Nicholas Halter, '"Cannibals and Convicts": Australian Travel Writing about New Caledonia', in *The Palgrave Handbook of Prison Tourism*, ed. Jacqueline Z Wilson, Sarah Hodgkinson, Justin Piché and Kevin Walby (London: Palgrave Macmillan, 2017), 867–84, doi.org/10.1057/978-1-137-56135-0_41.
108 White, 'The Subversive Tourist'.
109 Burchett, *Pacific Treasure Island*, 104.

> There are not many of the old convicts left now … most of them are well-known characters and can always rely on a few francs a day from former employers or workmates.[110]

His efforts produced mixed results. Henri Tartas offered an interesting story of escape and intrigue, while Quer Urbain's story was 'dreary rather than exciting', with 'much rambling and many repetitions'.[111] Even the sublime charm of the prisons had been lost, as the buildings were re-used for alternative purposes:

> To-day Ile Nou has been converted by Pan American Airways into a modern air base … Ile des Pins, where most of the Communards were imprisoned, is a charming island visited by young couples on their honeymoon, and once or twice a year the object of a specially organized tourist excursion from the mainland. The Peninsula Ducos, the site of the third main penitentiary hasn't had as happy a fate as the other two—it now houses New Caledonia's leper colony.[112]

For these reasons, Burchett recommended to his readers that they visit French Guiana or read other books to experience the French penal system.

In addition to its historic convict attractions, French culture was becoming identified by Australians increasingly as an admirable and attractive characteristic of the colony in the 1900s. These features pushed the island's Pacific characteristics into the background. Burchett remarked that:

> Added to the delights of living French, eating and drinking French, hearing and speaking French, is the attraction that in New Caledonia all these things can be enjoyed in the most perfect South Sea background.[113]

French culture, fashion and food were popular in Australia at the turn of the century and were considered symbolic of high art, culture and modernity.[114] It is thus unsurprising that visitors to New Caledonia described their daily routine in vivid detail, as they relished French food and drinks and enjoyed the novelty of reading French menus and street names. Fitzpatrick's description of the daily practice of midday siestas was

---

110 Burchett, *Pacific Treasure Island*, 101–2.
111 Burchett, *Pacific Treasure Island*, 93, 101–2.
112 Burchett, *Pacific Treasure Island*, 100.
113 Burchett, *Pacific Treasure Island*, 20.
114 Bergantz, 'French Connection', 43.

common in travel accounts, and he enjoyed the choice of cafes and bars in Noumea.[115] Phillips also admired French dining habits, noting that 'a French breakfast is a very serious undertaking … but remember that one French meal is equal to two English ones'.[116]

Favourable descriptions of French culture were accompanied by an admiration of French sensibilities. Wragge was explicit in his admiration of the French, describing them as 'a grand and noble people' who were 'liberal and broad-minded'; he argued that 'France can teach us to live in the pure enjoyment of life'.[117] James, writing much earlier, had acknowledged that 'France is lovingly known by her sons as the country *"la belle" par excellence*. And she deserves the title'.[118] In Burchett's case, his admiration of the French was expressed with reference to the nation's convict past: 'Because the Old World rejected—or ejected—many of the finest spirits of the age, the New World bordering the Pacific has a virile, liberty-loving ancestry'.[119] Others felt an affinity with the French because they shared a common European civilisation. James expressed this sentiment when he wrote about the New Hebrides: 'White blood is thicker than water, and Englishman and Frenchman are akin when brought face to face with savages'.[120]

Travellers also noted the influence of French colonialism, enjoying the architecture and modern advancements. Many commented on the adequate water and sewerage systems, clean streets, electric lighting, suitable roads and impressive buildings such as churches, government offices, restaurants and hotels. In 1912, Rannie remarked:

> The hotels are good and the tariff uncommonly moderate. I had a bedroom and sitting-room to myself, and an excellent table, for the moderate sum of ten francs per day in a first-class hotel. The town is beautifully laid out, and fine shade trees are planted along the streets. Most enjoyable drives can be had in all directions, as the roads are kept to perfection.[121]

---

115 Fitzpatrick, *Notes on a Trip to New Caledonia and Fiji*, 45.
116 Phillips, *Notes on a Visit to New Caledonia*, 3.
117 Wragge, *The Romance of the South Seas*, 36.
118 Thomas, *Cannibals and Convicts*, 49.
119 Burchett, *Pacific Treasure Island*, 122.
120 Thomas, *Cannibals and Convicts*, 162–3.
121 Rannie, *My Adventures among South Sea Cannibals*, 242.

Figure 19: On the Quayside, Noumea.
Source: Stephen Henty, 'New Caledonia', *Walkabout* (November 1935): 29, 31.
Image courtesy of the Australian National Travel Association.

These observations reflect the pace at which French colonial officials were developing the colony, with the help of convict and foreign labour. New Caledonia's importance as a penal settlement and the growth of its mining industry signified that it was much more developed and populated by the French than the isolated Islands of French Polynesia. Photographs of New Caledonia taken by travellers frequently included images of the indigenous police forces, who were regarded as a sign of progress, development and law and order (see Figure 19). This also reinforced a message of successful French colonialism when, in fact, Kanak resistance continued in the early twentieth century. Images of the police were not an exclusive feature to New Caledonia, but their prevalence in travel accounts is more noticeable than in other Islands in the Pacific. They should thus be considered within a broader context in which Australians imagined the Island as a space of conflict and convicts since the mid to late 1800s.

Travellers could visit more parts of the mainland by car, as the French extended their network of roads. George Meudell, another steamer tourist, commented on the prospects for a day trip by car: 'Noumea is a delightful centre for a holiday. There are two good hotels, excellent roads for motoring, and the scenery is right for motorists.'[122] This scenery was

---

122 Meudell, *The Pleasant Career of a Spendthrift*, 146.

often noted for its European rather than Pacific characteristics. Travellers drew similarities between the niaouli tree and the Australian eucalyptus, as well as the lush hills of the mainland (and the cattle they supported), were compared to familiar European and Australian landscapes.[123] Visitors also remarked on the prevalence of mining to a greater extent than in any other Pacific Island. These observations generally dominated Australian travel accounts, with limited descriptions of Kanaks. Visits to coffee or copra plantations warranted few comments about the labourers, instead focusing on their profitability or 'picturesque' qualities. Few also visited or commented about Kanak villages or mission stations. This suggests that as New Caledonia increasingly became marketed as a French holiday destination rather than as a Pacific reality, travellers were less inclined to report on its island characteristics.

Fading from View

From the beginning of World War I, Australian public interest in New Caledonia and the New Hebrides declined. The conflict in Europe had shown France to be an ally rather than an enemy, and the Australian government was preoccupied with the mandate for New Guinea that it had acquired in the aftermath. This decline was more pronounced in New Caledonia since Australian missionaries, businesses and residents continued to contest the condominium in the New Hebrides. Even a large-scale Kanak rebellion in 1917 did not elicit the same response in Australia as the 1878 conflict had, presumably because it was overshadowed by news from the front in Europe. Max Quanchi has shown in his study of Australian illustrated magazines that New Caledonia went virtually 'unnoticed' by Australians during the interwar period.[124] This was observed by Burchett when he visited in 1939 and 1941, noting that:

> For many years this island has been but a name to most of us … a name that featured once or twice a year as the goal of a tourist cruise to the South Seas … [it] vaguely recalled the site of a particularly odious convict prison.[125]

---

123 Thomas, *Cannibals and Convicts*, 45; Burchett, *Pacific Treasure Island*, 20, 40.
124 Max Quanchi, 'A Name That Featured Once or Twice a Year: Not Noticing French New Caledonia in Mid-20th Century Australia', *Journal of Pacific Studies* 29, no. 2 (2004): 196.
125 Burchett, *Pacific Treasure Island*, 11.

Australians still retained greater economic, religious and political interests in the New Hebrides than in New Caledonia, but economic investment in the Island group was diminishing and political will was intermittent. Australian travellers continued to describe the confusion that was created by the condominium in the 1940s, such as Woodburn, who described it as 'cumbersome, awkward, uneconomic and Gilbertian, but still existing'.[126] Yet these travel accounts about the New Hebrides were not as prolific as those of other Pacific Islands. This may have reflected the slow development of tourist routes and infrastructure due to the condominium, or to the topography of the Island group, signifying that there were numerous ports of call and no particular site or attraction that appealed to Australian travellers. Although Vila did have some French characteristics to satisfy Australian tourists who sought the 'exotic', French culture and influence were less pronounced in the New Hebrides than it was in New Caledonia. These factors were visible in BP's advertisements of its cruises through the New Hebrides, which promoted the 'absorbing interest and changing scene' provided by 'over one hundred calls' that took the traveller 'quite out of the beaten track'.[127] BP also tended to focus on the potential for encounters with Melanesian inhabitants, rather than on an authentic experience of French food and culture. In fact, by 1925, BP's advertisements downplayed the condominium, remarking in one short sentence that the New Hebrides were of 'special interest as the theatre of a remarkable experiment in Government'.[128] This starkly contrasted previous claims in 1903 that 'British supremacy [in the New Hebrides] … is undoubted', a statement that was questionable by the 1920s.[129]

BP's promotion of New Hebrideans as a tourist attraction contributed to essentialised and racialised stereotypes of the Melanesian savage that were repeated by Australian travellers. Abbott stated that 'a native of the group is a Melanesian before he is a New Hebridean'.[130] Apart from these formulaic tropes, Islanders were frequently absent from travellers' descriptions of the condominium. Rather, they were commonly portrayed as a subjugated and silent people. Rannie believed that Islanders had 'no idea of what the annexation of their island means', and James doubted that they could

---

126 Woodburn, *Backwash of Empire*, 44.
127 Burns, Philp & Company, Limited, *Picturesque Travel*, no. 5 (1925), 44.
128 Burns, Philp & Company, Limited, *Picturesque Travel*, no. 5 (1925), 43.
129 Burns, Philp & Company, Limited, *All About Burns, Philp & Company, Limited: Their Shipping Agencies, Branches and Steamers* (Sydney: John Andrew & Co., 1903), 106.
130 Abbott, *The South Seas (Melanesia)*, 25.

express their views, if they had any.[131] This supposedly silent Islander was preferable in James's opinion: 'In Australia we have solved our native difficulty by never allowing that the blacks have any rights in the soil at all'.[132] However, James was also willing to use them where necessary to support his criticisms of French rule. He claimed that every Islander disliked the French, and even overlooked the purportedly savage and childlike nature of New Hebrideans to emphasise the superiority of the British claim: 'They were not fools; they were bloodthirsty and brutal; but they had a sense of their own rights and their own liberties'.[133]

The trope of the Melanesian savage was more often applied to the New Hebrideans than to the Kanaks, with the emphasis on French culture being extended at the expense of the Kanak population, about whom little is written. The Islanders who Australians most commonly met in Noumea were foreign workers, mostly drawn from the nearby Loyalty Islands and New Hebrides. Burchett described many 'boys' at the Noumea wharf who were waiting to carry passengers' bags but noted that they were Loyalty Islanders. Fitzpatrick listed the variety of nationalities in Coconut Square, to which he added, 'A few, only a few, New Caledonians'.[134] This did not reflect the actual population, in which Kanaks outnumbered white residents. Other foreign labourers from Japan, Indochina, Réunion Island and Java also drew the gaze of Australian travellers away from the Kanak. The colony's development, particularly in regard to the mining industry, was built on cheap imported labour. In 1932, *The Pacific Islands Yearbook* reported statistics from the previous year that 6,198 Javanese and 5,026 Tonkinese labourers were part of a total population of 57,165.[135] Travellers viewed the preference for foreign imported labour as the result of the innate laziness of the Melanesian, an observation that overlooked the role that Kanaks had played in the New Caledonian economy.

The omission of Kanaks in Australian travel accounts was symptomatic of a gradual process in which Kanaks were slowly isolated and marginalised over time by the French colonial administration. As a result of disease, warfare and violent encounters with French settlers and authorities, the Kanak population had been gradually forced into reserves. These were

---

131 Rannie, *Notes on the New Hebrides*, 6–7; Thomas, *Cannibals and Convicts*, 202.
132 Thomas, *Cannibals and Convicts*, 275.
133 Thomas, *Cannibals and Convicts*, 247.
134 Burchett, *Pacific Treasure Island*, 20, 184; Fitzpatrick, *Notes on a Trip to New Caledonia and Fiji*, 43.
135 Robson, *The Pacific Islands Yearbook*, 297.

situated away from the major towns and urban areas, including the capital.[136] In 1924, Smith observed these controls, noting that a 'kanaka curfew' from 8 pm was in effect in Noumea.[137] French control of the northern districts remained intermittent in the 1920s, and combined with the remoteness of some reserves, Australians were less inclined to move beyond Noumea to meet Kanaks. Those few Kanaks who Australians did encounter were usually given reductive descriptions that repeated Melanesian stereotypes—Burchett described 'negroid' physical features, claimed to discover cannibal 'feasting grounds' and met one Islander guide who was allegedly 'the perfect caricature of a missionary-filled cannibal'.[138] Even in light of the French government's efforts to downplay past violent conflicts with Kanaks, Muckle argued that 'the idea of a recent savage past was too tempting to ignore altogether' in European literature, and recollections of past conflicts continued to label Kanak rebels as cannibals and savages from the 1920s to the 1940s. Australian travel accounts confirm a similar obsession with this 'trope of reawakened savagery'.[139]

In light of diminishing Australian public interest in New Caledonia and in the New Hebrides after World War I, it is unsurprising that generalisations about Melanesians in these Island groups persisted. Yet, given the historical relationship between Australia, these Islands and their colonial masters, it is remarkable that they could drift out of the Australian consciousness so rapidly. The historical legacy of French, British and Australian competition over these two Island groups before 1914 explains why Australian travel writing about New Caledonia and the New Hebrides was distinct from other Pacific Islands. New Caledonia was chiefly known for its convicts and its incidences of conflict between Europeans and Kanaks. These were issues of contention in Australia during the late nineteenth century until the early 1900s, when New Caledonia was transformed into a tourist destination; its convict heritage and French culture were becoming popular attractions. In the New Hebrides, Australian descriptions were marked by uncertainty and confusion, reflecting the controversial and contested nature of the Anglo-French condominium arrangement. Representations of both these Island groups were closely intertwined, and New Caledonia was frequently used as a device for justifying or criticising French control of the New Hebrides. Although popular opposition to French colonialism

---

136 Muckle, *Specters of Violence*, 5, 11.
137 Smith, *In Southern Seas*, 22.
138 Burchett, *Pacific Treasure Island*, 41, 64.
139 Muckle, *Specters of Violence*, 170.

in these Islands was intermittent and temporary, they occurred at a crucial time in the development of the Australian nation. As such, these Islands were significant in shaping early Australian perceptions of the Pacific, and in providing a setting for Australian individuals, groups and governments to debate Australia's role in the region.

7

Preserving Health and Race in the Tropics

At present it is a contest between racial debility and modern science. In places where the racial debility is far advanced, one sees the writing on the wall, though those concerned in the tragedy are not aware of it. But in the case of those who are not too far gone science will win in the long run. Some of the best brains in the world are at work on the matter, and the inhabitants of the Pacific will reap the result … It is only a matter of time before science will overcome the inertia at the fringes of civilisation and the abuses and mistakes of the past are replaced by the benefits that the white man's knowledge can and should bring to his brother of the stone age.[1]

M Kathleen Woodburn published this evaluation of the Pacific Islands based on her experience living on a farm in Erromango (in the New Hebrides) with her son in the 1930s. From her perspective on 'the fringes of civilisation', this inquisitive traveller blended personal narrative and scientific observations—a common technique in Australian travel writing. Pseudo-scientific practice was popular among Australian travellers, both amateur and professional, and scientific language provided an authoritative legitimacy to ordinary tourist impressions. It also formed part of a discourse from which Australian travellers drew when confronted with the reality of human difference. This extensive and racialised discourse had developed throughout 200 years of European exploration and travel in the Pacific. By the 1900s, a racial lexicon had permeated Australian travel writing that informed expectations, predetermined encounters and

---

1   Woodburn, *Backwash of Empire*, 223.

shaped reflections. The taxonomy of race as it was used in the twentieth century was sanctioned by science and considered authoritative and absolute despite its erroneous assumptions and inherent ambiguities. For Australians in foreign environments, race was a constant, a lens through which to observe and a standard by which they could compare themselves to others and reassure themselves of their superiority.

Popular ideas of race and science informed three issues that regularly featured in Australian travel accounts: disease, depopulation and ethnic diversity. Australians instinctively remarked on their own health when first travelling in a foreign and tropical environment. As they acclimatised, their initial concerns about disease were replaced by observations of the health of Pacific Islanders. In particular, Australian travellers commented on the widely perceived trend of depopulation in the region, providing their own verdict on popular explanations of its causes and influence. In doing so, travellers compared the progress of Europeans and Islanders to other foreign populations in the Pacific, particularly Japanese, Chinese and Indian. As Australians remarked on these issues, they fell back on 'scientific' assumptions that were considered self-evident and absolute. However, complex individual encounters of travel produced a diverse range of responses, with scientific theories and racialist terminology being used, misused, conflated, indiscriminately applied and occasionally challenged by Australian travellers.

Science and Stasis

The role of the Pacific Islands in complex racial debates that occurred in Europe and the US have been the subject of much scholarly study, but how these ideas were applied by ordinary travellers from the periphery of empire is less clear. The discourses of science and travel have remained intertwined in representations of the Pacific since early exploration. Initially, the collection of new information from the 1760s onwards about non-white people from a stream of naturalists, anthropologists, surveyors, missionaries and ethnographers (both amateur and professional) informed scientific debates and encouraged subsequent travel to Oceania to verify racial theories. As travel writing became increasingly valued as a form of education and as a valid contribution to the public record, the objective and scientific traveller's account was perceived to be more accurate and trustworthy.² By the 1880s, Australian travellers were influenced by new scientific disciplines that had been developed in Europe; this can be evidenced in the growth of domestic scientific associations, the adoption of scientific language in twentieth-century tourist accounts and the popularity of certain practices (e.g. collecting human skulls).³ Science was gradually adopted as a tool for travellers to authenticate their experiences and legitimate their work, as well as a method for writers to publicise their accounts as educative and informative.

Ordinary travellers' interpretation and application of scientific theories were varied. Warwick Anderson demonstrated that an individual's understanding of human difference was 'a situated knowledge'; Anderson had used the example of Australian doctors who were influenced by local training, clinical observations and their own personal experiences as much as they were by European theories.⁴ Similarly, Australian travellers did not often refer to 'key' figures or debates in academic disciplines and had used classification terms interchangeably and indiscriminately. A history of race relations in colonial Queensland argued that weekly periodicals provided readers 'with a wealth of illustrative material which both popularised scientific racist theories and provided plenty of local examples to bear these theories out'.⁵ Evans, Saunders and Cronin argued that phrases such as 'survival of the fittest' and 'white superiority' were widely adopted due to the popularisation and simplification of scientific theories by journalists and politicians. This simplification obscured the complex debates about human difference and development that had occurred since the fifteenth century and contributed to fixing the Islander as a static ideal in the eyes of Australian travellers.

Bronwen Douglas has outlined the history of the term 'race' and the development of what she called 'the science of race' in Europe—namely, the 'systematic efforts in the new 19th-century disciplines of biology and anthropology to theorize collective physical differences between broad human groups as innate, morally and intellectually determinant, and possibly original'.⁶ It was this science of race that Australian travellers in the twentieth century took for granted before embarking on their

---

2   Hulme and Youngs, *The Cambridge Companion to Travel Writing*, 20, 53.
3   Michael E Hoare, 'Science and Scientific Associations in Eastern Australia, 1820–1890' (PhD thesis, The Australian National University, 1974).
4   Anderson, *The Cultivation of Whiteness*, 4.
5   Evans, Saunders and Cronin, *Race Relations in Colonial Queensland*, 15.
6   Douglas, *Science, Voyages, and Encounters in Oceania*, 7; Douglas, 'Climate to Crania'.

journeys. They often overlooked the complex philosophical debates that had occurred over several hundred years. Measuring human difference according to physical appearance (particularly skin colour) had much older origins, with comparisons of bodily characteristics between black and white to be found as early as the mid-fifteenth century, in references to the slave trade in West Africa. Although this dichotomy bore connotations that privileged white-skinned people, collective terms used by explorers to describe people were nominalist and neutral in the sixteenth and seventeenth centuries. A Christian theological perspective of a common humanity remained influential until the late eighteenth century. It was a position that attributed human diversity to external factors and that supported humanity's universal potential for progress.[7]

Douglas identified a major discursive shift from human similitude to difference in the late eighteenth century, towards the assumption that rather than being subject to external change, race was innate and hereditary. This is evident in the meaning of the term itself, which shifted from a broad definition to a more specific anatomical and biological definition. No longer a general grouping, 'race' was a specific and essentialising label that was later indiscriminately applied by Australian travellers:

> Thus naturalized as an invariable, fundamentally differentiating, measurable human physical quality with axiomatic social, moral, and intellectual correlates, the idea of race acquired the scientific authority which guaranteed its unquestioned realism over at least the next century.[8]

Consequently, attitudes to human difference hardened, with the inferiority of non-Europeans being attributed to human deficiencies rather than environmental or historical factors.

According to popular theories of race, the Pacific Islander became locked in a racial hierarchy in which Melanesians were inferior to Polynesians. This relationship remained unquestioned by travellers from the Australian mainland from 1880 to 1941. White supremacy was assured on this ladder, and Aboriginal Australians were relegated to the very bottom. This view was articulated by the first European settlers in Australia, such as British marine officer Watkin Tench, who believed in 1793 that Aboriginal Australians 'rank very low, even in the scale of savages' and that they were

---

7   Douglas, 'Climate to Crania', 35.
8   Douglas, *Science, Voyages, and Encounters in Oceania*, 14.

inferior to 'the subtle African; the patient watchful American; or the elegant timid islander of the South Seas'.[9] Developments in stadial theory and natural history had encouraged the popular concept of human varieties that are differentiated according to stages of progression from savagery to civilisation.[10] Australian anthropologist Alfred William Howitt was an early authority on Aboriginal culture in the 1880s, who wrote:

> The progression theory … is of modern origin, and has arisen through the scientific investigation and comparison of the social condition and customs of savage and barbarous races, of the survivals of archaic customs still met with among civilised peoples, and of the most ancient written records left to us from the past.[11]

The subtle differences that are perceived to separate these varieties based on physical appearance, moral and intellectual development, political organisation, agricultural production and the nuances of scientific debate and classification were often overlooked by non-scientific travellers. This is evident in the indiscriminate use of various classifying terms such as 'Malay', 'Negro', 'Ethiopic', 'Papuan' and 'African'. The potential for confusion was highlighted by British anthropologist Charles Gabriel Seligmann, whose work, *The Melanesians of British New Guinea* (1910), proposed the idea of renaming Papuans (the inhabitants of New Guinea) to 'Papuasians' and of dividing them into 'western Papuasians' and 'Papuan-Melanesians'.[12] Not all Australian travellers made the distinction between Papuans and Melanesians, let alone using Seligmann's specific categories. Similarly, the terms 'Polynesian', 'Kanaka' and 'South Sea Islander' had different usages over time. They were applied to specific regions within the Pacific and were then used more generally as a reference to all Pacific Islanders.

---

9   Watkin Tench, *A Complete Account of the Settlement at Port Jackson in New South Wales: Including an Accurate Description of the Colony; Of the Natives; And of Its Natural Productions/Taken on the Spot* (London: G. Nicoll and J. Sewell, 1793), 187.
10   Bronwen Douglas, 'Philosophers, Naturalists and Antipodean Encounters, 1748–1803', *Intellectual History Review* 23, no. 3 (2013): 389–91, doi.org/10.1080/17496977.2012.723343.
11   Alfred William Howitt, in Lorimer Fison and Alfred William Howitt, *Kamilaroi and Kurnai: Group-Marriage and Relationship, and Marriage by Elopement, Drawn Chiefly from the Usage of the Australian Aborigines: Also the Kurnai Tribe, Their Customs in Peace and War* (Melbourne: George Robertson, 1880), 339.
12   Charles Gabriel Seligmann, *The Melanesians of British New Guinea* (Cambridge: Cambridge University Press, 1910), 1.

Evidence of the influence of racial thinking on Australian travellers is difficult to find in their written accounts. As Angela Woollacott argued, white Australian travellers in the 1900s frequently came from urbanised areas and were unfamiliar with other ethnicities; therefore, 'whiteness was more an assumed superiority than a frequently practiced subordination of others'.[13] A common practice after arrival was to situate Islanders within a racial order, often in comparison to others that had been encountered along the journey. This was accomplished with short, matter-of-fact statements that were usually based on physical characteristics. Whether this was an unconscious process or a tool to qualify one's first impressions by making a scientific reference is unclear. For example, naturalist Albert Stewart Meek wrote in his 1913 travel account:

> There are two distinct types of native in the Solomons. At the west end of the Solomons … they are much darker than the Papuan. At the east end of the group they are more like the Papuan in colour and in character.[14]

References to 'types' and shared racial characteristics, both physical and mental, reinforced the common assumption that Islanders were fixed within a rigid racial hierarchy. This resonated with popular tropes within the literature that portrayed Islanders as primitive, frozen in time and infantile—'an idle people, living in the most primitive condition, so luxuriously supplied by nature that they are dying off, mainly from pure inertia'.[15]

Strict racial categories also served a colonial purpose. Damon Salesa argued that race was 'a comparative dimension that made the Empire easier to archive, signify, consume, integrate and administer'.[16] The need to train colonial officers for the mandated territory of New Guinea stimulated the creation of the first anthropology department in Sydney in 1925.[17] For other groups with vested interests in the Pacific (most notably missionaries and businesses), signs of progress or stagnation among races were highly contested. People were assigned traits and were forced

---

13 Woollacott, *To Try Her Fortune in London*, 175.
14 Meek, *A Naturalist in Cannibal Land*.
15 Reverend AS Webb, in Allen, *Stewart's Handbook of the Pacific Islands*, 54.
16 Damon Ieremia Salesa, *Racial Crossings: Race, Intermarriage, and the Victorian British Empire* (Oxford: Oxford University Press, 2011), 12.
17 McGregor, *Imagined Destinies*, 103.

into types to support a claim to authority. For individual travellers, as Woollacott demonstrated, how they articulated their own whiteness in comparison to others asserted privilege and power.[18]

Armed with several scientific theories that have established ordered racial hierarchies in the Pacific, Australian travellers were reluctant to contradict these categories. Yet, their travel accounts described a vibrant and ethnically diverse Pacific. They revealed the difficulties of fitting particular Islands and Islanders into types and models, which proved to be much more ambiguous and contested than the popular Melanesian–Polynesian dichotomy. Even some Australian researchers wrote travel accounts for a broader public market, choosing to avoid (or criticise) the constraints of scientific discourse. Australian naturalist (and amateur anthropologist) William Ramsay Smith was one of these travellers. He reflected on the value of travel accounts in his own travelogue, based on his tour of the Pacific Islands in the early 1920s:

> Travellers provide much information of a scientifically trustworthy nature when they record their own observations among various peoples in different parts of the world and the comparisons they have drawn from these observations. And their evidence is almost of a different sort for what is collected by an investigator in a central anthropological laboratory, being a sort of intuitive spark that lights up a conclusion without a long and painful investigation ending in perhaps doubtful inferences.[19]

For Smith, Captain Cook was the 'ideal traveller, observer and reporter' because he embodied the ideals of both a scientific mind and an adventurous spirit.

Subsequent Australian travellers expressed a similar sentiment in their travel accounts. Although many were excited by the promise of adventure in a foreign environment, they were also informed by scientific knowledge, including medical theories of disease and the effects of the tropical climate on European bodies. Many Australian travellers faced a similar process of acclimatisation while they travelled to the Islands—their accounts revealed a general concern with preserving their health as they travelled in a foreign and potentially threatening environment.

---

18   Woollacott, *To Try Her Fortune in London*, 44.
19   Smith, *In Southern Seas*, 225.

Disease in the Tropics

Disease was a common topic of observation within Australian travel accounts. Travel to any foreign environment prompted an instinctive response, as travellers expressed feelings of vulnerability and a fear of contagion. So prevalent was this response that the *Oxford Book of Australian Travel Writing* argued that cleanliness was a major theme.[20] With the exception of labour recruiters, who frequently wrote about the health of the recruits that they were transporting, Australian travellers did not often dwell on this subject. They instead preferred to focus on more exotic and pleasing subjects. It is likely that most Australians were unfamiliar, if not unconcerned, with medical explanations of disease. Rather, concern for health and disease in travel accounts reflected a broader colonial discourse that Rod Edmond argued was 'central to the construction of boundaries in both nation and empire'.[21] Disease was racialised and sexualised, and the health of Australians became a standard against which to make judgements about the inferiority of Pacific Islanders and the superiority of the Australian 'stock'. These judgements reflected debates within Australia about the northern tropical region and the suitability of white settlement in the tropics.

Prospective travellers to the Pacific Islands were usually well informed about the prevalence of disease and the potential dangers that were specific to the Pacific. They could read news reports of contagion outbreaks, anthropological and historical documents recording the spread of disease, fictional tales of fevers and leprosy and the observations that were detailed in travel accounts. Commentary on Island hygiene and disease was also a crucial part of the discourse of settlement. Guidebooks had sections subtitled 'health' and 'climate', which explained the various diseases that were prevalent in specific islands, as well as the hospital and medical services available. *The Pacific Islands Yearbook* in 1932 pronounced that Fiji was 'probably the healthiest tropical climate in the world', that Hawai'i was 'famed for its climate', that the New Hebrides was 'unhealthy' (although 'not worse than that of many other tropical places'), that Samoa was 'mild and equable' and that the Solomon Islands were 'unfavourable for Europeans on account of its humidity and constant heat, and particularly

---

20   Pesman, Walker and White, *The Oxford Book of Australian Travel Writing*, xv.
21   Rod Edmond, *Leprosy and Empire: A Medical and Cultural History* (Cambridge: Cambridge University Press, 2006), 11.

on account of the prevalence of malaria', while Tahiti's climate was not mentioned at all.[22] Shipping advertisements and travel handbooks responded by promoting the health benefits of visiting a tropical climate during the Australian winter months:

> Enabling the people of Australia to escape the cold winter months and visit the tropics during the continuance of the cool and healthy south-east trade winds, which blow from the South Pacific from April to November.[23]

Passage on a ship was the first environment in which Australians encountered disease. Sea travel allowed for more gradual acclimatisation to the tropical climate, although conditions on the ship varied from luxurious to overcrowded and stuffy. The oppressive weather was a common complaint, with heat and dampness making the voyage uncomfortable and tiresome, and seasickness leaving passengers weak. Close-quartered living facilitated the spread of disease, with travellers sometimes refused entry ashore because of sickness onboard.[24] Absent from the accounts of travellers is any concern with the quality of food and water (both on and offshore) in relation to gastrointestinal illnesses. Only artist Aletta Lewis recalled consuming infected food aboard the American warship USS *Ontario* in 1929.[25] Instead, malnutrition and dysentery were frequently observed in the Islander population, often as part of an evaluation of their suitability for labour.

The threat of disease transmission was reinforced by strict quarantine regulations that were imposed before passengers could disembark. The devastating effects of highly contagious diseases such as influenza or measles were demonstrated in mass epidemics in the world and in specific outbreaks in the Pacific Islands. The 1918 flu pandemic spread throughout the Pacific Islands, with only American Samoa and New Caledonia employing effective quarantine that prevented outbreaks.[26] Similarly, 13 per cent of the Rotuman population died in 1911 from the measles because the medical staff of the port authority were absent when

---

22 Robson, *The Pacific Islands Yearbook*, 55, 101, 186, 211, 231, 263, 309.
23 Allen, *Stewart's Handbook of the Pacific Islands*, 85–6.
24 For example, see Nossiter, *Southward Ho!*, 103; Doorly, *In The Wake*, 294; Chewings, *Amongst Tropical Islands*, 27, 31.
25 Lewis, *They Call Them Savages*, 231.
26 Sandra M Tomkins, 'The Influenza Epidemic of 1918–19 in Western Samoa', *The Journal of Pacific History* 27, no. 2 (1992): 181, doi.org/10.1080/00223349208572706.

a passenger boat arrived.[27] Quarantine control was essential for protecting the Australian mainland, as much as it was for protecting the Islands. The transfer of the bubonic plague to San Francisco from a steamship returning from Honolulu in 1900 was a reminder of the potential dangers that unrestricted mobility in the Pacific Ocean posed.[28]

Once ashore, the most obvious signs of disease were visible skin diseases. Travellers noted rashes, lumps, boils and sores, such as yaws (a common infectious disease prevalent until the 1950s and 1960s). As Caroline David explained in 1899:

> There were Fiji sores, sprained ankles, tropical bilious attacks and sunburn, yaws or tonu, as the Funafutians call it, lafa and magesu (Tokelau ring-worm and itch) ... [T]he tropical sores were the most troublesome ailments; the least scratch, unless at once disinfected and covered from flies, would inflame and develop into an ulcer needing constant care.[29]

Skin diseases were commonly attributed to poor cleanliness and personal hygiene standards, with colonial travellers articulating their judgements in racial and denigrating language. Julian Thomas claimed that New Hebridean labour recruits 'ate their meals like apes', while Beatrice Grimshaw made the following observation in a Fijian village:

> Their clothes—only a loin-cloth apiece—were unspeakably dirty, and every unoccupied moment seemed to be spent in hunting through each other's huge frizzled heads for certain small game, which when found, was immediately eaten by the finder![30]

Such biased criticisms contradicted popular romantic notions of naked freedom and primitivism in the Islands.

Although not as common, the stigma that was attached to the incurable diseases of leprosy and elephantiasis, and the physical deformities that they caused, made them a subject of fear and fascination for travellers. Elephantiasis, also known as lymphatic filariasis, is caused by parasitic worms that are spread by the bites of infected mosquitoes; its cause and remedies were not well known in the early twentieth century. Australian

---

27 G Dennis Shanks et al., 'Measles Epidemics of Variable Lethality in the Early 20th Century', *American Journal of Epidemiology* 179, no. 4 (2014): 2, doi.org/10.1093/aje/kwt282.
28 James K Ikeda, 'A Brief History of Bubonic Plague in Hawai'i', *Hawaiian Entomological Society* 25 (1985): 75–81.
29 Edgeworth David, *Funafuti*, 48.
30 Thomas, *Cannibals and Convicts*, 336–7; Grimshaw, *From Fiji to the Cannibal Islands*, 120–1.

meteorologist Clement Lindley Wragge in 1906 expressed anxiety when sharing food with an infected person and Lewis was upset in 1929 when her friend contracted the disease in American Samoa: 'It was intolerable to think of Ava's straight, well-formed body falling into the clutches of this inexorable disease'.[31] Descriptions of the disease emphasised 'the horrifying proportions that made a grotesque of a man', in the words of plantation overseer Eric Muspratt, who observed in the 1920s disfigurement so extreme that one man carried his swollen parts in a wheelbarrow.[32] Although it was not fatal, elephantiasis caused poverty and social stigma—a consequence that Sydney Walter Powell feared in the 1910s, when he was diagnosed in Tahiti: 'I have elephantiasis, an abominable disease, which for months past I have dreaded … when the doctor told me I must leave here I dreaded banishment and forgot the disease'.[33]

Leprosy was also a widespread disease with a severe social stigma. The first International Leprosy Congress in 1897 in Berlin recommended the isolation of patients, based on medical thought that the disease was highly contagious and incurable. Consequently, colonial governments established quarantine stations on small, remote Islands throughout the Pacific for leper isolation.[34] Fear of contagion meant that missionaries and volunteers often provided care to these people. These Islands fascinated Australian travellers who passed by at a distance, in a similar way that the sublime decay of ruins and prisons attracted the subversive tourist, though face-to-face encounters were avoided. Arnold Safroni-Middleton, a wandering artist and musician in the late nineteenth century, wrote tales that featured a Hawaiian leper girl who was symbolic of the romanticism of 'martyrdom' and forbidden romance.[35] The leper colony on Moloka'i Island in Hawai'i was the most well known to Australians, made famous by the popular figure of its caretaker, Father Damien DeVeuster. The example of Moloka'i highlights the importance of Christian charity and sympathy, while also demonstrating how colonial governments regarded the disease as 'a symbol of native inferiority and ineptitude, requiring the custodial attention of foreigners with their assumed superior intelligence'.[36]

---

31 Wragge, *The Romance of the South Seas*, 108; Lewis, *They Call Them Savages*, 235.
32 Muspratt, *Fire of Youth*, 43.
33 Powell, *A South Sea Diary*, 62.
34 Jane Buckingham, 'The Pacific Leprosy Foundation Archive and Oral Histories of Leprosy in the South Pacific', *The Journal of Pacific History* 41, no. 1 (2006): 82. doi.org/10.1080/00223340600652441.
35 Safroni-Middleton, *In the Green Leaf*, 135, 197.
36 Gavan Daws, *Holy Man: Father Damien of Molokai* (New York: Harper & Row, 1973); Pennie Moblo, 'Leprosy, Politics, and the Rise of Hawai'i's Reform Party', *The Journal of Pacific History* 34, no. 1 (1999): 88, doi.org/10.1080/00223349908572892.

Although encounters with elephantiasis and leprosy were limited, it was the threat of fever that posed a greater danger to Australians—the most common being malaria, consumption (i.e. tuberculosis) and 'blackwater fever' (a complication of malaria). Other fevers included yellow fever, scarlet fever, cholera, chicken pox, typhoid, smallpox and polio. Labour recruiter A Nixon noted on 2 July 1877 about Erromango that 'it is a most unhealthy island. Fever ague and chest diseases seem to be … prevalent'.[37] In 1897, fevers were known to be spread by mosquitoes and were endemic in certain regions, so travellers were aware of the need for mosquito nets while visiting the Pacific Islands. Those who fell ill in the Islands wrote vivid accounts of their experiences and strong warnings to prospective travellers. Jack McLaren, who suffered malaria and yaws in the 1900s, explained how 'despite the barbarity, treachery and cunning of the natives, I think the greatest danger in the Solomons was from disease'.[38] In 1934, British traveller Richard Reynell Bellamy recalled the climate in Australia and in the Pacific, admitting that his health had influenced his observations:

> Perhaps it was not actually so hot as places I had been in on the Queensland coast, and my bad health might have been the reason for my feeling it to such an extent. Certainly I found it unbearable.[39]

Similarly, Meek looked forward to returning to Australia to 'recruit my shattered health'.[40]

Fear of fever was linked to a fear of the tropical environment as a cause of disease, and early colonial settler discourse about the northern Australian tropics informed expectations and observations about the Pacific. Acclimatisation to new and foreign environments was a slow and inconsistent process, as Anderson revealed in his history of the early colonial settlement of Australia.[41] Although the temperate southern climate of the continent had become normalised by the 1870s, the suitability of the tropical north for European settlement was still contested. This concern also applied to the tropical Pacific Islands, as one 1920 handbook noted:

---

37   A Nixon, 'Inwards Correspondence', in Colonial Secretary's Office, Series ID 5253, Item ID 846982 (Brisbane: Queensland State Archives, 1877).
38   McLaren, *My Odyssey*, 244.
39   Bellamy, *Mixed Bliss in Melanesia*, 267–70.
40   Meek, *A Naturalist in Cannibal Land*, 196.
41   Anderson, *The Cultivation of Whiteness*, 37.

> It [New Caledonia] would not be so healthful as Australia, which has its cleansing and purifying hot, dry winds, and its health-giving odours from eucalypt forests as well as a population rather more observant of sanitary conditions, and, perhaps, the practice of the virtues.[42]

Fears of disease were founded on actual incidences of European deaths in tropical climates, yet this anxiety was also encouraged by exaggerated and distorted stories. Raphael Cilento, an Australian medical administrator and tropical health expert in the 1920s and 1930s, believed that the tropics were a region of imagined danger:

> To the great majority of the inhabitants of temperate climates, the word 'tropical' conjures up visions of sweltering mangrove flats, the haunts of the crocodile; of rank and steaming forests that exhale the musky odour of decaying vegetation and conceal within their leafy depths 'miasmic' swamps; of deadly snakes and of the skulking savage with his poisoned spear.[43]

Indeed, these notions often appeared in Australian travel accounts. Trader Joseph Dickinson described 'an abomination of stench and flies' in Ugi, while Thomas was wary of 'noxious odours' that emanated from the ground in Tanna. Powell believed that the soil of Tahiti had caused elephantiasis in his foot.[44] Travellers regularly warned readers about the dangers of the tropics and suggested preventative measures.

The hot environment was also believed to affect the body and mind, sometimes termed 'colonial fever' or, in Cilento's case, 'heat stagnation'. From 1899 to 1906, colonial governments established schools in tropical medicine to test the suitability of races in tropical environments and the use of vaccines. These schools provided scientific backing to the notion that the tropical environment could induce laziness and physical, moral and psychological degeneration.[45] The fear of 'going native'—which had long been expressed as both fantasy and anxiety in European literature about the Pacific—became scientifically verified and located in the tropics. By World War II, Australian troops fighting in the Pacific Islands

---

42 Allen, *Stewart's Handbook of the Pacific Islands*, 62.
43 Raphael Cilento, *The White Man in the Tropics: With Especial Reference to Australia and Its Dependencies* (Melbourne: H.J. Green, Commonwealth Department of Health, 1925), 7.
44 Dickinson, *A Trader in the Savage Solomons*, 128; Thomas, *Cannibals and Convicts*, 292; Powell, 'Each to His Taste', 200.
45 Anderson, *The Cultivation of Whiteness*, 119.

used the phrase 'to go troppo' to describe a loss of sanity. Australian travel accounts frequently reiterated fears of white degeneration. Muspratt observed one Australian plantation overseer in the Solomon Islands who had 'practically gone native struggling with a poorly-equipped and fever-stricken plantation' and blamed the environment for leaving him 'broken' and 'so full of fever that he trembled continually'.[46] On his solo sailing voyage from Sydney to California, Fred Rebell claimed to feel 'Malua fever', an imagined disease 'of procrastination and disinclination to work'.[47] Travellers also described beachcombers and residents who were 'wrecked by alcoholism' and who warned travellers that the Islands were not suitable for women or children. Powell's criticism of European weaknesses was framed in terms of progress:

> The European can rise higher than the Tahitian, but he can sink immeasurably lower. It makes me wince to see the common white man beside the common native; physically, mentally and morally he is the native's inferior. It is not his fault: degeneration has followed degradation, as nothing can prevent it from doing.[48]

As racial theory gained popularity, a more hereditary perspective of disease shaped medical thought in Australia from the 1880s onwards. This did not completely displace environmental factors, nor did it become conventional until the early twentieth century. For example, germ theory was also influential in identifying other humans (and animals) as potential carriers of disease, rather than genetics. Yet policies of racial segregation could be justified by both hereditary and environmental explanations. This became formalised with the White Australia policy, as immigration and quarantine acts restricted the flow of people, particularly Asian immigration. As Anderson demonstrated, Federation became couched in scientific terms and white Australia was represented as a scientific experiment. In this experiment, the tropics were situated on the boundary and were considered distinctly as a 'separate, racially dubious territory'.[49] In some cases, the tropics were argued to consume the white race—a belief that was used by many proponents of the Queensland labour trade from 1863 to 1906 to justify their claim that white labour was unsuitable for the tropics. The trade, which was driven by the demand for cheap Islander labour on Queensland's sugar plantations, was vigorously debated in public.

---

46   Muspratt, *My South Sea Island*, 45, 48.
47   Rebell, *Escape to the Sea*, 88–9.
48   Powell, *A South Sea Diary*, 42.
49   Anderson, *The Cultivation of Whiteness*, 73–4, 114.

An alternative response was that the tropics would cultivate a new version of the 'coming man', or as Cilento described him, 'a definite type of North Queenslander, or tropical-born Australian'.[50] A growing number of Australians visiting and residing in the tropics from the 1900s onwards proved this point. In northern Queensland, the collapse of the labour trade had forced more white settlers to work, which undermined the notion that white labour was unsuitable in the tropics. In the Pacific Islands, the experiences of resident traders, plantation overseers, missionaries and colonial officials provided additional evidence that challenged this assumption. Their accounts describing day-to-day life often discussed the effects of European disease, as their engagement required them to sustain a healthy labour force for the plantation (as in the case of Muspratt), supervise and educate a congregation for the mission (as in the case of Helen Cato) or maintain good relationships with their neighbours (as in the case of David).[51] Concerted efforts by governments and businesses to encourage tourism and economic investment in the region by promoting a healthy climate contributed to the tropics and tropical diseases becoming less feared over time.

Depopulation

Depopulation was a trend widely believed to exist in the region, with Australian travellers often drawing on misguided racialist assumptions to understand and explain it. Australian anthropologist Herbert Ian Hogbin wrote in 1939, 'Everyone who has the smallest acquaintance with the literature of the Pacific is familiar with one at least of the effects of contact with the outside world, depopulation'.[52] Depopulation was accepted by most Australians as being self-evident, and as such, travellers often referred to the issue, but rarely dwelled on it. This was a notion applied to Aboriginal Australians as well, as Woollacott argued:

> By the last decades of the nineteenth century, white Australians, with Western beliefs in social Darwinism and eugenics supporting them, assumed that Aboriginal people were dying out. That assumption was so pervasive and secure that the fate of Aborigines was little discussed.[53]

---

50   Cilento, *The White Man in the Tropics*, 73–4.
51   Muspratt, *My South Sea Island*; Cato, *The House on the Hill*; Edgeworth David, *Funafuti*.
52   Herbert Ian Hogbin, *Experiments in Civilization: The Effects of European Culture on a Native Community of the Solomon Islands* (London: Routledge & Sons, 1939), 125.
53   Woollacott, *To Try Her Fortune in London*, 173.

Scholars such as Norma McArthur and Donald Denoon have since shown that population estimates that were made before European contact and during the colonial period were plagued by absences, inaccuracies and inconsistencies.[54] Nonetheless, it was a popular and pervasive idea on which Australians frequently commented.

The most common explanation for depopulation that travellers cited was European disease. Many were well aware of the disastrous effects of past epidemics that were caused by early explorers and more recent visitors (e.g. the outbreak of measles in Fiji in 1875). These events were highly publicised and well known within Australia, and accounts usually stressed the immediate and detrimental effects on the population, overlooking other factors such as population growth and recovery. Frank Coffee offered one example that reminded readers of the high death rates in Fiji in 1875 (which he estimated to be 40,000):

> Fiji affords a striking example of the direful results to be apprehended from exposing a race to a new disease, even though such a malady is comparatively harmless in respect to those who have become in the course of ages accustomed to its effects.[55]

Although improvements in quarantine were significant in preventing widespread outbreaks of diseases across island groups, some Australians also believed that Islanders had developed a resistance to European diseases as part of the evolutionary process. In 1932, Bishop Cecil Wilson discounted 'illnesses which steamers from Sydney often brought with them' as a factor that contributed to depopulation. He argued that Islanders were 'hardy and did not seem to be much affected'.[56] Only in very isolated Islands could a contemporary effect be observed, such as David's visit to Funafuti in 1897:

> We were thoughtful enough to bring with us from Fiji a fine assortment of influenza germs, and these ran riot among the native population. A few days after our arrival two-thirds of the people were down with it, and dismal objects they looked.[57]

---

54 Norma McArthur, *Island Populations of the Pacific* (Canberra: Australian National University Press, 1968), 345–54; Donald Denoon, 'Pacific Island Depopulation: Natural or Un-Natural History?', in *New Countries and Old Medicine: Proceedings of an International Conference on the History of Medicine and Health*, ed. Linda Bryder and Derek A Dow (Auckland: Pyramid Press, 1995).
55 Coffee, *Forty Years on the Pacific*, 171.
56 Wilson, *The Wake of the Southern Cross*, 184.
57 Edgeworth David, *Funafuti*, 52.

A more probable encounter was with diseases that were caused by poverty, malnutrition, overcrowding and dispossession. Growing urban centres and plantations were potential sources of diseases like tuberculosis because of their higher population density. In the case of plantations, poor working conditions placed Islanders at increased risk. This was framed as a clash of primitive and modern, in which 'civilisation intrudes with toil, disease and drabness and the Pacific yields to its advance'.[58] Comments were more often focused on moral corruption in the main urban centres, with descriptions of sexual promiscuity and alcohol abuse attributed as both cause and symptom of depopulation. For government agent Douglas Rannie, depopulation in the New Hebrides was a combination of 'natural laziness, filthy habits and syphilis … and from the vices of drink introduced by white men'.[59] He was also critical of mission rules that forced Islanders to wear ill-fitting clothes—which was a criticism regularly applied by others opposed to missionary influence and then reiterated in the 1920s and 1930s by those lamenting the erosion of traditional ways of life. Diseases of development may have been easily observable in the main towns and ports, but travellers' ability to evaluate the healthiness of an Island was limited, as they did not often venture further inland. In some cases, a traveller could misinterpret the absence of sick people in villages as a sign of healthiness, rather than as one of low life expectancy.[60]

Depopulation was also blamed on generalised racial deficiencies that were attributed to Pacific Islanders—including their supposed physical weakness, moral and psychological immaturity and primitive behaviours and customs. Coffee's explanation of Fiji's depopulation was typically vague, placing blame on both parties by describing:

> The comparatively weak maternal feeling of Fijian women (the infant mortality being very high), the introduction of new diseases, such as measles, whooping-cough, influenza, etc., with which the natives cannot cope, and the disappearance of many of their old social customs.[61]

---

58 Fox, *Oceania*, 3.
59 Rannie, *Notes on the New Hebrides*, 25.
60 Denoon, 'Pacific Island Depopulation', 329.
61 Coffee, *Forty Years on the Pacific*, 171.

The supposed childlike, irresponsible and lazy racial characteristics of Islanders were frequently cited as a major cause. In the 1910s, Ralph Stock described 'an irresponsible child, and, alas, a child who is dying', while Reverend John Wear Burton noted that:

> If the average white resident of Fiji is questioned as to the prime cause of the decrease of the population, in four cases out of five the reply will be, '*Laziness*—pure unadulterated laziness'.[62]

Travellers who applied these racial stereotypes to Pacific Islanders found support in local government officials and missionaries, who stood to benefit from entrenched notions of Islander inferiority. Depopulation was a convenient tool for justifying colonial rule. For example, in response to the measles outbreak in Fiji in 1875, a Royal Commission was established in 1893 'to inquire into the decrease of the native population'. Three years later, it reported:

> Consequently many must have died of starvation and neglect; but the heavy mortality was also attributable in great measure to the people's dire ignorance of the simplest nursing precautions, to their blind unimpressiveness, their want of ordinary foresight, their apathy and despair. They became at once … overwhelmed, dismayed, cowed, abandoning all hope of self-preservation, and becoming incapable of any effort to save themselves or others.[63]

This report was widely circulated and interpreted by other travellers and residents in the early twentieth century, such as by Burton, whose mission publication, *Fiji of To-Day*, reviewed the commission's conclusions. In his summary, he represented mission work as necessary for combatting many of the alleged causes of depopulation ('inbreeding', 'epidemic diseases', 'the condition of women', 'the narcotic influence of the communal system', 'sexual depravity', 'premature civilization' and 'ignorance in the treatment of disease').[64]

Causes of depopulation in the Pacific may have been unclear to Australian travellers, yet it was frequently assumed that all Pacific Islanders uniformly experienced the process. The supposed racial superiority of Polynesians did not make them more resistant to the 'inevitable' racial decline. In fact, the depopulation in Polynesia may have been in part due to the smaller

---

62 Stock, *The Confessions of a Tenderfoot*, 206; Burton, *The Fiji of To-Day*, 213.
63 BG Corney, J Stewart and BH Thomson, *Report of the Commission Appointed to Inquire into the Decrease of the Native Population: 1893* (Suva: Edward John March, 1896), 36.
64 Burton, *The Fiji of To-Day*, 197–216.

size and higher population density of the Islands and the longer period of European contact compared to Melanesia.[65] The European myth making of Tahiti and French Polynesia as sites of desire were influential in shaping Australian attitudes to diseases there. The Polynesian region was idealised as a primitive paradise, and travellers who were disappointed upon arrival blamed disease and corruption, among other factors. As Muspratt noted: 'Some strange quality dwelt here, a lonely forgotten spirit now dying in isolation in this modern world. Like Honolulu, only more so.'[66] A longer period of European contact with Polynesia resulted in a larger body of literature written by explorers and missionaries about disease and depopulation. In the literature, Polynesia was enshrined as being superior to Melanesia and was described as a land of sexual desire, with subsequent travellers aware of the European legacy of venereal disease. Powell noted that Tahiti suffered from 'disease due to debauchery' and that, for Tahitian women, 'to associate with foreign sailors is the utmost degradation'.[67] For the missionaries who established themselves in French Polynesia before moving west, depopulation was a convenient myth to justify their work.[68]

If the Polynesian ideal was degraded by its long association with Europeans, then the Melanesian was supposedly doomed to die because of his or her racial inferiority. As a region less known to Europeans, Melanesia was imagined as being more diseased and more dangerous than Polynesia. It was bestowed the tropical imagery of decay and rottenness, and then it was compared to an idealised east that had 'higher and more vigorous races'.[69] This was supported by the presence of diseases that were not commonly found in the eastern Islands (e.g. malaria). Its proximity to Australia—and reports from sandalwood, *bêche-de-mer* and labour trading within the region—had introduced stereotypes of Melanesian savagery and backwardness into the Australian public consciousness. According to Coffee:

> The [Queensland] plantations turned out some of the most accomplished specimens of savage scoundrels imaginable—men who had grafted on to their originally depraved natures the vices of civilization, but none of its virtues.[70]

---

65 Denoon, 'Pacific Island Depopulation', 405.
66 Muspratt, *Fire of Youth*, 181.
67 Powell, *Adventures of a Wanderer*, 165.
68 McArthur, *Island Populations of the Pacific*, 160.
69 Burton, *The Fiji of To-Day*, 16.
70 Coffee, *Forty Years on the Pacific*, 105.

Due to the scientific theories that situated people according to stages of development from savage to civilised, depopulation was considered a symptom of stagnation—or worse, degradation. In some cases, this became a call to action for Australians. For Presbyterian minister Charles Stuart Ross, the merits of Christian education were emphasised by describing the Fijian as being disadvantaged by 'centuries of moral degradation and intellectual atrophy'.[71] For other travellers, it was accepted that extinction was the only outcome.

Australian attitudes to the Pacific Islands were informed by domestic policies and debates about Aboriginal Australians, who were assumed to be the most primitive and savage of races, and thus doomed to extinction. Considered inferior to Pacific Islanders (both Melanesian and Polynesian), Aboriginal Australians were widely expected to become extinct from the 1830s, an assumption that hardened throughout the early twentieth century. Although the Melanesian race of peoples was believed to possess the same ability to stagnate or degrade as Aboriginal Australians, white Australian attitudes towards the Pacific Islands were generally more positive. This was evident in government policies towards the territories of Papua and New Guinea. These were motivated by a concern for Australia's international image and a belief that Melanesians could be 'civilised' in a way that Aboriginal Australians could not. For example, in practice, this meant that only colonial officers working in Papua and New Guinea received specialised training in anthropology, geography and hygiene, despite the welfare of Papuans and Aboriginal Australians frequently coming under the control of the same ministerial office.

Comparisons between Pacific Islanders and Aboriginal Australians were rare in Australian travel accounts. This may be attributed to the focus on more exotic foreign images or the reality that few urban white Australians came into contact with Aboriginal Australians.[72] Even for travellers who described their encounters with Aboriginal Australians and Pacific Islanders within the same text, they tended to confine each meeting to separate chapters and observed racial characteristics without cross-comparison. This suggests that the broader Australian population considered Aboriginal Australians and Pacific Islanders distinct and separate races, preferring Islanders because they were supposedly superior

---

71 Ross, *Fiji and the Western Pacific*, 133.
72 Woollacott, *To Try Her Fortune in London*, 175. Only William Ramsay Smith and John Wear Burton described encounters with Aboriginal Australians in detail.

or more exotic. In these decades, Australians displayed a more active interest in civilising the Pacific than they did in advancing the Aboriginal Australian cause.

Australians began to articulate more clearly their roles and responsibilities in civilising the Pacific from the 1920s. War had energised a sense of Australian racial character, and the acquisition of new Pacific Island territories post–World War I gave further impetus to a more involved Australian position in the region. Writing in 1939, Hogbin argued that:

> A definite obligation exists to encourage the social development of the natives so that they can eventually, after perhaps several generations, participate in the life of the world on the same sort of footing as ourselves.[73]

Depopulation provided a convenient cause for justifying Australian colonial presence (and, in some cases, a measure of its success). It resonated with the concerns of travellers post–World War I that the primitive and natural Pacific ideal was threatened.

Progress was encouraged in Pacific health and development, in the hope of arresting the alleged trend of depopulation. In Australia, doctors returning from the war felt empowered in managing populations, with the Australian government displaying a greater interest in tropical health, particularly driven by Cilento. Although this government interest faded by the end of the 1920s, Anderson argued that:

> It was the biological utopianism of Cilento and his coterie that resonated most loudly outside the medical profession and health bureaucracies, as it appealed especially to those political radicals and bohemian writers who were trying in the 1930s to distinguish a new national character.[74]

Other nations were concurrently influencing health and disease in the Pacific, prompted by advances in medicine and postwar humanitarian sentiment. The Central Medical School in Fiji was the first of its kind in 1929, funded by the US philanthropic organisation, the Rockefeller Foundation. Building on the training programs developed in Fiji since the 1880s, the school began training 'native medical practitioners'.[75]

73　Hogbin, *Experiments in Civilization*, 231.
74　Hogbin, *Experiments in Civilization*, 129–36, 176.
75　Annie Stuart, 'Contradictions and Complexities in an Indigenous Medical Service', *The Journal of Pacific History* 41, no. 2 (2006): 143.

Australian missions and businesses were also eager to broadcast their roles in developing health facilities and programs to combat depopulation. This is evident in a statement by Bishop Cecil Wilson in 1932, which was published in a children's reference book that promoted Anglican mission work in the Pacific:

> I do not think that at the end of my seventeen years there had been any great decrease in the population … Our Mission, with its doctors, its medicines, its high standard of family life … and its opposition to harmful customs, could only help to stabilize the people, neutralize adverse influences and prevent the depopulation which so-called civilization, with its shoddy clothes, alcohol, firearms, and diseases, almost invariably brings to child races.[76]

NSW state politician Thomas Henley visited a Methodist mission hospital in Fiji in 1926 and praised the work of Australian staff there (see Figure 20). He published an account of his trip to promote the strategic value of the British colony to Australians. Similarly, businesses also referred to medical aid to promote and justify their colonial works. Albert Fuller Ellis's account of Ocean Island and Nauru attributed health and hygiene improvements in mining labour camps to the efforts of British colonisers—to justify the exploitative phosphate mining operations that were conducted on these Islands.[77]

Improved medical knowledge and treatment in the early twentieth century also shaped perceptions of disease in the Pacific, resulting in a diminishing fear of human carriers of disease and greater confidence in medicine. Further, medical and scientific discourses in the 1930s began to challenge 'formalist taxonomies of race', according to Anderson; he identified a shift in government policies towards Aboriginal Australians from isolation to assimilation.[78] However, stereotypes remained persistent, as Stuart revealed in the records of the Fiji Annual Medical and Health Report of 1936 and 1938—these reports applied racialised traits to students, classifying Polynesians as 'sanguine', Melanesians as 'phlegmatic' and Micronesians as 'choleric'.[79]

---

76   Wilson, *The Wake of the Southern Cross*, 184.
77   Ellis, *Ocean Island and Nauru*, 135, 138.
78   Anderson, *The Cultivation of Whiteness*, 206.
79   Stuart, 'Contradictions and Complexities', 132.

7. PRESERVING HEALTH AND RACE IN THE TROPICS

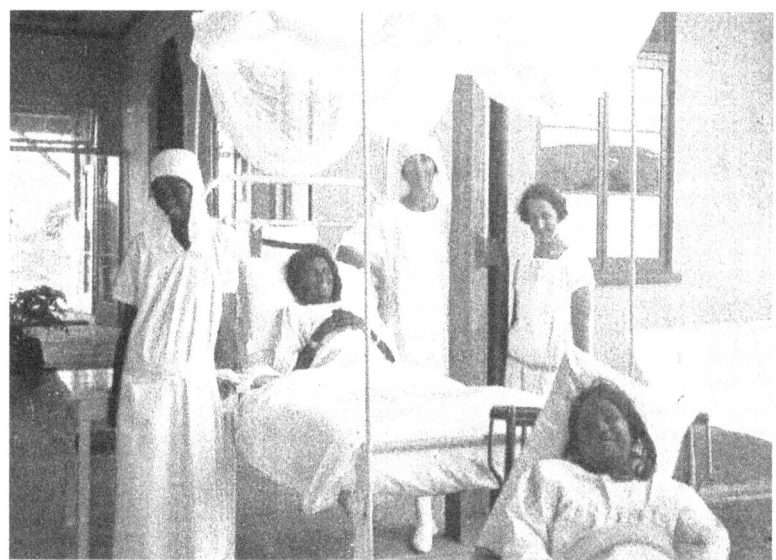

One of the Wards of the Methodist Mission Hospital, Ba, Fiji.
Dr. Doreen Hensley, Resident Medical Missionary, late of Melbourne (standing behind the patient in chair); Matron Miss Clare Spencer, of Burwood, Sydney (standing at the head of the bed).

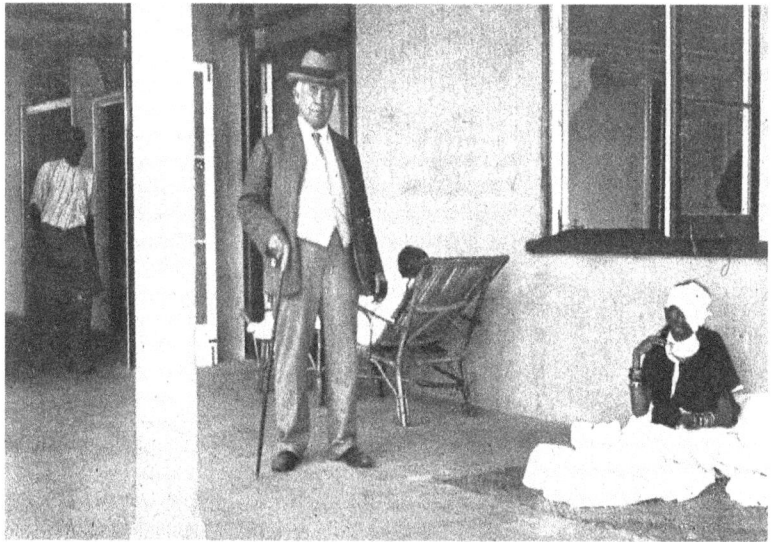

Sir Thomas Henley visiting the Hospital—July, 1926.
(One of the Sleeping-out Verandahs)

Figure 20: One of the Wards of the Methodist Mission Hospital, Ba, Fiji.
Source: Thomas Henley, *Fiji—The Land of Promise* (Sydney: John Sands Ltd, 1926), 48.

For Australian travel writers, evidence of depopulation, degradation or progress was difficult to observe during their momentary encounters in the Islands. As sailor Alan John Villiers observed in the Solomon Islands in 1937, 'Tulagi is frankly and plainly a headquarters for white living … where white meets white, lives with white, thinks white, and plays golf and tennis and cricket and so forth'.[80] The nature of travel thus reinforced the racialist assumptions that were popular in Australia at the time. Occasionally, some travellers would depart from these conventions. For example, Villiers's narrative of yachting in the Pacific was critical of the Australian administration and of its effects in the Solomon Islands, which led him to question 'whether new countries … ought ever to be entrusted with the control of native races'.[81] Gold prospector John Archibald Fraser wrote in the 1930s that he considered the Fijian his 'brown-skinned brother', finding Fijian cannibalism to be no less moral than the British treatment of Aboriginal Australians.[82] Similarly, young artist Aletta Lewis became deeply attached to the Samoan community with whom she temporarily lived in 1929, to the extent at which she forgot the division between 'his race and mine'.[83] In 1939, lone adventurer and sailor Fred Rebell remarked:

> There is something in those natives [of Fiji] which makes them accept life without a struggle … And yet how much are these tendencies racial? How much are they merely climatic and geographical?[84]

The few travel accounts that depart from the conventional narrative of racialised human difference suggest that the contradictions of racial theory and policy in the Pacific were more clearly visible by the 1920s and 1930s.

The Asian 'Invasion'

Australian travel writers also noted the growth of the other populations in the Pacific Islands. Expecting a Pacific that was populated entirely by primitive Islanders and colonial white masters, travellers were instead surprised to find evidence of substantial Asian immigration throughout

---

80   Villiers, *Cruise of the Conrad*, 173.
81   Villiers, *Cruise of the Conrad*, 175–6.
82   Fraser, *Gold Dish and Kava Bowl*, 131.
83   Lewis, *They Call Them Savages*, 76, 109.
84   Rebell, *Escape to the Sea*, 88–9.

the region. The economic success and population growth of Asian people in the Pacific were attributed to the assumed depopulation of Pacific Islanders, which made Asian peoples the target of negative and derogatory labelling. Specifically, Australian travellers commented on the high concentration of Japanese people in Hawai'i, Chinese in Tahiti and Indians in Fiji. These were high-profile stopover destinations for travellers, and Australians had different responses to each group, as well as a more general aversion to a perceived external Asian threat. Anti-Asian immigration policies in Australia were used by Australian travellers to justify colonial oversight of the Pacific to protect indigenous people and to reassure themselves of their own national policy of a 'White Australia'. The White Australia policy was a source of pride for many Australians who believed that it protected the nation from an Asian invasion. Historian David Walker characterised Australia as an 'anxious nation' at the turn of the twentieth century, with the imagined geopolitical threat of Asia propelling a 'powerful masculinising and racialising impulse in Australian nationalism'.[85] Journalist Frank Fox expressed this sentiment in his 1912 travelogue: 'Australia is at once the fortress which the White Race has thinly garrisoned against an Asiatic advance southward, and the most tempting prize to inspire the Asiatic to that advance'.[86] This racial preoccupation with Asia influenced the travel accounts of the Pacific Islands.

Australian reactions to Japanese migrants in Hawai'i were characterised by a disappointment that their expectations of Hawaiian and/or American society were not met, or by a general concern about the growing military threat that Japan posed post–World War I. Japanese migration was most visible in Hawai'i, though they were spread extensively throughout the Pacific Islands. They were also visible in smaller concentrations in pearling stations along the north Queensland coast, as labourers in New Caledonia, Banaba, Nauru and Queensland (on sugar plantations) and as traders in Micronesia. Their population in Australia was relatively small, numbering only 3,489 in the 1911 census.[87] This explains why few Australians who travelled to the Pacific were familiar with Japanese culture and why they relied instead on generic stereotypes.

---

85 David Walker, *Anxious Nation: Australia and the Rise of Asia, 1850–1939* (St Lucia: University of Queensland Press, 1999), 5.
86 Fox, *Problems of the Pacific*, 107.
87 'Japan-Born Community Information Summary', Commonwealth of Australia, www.homeaffairs.gov.au/mca/files/2016-cis-japan.PDF.

Sustained labour migration from Japan to Hawai'i began from 8 February 1885, as contract labour for sugar and pineapple plantations. By 1920, the Japanese constituted 43 per cent of Hawai'i's population. This numerical dominance was a frequent observation of many Australian travellers who passed through Hawai'i. As Anne Rees revealed in her study of Australian female travellers to the US, expectations of an exclusively white and American nation that was similar to Australia were shattered by the racial and cultural hybridity of Hawai'i.[88] Many Australians represented the Japanese threat as a reproductive one. The notion that Japanese people would 'out-breed' other races was one also applied to Chinese and Indian people in the Pacific. In 1929, George Meudell remarked that they 'breed quicker than flies or rabbits' and, in a patriotic treatise, he argued that the Australian 'doors' of immigration not allow 'inferior, ignorant humans'.[89] Meudell observed that 'the aborigines [indigenous Hawaiians] are decadent and will shortly vanish as a race'. Yet, his concern for the indigenous population of Hawai'i was uncommon, as few travellers encountered Islanders during their transit at the port in Honolulu. Rather, the Japanese were perceived as spoiling the Island paradise that many Australians sought, possessing a 'pervasive, acrid smell of Asia' that was 'haunting, persistent, disquieting'.[90]

Not all Australian accounts were as damning and vehement in their opposition to Japanese people. Some understood the racial tensions that existed within Hawai'i, caused by the population growth and economic prosperity of Japanese residents. Although many Japanese labourers worked on plantations, Australian tourists frequently observed them working at the docks and within the town. In 1925, politician Richard Meagher noted that 'there is an enormous distrust of the Japanese. Rightly or wrongly they get the credit of being at the back of various industrial disturbances'.[91] Robert McMillan, who visited Hawai'i in 1903, argued that the Islands were 'just simmering in destructive discontent'.[92] Others, such as Paul McGuire, predicted a more mixed future race, arguing that 'He is a Chinese–Japanese–Scandinavian compound with flecks of Polynesian, and he is, I suspect, Pacific Man of to-morrow'.[93]

---

88   Rees, 'Ellis Island in the Pacific'.
89   Meudell, *The Pleasant Career of a Spendthrift*, 144.
90   Fox, *Oceania*, 9.
91   Richard Denis Meagher, *American Impressions* (Sydney: Gordon & Gotch, 1925), 8.
92   McMillan, *There and Back*, 358. He further added that 'the little brown man is absolutely wicked'.
93   McGuire, *Westward the Course*, 44.

The establishment of Pan-Pacific conferences in the 1930s, many of which were based in Hawai'i, also encouraged cross-cultural encounters and sympathetic understanding to a degree.[94]

The 1930s were marked by fears of war, colouring Australian attitudes to Japanese residents in Hawai'i. When journalist Eric Baume visited Hawai'i in 1937, he proudly stated that Australia did not have 'any Japanese problem because we took good care we would not'.[95] Although potential enemies were vaguely located in Asia in the 1920s and 1930s, by the end of the decade, the military strength of the Japanese attracted the most concern. Their skill had already been proven in the Russo–Japanese War of 1904–1905, and their acquisition of Micronesian Islands after World War I was well known among Australians. This was evident in certain travel accounts, such as those by Villiers, who avoided the Caroline Islands for fear of being called a spy, and Marshall, who, although expressing anti-colonial sentiments, argued for Australian settlement in New Guinea to protect it from Japanese hands.[96] Books with titles such as *Pacific Peril* contributed to a sense of panic in Australia—which was reflected in comments made by travellers like Thomas McKay, who explicitly warned his readers that 'Australians may wake up some fine morning to find Japan installed as their next-door neighbour'.[97]

The Chinese influence in the Pacific Islands was also frequently noted by Australian travellers. However, the Chinese were more often identified with economic prosperity than the Japanese. Chinese, 'Chinamen' or 'Orientals' were described in various locations: 'John Chinaman' fishing in Hawai'i, eating at 'Sam Doos' restaurant in the Solomon Islands, walking through 'Chinatown' in Suva, working as a trader in the Gilbert Islands and with an 'Asiatic' crew onboard ships.[98] If they were represented pictorially, they would be decoratively adorned and usually in masculine form, with exaggerated or distorted body shapes and facial features. Australians were

---

94   Janet Mitchell, *Spoils of Opportunity: An Autobiography* (New York: Dutton, 1939); Paisley, *Glamour in the Pacific*.
95   Baume, *I Lived These Years*, 167.
96   Villiers, *Cruise of the Conrad*, 133; Jock Marshall, *The Men and Birds of Paradise: Journeys through Equatorial New Guinea* (London: William Heinemann, 1938), 131. See also Ernest George Marks, *Pacific Peril, or, Menace of Japan's Mandated Islands* (Sydney: Wynyard Book Arcade, 1933).
97   Marks, *Pacific Peril*; McKay, *Seeing the World Twice*, xv.
98   James Park Thomson, *Round the World* (Brisbane: Outridge Printing Co., 1904), 8; Villiers, *Cruise of the Conrad*, 172; Allan, *Homeward Bound*, 24; Rosa Angela Kirkcaldie, *In Gray and Scarlet* (Melbourne: Alexander McCubbin, 1922), 30; Osborne, *Through the Atolls of the Line*; Thomas, *Cannibals and Convicts*, 49.

also familiar with the Chinese people since their immigration to the New South Wales and Victorian goldfields in the 1850s. They were the largest ethnic minority in Australia, other than Aboriginal Australians. By the late 1870s, their population peaked to 38,553.[99] Their wide geographical distribution encouraged fears of a racial overpowering of the Pacific Islands and Australia.

The Chinese had a long history of contact with the Pacific Islands, first as carpenters and cooks who travelled with sandalwood traders in the mid-nineteenth century, then as traders and indentured labourers in French Polynesia, New Guinea, Samoa and the Gilbert Islands. Their numbers remained relatively small until the 1930s, but they were noted for their economic enterprise (as cooks and store owners), incurring the enmity of Europeans because they were frugal, willing to work long hours, lived more simply and could undersell European traders.[100] These concerns were evident in the 1932 article 'Chinese Problem in the South Seas', in the *Pacific Islands Monthly*.[101] The Chinese were also vocal and active in defending their rights—this was demonstrated when the Chinese consul-general in Australia sent a representative to the Solomon Islands to challenge discriminatory policies, and in the New Hebrides, when Chinese residents formed a 'Chinese club' in 1932 in response to anti-Chinese sentiment.[102]

Australians criticised the Chinese in particular because of their dominance in Tahiti. This was due to the highly romanticised Polynesian ideal, the large population of Chinese people residing there, their relative economic prosperity and the low visibility of other Asian cultures.[103] Initially, Australian tourists resented the Chinese for spoiling the primitive ideal that they expected in Tahiti, though this was only one of many corrupting influences to be blamed. More threatening to Australians was the potential for interbreeding, with the Chinese having intermarried freely with Polynesians in Tahiti from the late nineteenth century to the extent that Powell wrote in 1942: 'The Chinese … are in Tahiti absorbed'.[104]

---

99 Woollacott, *To Try Her Fortune in London*, 173.
100 William E Willmott, *A History of the Chinese Communities in Eastern Melanesia: Solomon Islands, Vanuatu, New Caledonia* (Christchurch: Macmillan Brown Centre for Pacific Studies, University of Canterbury, 2005), 13.
101 'Chinese Problem in the South Seas', *Pacific Islands Monthly* 3, no. 5 (December 1932): 33.
102 Willmott, *A History of the Chinese Communities*, 16, 39.
103 Newbury, *Tahiti Nui*, 263–71.
104 Powell, *A South Sea Diary*, 24.

7. PRESERVING HEALTH AND RACE IN THE TROPICS

This reflected a wider concern about the fragility of the Pacific Islander races and the proliferation of 'half-breeds of various colours'.[105] Some, like Powell, believed that 'the Chinese and the Europeans here have saved the Tahitian race from its threatened extinction',[106] but this view belonged to a minority. Concerns about interbreeding were not as prevalent in Melanesia, where William E Willmott demonstrated that, although most Chinese migrants were single men, intermarriage was rare.[107]

Much more common and widespread was a fear of Chinese dominance, both in the Pacific Islands and in Australia. This reflected the broader concern of an Asian 'invasion' in the region. This was suggested by travellers like Safroni-Middleton, who indiscriminately blended racial characteristics to imagine a hybrid race of 'several stealthy-footed followers of Mohammed, a kind of mongrel, half-caste Chinese-Indian'.[108] Although these exaggerated and blended stereotypes were common, other travellers experienced genuine surprise and ambivalence, as tourist Alfred Hill's account in 1927 demonstrated:

> He is quiet, law-abiding, patient and persevering, biding his time and opportunity and then seizing it with both hands and coming out on top. This is the history of almost every island in the Pacific, and gives thought to those who consider the ultimate destiny of the lands bordering it. It comes as rather a rude shock to an Australian to find that the Chinese are treated by the whites and natives with the same deference as is extended to the white man. They also travel first class on the steamers, dine in the saloon, and frequent the smokerooms and lounges, also best seats in the pictures. At first one feels a repugnance, but, finding it is the accepted custom, one gradually sees the sense, and the Chinaman is treated an equal, which, in most cases he is, if not a superior.[109]

As Hill's comments suggest, the clearest danger that Australians perceived was the Chinese work ethic and their subsequent economic prosperity. Australians frequently identified Chinese people as business owners throughout the region, describing them as hardworking and shrewd, yet cunning and undermining. In Nossiter's perspective, the Chinese took advantage of the weak:

---

105 Irwin and Goff, *No Longer Innocent*, 90.
106 Powell, *A South Sea Diary*, 24.
107 Willmott, *A History of the Chinese Communities*, 17.
108 Safroni-Middleton, *Wine-Dark Seas and Tropic Skies*, 29.
109 Hill, *A Cruise among Former Cannibal Islands*, 43–4.

> The Chinaman works hard wherever he goes, keeps his shop open for trade day and night and quickly becomes the shopkeeper of a town or village. They undersell the other traders, whom they put out of business … In the old civilized countries as India, Ceylon, Egypt and Arabia, they are not to be found in any numbers, neither does one come across them in Europe. It seems to me the Chinaman selects the newer civilisation where the people are unsophisticated and careless.[110]

Many travellers commented on 'Chinese trade robbers', who were considered corrupt and amoral, or Chinese storekeepers, who would manipulate or trick customers. However, this resentment was tempered by the view that the Chinese were necessary in the Pacific because they were racially superior to the Islanders, and thus a more capable and reliable labour force. After leaving Circular Quay for the Pacific Islands in 1878, Thomas noted many Chinese people ashore and remarked: 'He, like the poor, is always with us; and, like poverty, we look upon him as a disagreeable necessity'.[111]

This ambiguous attitude was also directed towards Indians in the Pacific Islands, particularly the large population living in Fiji. The nation's proximity to Australia and its close relationship with Australian business, trade, Christian missions and tourism signified that race was an issue that Australian travel writers in the Pacific most frequently associated with Fiji. Fiji's location on the border of Melanesia and Polynesia also generated uncertainty among Australians who were unsure how to regard people who were physically darker, yet who shared similarities in kinship systems, language and traditions with Polynesia, as well as having British colonial affinities. United by their shared British colonial heritage, Australians approached Fiji (and its Indian population) with greater familiarity and confidence to pronounce judgement on the merits and faults of its people and its colonial masters.

Henley noted this colonial familiarity when he wrote about Fiji in 1926: 'The Fijians regard Australia as the big brother, and ask for a brotherly consideration in trade matters'.[112] Trade and business underpinned Australian engagement with the colony, and it promoted the exchange of people as well as goods. This British imperial connection even prompted

---

110 Nossiter, *Southward Ho!*, 152.
111 Thomas, *Cannibals and Convicts*, 49.
112 Henley, *Fiji—The Land of Promise*, 58.

some people, like JS Griffiths, to argue for Australian annexation of Fiji: 'More than two-thirds of the total trade of Fiji is with Australia, and it is largely the sons of Australia who carry on the work in the islands as overseers or clerks'.[113] Crucial to Fiji's economic success was Indian indentured labour, which had been employed from 1879 to provide a labour force that was considered more reliable than Fijian and other Pacific Islander labourers (as well as ensuring the protection of the indigenous population). By the time that indentured labour immigration ceased in 1916, over 60,000 Indians had immigrated to Fiji.[114] Despite their numerical dominance, Indians drew little, if any, comment from Australian travellers. When they did, the observations were overwhelmingly negative, repeating the commonly held belief that Indians were 'beasts of burden' who served a primarily commercial purpose.[115]

Encounters with Indians in Fiji were unsurprising to Australian travellers, who were knowledgeable about the indentured labour trade and familiar with Indians living in Australia. The British Empire network had facilitated the exchange of people, goods and ideas between India and Australia since the early nineteenth century. Suzanne Rickard highlighted the migration of Indian seamen, servants, convicts and traders to Australia.[116] They were followed by an influx of Indian indentured labour that New South Wales pastoralists employed in the 1830s and 1840s, as well as camel handlers and traders from the north-west provinces of India from the 1860s to the 1890s.[117] Indians were also visible on cruise ships that travelled to and from Australia; they were preferred as servants in the saloon and on deck, as opposed to other workers who were confined below to the engine

---

113 JS Griffiths, 'Fiji: The Eastern Outpost of Australia', *The Lone Hand* (April 1912): 508.
114 See Kenneth Lowell Oliver Gillion, *Fiji's Indian Migrants: A History to the End of Indenture in 1920* (Melbourne: Oxford University Press, 1962), 76; Brij V Lal, *Chalo Jahaji: On a Journey through Indenture in Fiji* (Canberra: ANU E Press, 2012), 69, 138, doi.org/10.22459/CJ.12.2012.
115 Gillion, *Fiji's Indian Migrants*, 18.
116 Suzanne Rickard, 'Lifelines from Calcutta', in *India, China, Australia: Trade and Society 1788–1850*, ed. James Broadbent, Suzanne Rickard and Margaret Steven (Glebe: Historic Houses Trust of NSW, 2003), 66, 71, 75, 82.
117 Christine Stevens, *Tin Mosques and Ghantowns: A History of Afghan Camel Drivers in Australia* (Melbourne: Oxford University Press, 1989), 26. For further discussion, see Michael J Cigler, *The Afghans in Australia* (Melbourne: AE Press, 1986); Pamela Rajkowski, *In the Tracks of the Camelmen* (North Ryde: Angus & Robertson, 1987); Peter Scriver, 'Mosques, Ghantowns and Cameleers in the Settlement History of Colonial Australia', *Fabrications: The Journal of the Society of Architectural Historians, Australia and New Zealand* 13, no. 2 (2004): 19–41, doi.org/10.1080/10331867.2004.105 25182; Heather Goodall, Devleena Ghosh and Lindi R Todd, 'Jumping Ship-Skirting Empire: Indians, Aborigines and Australians across the Indian Ocean', *Transforming Cultures eJournal* 3, no. 1 (2008): 44–74, doi.org/10.5130/tfc.v3i1.674.

rooms.[118] When the Australian colonies federated in 1901, the number of Indians was estimated at 7,637. This number dropped to 3,698 by 1911 due to the *Immigration Restriction Act* (1901), which overlooked their status as British subjects and classified Indians as 'natives of Asia'.[119] Their controlled mobility starkly contrasted the unrestricted movement of Australians to India, many of whom were missionaries.

This discrimination was evident in Australian representations of Indians, which emphasised their role as subservient workers. This image was prompted by the jobs in which most Indians were employed, which encouraged a stereotype of Indians as being docile, compliant and hardy.[120] The terms 'lascars' (sailors), 'Afghans' (cameleers), 'hawkers' (traders) and 'coolies' (unskilled labourers) not only became synonymous with Indians, but they also became racialised categories that relegated the Indian to an inferior status to white Australians. Despite this assumed inferiority, Australians expressed their concern about the ascendancy of Indians, most commonly in objection to the dominance of lascars on ships.[121] Like the Chinese and Japanese, Indians were part of the general notion of an Asian menace that served to reinforce a nationalist ideology of racial purity and control in Australia. Apart from lascars, Indian migrants living in Australia did not constitute a large enough group to prompt the same hostility from Australians that was reserved for Fiji.

After arriving in Suva, Australians' first impressions reveal an immediate awareness of the multi-racial nature of the Fijian community. A 'medley of races' was a phrase commonly used to describe Suva wharf, a place at which the prevalence of Chinese and Indians was often noted. During his gold prospecting in the early 1930s, Fraser recalled:

> The streets of Suva were busy, and the medley of people in their distinctive costumes presented a lively and colourful picture … But by far the greatest part of the population seemed to be made up of Indians, Fijians, and Chinese, in about that order numerically. Every waiter and taxi-driver we saw was an Indian, and we

---

118 Goodall, Ghosh and Todd, 'Jumping Ship-Skirting Empire', 54.
119 Margaret Allen, '"Innocents Abroad" and "Prohibited Immigrants": Australians in India and Indians in Australia 1890–1910', in *Connected Worlds: History in Transnational Perspective*, ed. Ann Curthoys and Marilyn Lake (Canberra: ANU E Press, 2006), 120, doi.org/10.22459/CW.03.2006.
120 Ravi Ahuja, in Goodall, Ghosh and Todd, 'Jumping Ship-Skirting Empire', 47; Scriver, 'Mosques, Ghantowns and Cameleers', 26.
121 Goodall, Ghosh and Todd, 'Jumping Ship-Skirting Empire', 56.

learned that the most skilled work, such as that of carpenters and mechanics, was in their slim dark hands. They usually looked much the same as the Hindu hawkers of Australia.[122]

It is evident from Fraser's statement that Indians were clearly visible in Suva by the 1930s. This was not the case in the 1880s and 1890s, when the Indian population was small, isolated and dispersed across Fiji. The difficulty of access to other districts on the main island of Viti Levu explains the absence of Indians from Australian travel accounts during this time. However, by the 1910s, Australian visits were more frequent, more prolonged and more probing. Consequently, visitors wrote of short, glancing encounters with Indian taxi drivers, Indian shopkeepers, Indian housekeepers and Indian waiters. In 1924, Meagher visited the Grand Pacific Hotel and observed:

> The attendants, all Hindoos in immaculate white garb with coloured sashes, prove excellent waiters. Nearly all the motor-car drivers are Hindoos, the one I employed to drive around the island being particularly intelligent. The number of Hindoos in the place is astounding.[123]

It was also possible to visit the sugar mills of CSR, which offered a passenger service on its commercial line. Harriet Ponder was an experienced traveller who fondly remembered travelling on the train in 1924:

> You can travel (free) over the hundred miles of two-foot-gauge railway built by the Colonial Sugar Refining Company to serve the coastal sugar districts of Viti Levu … for a trip on this train provides a miniature pageant of island life that it would not be easy to equal … At every plantation at which the train stops to hand out the week's pay, the stranger feels inclined to rub his eyes and wonder whether he is travelling in India by mistake.[124]

The observations of Indians when they were noticed were casual, essentialist and negative. Few Australian visitors had sustained contact with Indians in Fiji. Instead, they drew on the stereotypes that were used in previous European literature, which reinforced an anti-Indian prejudice. This image was enhanced by comparisons to the indigenous Fijian population, who were romanticised as primitive and innocent and who were framed within a discourse of protectionism in response to their perceived depopulation.

---

122 Fraser, *Gold Dish and Kava Bowl*, 45.
123 Meagher, *American Impressions*, 6.
124 Ponder, *An Idler in the Islands*, 18, 56, 61.

Australian travellers seeking the exotic Islander were uninterested in Indian culture or traditions, and rarely described Indian houses, clothes, food or cultural traditions. Indians were considered a foreign intrusion in the Pacific Islands, their population described by Robert Brummitt as 'the Indian Invasion' in 1914.[125] When Indian women were described, it was to note the common practice of wearing jewellery while working on the plantations. In contrast to their 'innocent' Fijian neighbours, Indians were represented as treacherous and cunning, waiting to take advantage of gullible tourists or naive overseers. These ideas were fuelled by speculative reports in the local press and planters' fears of Indian uprisings, especially in the 1900s.[126] Stock made dismal and degrading remarks about Indians at work in 1913:

> Here were the sullen, the cunning, the murderous, the fawning and the banal ... culled from the dregs of central India ... The islander is a child throughout life, the coolie, for the most part, a snake.[127]

As Stock's comment suggests, the threat was emphasised by comparing Indians to the innocent Fijians. It also highlights a commonly held belief that Indians living in Fiji were outcasts who were 'crowded out' from their 'old land'.[128]

Portrayals of Indians living in Fiji as outcasts conflicted with conventional representations of India in Australia and the broader British Empire. As Walker revealed, Indians were admired for their ancient cultural traditions, with Australian travellers to India emphasising the nation's 'antiquity and spiritual wealth'.[129] Racial notions of Aryanism proposed that Europeans shared a common Aryan heritage with Indians and that Asia (specifically central Asia/north India) was identified as the cradle of humanity. Tony Ballantyne argued that this racial connection was amplified by the colonial exchange between India and the rest of the Empire, not only of goods and people but also of ideas.[130] Travellers to India, like GT Garratt, admired the cultural legacy of the subcontinent, Garratt remarked in 1937 that:

---

125 Brummitt, *A Winter Holiday in Fiji*, 132.
126 Gillion, *Fiji's Indian Migrants*, 156–7.
127 Stock, *The Confessions of a Tenderfoot*, 174, 176.
128 Fraser, *Gold Dish and Kava Bowl*, 237.
129 Walker, *Anxious Nation*, 19. See also Allen, '"Innocents Abroad" and "Prohibited Immigrants"', 112.
130 Ballantyne, *Webs of Empire*, 30–3. Ballantyne's description of Aryanism in New Zealand can be applied to the Australian context.

> More and more, however, we are beginning to realize the innumerable contacts, throughout the course of history, between East and West, and their mutual indebtedness in language, literature, art and philosophy.[131]

In comparison, Indians in Fiji did not receive the same treatment, attracting mainly hostile and disparaging judgements.

The strong religious and cultural traditions that Indian migrants brought with them to Fiji made the conversion efforts of European missionaries difficult. Reverend Burton noted the difficulty of converting Indians to Christianity in 1914 (a task that had not been undertaken by missionaries until 1892):

> The results, statistically, are small, and it is to be feared the impression made upon the population is only slight ... So far, the Hindu and Muhammadan influences of the home and parents have been stronger than the Christian influence in the school.[132]

Consequently, Indians were represented by missionaries more negatively. Missionaries emphasised their stubbornness and heathenism and compared them to indigenous Fijians, who were often described as the model Pacific Islander because they had been Christianised.[133] These descriptions filtered into Australian travel accounts, like those of Methodist doctor Brummitt, who concluded that Indians were 'often very ignorant and superstitious ... subject to the most violent passions, which often find expression in violent deed ... under the influence of jealousy or of revenge'.[134] Safroni-Middleton's comparison emphasised the fragility of Fijians, arguing that the Eastern religions that were introduced threatened traditional religious beliefs:

> The Indian sadhu (saint) sits by the line of dens and stores under the palms; he looks like some carved holy image as he stares with bright, unblinking eyes. The natives' wooden idols have long since been smashed, or have rotted away and that living idol of the East is one from many cargoes that have arrived to take the place of the old deaf South Sea idols. The new idols are real ... the deaf, dumb wooden gods of heathen times were sanctified compared with these new immigrant idols that breathe![135]

---

131 HG Rawlinson, 'Indian in European Literature and Thought', in *The Legacy of India*, ed. GT Garratt (Oxford: The Clarendon Press, 1937), 37.
132 Burton, *The Call of the Pacific*, 110, 112.
133 Paton, *Thirty Years with South Sea Cannibals*, 108.
134 Brummitt, *A Winter Holiday in Fiji*, 138.
135 Safroni-Middleton, *A Vagabond's Odyssey*, 56.

The perpetuation of negative Indian stereotypes was closely connected to Indians' association with hard labour and industry. They were often overlooked because they did not match the exotic imaginings of a carefree island way of life, and the reality of life while working on sugar plantations and mills was not appealing or picturesque. Burton was one of the earliest Australians to detail the terrible living conditions of indentured labourers:

> The coolie 'lines' (as they are called) are long rows of tarred, wooden buildings, which might be taken as the very apotheosis of architectural ugliness ... In each of these miserable kennels three men, or one family, have to eat and sleep ... Vice, wickedness, and abjectness abound. Personal filth is ever in evidence, and life seems to have turned rancid.[136]

Framed within a discourse of labour and commerce, the Indian work ethic reinforced the undisputed assumption of the Fijian's unwillingness to work.[137] Like most Europeans, Henley considered idleness a natural trait of the Fijian race, and attributed it to the natural abundance of the Islands and an 'ingrained conception of communal rights'.[138] Journalist Charles Edwin Woodrow Bean commented in 1909 that, 'The Fijian is a gentleman, and lives in comfort ... [he] is there for ornament, not for use'.[139] Similarly, Indians were believed to have a natural affinity for hard labour and to 'possess powers of endurance which make them suitable plantation workers'.[140]

With this potential came a warning regarding their supposed tendency for violence and the need for strict discipline—a stereotype that originated from planters' fears of Indian uprisings. Fears of violence may also have been stoked by anti-colonial protests in India during the 1920s and 1930s.[141] It was a common assumption in Australian travel writing that Indians committed many murders, often of their overseers or of Indian women. For example, Bean wrote:

---

136 Burton, *The Call of the Pacific*, 107.
137 Lal, *Chalo Jahaji*, 69.
138 Henley, *Fiji—The Land of Promise*, 56.
139 Bean, *With the Flagship of the South*, 57.
140 Burton, *The Call of the Pacific*, 104.
141 Lal, *Chalo Jahaji*, 174; John Dunham Kelly, *A Politics of Virtue: Hinduism, Sexuality, and Countercolonial Discourse in Fiji* (Chicago: University of Chicago Press, 1991), 142.

> The strange part of it is that, though he seemed so spiritless, he had been committing nearly all the murders in the island … the Indian murders simply because he is passionately moral.[142]

Realistically, Australian travellers did not encounter violent Indians. Instead, contact was usually momentary and superficial, with Indians being described as serious and unfriendly. This may have been partly due to the general European prejudice towards Indians and the lack of sustained engagement with them. However, it also resonates with Brij V Lal's summary of Indian responses to overt prejudice and oppression, particularly in the plantations, whereby 'active non-resistance, thus, became a strategy for survival'.[143] The mistreatment of Indian indentured labourers, often under the supervision of the CSR or at the hands of Australian overseers, contributed to an Indian distrust of white men.

Although most Australian travel writing overlooked Indians in Fiji, there were some perceptive travellers who described the Indian population in more generous terms. Unlike the 1880s and 1890s, when little information about Indian indentured labour was available to British and Australian audiences, Australian interest in the indenture issue increased during the 1910s and 1920s. The decline of the Fijian population and the growth of the Indians became a major concern for the British administration, which was a concern echoed in other travel accounts. Burton was a particularly influential Australian Methodist who highlighted the 'dehumanising' indenture system. Australians were well informed of the nationalist movement in India at the time, and the plight of Indo-Fijians became part of this international political discourse. Indians were active in organising themselves in Fiji and in forming connections with the Indian nationalist movement abroad, raising the profile of their cause. Indian barristers, missionaries, teachers and lawyers were sent to Fiji under the sponsorship of Indian organisations to document the circumstances of indenture and support Indian labourers who were persecuted by colonial masters.[144] At home, some Australians offered sympathy and support. Gillion offered an example of 46 women's organisations from Australia and New Zealand who sent a delegate to Fiji to investigate indenture conditions in 1919.[145] Within the body of Australian travel writing are examples of this growing

---

142 Bean, *With the Flagship of the South*, 58.
143 Lal, *Chalo Jahaji*, 168.
144 Kelly, *A Politics of Virtue*, 115, 142.
145 Gillion, *Fiji's Indian Migrants*, 187.

Australian concern for Indians' welfare and a softening of racialist attitudes towards them. Brummitt echoed Burton's concerns that indenture was dehumanising in 1914; Henley's account argued for a better organised and regulated administration in 1926; and, in 1935, Bendigo miner WJ Stephens demanded that the British government make reparations to indentured labourers.[146]

Whether encountering Indians, Chinese, Japanese or other 'Asiatic' types, Australian travellers were generally surprised to find racial and cultural hybridity in the Pacific Islands. Their experiences of travel tested their understanding of race and human difference, forcing them to consider the merits of maintaining a racially pure, white Australia. Race was an integral part of Australian travel writing, informing Australians throughout their Pacific journeys. Travel literature and science in the Pacific have been historically intertwined; travellers adopted scientific practices and language with ease, yet applied scientific ideas indiscriminately and ambiguously. The most significant assumption that Australians carried with them was that race was an uncontested category, a rigid hierarchy in which Pacific Islanders were static, timeless and locked into a particular position. Their observations of disease and the tropical environment, of depopulation and of other foreigners were informed by this assumption, one that had hardened over time from the 1880s to the 1940s.

Although many travel accounts repeated these racialist assumptions and stereotypes, some Australians struggled to reconcile strict racial categories with the multi-racial reality of the Pacific Islands. In 1934, in the New Hebrides, zoologist Alan John Marshall and his British companion, Tom, ridiculed a pamphlet that was given to him by a customs official titled *Talking Points of Australia*:

> 'Do you realise, Tom,' I held forth, 'that my country is the healthiest in the world; that my city, Sydney is the second greatest in the British Empire? … [and] you should certainly know that our White Australia policy ensures that we shall have no "colour problem" … Again, the booklet says (and it must be right) that we are rapidly developing into a distinctive race—tall, strong and athletic; proud of our freedom and progress, yet loyal, dear Tom, and living up to the best traditions of justice, humanity and hospitality!'[147]

---

146 Henley, *Fiji—The Land of Promise*; Brummitt, *A Winter Holiday in Fiji*; Stephens, *Samoan Holidays*.
147 Marshall, *The Black Musketeers*, 168.

In reply, Tom remarked, 'I haven't noticed any of those traits in you'. Such criticisms revealed the flaws in Australia's efforts to preserve health and race at home and abroad. The limited number of these accounts means that it is difficult to identify whether travellers like Marshall were exceptional, or whether they represent a broader trend in Australia in the 1920s and 1930s. This period was a time of great social and economic change in Australia after World War I, and the acquisition of new mandates in the Pacific encouraged a more internationalist outlook among Australians. Anderson's history of Australian medical theory and practice suggested that the interwar period was a significant time when conventional knowledge and racial policies were contested and negotiated within medical establishments. In the same way that the practical experience of doctors contributed to changes in medical theory, the experience of Australian travellers who witnessed the growth of European and Asian populations in the tropical Pacific began to undermine popular views at home of a static or hostile neighbouring region.

Conclusion

Australian travel writing forms a rich and diverse collection of the impressions and observations of Australians abroad. These stories of travel are significant because they can extend our historical understanding of Australian engagement with the Pacific Islands. They are also important because they enrich the broader narrative of European colonial encounters in the region, as well as offer an alternative perspective from the periphery of the Empire. Once dismissed for its momentary, superficial and touristic nature, travel literature can now offer new information about encounters with, and representations of, the Pacific Islands. These accounts challenge the notion that engagement was restricted to political and economic channels only. Ordinary Australians regularly discussed and encountered the Pacific Islands outside official or business capacities, and their accounts were crucial avenues for informing Australian readers at home.

These sources illuminate an important period in Australia's national history, one in which a growing, Australian-born population began to negotiate its own sense of identity and articulate its role in the broader region. Between c. 1880 and 1941, Australian engagement with the Pacific Islands increased dramatically due to improvements in transportation, the growth of trade and business, Christian outreach and colonial administration in the region. Further, the development of the publishing industry and literacy in Australia facilitated the circulation of travel accounts around the country. During this time, Australians were closely connected to the Pacific Islands and were well aware of their neighbours. Of course, stereotypes and misunderstandings persisted and, in some aspects, Australian knowledge of the Islands was rudimentary or simplified. However, Australian travel writing contributed to an increasingly informed Australian public. This was accomplished at a time that has often been overlooked by historians who were more concerned with the legacy of the Pacific War in transforming Australian perceptions of the Islands. Although this war had significant consequences for the region, it should not overshadow the long-term engagement between Australians and the Pacific before 1941.

Travel writing provides a more nuanced and complex perspective of Australians and how they perceived their place in the region. Analysis of this genre must maintain a balance between acknowledging the individual experiences of travel and situating travellers within a collective historical context. These individual impressions formed layers of representations over time, substantiating and perpetuating particular tropes and stereotypes that ultimately contributed to a broader Australian literary corpus. Australian travel accounts suggested that most travellers conformed to popular tropes and stereotypes when representing the Pacific Islands. The development of steamship travel and tourism shaped Australian expectations and impressions of the Pacific Islands, with travellers often following well-worn paths and making similar remarks about the voyage and the moment of first arrival. Australian travellers shared expectations of the Pacific as a place of economic prosperity and potential wealth, embodied by the figure of the enterprising trader, prospector, planter and overseer. This extended to Polynesia, which was commonly idealised as alluring and idyllic, despite the effects of European contact and development. Australian travel writers were also united in their criticisms of French colonial ambitions in the Pacific before World War I. The clearest commonality that Australian travel writers shared was popular attitudes to race and racial theory. Observations of disease, depopulation, ethnic diversity and Islander savagery reflected widespread assumptions of the perceived stasis of the Pacific in comparison to Australian progress and superiority.

Yet, there were cases of dissent and difference too. In response to the growth of tourism, many rejected the tourist label because it contravened the ideals of adventure and exploration that were traditionally associated with the Pacific. Similarly, idyllic tropes of economic wealth or of an alluring Polynesia were challenged by the accounts of travellers who reported on the realities of commerce in the Pacific, and on the difficulties of realising a utopian life in the Islands. Closer inspection of the accounts of the Queensland labour trade and the New Hebrides condominium also suggest that Australian travellers and readers were just as likely to be confused as they were to be convinced or conformist in their views. While the science of race was popularly regarded as absolute, face-to-face encounters in the Pacific could unsettle Australians' racialist assumptions of Islander savagery and inferiority. Though the travellers who expressed uncertainty and doubt were a minority, they offered a more complex understanding of how Australians negotiated and contested popular themes and narratives about the Pacific Islands.

This study has provided glimpses of the numerous accounts of travellers in the Pacific Islands, showing that the most well-known travel writers were not isolated cases. The travel accounts that were highlighted represent only a small fraction of a wider body of European and American literature that had described and entrenched images of the Pacific. They also represent an even lower percentage of the Australian travellers who move across the Pacific Ocean. Though they were situated on the edge of the British Empire, Australian travellers were well informed about the region before embarking on their journeys, so that they were knowledgeable about the Islands themselves, about their relationship to Australia and about the travellers who preceded them. Their own accounts contributed to a growing body of knowledge about the Pacific that was accessible to a broader readership. It was preferred as truthful and educative over the exaggerated fictional tales that had been so popular in the 1800s.

Determining how widespread Australian interest in the Pacific was is problematic, as well as whether there was a particular time between 1880 and 1941 when Australians were more aware of the Pacific. The 1880s and 1890s were a time when Australian public interest in the Pacific Islands peaked due to French and German presence in Melanesia and the growth of the Queensland labour trade. Despite well-established maritime connections with the eastern colonies, Australian travel writing was limited in volume until the 1890s, and tourism in the Pacific was in its infancy. From these few accounts, it is evident that Australians continued to subscribe to conventional European tropes of the Pacific Island as a romantic and exotic location with the potential for savage encounters at the end of the nineteenth century.

From the 1890s until 1914, travel writing increased dramatically and the Pacific featured prominently in Australian public discourse. It was encouraged by economic prosperity and social mobility in Australia, the growth of publishing and the development of steamship and tourism industries. This was also a period of national self-confidence and optimism, as the newly federated nation articulated its own role in the Pacific. Australian-born travellers began to identify themselves as distinct from their European origins, and their travel accounts began to show evidence of a more localised and specific relationship with the Pacific Islands than previous European generalisations. This included making judgements on colonial rule in the region and discussing the potential benefits of Australian imperialism.

Australian interest in the Pacific Islands peaked in the interwar period between 1918 and 1941. Following World War I, Australians travelled to the Pacific Islands in higher numbers than ever before and subsequently produced more travel writing. After the social and economic upheaval of World War I, a white urban middle class in Australia drove demand for travel and literature simultaneously. Travel writers thus increasingly needed to distinguish themselves in a competitive commercial market. Concurrently, Australia acquired mandated territories in the Pacific, which was followed by greater interest in, and criticism of, the nation's new internationally sanctioned role in the Pacific. A growing number of travel accounts that were written during the interwar period conveyed uncertainty about conventional European and Australian assumptions and narratives about the Pacific Islands. These include accounts that challenged or rejected stereotypes emphasising Islander inferiority and savagery and that advocated a more humanistic identification with them.

These accounts may reflect a broader shift in Australian society during the 1920s and 1930s towards a cultural maturity, marked by a reaction against the racialised and essentialist assumptions that had underscored the White Australia policy. However, this response may have been limited to the cultural elite. A close analysis of travel writing reveals more broadly that Australian travellers and readers grew weary of the exaggerated and overused tropes about the Pacific Islands. A similar response had occurred 30 years earlier, when Australian readers chose literature that departed from the formulaic British fictions of the 1880s. This apparent trend towards a more critical and nuanced understanding of the Pacific Islands may also reflect the numerical growth of travellers and travel accounts in the 1930s, offering more occasions for intimate encounters in the Pacific that challenged individuals' preconceptions.

Our ability to understand the effects of these travel accounts on the wider Australian audience is limited by the availability of information about the publication, distribution and reception of these texts. It is important not to inflate the effects of Australian travel writing on the Pacific Islands, as argued in Hank Nelson's study of Australian descriptions of Papua and New Guinea. This suggested that even by the 1930s, most Australians rarely thought about the region at all.[1] Occasionally, clues point to the popularity of particular texts—the number of editions printed and where they were printed; book reviews listed in newspapers; references to particular authors or works in other travel accounts; and the persistence of certain themes or representations in the literature. However, the extent to which they influenced popular opinion is not always clear.

Australian readers were as diverse as those who were travelling and writing, with different responses to the Pacific Islands in the various Australian colonies and states over time. The eastern colonies of Victoria, New South Wales and Queensland were more closely connected to the Pacific Islands than South Australia and Western Australia. On the eastern seaboard, Sydney's maritime connections and its location as a centre of Pacific trade fostered a regard for the Pacific Islands that was distinct from the protectionist attitudes in Victoria. As the seat of the national government from 1901 to 1927, Victoria was also the location of vigorous lobbying by the Presbyterian Church for greater involvement in the New Hebrides. Similarly, Queensland's proximity to Melanesia, its tropical characteristics and its demand for cheap agricultural labour are just a few of the factors that distinguished its engagement with the Pacific Islands from others. Within these regions, the rural–urban divide complicates our understanding of Australian readers and responses. So too does the mobility of Australians, many of whom moved fluidly between countries, colonies and continents and cannot be pinned to a particular home or localised identity. These nuances within Australian readerships and travellers require further exploration in the future.

Travel writing is an ideal source for contemporary historical studies that recognise the mobility of Australians and the need to consider Australian history in a transnational context. Australians were, and continue to be, exceptionally mobile—to the point that this has become part of what it means to be Australian.[2] This brief survey of the Pacific Islands is a small contribution to a broader study of Australian travel writing, one that explores how travel to Asia, Europe and North America shaped the nation. There is merit to considering the views of those on the periphery of empire, and to considering the distinct historical contexts that shaped

---

1   Nelson, 'Looking Black: Australian Images of Melanesians', 156.
2   Agnieszka Sobocinska and Richard White, 'Travel and Connections', in *The Cambridge History of Australia*, vol. 2, ed. Alison Bashford and Stuart Macintyre (Port Melbourne: Cambridge University Press, 2013), 493, doi.org/10.1017/cho9781107445758.051.

Australian perceptions of the world. At the turn of the twentieth century, an emerging Australian nation began to consider itself at the centre of an oceanic region. The scale and geography of the region necessitate a more sophisticated understanding of the Pacific Islands, one that recognises the specific historical relationships between particular Islands and Australian localities. This was especially the case in Melanesia, where Australians associated individual Islands with specific historical encounters, often marked by trade, conflicts, murders and reprisals. Queenslanders were familiar with the New Hebrides due to labour traders, and caricatures such as 'Tommy Tanna' demonstrate that Australians did not always consider the Islands according to regional or colonial boundaries. Australians distinguished specific Islands as more or less savage than others in recognition of the past martyrdom of a particular missionary or official, or in an attempt to justify their own ambitions or achievements. There is the need for a more localised and specific history of Australian encounters in the Pacific that recognises that while generalisations and stereotypes continued to persist in Australian representations of the Islands, there were local influences in both regions that challenged and modified popular notions.

Pacific Islanders were also extensive travellers, and their historical mobility within Australia and the Pacific is a burgeoning area of study. Indigenous crews on ships, missionaries and political leaders offer important counter-narratives that enrich our understanding of colonial mobility at this time. They also highlight how visiting Australia might have unintentionally shaped the ways in which Pacific people have viewed their neighbour. The changing reactions and responses of Pacific Islanders to Australian visitors in their Islands also require further attention in the future, particularly as tourism has become a significant part of Pacific Island economies at present.

Determining the influence of Pacific travel on itinerant Australians is fraught. Australian travel writers dedicated comparatively little space to describing their departure from the Pacific Islands than they did to describe their arrival. The moment of departure often abruptly ended the travel account—there were few reflections on steaming back into Sydney harbour, or about settling back into life at home in Australia. For those embarking on, or returning from, their grand tours, the Pacific Islands were a brief chapter or subheading within a broader account, overlooked in the travellers' excited anticipation of reaching Europe or returning home. Some travellers ended their accounts with a short summative statement or paragraph, while published books usually included a reflection in the preface or final chapter. These remarks varied in their content and purpose, from simplistic short impressions to more well-planned observations about the Islands, the travellers or their future. The author's views were frequently unclear, such as those of politician Thomas Henley, who warned 'readers of the foregoing generalizations may, and probably will, conclude that I have presented to them a hotchpotch collection—a mixture of many thoughts about many things, from many sources. I admit the impeachment'.[3]

In some cases, travellers remained unmoved by the Pacific Islands. But, more commonly, authors argued that the Pacific Islands had something to offer to the Australian traveller. In attempting to justify their travels and distinguish their writing from others, many Australians argued that the Pacific Islands (or, more accurately, *their* experience of the Pacific Islands) could satisfy the 'enquiring mind'. Henley claimed:

> My object in writing has been to present in as simple a form as possible some of the answers to the questions propounded to enquiring minds when travelling in the great archipelago of the Pacific in search of information and recreation.[4]

Beatrice Grimshaw framed her own journey as 'a quest after information spiced with amusement', in accordance with conventional notions of travel as an activity in self-improvement.[5] For this reason, travellers frequently reiterated the accuracy of their accounts and explained their attempts to be objective. Dr Casey Albert Wood remarked:

> Possibly the following descriptions, that I jotted down in my notebook from time to time may appear to be sentimental exaggerations and worthy of being classed with the productions of South Sea 'fakirs', but they were, at the time of observation at least, genuine impressions.[6]

Although most travellers tried to justify their recollections as being honest, accurate and authentic, few could resist relying on the familiar descriptions of the 'indescribable' or 'picturesque', or alluding to European

---

3   Henley, *A Pacific Cruise*, 155.
4   Henley, *A Pacific Cruise*, 155.
5   Grimshaw, *From Fiji to the Cannibal Islands*, 29.
6   Casey Albert Wood, Letter, 1923–1924, MS 3526 (Canberra: National Library of Australia, 1923–1924), 8.

fantasies such as 'the lure of the Pacific Islands'.[7] A few accounts were more explicit in embracing the romance that imbued the Pacific and the travellers' memories, who sometimes wrote years after their travel. Arnold Safroni-Middleton was upfront with the reader about his 'half-remembered romance'.[8] Elinor Mordaunt was explicitly nostalgic, writing that 'one is not really happy traveling, one is most happy in remembering'.[9] For others, the process of writing and remembering was cathartic. Eric Muspratt described this in his autobiography, *Fire of Youth*: 'One had wanted to build so much into a book, the fire of youth, smokelike dreams, and the creeping shadows of final darkness'.[10] John Fraser completed his account before departing for war and noted that:

> Many threads go to weave the fabric of memory, and I have found the unravelling of these, during odd times of leisure, so absorbing a pastime that I have to go on and on like the Ancient Mariner who *had* to tell all he knew.[11]

For these Australians, it was a reflection on their personal journey rather than the physical voyage that brought their accounts to a close.

These personal reflections—hidden among the sterile observations and predictable tourist tropes of the overwhelming majority of Australian travel writing—are much more difficult to find. Few travellers wrote reflections about themselves or how their experiences of the Islands changed their worldview. This is not to say that travel to the Pacific did not prompt introspection, but perhaps that it was not articulated openly in the literature. Travel writing provided a sense of escapism, and travellers were reluctant to disturb the exotic fantasy by revealing personal anxieties or conflicted feelings. Racialised scientific language was a convenient tool to disguise the heightened emotional state of travellers during human encounters. Such responses reinforced popular and misguided notions of the Pacific that were peddled by the accounts of government officials, missionaries and residents—who possessed vested interests that prevailed in the discussion of broader issues relating to Australia and the Pacific Islands. As racialist views of the Pacific

---

7   Dickinson, *A Trader in the Savage Solomons*, 206–7.
8   Safroni-Middleton, *Wine-Dark Seas and Tropic Skies*, 12.
9   Mordaunt, *The Venture Book*, vi.
10 Muspratt, *Fire of Youth*, 189.
11 Fraser, *Gold Dish and Kava Bowl*, 252.

progressively hardened in Australian public discourse, so too did travellers struggle to reconcile such judgements with the realities they faced during close encounters with Pacific Islanders.

The emotional power of human encounters can be observed in some accounts in which Australians expressed deeper sentiment than simply disillusionment. In some cases, the experience of travel destabilised certain conventional assumptions while leaving others intact. Jack McLaren was one such example. He retained a colonial view of Islanders and used colonialist language, yet recognised their basic equality:

> And I, watching, concluded that in the matters of superstition, tradition and, above all, keen sensibility to scorn the man of the Palaeolithic Wild and the man of the Civilized Wild were brothers all the while.[12]

Ralph Stock maintained racialised and essentialised views of Pacific Islanders, yet recognised that Islanders must have regarded European practices as 'equally ludicrous to them'.[13] Henley was also moved by empathy during his travels, noting that, 'something may be said or written which will make for a better understanding of our relations one with the other. To that end we must work'.[14] This compassionate view must also be weighed against his belief that the British Empire had a 'divine' responsibility to the Pacific.

Occasionally in face-to-face human encounters, the expected stereotype of savage or primitive was deeply unsettled. Aletta Lewis endeavoured to abandon her European-ness in American Samoa completely but was dismayed to find that task impossible.[15] Alan John Marshall was critical about the influence of European colonialism in the Pacific:

> In all my writings and lectures I have been a friend of the native, and nobody is more interested in his cultural and physical welfare than I am. I loathe that spreading rash of civilisation which is smashing the slow sure rhythm of stone.[16]

---

12   McLaren, *My Odyssey*, 256.
13   Stock, *The Cruise of the Dream Ship*, 222.
14   Henley, *A Pacific Cruise*, 174.
15   Lewis, *They Call Them Savages*.
16   Marshall, *The Men and Birds of Paradise*, 130.

Muspratt's account vividly described his shock when he returned home:

> Returning to civilization was a painful experience. Again one felt the unpleasantness and the unfairness of the money standard and all the meannesses it involves. Hurt by these things I retired into quiet corners, and withdrew into myself, ashamed of myself and ashamed of humanity. Once I had belonged quite splendidly in the scheme of things but now I belonged quite badly. And so the whole scheme seemed to be bad because I had lost my place in it. It was the first taste of bitterness of life for a young man hitherto rather successful, rather self-satisfied, and rather arrogant.[17]

These are rare and brief glimpses of the emotional vulnerability of travellers when they are placed in foreign environments and face the potential for disillusionment with notions of a supposedly 'superior' European or Australian society.

For a historian sifting through a vast catalogue of texts, these particular voices stand out. This is not due to their progressive views of Pacific Islanders, nor their willingness to challenge the mainstream assumptions of the time. Rather, these Australians are notable because they openly admitted the uncertainties and fragilities of travel abroad. We can learn more from those whose assumptions were unsettled by the travel experience than from travellers who were utterly convinced before and after their voyage. These ambiguous accounts more accurately reflect the feelings of temporary uncertainty and flux that travel provokes. This is evident in not only these travellers' physical mobility between two different worlds but also the fluid nature of the texts that they write, which blend fact and fiction, imagination and reality, and emotion and reason.

The travellers studied here were products of different times to our own. Assumptions and expectations have dramatically shifted and the 'lure' of the Pacific Islands, with its myths of hidden riches, lost tribes and pristine utopias, has long been debunked. Yet, there were also many similarities for all these differences. Their journeys have often followed the same process of anticipation, encounter and reflection that all travellers undergo. Some stereotypes persist today, despite the condensing of time and space by ships and planes. Images of vastness, distance, isolation and timelessness continue to challenge contemporary notions of a globalised world. The Pacific Islands remain a place of sojourn or transit for Australians,

---

17 Muspratt, *My South Sea Island*, 256.

rather than a place in which to live. The promise of adventure and freedom lingers because these Islands remain largely unknown to their Australian neighbours.

Through travel writing, this book attempted to address the lack of historical memory regarding Australia's close and sustained relationship with the Pacific Islands. The vast archive of Australian travel accounts reveals that Australians were more closely connected to and aware of the Pacific Islands than previous studies have acknowledged. By recognising the historical legacy of the encounters and exchanges between Australians and Pacific Islanders, we can better understand and critically evaluate former and contemporary Australian attitudes and policies to the Pacific. This is not only important because Australian officials continue to express their role in the Pacific region today, whether in the 'Arc of Instability' or as part of a broader recognition of the 'Asia-Pacific Century'; it is crucial because Australians continue to travel to the Pacific Islands. This means that Pacific Islanders continue to grow as a visible feature of our cultural landscape. Rather than considering these two regions as separate entities, future studies of this relationship must wholly acknowledge the complexities and diversities of peoples in Australia and in the Islands, their mobility within Oceania and the historical connections that bind them.

Appendix: An Annotated Bibliography of Australian Travel Writing

This appendix contains an annotated bibliography of Australian travel writing on the Pacific Islands from c. 1880 to 1941 (excluding Papua, New Guinea and fictional accounts). Some accounts published after 1941 that describe prior experiences of travel have been included. For further details about these texts and their authors, see the *Australian Dictionary of Biography* and the *Annotated Bibliography of Australian Overseas Travel Writing, 1830 to 1970*, edited by Terri McCormack, Ros Pesman, David Walker and Richard White.

Abbott, John Henry Macartney, *The South Seas (Melanesia)*. London: Adam and Charles Black, 1908.

> Born in New South Wales in 1874, Abbott worked as a jackeroo in the Hunter Valley until he started writing for *The Bulletin* in 1897. He fought in the South African War in 1900 and wrote about his experiences in the book, *Tommy Cornstalk* (1902). His success took him to England as a freelance journalist, where he wrote four books, including *The South Seas (Melanesia)*. This was part of the 'Peeps at Many Lands' series for children, which was based on his travels in c. 1907. It was illustrated by Norman Hardy. Abbott spent the rest of his life writing in New South Wales and died in Sydney in 1953.

Allan, William, *Homeward Bound, from Australia to Scotland: Impressions by the Way*. Helensburgh: Helensburgh and Gareloch Times, 1915.

> Born in Scotland, Allan lived in Queensland as a journalist for *Warwick Argus*. Reprinted from the *Helensburgh and Gareloch Times*, this short book is an account of a holiday trip to Scotland via Canada and the US, beginning in Sydney on 8 July 1915. On his journey home, Allan visited Hawai'i and Fiji.

Allen, Percy S, *Stewart's Handbook of the Pacific Islands: A Reliable Guide to All the Inhabited Islands of the Pacific Ocean—For Traders, Tourists and Settlers, with a Bibliography of Island Works*. Sydney: Stewart McCarron, 1920.

Born in 1876, Allen was a journalist in Sydney, as well as a librarian for the *Sydney Morning Herald*. This handbook was reprinted in eight editions, beginning in 1907 and finishing in 1923. It includes descriptions of each Island or Island group, as well as trade statistics, travel advice, lists of residents, photographs and 'a bibliography of island works'. It also printed contributions from other writers, newspapers and Pacific experts, including Australians. Allen also published *Bibliography of Works on the Pacific Islands* (1900), *Cyclopedia of Fiji* (1907), *The Pacific Islands: Fiji and Samoa* (1908), *The Pacific Islands: New Zealand's Commercial Interests* (1908) and *The Late Mr. Louis Becke* (1921).

Anderson, J Mayne, *What a Tourist Sees in the New Hebrides*. Sydney: W.C. Penfold & Co., 1915.

This 'deck observation' was originally written for family, but was later published in a newspaper series. It is an account of a tourist cruise from Sydney in 1914 for seven weeks, in which the author visited Lord Howe Island, Norfolk Island and the New Hebrides.

Arthur, James, 6940 James Arthur Papers, Box 14302, Manuscript Number 6940. Brisbane: Queensland State Library, 1899–1900.

Arthur was an English-born lawyer who moved to Australia with his Irish wife and became a labour recruiter. These papers contain letters to his wife, family photographs and newspaper clippings, with evidence of his time aboard the *Lady Norman* in 1899 and the *Fearless* in 1900. While travelling on the *Sydney Belle*, he was shot dead in Malaita (Solomon Islands) on 19 April 1901 and was buried at sea.

Atkin, Charles Ager, *A Trip to Fiji via East Coast of New Zealand*. Melbourne: Massina, 1885.

Born in 1829, Atkin was a chemist from Melbourne who went on a two-month cruise on a USSCo. vessel in 1884. Atkin visited New Zealand, Fiji, Samoa and Tonga. He died in 1898.

Baker, HE, *World Ramblings: Follow the Trail through Forty-Four Countries with Impressions and Experiences*. Brisbane: Globe Printing, 1939.

Baker describes himself as a grazier from Queensland. In this account of his grand tour, he describes Hawai'i, the Midway and Wake Islands, Guam and Dutch New Guinea.

Baume, Eric, *I Lived These Years*. Sydney: George G. Harrap & Co., 1941.

> Frederick Ehrenfried Baume was born in 1900 in Auckland. He worked as a reporter and broadcaster, first in New Zealand and then in Australia, from 1923 to 1939. Baume was fond of Australia, writing that 'Australia breathes freedom at a man'. He then spent time in England as a war correspondent, where he wrote two memoirs and several short stories and works of fiction. He returned to Australia in the 1950s and became a television celebrity. He was also a Fellow of the Royal Geographical Society. This autobiography recalls two of his Pacific voyages. The first a trip to San Francisco when he was a child, passing the Cook Islands, Tahiti and American Samoa. The second voyage was in 1937, when Baume passed Fiji and Hawai'i en route to the US.

Bean, Charles Edwin Woodrow, *With the Flagship of the South*. Sydney: William Brooks, 1909.

> Born in Bathurst in 1879, Bean is popularly remembered for his role as an Australian official war correspondent in World War I. He was also a trained lawyer before he began his journalism career in 1908. In August that year, he was assigned as a correspondent to the HMS *Powerful*, flagship of the Royal Navy squadron on the Australian Station. In his account of this time, he describes Fiji. He died in 1968.

Beattie, John Watt, 'Journal of a Voyage to the Western Pacific in the Melanesian Mission Yacht Southern Cross'. Project Canterbury. anglicanhistory.org/oceania/beattie_journal1906.html.

> Beattie was born in 1859 in Scotland. He migrated with his family to Tasmania in 1878 and became a professional photographer in 1882. He married in 1886 and had two children. He was appointed Tasmania's official photographer in 1896 and worked hard to foster tourism there. In 1906, he toured the Pacific Islands aboard the Melanesian Mission ship, *Southern Cross*. He described New Zealand, Norfolk Island, the Solomon Islands, New Hebrides and Santa Cruz Islands. He died in Hobart in 1930.

Becke, Louis, *By Reef and Palm*. London: T. F. Unwin, 1894.

Becke, Louis, *Notes from My South Sea Log*. London: Laurie, 1905.

> Born in New South Wales in 1855, George Lewis Becke (later changed to Louis) was a popular Australian travel writer. In 1869, he travelled to San Francisco with his brother, then stowed away to Samoa aboard a ship, taking a job in Apia as a bookkeeper. He was 18 when he met the notorious Captain 'Bully' Hayes, who was to become a central character

in his later writings. In 1874, Hayes signed Becke on as supercargo on the *Leonora,* which was later shipwrecked. Becke was arrested for piracy by a British warship, but was later acquitted. In 1880, he worked in the Ellice Islands as a trader, then moved to New Britain and the Marshall Islands. In 1885, he returned to New South Wales, but then worked in New Caledonia from 1890 to 1892. Unemployed, Becke turned to writing, with *The Bulletin's* editor, JF Archibald, helping him launch his career. In addition to numerous newspaper and magazine articles, Becke published 34 books (including six in collaboration with WJ Jeffrey). Becke was known for his simple and realist writing style, with *By Reef and Palm* (1894) becoming one of his most successful texts (it was republished in several editions). After various worldwide travels, he returned to Sydney, moneyless, in 1909 and then died in 1913.

Belbin, Robert James, Papers, 1881–1883, MS 6466. Canberra: National Library of Australia, 1881–1883.

Belbin was a master mariner engaged in the Queensland labour trade. These papers contain Belbin's official log book from 1881 to 1883 aboard the *Barough Belle*, his ship diaries from 1881, 1882 and 1883, and his last will and testament, dated 1883. He visited the New Hebrides and Solomon Islands from Port Mackay.

Blakiston, J, *Seeing the World Today: An Unconventional Travel Book*. Melbourne: E.A. Vidler, 1930.

Blakiston was a businessman from Geelong who went on a grand tour to Europe in the 1930s for eight months. He was 78 years old and accompanied by his daughter. His account describes Fiji and Hawai'i and promotes the Australian Travel Service for organising his itinerary.

Bollard, Arthur Ross Bramwell, Private Record, 3DRL/6061. Canberra: Australian War Memorial, 1914.

Bollard was born in 1894 and was a bandsman on HMAS *Australia* during World War I. In his diary, he describes spending time in Fiji and New Caledonia. He died in 1952.

Bond, Florence, Diaries and Autograph Book, 1904–1955, MS 9196. Canberra: National Library of Australia, 1904.

Bond was a wealthy woman from Adelaide who made frequent travels to England, usually via the Suez Canal. One of her diaries describes her trip on the *Rotorua* from England to Adelaide, during which time she wrote about Pitcairn Island. Her papers include other travel ephemera, such as postcards, photos, menus, pressed flowers, tickets and letters.

Brummitt, Robert, *A Winter Holiday in Fiji*. Sydney: C.H. Kelly, 1914.

Brummitt was born in England in 1851 and worked as a doctor in Adelaide, living with his Australian wife. He was also a fervent Methodist. His account of a five-week holiday to Fiji in 1912 was based on a series of articles that he wrote for the periodical, *Australian Christian Commonwealth*. It includes an introduction by Reverend George Brown. Brummitt also published an article, 'Fiji and Its People', in the *Proceedings of the Royal Geographical Society of Australasia, South Australian Branch* (1915). He died in 1927.

Burchett, Wilfred, *Pacific Treasure Island: New Caledonia; Voyage through Its Land and Wealth, the Story of Its People and Past*. Melbourne: Cheshire, 1941.

Born in Melbourne in 1911, Burchett worked in the travel industry in Europe in the 1930s before returning to Australia in 1939 to work as a journalist. In 1941, he visited New Caledonia and recorded his experiences in *Pacific Treasure Island*. He also wrote articles for *Walkabout*, *Pix* and other Australian newspapers. He was particularly concerned by Australian apathy towards German and Japanese hostility. He later sailed with American naval fleets and reported on the Pacific War (see *Democracy with a Tommy Gun,* 1946). His autobiography, *Passport*, was published in 1969 and recalled these travels and a previous sojourn in Tahiti in 1936. From 1945, Burchett lived and worked in Britain, Berlin, Korea, Vietnam, Moscow, South Africa, Cambodia and Bulgaria. He wrote over 35 books, two which responded to the government's refusal to grant him a passport from 1955 to 1972 due to alleged communist sympathies. He died in Bulgaria in 1983.

Burrowes, JA, 'Briefs and Associated Papers in Cases Involving Pacific Islanders'. In Crown Solicitor's Office, Series ID 12102, Item ID 7866. Brisbane: Queensland State Archives, 1883–1884.

Burrowes was a government agent aboard the *Ceara* and the *Lizzie*, visiting Papua, New Guinea and the Solomon Islands. On the latter journey, he travelled with Captain William Wawn.

Cheeseman, Richard, *The South Sea Islands: Notes of a Trip*. Brighton: publisher unknown, 1901.

Born in 1855, Cheeseman migrated to Brighton, Victoria, in 1867. He became a well-known horticulturist, becoming president of the Royal Horticultural Society of Victoria and a member of the local Brighton council. He died in Victoria in 1916. This is an account of his seven-week tourist cruise through New Caledonia and the New Hebrides, beginning in December 1900. It was also printed in the *Brighton Southern Cross*.

Chewings, Hannah, *Amongst Tropical Islands, or, Notes and Observations Made during a Visit of the S. S. 'Moresby' in 1899, to New Guinea, New Britain and the Solomon Islands*. Adelaide: publisher unknown, 1900.

Residing in South Australia, Hannah is possibly related to geologist and anthropologist Charles Chewings (1859–1937). This account describes a three-month voyage in 1899 from Sydney to New Guinea and the Solomon Islands. It was reprinted from articles that were sent to *The Advertiser*. Chewings was a devout Christian and noted that Reverend George Brown had chartered the boat.

Coffee, Frank, *Forty Years on the Pacific: The Lure of the Great Ocean; A Book of Reference for the Traveller and Pleasure for the Stay-at-Home*. Sydney: Oceanic, 1920.

Born in 1852 in the US, Coffee came to Sydney in 1881 and left his journalism career behind to create the Oceanic Publishing Company. He settled in Artarmon and his success in business allowed him to travel around the world several times. These experiences formed the basis of his book, *Forty Years on the Pacific*. A second edition was published in 1925. His two sons fought in World War I and he published the letters of Frank Jnr, who died at Gallipoli. Coffee died in Sydney in 1929.

Collingridge, George, *Round and Round the World*. Sydney: George Collingridge, 1925.

George Alphonse Collingridge de Tourcey was born in 1847 in England. He was an artist, historian, teacher and cartographer who lived in the Sydney area from 1879. He was particularly interested in Portuguese maritime exploration, writing books and articles on the subject, as well as novels for children. He sometimes used the pseudonym, 'The Hermit of Berowra'. This text describes a grand tour that included visits to New Guinea, New Caledonia, Micronesia, Hawai'i and Easter Island. It is an unusual and frequently incoherent collection of childhood memories and varied travels, some with a fictitious Martian companion. Collingridge died in 1931.

Collins, Dale, *Sea-Tracks of the Speejacks Round the World*. Garden City: Doubleday, Page & Co., 1926.

Cuthbert Quinlan Dale Collins was born in 1897 at Balmain, Sydney. He joined the *Melbourne Herald* as a reporter and contributed stories to *The Bulletin*. In 1922, he was engaged by AY Gowen, an American millionaire, to accompany him on a world tour aboard his yacht, *Speejacks*. This trip inspired *Sea-Tracks of the Speejacks Round the World*, in which he described New Guinea and the Trobriand Islands. Although moving to London in 1923, Collins returned to Melbourne in 1948, where he died eight years later. He wrote 37 books in total, including the autobiographical *Bright Vista* in 1946 and 10 novels for children. Other pseudonyms include 'Stephen Fennimore' and 'Michael Copeland'.

Cook, May, *Fijian Diary 1904–1906: A Young Australian Woman's Account of Village Life in Fiji*, edited by Leigh Cook. Ashwood: PenFolk, 1996.

Elinor Violet May Cook was born in 1877 in Victoria. She became engaged to Wesleyan minister Richard Osbourne (whom she called 'Oz') in 1899. She and Oz travelled from Melbourne to Sydney, and then to Suva. They were married on 15 April 1904, then went to Macuata (near Labasa). She gave birth to her first child there, and moved to Lakeba Island in the Lau Group in 1905. The diaries end abruptly in September 1906 and she does not mention having to return to Australia for the birth of her second child. She did not return to Fiji and died in Victoria in 1958. This edited edition also contains several letters that were published in the Methodist publication, *The Spectator*, as well as some personal photographs.

Combes, Alice Herminie, *Diary of a Trip to the South Sea Islands*. Lithgow: T.T. Wilton, 1898.

Combes was a landscape painter who lived in Lithgow, New South Wales. She exhibited with the Art Society of New South Wales during the 1880s. Her account describes a trip in 1895 with her father, Edward Combes, from Sydney on a USSCo. vessel. She writes about Fiji, Samoa and Tonga. She died in 1924 in Sydney.

Coombe, Florence, *Islands of Enchantment: Many-Sided Melanesia*. London: Macmillan, 1911.

Coombe was an Anglican missionary on Norfolk Island and in the Solomon Islands. In 1907, Coombe visited the New Hebrides, Banks Islands, Torres Islands, Santa Cruz Islands and Solomon Islands. She could speak Motu, a language used by many missionaries in the region. She also wrote *Schooldays in Norfolk Island* (1907), as well as other books about her schooling experience. This text contains illustrations by John Watt Beattie.

Craig, James Kirkpatrick, 'Briefs and Associated Papers in Cases Involving Pacific Islanders'. In Chief Secretary's Department, Series ID 12102, Item ID 861839. Brisbane: Queensland State Archives, 1904.

Craig, James Kirkpatrick, 'Logbook of Vessels *Helena* and *Lochiel*'. In Inspector of Pacific Islanders, Maryborough, Series ID 16998. Brisbane: Queensland State Archives, 1903.

> These are the logbooks of Craig, a government agent aboard the *Clansman*, *Helena* and *Lochiel* in the Solomon Islands, New Hebrides, Papua and New Guinea. They also include material relating to Craig's debarment from the labour trade in 1905.

Cromar, John, *Jock of the Islands: Early Days in the South Seas: The Adventures of John Cromar, Sometime Recruiter and Lately Trader at Marovo, British Solomon Islands Protectorate, Told by Himself*. London: Faber & Faber, 1935.

> John ('Jock') Cromar was born in Scotland in 1860 and visited Australia numerous times from 1875 as a sailor working on steamers from London. When he was 23 years old, he joined a labour-recruiting vessel, the *Forest King*, and continued to recruit in the New Hebrides and Solomon Islands until the end of the labour trade in 1904. He was a crewman aboard the vessels *Madeline, Storm Bird, Helena, Fearless* and *Seashell* during this time. This is an account of his encounters as a recruiter, and although Cromar identified himself as a trader in the Marovo area of New Georgia, this book does not record these experiences.

David, Edgeworth, Mrs, *Funafuti, or, Three Months on a Coral Island: An Unscientific Account of a Scientific Expedition*. London: J. Murray, 1899.

> Born in England in 1856, Caroline Martha ('Cara') Mallett emigrated to Australia in 1882 to be the principal of a teacher training college in Sydney. Her husband was the chair of geology at the University of Sydney, and she accompanied him for three months on the 1897 Royal Society expedition to bore coral reefs at Funafuti in the Ellice Islands. She also visited Fiji, Tonga and Samoa along the way. Back home, Caroline wrote 'Mission Work in Funafuti' for the *Australian Christian World* (1897) and then published *Funafuti*, first in 1899 and then as an abridged edition in 1913. The Davids accepted responsibility for educating a Fijian woman, Adi Elanoa, who later died of influenza while holidaying in Fiji. They moved to the Blue Mountains, where Caroline was active in the girl guides, as well as president of the Women's National Movement for social reform. She also turned her residence into a convalescent home for soldiers. She died in Sydney in 1951.

Dean, Ruth Mansel, *Some Memories of Life on Tanna and Norfolk Island,* PMB 1022, c. 1911. Pacific Manuscripts Bureau, Australian National University, Canberra.

Dean was born in the Paton Memorial Hospital at Port Vila, Vanuatu, in 1914. She was the daughter of David and Winifred Griffiths and spent her childhood with her sister on her parents' plantation at Lenakel, Tanna. Due to repeated attacks of malaria, her family moved to Norfolk Island, where they owned a banana plantation for a short time. These papers include Dean's letters and notes recalling her time in Tanna as a child; notes from when she returned with her husband in 1963; a letter written by her mother on Christmas Day in 1911; a photograph of her parents at Tanna in 1911; and birth certificates for Dean and her sister.

Dickinson, Joseph HC, *A Trader in the Savage Solomons: A Record of Romance and Adventure.* London: H.F. & G. Witherby, 1927.

Dickinson's background is unknown. In this book, he describes 18 years that he spent in the Solomon Islands (c. 1908–1926), working as a trader, planter and labour recruiter. In his account, he describes his admiration for Australia when he departs Sydney for the Islands.

Doorly, Gerald Stokely, *In the Wake.* London: Sampson Low, 1937.

James Gerald Stokely Doorly was born in Trinidad in 1880 and became a seaman and master mariner. Based in New Zealand, he worked for USSCo., commanded New Zealander troop transports during World War I and accompanied an expedition to Antarctica. He then migrated to Melbourne in 1925 and worked as a maritime pilot. He wrote two books, various short stories and articles for *Blackwood's Magazine*, *The Bulletin*, *Argus* and *Herald*, and he composed music. This autobiography was primarily written for his daughters and describes Honolulu, Tonga, Samoa and Tahiti. Doorly moved to Wellington in 1951 and died there five years later.

Dyring, *Our Island Trip: S. S. 'Manapouri', July 1904.* Sydney: W.A. Pepperday, 1904.

An account of a round trip aboard the USSCo. Vessel, *Manapouri*, from Sydney to New Zealand, Suva, Tonga and Samoa in 1904. This text was part of the 'Manapouri Messenger', a booklet that was published privately by the passengers onboard the ship. The author is possibly Dr CPW Dyring of Coburg, Victoria.

Ellis, Albert Fuller, *Adventuring in Coral Seas*. Sydney: Angus and Robertson, 1936.

Ellis, Albert Fuller, *Ocean Island and Nauru: Their Story*. Sydney: Angus and Robertson, 1935.

Sir Albert Fuller Ellis was born in Queensland in 1869 and moved to New Zealand the same year. When he was 18 years old, he joined John T. Arundel and Co. as a phosphate prospector. He spent three years in the Phoenix Islands, then worked on the north Queensland coast. In 1899, he was transferred to Sydney and found phosphate rock from Nauru propping open a door. In 1900, he sailed for Ocean Island and Nauru, confirmed the existence of phosphate and began mining operations there. He managed mines from 1906 to 1911 and returned to Auckland. Ellis was appointed phosphate commissioner for New Zealand in 1920, a position that he held until his death in 1951. Ellis was an avid publicist for the phosphate and fertiliser industries, contributing frequent journal articles and three books. The first two books in 1935 and 1936 described his Pacific voyages from 1887 to 1911, in which he visited Ocean Island, Nauru, Fiji and the Phoenix, Marshall and Gilbert Islands. His other book, *Mid-Pacific Outposts* (1946), focused on World War II. Ellis was an active member of the Presbyterian Church, as well as a fellow of the Royal Geographical Society. It is unclear from his texts whether he considered himself Australian or New Zealander.

Farquhar, WG, *Diaries 1870–1872*, PMB 496. Pacific Manuscripts Bureau, Australian National University, Canberra.

Farquhar was a farmer of Maryborough, Queensland. He visited New Caledonia, the Loyalty Islands and the New Hebrides in the schooner, *City of Melbourne*, from November 1870 to January 1871 to recruit labourers for himself and for other farmers in his region. He made a second voyage to New Caledonia, the New Hebrides and Banks Islands in the schooner, *Petrel*, from September 1871 to January 1872 as a government agent. These diaries record his two voyages.

Fehon, William Meeke, *Six Weeks' Excursion to the South Seas and Eastern Pacific Islands: Comprising Raratonga, Tahiti, Raiatea, Samoa and the Friendly Islands, by the New Steamer 'Waikare', 3,000 tons: (Union Steam Ship Company of N. Z., Ltd) from Sydney, 30th June, 1898*. Sydney: S.D. Townsend and Co. Printers, 1898.

Fehon was born in London in 1834 and moved to Melbourne in 1858 to work on the railways. He eventually became the railways commissioner and died in Sydney in 1911. This account describes a six-week trip he took in 1898 on a cruise ship to the Cook Islands, Tahiti, French Polynesia, Samoa and Tonga. Fehon was commissioned by USSCo., and his book contains several promotions and a passengers list.

Fitzpatrick, John Charles Lucas, *Notes on a Trip to New Caledonia and Fiji*. Windsor: Hawkesbury Herald, 1908.

Fitzpatrick was born in New South Wales in 1862. He worked as a journalist and eventually owned a newspaper. In 1895, he was elected as a New South Wales politician until 1930. He was also a trustee of the Public Library of New South Wales and was passionate about Australian history. He compiled several books of local reminiscences, two poetry volumes and two travel books: *Eastward Ho* (1905) and *A Jaunt to Java* (1908). This small pamphlet records his 1907 trip to New Caledonia and Fiji. Fitzpatrick was also chairman of the Lord Howe Island Board. He died in 1932.

Fox, Frank, *Oceania*. London: A&C Black, 1911.

Fox, Frank, *Problems of the Pacific*. London: Williams & Norgate, 1912.

Sir Frank Ignatius Fox was born in 1874 in Adelaide. He worked as a journalist for several papers in Tasmania, Bathurst and Sydney, including *The Bulletin* and *Lone Hand*. He moved to London in 1909 and wrote several imperialist books, such as *Ramparts of Empire* (1910), *Australia* (1910) and *The British Empire* (1914). He served in World War I and continued writing in England until his death in 1960. *Oceania* is part of the 'Peeps at Many Lands' reference series for children, illustrated by Norman Hardy. It includes personal experiences from Fox's trip to Fiji and Hawai'i en route to Vancouver in 1909. There were four editions (1911, 1912, 1913 and 1919), with the second being 'specifically printed for the Salvation Army, Australasia'. Other publications such as *Problems of the Pacific* (1912) and *The Mastery of the Pacific* (1928) focused on the strategic value of the region.

Fraser, John Archibald, *Gold Dish and Kava Bowl*. London: Dent, 1954.

Fraser was born in Victoria and worked as a miner in Australia from 1927 to 1933, before accepting a position in Tavua, Fiji, prospecting for gold. He stayed for approximately nine months, returned to Australia and then visited Fiji again in 1935 with his brother. He travelled around Viti Levu in search of gold for a Melbourne company. After a year, he went prospecting in Guadalcanal in the Solomon Islands and returned to Australia unsuccessful. He served in an anti-aircraft battery in the Middle East and in New Guinea during World War II, and died in 1946. This manuscript was published posthumously by Terence O'Brien at the request of Fraser's sister.

Gaggin, John, *Among the Man-Eaters*. London: T. Fisher Unwin, 1900.

> John Gaggin was a labour recruiter from Melbourne. According to this autobiography, he worked on Fiji cotton plantations from 1871 and then spent six years as a government agent on Australian recruiting ships. He visited Fiji, the Solomon Islands and the New Hebrides. Parts of this text were originally published in *Chamber's Journal*, *The Age*, *The Argus* and *The Leader*.

Garran, Andrew, ed., *Australasia Illustrated*. Sydney: Picturesque Atlas Publishing Company, 1886.

> Garran was born in 1825 in London. He arrived in Adelaide in 1848, working as a journalist in small newspapers until he joined the *Sydney Morning Herald* as assistant editor in 1856 and then the *Herald* in 1873. Failing health forced him to resign at the end of 1885, and he edited three volumes of *Australasia Illustrated* the following year. He was a member of the Legislative Council from 1887 to 1895 and died in 1901. Under the title 'Insular Territories', Garran makes references to Papua and New Guinea, the Solomon Islands, the New Hebrides, Fiji, Samoa, Tonga, Lord Howe and Norfolk Islands and New Caledonia.

Gay, John J, *Through Other Lands*. Sydney: Edwards, Dunlop, 1931.

> Gay was an Australian journalist and proprietor of the *Lane Cove Herald*. This text was based on letters that he sent to his sons while he was on a grand tour, presumably in 1930. Gay was elderly at the time and gave descriptions of Fiji, American Samoa and Hawai'i.

Giles, William E, *A Cruize in a Queensland Labour Vessel to the South Seas*, edited by Deryck Scarr. Canberra: Australian National University Press, 1970.

> Giles spent five months on a Queensland labour vessel recruiting in the New Hebrides in 1877 because he was 'in want of a holiday'. His account was written in 1880 and was probably intended for publication, though the manuscript is anonymous and the name of the boat was concealed. Giles's background is unknown. In his account, he mentioned that he spent four years working in 'a back district of Western Queensland' on sheep stations, where he met many Pacific Islanders. After the voyage, he bought land on Emae in the New Hebrides and grew maize. In 1879, suffering from malaria, he sailed to Levuka and then to New Zealand, arriving moneyless. In 1880, he went back to Fiji and settled at Lomaloma on a plantation, after which he ran a small schooner between the Islands. By 1884, he also had business in Nukualofa, Tonga, and in 1885, he became an agent for USSCo. From 1886 to 1887, he served as British Vice Consul in Tonga.

Grimshaw, Beatrice, *From Fiji to the Cannibal Islands*. London: Eveleigh Nash, 1907.

Grimshaw, Beatrice, *In the Strange South Seas*. London: Hutchinson & Co., 1907.

Grimshaw, Beatrice, *Tours to the South Sea Islands, Tonga, Samoa, Fiji*. Dunedin: Union Steamship Company of New Zealand, 1914.

> Beatrice Ethel Grimshaw was born in 1870 in Ireland. She initially worked as a sports journalist in Dublin, before working for various shipping companies and then reporting on the Pacific Islands for the *Daily Graphic*. In 1904 and 1905, she accepted government and company commissions to write tourist publicity for the Cook Islands, Tonga, Samoa, Niue and New Zealand, as well as on the prospects for settlers in Fiji. She completed three books in Europe before returning to the Pacific. Commissioned by the *Times* in London and the *Sydney Morning Herald*, she sailed late in 1907 to report on Papua, intending to stay only two or three months. She lived in Port Moresby for the next 27 years and formed a close friendship with the acting administrator, Sir Hubert Murray. Grimshaw was commissioned by Australian Prime Minister Alfred Deakin to advertise Papua's need for white settlers and capital. She published pamphlets in 1909 and a book, *The New Guinea*, in 1910. Afterwards, Grimshaw concentrated on fiction writing (which she preferred), with most of her texts being romances in Pacific settings. One was even produced into the movie: *The Adorable Outcast* (1928). Grimshaw also managed a plantation near Samarai from 1917 to 1922. She accompanied exploring parties up the Sepik and Fly rivers in 1923 and 1926 and, in 1933, she took up tobacco growing. In 1934, she left Papua, visiting Fiji, Samoa and Tonga one last time before retiring in Bathurst, New South Wales, in 1936. She died in 1953. In total, Grimshaw wrote four travel books, 24 novels, 10 volumes of short stories and countless articles for newspapers and magazines. These included the travelogues, *In the Strange South Seas* (which focuses on Polynesia); *From Fiji to the Cannibal Islands* (which focuses on Melanesia and which was also published in New York under the title *Fiji and Its Possibilities*); a part-autobiography titled *Isles of Adventure*; and her first Pacific fiction, *Vaiti of the Islands*.

Grundy, Joseph Hadfield, *A Month in New Zealand; A Trip to Fiji, Tonga and Samoa*. Adelaide: Hunkin, Ellis & King, 1931.

Grundy, Joseph Hadfield, *The New Hebrides Group of Islands*. Adelaide: Hunkin, Ellis & King, 1933.

> Born in England in 1856, Grundy arrived in South Australia at the age of 19, later founding a jeweller and druggist firm. He travelled in Europe and in the Pacific, writing several travel pamphlets and a book

of verse afterwards (some with the help of his nephew as he became blind). *A Month in New Zealand: A Trip to Fiji, Tonga and Samoa* recalled a month's holiday in 1914. *The New Hebrides Group of Islands* described another voyage, though it is unclear when it was undertaken. He also wrote *More about Australia and the Pacific* in 1929 (with a short reference to his travels to Tahiti) and *Lord Howe Island and Norfolk Island* in 1933.

Gunga, *Narrative of a Trip from Maryborough to New Caledonia*. Maryborough: publisher unknown, 1878.

This is a collection of letters that were printed in the *Wide Bay and Burnett News*. The author, 'Gunga', occasionally addresses these letters to 'Mr Editor'. Gunga was sent to New Caledonia to investigate nickel deposits and arrived when the so-called 'native insurrection' was at its height. His identity is unknown.

Hamilton, William, *Diaries and Pearling Logs, 1882–1905*, PMB 15. Pacific Manuscripts Bureau, Australian National University, Canberra.

Hamilton was born in Scotland and came to Australia at the age of 10. From 1882 to 1883, he voyaged from Brisbane to the New Hebrides, New Britain and New Ireland in labour recruiting vessels. From the late 1890s, he ran the Hamilton Pearling Company, with luggers operating out of the Admiralty Islands and Solomon Islands. Later, Hamilton invested in plantations in the Solomon Islands, mainly on Choiseul. He died in Sydney in 1937. These papers include two diaries of recruiting voyages to the New Hebrides (1882–1883); a report and diary on a voyage prospecting for pearl shell in New Guinea and the Solomon Islands (1899–1901); two logs kept by the Hamilton Pearling Company in the Admiralty Islands; and logs and diaries for four vessels in New Guinea and the Solomon Islands (1903–1905).

Hayball, Doris, *Strawberries in the Jam: Being Intimate Notes about Interesting People*. Melbourne: Sunsphere Press, 1940.

Born in Melbourne in 1909, Doris ('Ada') Hayball was a playwright, author and poet. This is an anecdotal account of a one-year grand tour taken in 1937. On the return trip to Australia, she visited Hawai'i and Fiji. She died in 1948.

Henley, Thomas, *Fiji—The Land of Promise*. Sydney: John Sands Ltd, 1926.

Henley, Thomas, *A Pacific Cruise: Musings and Opinions on Island Problems*. Sydney: John Sands Ltd, 1930.

Sir Thomas Henley was born in England in 1860 and migrated to Sydney in 1884. Beginning as a building contractor, he eventually became a state politician in 1904. In *Fiji—The Land of Promise*, Henley describes a trip to Fiji that he took in 1926, specifically focusing on the strategic value of the country to Australia. It includes a preface by John Wear Burton. In *A Pacific Cruise*, Henley describes a circuit of Fiji, Tonga and Samoa in 1928. He also wrote a book titled *New Guinea and Australia's Pacific Islands Mandate* in 1927, as well as some articles commenting on Samoan politics. He fell from a Manly ferry and drowned in 1935, leaving money from his estate to the Congregational and Presbyterian Churches.

Hickson, JC, *Notes of Travel: From Pacific to Atlantic, with Description of the World's Fair at Chicago; Also Travels by Sea and Land round the World*. Parramatta: Fuller's Lightning Printing Works, 1894.

This is an account of Hickson's 'hurried trip round the world' in 1893 on the *Monowai* with his eldest daughter. The letters he sent home during the trip were published in the local paper, *The Australian Currier*. He describes Samoa and Hawai'i. His identity is unknown, though the preface refers to his residence in Enfield, New South Wales.

Hill, Alfred William, *A Cruise among Former Cannibal Islands, Fiji, Tonga, Samoa: A Glimpse at the Countries, People, Customs and Legends*. Adelaide: W.K. Thomas, 1927.

Hill was born in 1863 in Adelaide and was trained as a doctor in England. He was an officer in the First Australian Imperial Force and a surgeon in Adelaide from 1897 to 1922. This text describes his 30-day steamer trip in the *Tofua* to Fiji, Tonga and Samoa in 1927. He died in South Australia in 1933.

Holmes, Charles Henry, *A Passport round the World*. London: Hutchinson, 1937.

Born in 1891 in Melbourne, Holmes was an editor of the magazine *Walkabout* and the managing director of the Australian National Travel Association from c. 1930 to 1957. Holmes spent three months on a grand tour in the 1920s visiting Hawai'i, American Samoa and Fiji on his way back to Sydney. He also wrote a travelogue titled *We Find Australia* in 1932.

Hore, Edward Coode, *S. S. John Williams: Captain Hore's Narrative of the Leading Incidents of Voyage no. 2*. Sydney: William Brooks & Co., 1895.

Hore was born in 1848 in London and arrived in Australia in 1890. He was a Congregational missionary and seaman, working with the London Missionary Society in Africa in 1877 and on the mission ship, *John Williams*, from 1893 to 1900. This is a report of a six-month visit in 1895 to 36 missionary stations in the Pacific, including New Guinea, Niue, Samoa, the Ellice and Gilbert Islands and the Cook Islands. Hore wrote one other book about his African mission work and died in Hobart in 1912.

Hoskin, Aaron, *With Other Races*. London: Watts, 1913.

Born in South Australia in 1862, Hoskin was a grazier and archaeologist who lived in Mitchell, Queensland. This is an account of his 1910 grand tour to London via Fiji and Hawai'i. His other publication, *My Trip Round the World* (1917), described a journey from the Philippines to San Francisco via Hawai'i.

Ievers, William, *Fifty Years after, or, Old Scenes Revisited A. D. 1890*. Melbourne: Ford & Son, Printers, 1894.

Born in 1818 in Ireland, Ievers arrived in Australia in 1855. He worked as a merchant, sailor, auctioneer and estate agent. This is a travel diary that was published for private distribution. Ievers describes his nine-month grand tour with his eldest son, beginning in 1890. He visited Honolulu and American Samoa aboard the *Mariprosa*. He died in Melbourne in 1901.

Irwin, Edward Way, and Ivan Goff, *No Longer Innocent*. Sydney: Angus & Robertson, 1934.

Bill Irwin and Ivan Goff were shipping reporters living in Fremantle, Western Australia. Only 18 years old, they travelled to Fiji and across the US and Canada in the 1930s with little money, apart from the commission earned from submitting articles to the *Western Mail* newspaper. This is an account of their journey.

Jamieson, A, *With the Scottish Delegation: Impressions of the Sea Voyage, Egypt, Great Britain, the Continent, the Battlefields of France, America, Honolulu, Fiji and New Zealand*. Ashfield: A. Jamieson, 1929.

This is a report of a pilgrimage by Scottish descendants carrying samples of Australian products to Europe to 'tell the people of the Old Land the wonderful possibilities and achievements of Australia'. Miss A Jamieson left Sydney in 1928 on the liner *Hobson Bay*. On the journey home, she visited Hawai'i, Fiji and New Zealand.

Joseph, Alfred, *A Bendigonian Abroad: Being Sketches of Travel Made during a Ten Months Tour through Europe and America*. Melbourne: Reardon & Mitchell, n.d.

Born in 1848 in London, Joseph was a financier, stockbroker and self-proclaimed 'Bendigonian'. This account of a seven-month grand tour in March 1890 was originally written for publication in the *Bendigo Advertiser*. His book was privately circulated. In it, he describes Hawai'i and American Samoa on the journey home.

Kingsford-Smith, Charles, *My Flying Life: An Authentic Biography Prepared under the Personal Supervision of, and from the Diaries and Papers of, the Late Sir Charles Kingsford-Smith*. London: Andrew Melrose, 1937.

Born in Brisbane in 1897, Kingsford-Smith served in the First Australian Imperial Force and later became a famous aviator, breaking several records in his inter-country plane trips. This autobiography was published posthumously after Kingsford-Smith's plane, *Lady Southern Cross*, disappeared in 1935. This account describes the first trans-Pacific flight from San Francisco to Australia in 1928, including stopovers in Hawai'i and Fiji.

Kirkcaldie, Rosa Angela, *In Gray and Scarlet*. Melbourne: Alexander McCubbin, 1922.

Kirkcaldie was born in Sydney in 1887 and worked as a nurse at the Royal Prince Alfred Hospital in Sydney. She served as an army nurse in World War I, then returned to nursing duties as a matron in Sydney afterwards. This is an account of her trip on the hospital ship, *Grantala*, which went to Fiji and German New Guinea from August to December 1914. She died in Sydney in 1972.

Lane, James, 'Briefs and Associated Papers in Cases Involving Pacific Islanders'. In Crown Solicitor's Office, Series ID 12102, Item ID 7866. Brisbane: Queensland State Archives, 1883–1884.

Journal of a government agent aboard the *Lizzie* and *Ceara* in 1884. He visited the Solomon Islands, Papua and New Guinea. His captain aboard the *Ceara* was William Wawn.

Lees, William, *Around the Coasts of Australia and Fiji Illustrated: A Handbook of Picturesque Travel and General Information for Passengers by Steamers of the Australasian United Steam Navigation Co. Ltd.* Brisbane: Robert McGregor & Co. Printers, 1916.

Lees was a proprietor and editor of the *Queensland Pastoral Gazette*. He published guides to the Queensland goldfields and railways in the late nineteenth century. According to this illustrated handbook, 'An effort has been made to place before the reader the scope of operations of this Company and a guide to the various places around the coast of Australia and Fiji, with which the Company's steamers have regular communication'. He died in 1939.

Lewis, Aletta, *They Call Them Savages*. London: Methuen, 1938.

Aletta M Lewis was born in England in 1904. She trained as an artist and arrived in Sydney in 1927, where she taught at the Sydney Art School. She was a regular exhibitor in Sydney, winning the Archibald prize in 1928. In 1929, the director of the Macquarie galleries funded Lewis to go to the Pacific Islands and fulfil her desire 'to paint brown people'. She recorded her six-month sojourn in American Samoa in this 1928 account. She also exhibited her paintings at a solo show in 1929 before returning to London (the artwork has since been lost). Although British, Lewis frequently questioned her own nationality while attempting to become a part of the Samoan communities in which she lived.

Littlejohn, George Stanley, *Notes and Reflections 'on the road'*. Sydney: Swift Print, 1911.

Born in 1862 in London, Littlejohn arrived in Sydney two years later and studied at Sydney Grammar School. He became a successful businessman until his death in 1923. Littlejohn travelled to the US via Fiji and Hawai'i in 1909 for four months on doctor's recommendations. This account was based on daily diary entries, with only 250 copies being printed for private circulation.

Livingston, John, John Thomson and D Livingston, *Three Australians Abroad*. Mount Gambier: publisher unknown, 1912.

John Livingston (1857–1935) was a stock agent, station manager, auctioneer and politician. His brother was a station manager in New South Wales. John Thomson (1862–1934) was a New South Wales politician. They travelled from Melbourne to 'the old country' in 1911 as part of a political delegation to attend the coronation of King George V. On the way home, they visited Hawai'i and Fiji.

Lloyd, M, *Wanderings in the Old World and the New*. Adelaide: Vardon and Pritchard Printers, 1901.

Lloyd was a South Australian and self-professed 'true Britisher'. This travel account describes Lloyd's grand tour with his wife in 1901 for six months. On the way to the US, he visited American Samoa and Hawai'i.

Lucas, Thomas Pennington, *Cries from Fiji and Sighings from the South Seas.* Melbourne: Dunn & Collins, n.d.

Lucas, Thomas Pennington, *Shall Australasia Be a Nation.* Brisbane: Edwards, Dunlop and Co., 1907.

> Lucas was born in Scotland in 1843. His father was a Wesleyan minister, and Lucas was convinced in his youth that he had a divine mission to save humanity. He studied medicine and joined the prestigious Linnean Society. After the death of his wife and his contraction of tuberculosis, he moved to New South Wales in 1877 and briefly visited the Methodist missions in Fiji the same year. *Cries from Fiji* defended the Methodist missionaries there and opposed the Queensland labour trade. Afterwards, he established a medical practice in Melbourne, then moved to Brisbane in 1886, where he promoted pawpaw ointment as a medical treatment. He was considered quite eccentric in his later life, until his death in 1917.

Mahlmann, John James, *Reminiscences of an Ancient Mariner.* Yokohama: Japan Gazette Printing & Publishing, 1918.

> Mahlmann lived in Australia and worked as a second officer on a trading ship between Sydney and Auckland. This text is the only source of information about his life. After a failed gold prospecting expedition to New Zealand in 1864, he joined a trading ship that took him to Japan, China and the Micronesian region (including the Gilbert and Marshall Islands, Ponape and Hawai'i). His reminiscences include being shipwrecked in the Marshall Islands, living in Ponape for two years, touring Hawai'i with a Japanese government delegation in 1885 and visiting his daughter in Europe. He lived in Japan from 1871 for 47 years.

Marks, Ernest George, *Pacific Peril, or, Menace of Japan's Mandated Islands.* Sydney: Wynyard Book Arcade, 1933.

> Marks was born in New South Wales in 1885. He was a journalist for the *Australian Star* from 1903 and for the *Sun* from 1909 to 1935. He was an amateur military historian, showing particular interest in the Napoleonic Wars. Marks authored six books, contributed articles on naval subjects to the *Navy League Journal* and was a founding member of the Australian Journalists Association. He died in 1935 in Sydney. This text warned readers about the Asian threat in the Pacific, and it is unclear whether it was based on his personal experience of travel in the region.

Marshall, Alan John, *The Black Musketeers: The Work and Adventures of a Scientist on a South Sea Island at War and in Peace*. London: William Heinemann, 1937.

Marshall, Jock, *The Men and Birds of Paradise: Journeys through Equatorial New Guinea*. London: Heinemann, 1938.

Alan John (Jock) Marshall was born in 1911 in Sydney. Despite having lost an arm in a shooting accident at the age of 16, he was active in several natural history expeditions as a zoologist. *The Black Musketeers* describes seven months that he spent with his colleague, Tom Harrison, living in Espiritu Santo (the New Hebrides) in 1934 on an Oxford University Expedition trip. Their goal was to research the effects of climate on animal reproduction. *The Men and Birds of Paradise* described Jock's travels through Papua and Dutch New Guinea in 1936, in which he conducted reconnaissance for a scientific expedition. He also published other books about Australia, such as *Australia Limited* (1942). He had a distinguished service record during World War II in New Guinea and worked in academia afterwards, becoming a Professor of Zoology at Monash University. He died in Victoria in 1967. A biography of his life was written by his wife, Jane Marshall, and is accessible online.

Matters, Charles Henry, *From Golden Gate to Golden Horn, and Many Other World Wide Wanderings: Or 50,000 Miles of Travel over Sea and Land*. Adelaide: Vardon & Pritchard, 1892.

Born in 1847 in England, Matters moved to Adelaide in 1853, where he worked as a land agent and manager. This is an account of his year-long grand tour to the US in 1891, in which he describes American Samoa and Hawai'i. Parts of his 'rapid sketches of travel' were published in the *Advertiser*, *Register* and *Christian Weekly*. He was a fellow of the Royal Geographical Society and gave public lectures on his travels.

McGuire, Paul, *Westward the Course: The New World of Oceania*. Melbourne: Oxford University Press, 1942.

Born in 1903 in South Australia, Dominic Paul McGuire was a journalist, writer, literary critic and diplomat. He worked as an overseas correspondent in Europe for several newspapers in the late 1920s and early 1930s, and was a diplomat in Europe in the 1950s. This text describes McGuire's travels in the Pacific and South-East Asia in the 1940s, including his visits to Hawai'i and Fiji. He frequently commented on the expansion and influence of Western empires, including Australia. He died in 1978.

McKay, Thomas Allan, *Seeing the World Twice 1926–1935*. Melbourne: Robertson & Mullens, 1936.

McKay was born in 1887 in New Zealand and worked in Melbourne as a publisher and businessman from the 1880s. He identified himself as a 'British–Australian' in his account of two grand tours in 1926 and 1935. He visited Hawai'i and Fiji in 1926, and Papua in 1935.

McLaren, Jack, *Gentlemen of the Empire; The Colourful and Remarkable Experiences of District Commissioners, Patrol Officers and Other Officials in Some of the British Empire's Tropical Outposts*. Melbourne: Hutchinson & Co. Ltd, 1940.

McLaren, Jack, *My Odyssey*. London: Jonathan Cape, 1923.

John (Jack) McLaren was born in Melbourne in 1884. He ran away from school when he was 16, working in various jobs in north Queensland, Papua and New Guinea, the Solomon Islands and Fiji—including mining, driving, pearling, trading, prospecting and labour recruiting. He described these experiences in the autobiography, *My Odyssey*. From 1911, he settled on a coconut plantation in Cape York and wrote articles for *The Bulletin* and other fiction and non-fiction books under the pseudonym 'McNorth'. In 1925, he moved to London for 30 years, where he remained publishing books, broadcasting radio and writing government propaganda during World War II. He died in 1954 in England. Of his many other books, *Gentlemen of the Empire* was devoted to Pacific subjects, describing the lives of patrol officers in Melanesia.

McMahon, Thomas John, *Pacific Islands Illustrated*. Sydney: McCarron, Stewart and Co., 1910.

Born in 1864, McMahon was a journalist for the *Cairns Post* and *Northern Herald*, and later a freelance author, photographer and speaker. He first visited Papua and New Guinea in 1915 and then spent the next seven years visiting the Pacific Islands, taking over 1,000 photographs that were published in newspapers, magazines and books between 1915 and 1924. Historian Max Quanchi has argued that McMahon's images promoted Australian colonialism in the Pacific. *Pacific Islands Illustrated* consisted of three photographic albums titled 'Gilbert & Ellis', 'Ocean Island' and 'Nauru'. Each album had between eight and 13 black and white images with short captions. They documented the phosphate mining industry and the indigenous people. The date of publication does not correspond to McMahon's actual travels, and it is more likely that these images were published in the 1920s rather than in 1910, as listed by the Barr Smith Library at the University of Adelaide. McMahon died in Brisbane on 12 August 1933.

McMillan, Robert, *There and Back: Or Notes of a Voyage round the World by 'Gossip'.* Sydney: William Brooks, 1903.

McMillan was said to have been born in Scotland in 1848, but he ran away from home at age 14. He lived in the US as a journalist, then returned to England before moving to New South Wales in 1890 for health reasons. He became editor and proprietor of the *Blue Mountains Express*, and further worked for another journal, *Stock and Station*. He often wrote under the pseudonyms 'Gossip' and 'Globe Trotter' and dedicated many books to children and to his beloved *Stock and Station* readers. He was also a founding member of the New South Wales Institute of Journalists, before he died in Sydney in 1929. In this text, 'Gossip' describes his travels to Hawai'i and American Samoa on an 11-month grand tour in the 1900s.

McWilliam, Henry Hastings, Private Record, 1DRL/0467. Canberra: Australian War Memorial, 1914–1915.

Sub-Lieutenant McWilliam was born in 1894 and served on HMAS *Australia* during World War I. A carbon copy of his diary from 27 July 1914 to 28 January 1915 is held by the Australian War Memorial. It records McWilliam's journey from Sydney to German New Guinea, New Caledonia, Fiji and Samoa as the ship patrolled for German vessels.

Meagher, Richard Denis, *American Impressions*. Sydney: Gordon & Gotch, 1925.

Born in 1866 in New South Wales, Meagher worked as a solicitor and state politician. This text describes his trip to the US in 1924, when he was Lord Mayor of Sydney. He visited Fiji and Hawai'i. Meagher published two other books about his political career, before his death in Sydney in 1931.

Meek, Albert Stewart, *A Naturalist in Cannibal Land*, edited by Frank Fox. London: T.F. Unwin, 1913.

Meek was born in London in 1872. He was a bird collector and naturalist who travelled across Australia, Papua, Dutch New Guinea and the Solomon Islands from 1889 to 1913. Many of the specimens were donated to the Rothschild Natural History Museum in England. Meek returned to England 'weary of the South Seas life', where he published this book with Frank Fox. Meek may be considered Australian because he spent six years working as a jackeroo on Queensland cattle stations, and because he uses Australian slang in his writing. He also visited Australia regularly between his travels in the Pacific and was married in Cooktown in 1898 (to whom it is unclear).

Melvin, Joseph Dalgarno, *The Cruise of the Helena: A Labour-Recruiting Voyage to the Solomon Islands*, edited by Peter Corris. Melbourne: Hawthorn Press, 1977.

Melvin was born in 1852 in Scotland. He worked as a journalist in Perth, then as one in Melbourne for the *Argus*. He was sent as a correspondent to report on the Sudan War in 1885 and on the Queensland labour trade in 1892, publishing 13 articles on the labour trade. His experience aboard a recruiting ship was positive, and he failed to observe any offences committed. He was an active Congregationalist and rebutted Australian missionaries who attacked his interpretation of the trade. He continued working as a reporter for various Australian newspapers, until his death in 1909.

Mercer-Smith, Sydney, OM76-04 Sydney Mercer-Smith Diaries 1892–1900, OM76-04. Brisbane: State Library of Queensland, 1892–1900.

Born in Sydney in 1857, Captain Mercer-Smith was appointed as a government agent onboard labour recruiting vessels from 1893 to 1902. These diaries record the author's recruiting experiences from 1893 to 1900. They were also personal diaries rather than official logs. He died in Brisbane in 1933. Carol Edmondson published an introduction to Mercer-Smith's diaries in 1984.

Meudell, George, *The Pleasant Career of a Spendthrift*. London: G. Routledge, 1929.

George Dick Meudell was a stockbroker and accountant, born in 1860 in Victoria. This autobiography is a disorderly collection of anecdotes and reminiscences of his life, including his visits to Samoa, Fiji, Tahiti, Hawai'i, New Caledonia and New Guinea. He reprinted a second edition in 1936, but removed references to certain prominent Melbourne families due to his controversial exposé of the Victorian land boom. He also published a book about banking and kept documents and souvenirs from his American and European travels. He died in Melbourne in 1936.

Mickle, Alan Durward, *Of Many Things*. Sydney: Australasian Publishing Company, 1941.

Born in 1883 in Melbourne, Mickle was a poet, novelist, playwright and literary critic. This book is divided into three parts: 'autobiographical', 'of places and people' and 'travel'. The travel section described his visits to Fiji in 1908. He visited Samoa on a later journey in 1935, on a grand tour to Europe with his wife. He died in 1969.

Millican, J, *Notes of Our Rambles*. Charters Towers: J. Millican, 1906.

Born in England in 1855, Millican was a businessman involved in Queensland mining, who later owned a Sydney hotel. This text was based on diary notes and a collection of press interviews from *The Northern Miner* and *North Queensland Register*, in which he offered his impressions of the British and American economies. The year-long journey was undertaken in 1905 with his family, for both a holiday and a trip to encourage investment in Queensland mines. They visited Hawai'i and American Samoa. Millican died in Sydney in 1934.

Mills, Christopher, 'Briefs and Associated Papers in Cases Involving Pacific Islanders'. In Crown Solicitor's Office, Series ID 12102, Item ID 7876. Brisbane: Queensland State Archives, 1884.

Mills was a government agent aboard the *Ethel* in 1884, which visited the New Hebrides, Solomon Islands and German New Guinea. These papers include files relating to a case of alleged kidnapping by Captain John Loutit and First Mate George R Burton.

Mitchell, Janet, *Spoils of Opportunity: An Autobiography*. New York: E.P. Dutton & Co. Inc., 1938.

Janet Charlotte Mitchell was born in 1896 in Melbourne. She graduated from university in London in 1922 and was education secretary of the Young Women's Christian Association in Melbourne from 1924 to 1926. She was active in the League of Nations Union and was an Australian delegate to conferences of the Institute of Pacific Relations in Honolulu (1925) and China (1931). In her autobiography, she describes her trip to Hawai'i, during which time she was 'keenly interested in the immigration question' and explored Japanese attitudes to the White Australia policy. She also briefly mentioned a trip to Rarotonga and Tahiti the following year, en route to England as part of her frequent lecture tours for the Institute. Mitchell published a novel, *Tempest in Paradise* (1935), based on her life as an English teacher in Manchuria, which she dedicated to her cousin, George Ernest Morrison ('Chinese George'), who was a popular reporter on the Queensland labour trade. She died in Melbourne in 1957.

Mordaunt, Elinor, *Sinabada*. London: Michael Joseph, 1937.

Mordaunt, Elinor, *The Venture Book*. New York: The Century Co., 1926.

Evelyn May Mordaunt was born in 1872 in England. In 1897, she went to Mauritius with her cousin and married a sugar planter the next year, though she suffered from malaria and returned to England alone. She then left for Melbourne in 1902 and, in 1903, gave birth to her son,

Godfrey, in Australia. In Australia, she refused all offers of help and lived in cheap lodgings, earning money by sewing and painting. She briefly edited a woman's monthly magazine. In 1909, she and her son left for England, though she continued writing to support herself. She published over 40 volumes, mainly novels and short stories. Her reputation as a travel writer resulted from her around-the-world trip for the London *Daily Mail* in 1923, which was later published in *The Venture Book* and *The Further Venture Book* in 1926. The first book described Tahiti, Samoa, Tonga and Fiji, while the second explored Dutch New Guinea and the East Indies. Her autobiography, *Sinabada*, recounted her Pacific travels, with additional descriptions of the Trobriand Islands and Papua. Mordaunt continued to travel throughout her life, and died in England in 1942.

Muspratt, Eric, *My South Sea Island*. London: Travel Book Club, 1931.

Muspratt was born in England in 1899 and, after travelling across Europe and North America, he joined the First Australian Imperial Force, from 1917 to 1919. He subsequently purchased a pineapple farm in Queensland in 1919, then moved to San Cristoval in the Solomon Islands the following year to work as a plantation manager for six months. *My South Sea Island* recounts his temporary stay in the Solomons. Muspratt continued to travel the world as a seaman and vagabond, returning to Australia twice before serving with the Australian forces during World War II. He recounted these experiences in several other books, including in his 1948 autobiography, *Fire of Youth* (with descriptions of American Samoa, Tahiti and Hawai'i). He died in 1949 in Sydney.

Napier, Sydney Elliott, *Men and Cities: Being the Journeyings of a Journalist*. Sydney: Angus & Robertson, 1938.

Napier was a lawyer, journalist and poet born in Sydney in 1870. He served in World War I and contributed articles to the *Sydney Mail*, *Sydney Morning Herald* and *BP Magazine* in the 1920s and 1930s. This text was one of his contributions, describing his voyage to the Panama Canal via Tahiti in May 1938. He also published some books of verses and travel books about Europe and the Great Barrier Reef. He died in Sydney in 1940.

Nicoll, George Robertson, *Fifty Years' Travels in Australia, China, Japan, America, Etc., 1848–1898*. London: George Robertson Nicoll, 1899.

Nicoll, George Robertson, The Life and Adventures of George Robertson Nicoll, 1824–1890, MS 3292. Canberra: National Library of Australia, 1824–1890.

Nicoll, JB, 'A Cruise through Some of the Pacific Islands in 1902 by Mr and Mrs J. B. Nicoll'. In The Life and Adventures of George Robertson Nicoll, 1824–1890, MS 3292. Canberra: National Library of Australia, 1902.

> George Robertson Nicoll was born in Scotland in 1824 and settled in Sydney in 1848. He was a wealthy shipwright and businessman. Nicoll privately printed a narrative of his worldwide travels for his family in 1899, containing descriptions of Tahiti, Hawai'i, Fiji, Wallis Island, Niue and Samoa. The manuscript was written in 1890, and the file contains another piece that was written in 1902 by his son and daughter-in-law, Mr and Mrs JB Nicoll, which described Norfolk Island, New Caledonia, the New Hebrides, Solomon Islands and Santa Cruz Islands. George Nicoll died in Sydney in 1901. Information about his son is unknown.

Nixon, A, 'Inwards Correspondence'. In Colonial Secretary's Office, Series ID 5253, Item ID 846982. Brisbane: Queensland State Archives, 1877.

> This diary belonged to a government agent aboad the *Bobtail Nag*, which visited the New Hebrides in 1877. The papers also include a newspaper clipping from the *Courier* on 23 January 1878, titled 'The True Story of a Recruiting Voyage', presumably written by Nixon.

Nossiter, Harold, *Southward Ho!* London: Witherby, 1937.

> Nossiter was an eminent yachtsman who sailed with his two eldest sons around the world from 1935 to 1937. They became the first Australians to circumnavigate the globe in a yacht. Nossiter was aware of the historical nature of their voyage and wanted to document the trip in two books. The first, *Northward Ho!*, recounted the initial voyage from Sydney to London. *Southward Ho!* described the homeward journey via the Marquesas Islands, Tahiti, French Polynesia, Rarotonga and Tonga. Both books were published in the US and UK.

Osborne, Ernest, *Through the Atolls of the Line*. Five Dock: publisher unknown, 1900.

> Details of Osborne's life are sketchy. He worked in the Pacific phosphate trade, was in Fiji in 1917 and was a trader in the Gilbert Islands in the 1930s. He also published several fiction novels for the New South Wales Bookstall Series, as well as short stories for *The Bulletin* and *Lone Hand*

from 1905 onwards. In this unpublished typescript, Osborne describes a leisurely cruise through the Gilbert Islands in search of a copra trading post in the 1930s.

Paterson, Andrew Barton, 'The Pioneers', Talks—AB Paterson, Australian Broadcasting Commission, Sydney: ABC, 1935. Series no. SP 1558/2, 629, National Archives of Australia.

'Banjo' Paterson was an Australian poet and journalist, born in 1864 in Orange, New South Wales. Paterson began writing for *The Bulletin* in the 1880s and his first collection of poems, *The Man from Snowy River, and Other Verses*, made him famous throughout the country in 1890. Paterson served as a war correspondent during the Boer War in 1899, and then travelled to China in 1901 as a journalist. Less well known is his trip to the New Hebrides in 1902 to report on a newly established settlement scheme by Burns, Philp and Company. His impressions were published in the *Sydney Morning Herald*, and later in unpublished radio broadcasts with the Australian Broadcasting Commission. He died in 1941 and was remembered as a great Australian ballad writer.

Paton, Frank Hume Lyall, *Glimpses of the New Hebrides*. Melbourne: Foreign Missions Committee, Presbyterian Church of Victoria, 1913.

Paton was born in Aniwa, the New Hebrides, in 1870, son of the Reverend John Gibson Paton. Educated in Melbourne and Scotland, he then worked as a missionary in the New Hebrides. His years on Tanna from 1896 to 1902 are described in *Lomai of Lenakel* (1903), and he further published several religious texts and translations. From 1902, he worked in administrative roles for the Australian Presbyterian Church, travelling extensively throughout Australia and the region. He also served overseas as a chaplain with the First Australian Imperial Force from 1918 to 1919. Paton published many books, magazines and pamphlets for children and adults on Pacific issues, taking a more moderate line than his father on the labour trade and on French influence in the New Hebrides. His publications included *Quarterly Jottings from the New Hebrides* (the magazine of the Paton mission fund published from 1895 to 1961), *Glimpses of the New Hebrides* (1913, based on his visit in 1913), *Kingdom of the Pacific* (1913, a reference book for children), *Slavery under the British Flag* (1914) and *Australian Interests in the New Hebrides* (1919). He died in 1938.

Pearse, Albert William, *Recent Travel*. Sydney: John Andrew, 1914.

Pearse, Albert William, *A Windjammer 'Prentice*. Sydney: John Andrews & Co., 1927.

Pearse was born in 1857 in London and moved to Australia in 1891. Initially an accountant, he went to sea in 1875 and worked with the Royal Mail Steam Packet Company and the Orient Steam Navigation Company, becoming a master mariner. He moved to Sydney in 1891, where he worked as an editor for several agricultural journals. He was politically ultra-conservative and hostile to unionism, writing several pamphlets on White Australia and state-owned railways. He was also a devout Anglican and a fellow of the Royal Geographical Society. *Recent Travel* describes a six-week cruise in 1911 to Tahiti, French Polynesia and the Cook Islands, as well as a visit to Fiji and Hawai'i en route to the US in 1913. His autobiography, *A Windjammer 'Prentice,* incorporated stories about the Pacific from the previous book. It was reprinted with an additional 13 chapters in 1932 due to popular demand. Pearse died in Sydney in 1951.

Phillips, George, *Notes on a Visit to New Caledonia*. Brisbane: Brisbane Telegraph, 1903.

Born in England in 1843, Phillips was a civil engineer and surveyor in Australia from 1851. This is a collection of six letters that he sent to the *Brisbane Telegraph*, describing his trip to New Caledonia in April 1903. He died in 1921.

Philp, John Ernest, *A Solomons Sojourn: J. E. Philp's Log of the Makira, 1912–1913*, edited by Richard Allen Herr and E Anne Rood. Hobart: Tasmanian Historical Research Association, 1978.

Born in 1869 in Tasmania, Philp was a railway surveyor before he left his wife and family in 1912 to work as a labour recruiter in the Solomon Islands. This is an edited copy of his private log that described his two years in the region. During his travels, he encountered other travel writers and famous personalities in the area, including Joseph HC Dickinson, Eric Muspratt, Osa Johnson and Clifford Collinson. Philp was also interested in collecting and sailing, and he occasionally wrote for the *Tasmanian Mail*. He returned to his family in December 1913, intending to take them back to the Solomon Islands; unfortunately, the outbreak of war changed these plans. He died in 1937.

Ponder, Harriet Winifred, *An Idler in the Islands*. Sydney: Cornstalk Publishing, 1924.

> Ponder (1883–1967) was originally a vocalist in England before she came to Australia in search of health when her voice broke down. She lived in Queensland for a time before travelling around Australia and the world, establishing a reputation as a journalist and author. She wrote several books about Java and Cambodia, as well as a biography of the singer, Dame Clara Butt. This account describes Fiji, Tonga and Samoa and includes parts that were published in the *Melbourne Herald* and *Adelaide Register*.

Powell, Sydney Walter, *Adventures of a Wanderer*. London: Jonathan Cape, 1928.

Powell, Sydney Walter, *A South Sea Diary*. London: V. Gollancz, 1942.

Powell, Sydney Walter, 'Each to His Taste'. In Papers of Sydney Powell [circa 1920–1950], MS10012. Canberra: National Library of Australia, 1920–1950.

> Powell was an Australian writer who is remembered for his descriptions of Gallipoli, where he fought in World War I. Born in England in 1878, Powell spent his childhood in South Africa, but was educated in England. He moved to Australia and worked in various jobs around the country until he joined the artillery. He was posted to Thursday Island, where he began writing for *The Bulletin* and developed an interest in the Pacific Islands. He visited Tahiti in 1912, where he (allegedly) married a Tahitian. He returned to Tahiti in 1916 after serving in World War I. He moved to England in c. 1926, where he became a prolific fiction and poetry writer. Many of his stories were about South Africa, but he also wrote Pacific fiction as well as three travel accounts of the same experience in Tahiti, one of which that was never published. There are inconsistencies between these three accounts regarding his marriage, the number of visits he made and the reasons why he left Tahiti. He died in 1952.

Rannie, Douglas, *My Adventures among South Sea Cannibals: An Account of the Experiences and Adventures of a Government Official among the Natives of Oceania*. London: Seeley, Service & Co., 1912.

Rannie, Douglas, *Notes on the New Hebrides*. Brisbane: Queensland Branch of the Royal Geographical Society of Australasia, 1890.

> Rannie was born in Scotland in 1860, but went to Brisbane in 1883 after the death of an acquaintance in the Solomon Islands; to 'make myself acquainted as well as I could with the particulars of the Queensland Labour Traffic'. He served as a government agent on Australian labour vessels from 1884 to 1892, then worked as an inspector at Mackay and

Charters Towers and then finally worked as a librarian at the Queensland museum. During his time as a government agent, he visited the Solomon Islands, the New Hebrides, New Caledonia, Bougainville and New Ireland. He died in Brisbane in 1915. His papers and photographs are kept by the University of Queensland Anthropology Museum.

Ravenscroft, Stan H, *A Trip Round the World*. Sydney: E.H. Hume, 1914.

Ravenscroft was born in Australia and lived in Sydney. He visited Fiji and Hawaiʻi on *RMS Niagara* in April 1914, during his grand tour to Europe. The National Library has a collection of letters, photographs and biographical cuttings related to his trip.

Rebell, Fred, *Escape to the Sea: The Adventures of Fred Rebell, Who Sailed Single Handed in an Open Boat 9,000 Miles across the Pacific in Search of Happiness*. London: Murray, 1939.

Born in 1886 in Latvia as Paul Christian Julius Sproge, Rebell changed his name and fled to Germany to avoid military conscription, before stowing away to Sydney in 1909. Until 1928, he worked as a railway construction worker, sawmiller, farmer and carpenter. He was also married and divorced. In Sydney, on the dole and desperate, Rebell decided to emigrate to the US. He bought a derelict 18-foot boat and left Sydney on 31 December 1931. He reached California in 1933, his voyage being the first recorded lone crossing of the Pacific Ocean from west to east. He was deported to Latvia, where he completed his book, and then returned to Australia in 1937. His account explains how the voyage prompted his conversion to Christianity, and he joined a Pentecostal church soon after. He was naturalised as an Australian in 1955 and died in Sydney in 1968.

Robertson, Macpherson, *MacRobertson Abroad: A Reprint of Mr. Mac. Robertson's Diary Written during His World Tour of 1926–1927*. Melbourne: 'Welcome Home' Committee, 1927.

Robertson was born in 1859 in Ballarat. He was a confectioner, industrialist and philanthropist, as well as a fellow of the Royal Geographical Society and a knight. This travel narrative was privately published by Robertson and describes a trip to the US and Europe via Fiji and Hawaiʻi in 1926. Robertson died in Melbourne in 1945.

Robson, Robert William, ed., *The Pacific Islands Yearbook*. 1st ed. Sydney: Pacific Publications Ltd, 1932.

Robson, Robert William, ed., *Handbook of New Guinea, Papua, British Solomon Islands, Norfolk Is., Lord Howe Is., New Hebrides, New Caledonia, 1933*. Sydney: Pacific Publications, 1933.

Robson (1885–1984) founded the *Pacific Islands Monthly* (PIM) in 1930—the Pacific's oldest news magazine—which continued until June 2000. It accepted contributions from many Australian travellers in the Pacific. Robson was a New Zealander who moved to Sydney during World War I. He published several handbooks about the Pacific Islands, including five editions of the *Pacific Islands Yearbook* (1932, 1935–1936, 1939, 1942 and 1944). These handbooks contained many articles of interest to planters and traders, and Robson publicly advocated for the formation of a regional organisation to benefit the European settlers in the Islands. Judy Tudor (1910–1997) joined his team in 1942 as assistant editor of PIM, then became sole editor from 1955 to 1962. Together, they published other books on Pacific subjects, such as *Where the Trade-Winds Blow* (1946), a compilation of stories taken from PIM.

Runcie, James, Diary of James Runcie, 1869–1892, MS 8984. Canberra: National Library of Australia, 1869–1892.

Born in Scotland, Runcie was a ship builder who first visited Australia aboard the *John Williams II*, and then again on the *John Williams III*. Later, as captain of the missionary schooner, *Ellengowan*, he accompanied Samuel McFarlane and Luigi D'Albertis on their trip to the Fly River, New Guinea, in 1875. After returning to Australia, Runcie spent the remainder of his career commanding cargo ships in the Pacific Islands for companies such as Burns, Philp & Company and the ANHC. Runcie died in Sydney, aged 80. This collection comprises the diary written aboard the *John Williams III*, on the voyage to Sydney from 1869 to 1870. It includes entries written while Runcie was at sea in 1878 and 1890 and account records for 1892.

Safroni-Middleton, Arnold, *A Vagabond's Odyssey: Being Further Reminiscences of a Wandering Sailor, Troubadour in Many Lands*. London: Grant Richards, 1916.

Safroni-Middleton, Arnold, *Sailor and Beachcomber: Confessions of a Life at Sea, in Australia and amid the Islands of the Pacific*. London: Grant Richards, 1915.

Safroni-Middleton, Arnold, *South Sea Foam: The Romantic Adventures of a Modern Don Quixote in the Southern Seas*. London: Methuen, 1919.

Safroni-Middleton, Arnold, *Tropic Shadows: Memories of the South Seas, Together with Reminiscences of the Author's Sea Meetings with Joseph Conrad*. London: Richards Press, 1927.

Safroni-Middleton, Arnold, *Wine-Dark Seas and Tropic Skies: Reminiscences and a Romance of the South Seas*. London: Grant Richards, 1918.

George Arnold Haynes Safroni-Middleton was born in England in 1873. He wandered around Australia and the Pacific Islands as a teenager, earning a living principally as a violinist. During this time, he met Robert Louis Stevenson and Joseph Conrad, who inspired him to write. He wrote several novels, poems, travel books and an autobiography, in addition to composing music. In his travelogues, he focused on Samoa, Fiji, Tahiti and New Zealand. He died in England in 1950, the same year that he published his autobiography, *In the Green Leaf*. Safroni-Middleton was included in Edmund Morris Miller's bibliography of Australian literature and in the AUSTLIT database, presumably due to his formative experience as a youth in Australia and his detailed descriptions of the country.

Smith, William Ramsay, *In Southern Seas: Wanderings of a Naturalist*. London: John Murray, 1924.

Smith was born in Scotland in 1859. Initially a school teacher, he studied natural sciences at university in England, then moved to Adelaide in 1904. In 1913, he qualified as a medical physician. He worked at the Adelaide Hospital from 1896 and was a specialist in infectious diseases (publishing in multiple medical publications), before retiring in 1929. He also served in the South African war in 1901 and commanded the First Australian Imperial Force hospital in Egypt in 1915. Smith belonged to the Royal Anthropological Society and recorded Aboriginal folklore in *Myths and Legends of the Australian Aborigines* (1930). *In Southern Seas* contains many anthropological observations of New Caledonia, the New Hebrides and northern Australia. In fact, Smith devoted several chapters to discussing methodological issues that are associated with anthropology and photography (five photo albums are held at the South Australian Museum). Smith died in 1937.

Somer, Henry Montague, *Amazing America*. Sydney: N.S.W. Bookstall, 1923.

Born in Victoria in 1860, Somer was a journalist and a newspaper editor. This travel account is reprinted from *Daily Telegraph* reports and describes Somer's journey to the US in 1923 for five months via New Zealand, the Cook Islands and Tahiti. He was sent to conduct research for the Royal Agricultural Society. He died in Sydney in 1924.

Stephens, Alfred George, *A Queenslander's Travel-Notes*. Sydney: Edwards, Dunlop, 1894.

Stephens was born in 1865 in Queensland and worked in various Queensland and New Zealand newspapers as a writer and an editor. He was an influential literary critic for *The Bulletin* from 1894 to 1906. This account, reprinted from articles in the *Cairns Argus* and the *Darling Downs Gazette*, describes a nine-month grand tour to the US and Europe in 1893 via Samoa and Hawai'i. He died in Sydney in 1933.

Stephens, William John, *Samoan Holidays*. Bendigo: Cambridge Press, 1935.

Born in England in 1873, Stephens moved to Victoria as a child, where he worked in the mines from age 12. He later became an accountant and eventually became a managing director and editor of the *Bendigo Advertiser* newspaper. He describes a round trip from Melbourne to Fiji, Samoa and American Samoa on the *Mariposa*, with his wife. He died in 1943.

Stock, Mabel M, *The Log of a Woman Wanderer*. London: William Heinemann, 1923.

Mabel was the sister of Ralph Stock and likely resided in England. It is unclear whether she stayed in Australia for an extended period of time, like her brother. She describes a yacht cruise from Europe to the Pacific Islands with her brother and his friend in 1914, visiting the Marquesas Islands, French Polynesia, Tahiti, Cook Islands, Niue and Tonga. In Tonga, her brother sold his boat and they caught a steamer to Sydney via Samoa and Fiji (which she did not describe in further detail).

Stock, Ralph, *The Chequered Cruise: A True and Intimate Record of Strenuous Travel*. London: Grant Richards Ltd, 1916.

Stock, Ralph, *The Confessions of a Tenderfoot: Being a True and Unvarnished Account of His World-Wanderings*. London: Grant Richards Ltd, 1913.

Stock, Ralph, *The Cruise of the Dream Ship*. London: William Heinemann, 1921.

> Ralph Stock was born in 1881 in New South Wales, according to Edmund Morris Miller's 1940 bibliography of Australian literature. However, the AUSTLIT database has identified this as incorrect, stating that he was actually born in London. In 1901, Stock worked his way across Canada and the Pacific Islands, before returning to Australia and buying a pineapple farm in Queensland. *Confessions of a Tenderfoot* describes this voyage. In 1914, he went on another Pacific voyage with a companion and his sister, Mabel, which he described in *The Chequered Cruise*. After a stay in England (invalided due to war service in France), he made yet another voyage to the Pacific Islands via Panama in 1920. This was recorded in *The Cruise of the Dream Ship*. These three travelogues mentioned the Marquesas and Cook Islands, French Polynesia, Niue, Tonga, Norfolk Island, Fiji, Hawai'i and Samoa. Stock also published three novels and four volumes of short stories that were set in Fiji, Queensland, Thursday Island, Papua and Hawai'i. Stock was better known for his short stories than his larger works. He contributed to the *Captain* and the *Wide World Magazine*, with some of Stock's stories having been adapted into screenplays from the 1930s to the 1950s. He died in London in 1962.

Syvertsen, Chris, Private Record, PR01438. Canberra: Australian War Memorial, 1917–1918.

> Syvertsen served on HMAS *Fantome* during World War I. This diary was kept from 27 October 1917 – 3 April 1918, containing daily entries. HMAS *Fantome* was a sloop based in Suva during the end of the war, which performed police duties in the Islands. Syvertsen describes the islands of Fiji, Tonga, Niue, Palmerston Island and Tahiti.

Taylor, George Augustine, *There!: A Pilgrimage of Pleasure*. Sydney: Building Limited, 1916.

> Born in 1872 in Sydney, Taylor worked as a cartoonist and journalist in the 1890s, and was also a town planner, inventor, engineer and draughtsman. He served in World War I and was a fellow of the Royal Geographical and Astronomical Societies. This account details a business journey to the US when he was a town planner in 1914. With two companions, 'The Master Builder' and 'The Engineer', Taylor visited Fiji and Hawai'i on the initial journey, and Tahiti on the return trip. He died in Sydney in 1928.

Taylor, Patrick Gordon, *Pacific Flight: The Story of the Lady Southern Cross*. Sydney: Angus & Robertson, 1935.

Sir Patrick Gordon Taylor was born in 1896 in Sydney. He was an aviator and navigator for Charles Kingsford-Smith, breaking several flight records. *Pacific Flight* describes the first Australia–US flight in the *Lady Southern Cross* by Taylor and Kingsford-Smith in 1934. Taylor recalled visiting Fiji in 1933 in preparation for the following year (as Fiji and Hawai'i were refuelling stations). The 1963 autobiography, *The Sky Beyond*, recalls similar events. He died in Honolulu in 1966.

Thomas, Julian, *Cannibals and Convicts: Notes of Personal Experiences in the Western Pacific*. Melbourne: Cassell & Company, 1886.

Thomas, Julian, 'On the War-Path in New Caledonia'. *Victorian Review* 8, no. 40 (1883): 357–66.

Julian Thomas was one of many pseudonyms that were used by John Stanley James. Born in England in 1843, James moved to Australia in 1875 and found work with newspapers in Melbourne and Sydney for three years. During this time, he became popular under the pseudonym, 'The Vagabond', for his stories about a life of poverty, as they were based on real experience (see *The Vagabond Papers*). James made several trips to the Pacific Islands: in 1878, he went to Noumea to report on native rebellions against French colonial rule; in 1883, he went to the New Hebrides to report on blackbirding; in 1884, he travelled to Port Moresby, accompanying an exploration party; in 1887, he went to the New Hebrides; and in 1889, he travelled to Samoa and Tonga to report on political events. He published several books about his Pacific travels before his death in Sydney in 1896.

Thomson, James Park, *Round the World*. Brisbane: Outridge Printing Co., 1904.

Thomson was born in 1854 in Scotland and moved to Australia in 1877. He was a seaman, surveyor, geographer and civil servant. He was also founder of the Royal Geographical Society of Queensland and worked as a land surveyor in Fiji from 1880 to 1884. In 1884, he travelled around the Pacific before settling in Queensland. He published three books on British New Guinea in the 1890s, three on Fiji and several papers for the Royal Geographical Society. *Round the World* describes a business trip to the US via American Samoa and Hawai'i in 1903, with Thomson's brother. It is dedicated to the Australian Commonwealth, which the author calls 'my adopted country'. Thomson died in Queensland in 1941.

Thomson, TAG, 'Briefs and Associated Papers in Cases Involving Pacific Islanders'. In Crown Solicitor's Office, Series ID 12102, Item ID 7866. Brisbane: Queensland State Archives, 1884.

Thomson was a government agent aboard the *Heath* who visited the Solomon Islands, Papua and New Guinea with Captain William Wawn in 1884.

Tichborne, Henry, *Noqu Talanoa: Stories from the South Seas by Sundowner*. London: European Mail Ltd, 1896.

Tichborne, Henry, *Rambles in Polynesia by Sundowner*. London: European Mail, 1897.

Tichborne, Henry, *Told by the Taffrail by Sundowner*. London: Chatto & Windus, 1901.

According to his accounts, Tichborne (also known as 'Sundowner') was born in England, but spent some time in Australia. There is evidence that he considered himself Australian, such as calling the British 'new chums' and writing that he wanted to be buried 'with my own folk under the old gum trees on the Kolarendabri [in Australia]'. It is likely that he worked as a journalist, as his name appears in several Australian newspaper columns. Some of his Pacific texts were composed of anecdotes and short stories, many of which had appeared in other periodicals and were randomly 'thrown together', according to the author. It is difficult to tell which tales are based on Tichborne's personal experience, but he claimed to have visited Fiji, the Solomon Islands, New Caledonia, Hawai'i, the New Hebrides, Tonga, Yap, Tahiti, French Polynesia, Samoa and the Gilbert and Ellice Islands.

The Vagabond, *Holy Tonga*. Melbourne: publisher unknown, 1890.

The Vagabond, *South Sea Massacres*. Sydney: 'The Australian' Office, 1881.

The Vagabond, *The Vagabond Papers*, edited by Michael Cannon. Melbourne: Hyland House, 1983.

Also known as John Stanley James or Julian Thomas. See entry for Thomas.

Villiers, Alan John, *Cruise of the Conrad: A Journal of a Voyage around the World, Undertaken and Carried Out in the Ship Joseph Conrad, 212 tons, in the Years 1934, 1935 and 1936 by Way of Good Hope, the South Seas, the East Indies and Cape Horn*. London: Hodder & Stoughton, 1937.

Villiers, Alan John, *Stormalong: The Story of a Boy's Voyage around the World in a Full-Rigged Ship*. New York: C. Scribner's Sons, 1937.

Villiers was born in 1903 in Melbourne. He worked in several ships since he was 15 years old, including a whaling ship, with a short stint as a journalist when he was injured. These texts are accounts of his voyage around the world in the *Joseph Conrad* from 1934 to 1936, which aimed to train young boys to sail. He passed through New Guinea, the Trobriand Islands, the Solomon Islands, the Caroline Islands and Tahiti. Villiers served in the Royal Navy reserve during World War II and later worked in a maritime museum, commanding sailing ships for famous films and re-enactments. He died in England in 1982.

Wawn, William Twizell, *The South Sea Islanders and the Queensland Labour Trade: A Record of Voyages and Experiences in the Western Pacific, from 1875 to 1891*, edited by Peter Corris. Canberra: Australian National University Press, 1973.

Wawn was a mariner and cartographer, born in England in 1837. In 1868, he made his first visit to the Pacific Islands (probably Samoa). From 1870 to 1900, he worked as a labour recruiter (for Queensland and Fiji, from 1876–1894), as a trader and as a salvager in the Pacific. This is an account of his labour-recruiting experiences, which were first published in London in 1893, with stories of shipwrecks, storms and violent encounters. Wawn mainly recruited in the Solomon Islands, the New Hebrides, Papua and New Guinea, but also visited Fiji, Samoa, New Caledonia and the Caroline, Marshall and Gilbert Islands. The original manuscript was lost at sea in 1890 and had to be rewritten. The final published account argued that labour recruiting was not slaving, but an equally beneficial trade. Wawn died in Sydney in 1901. His manuscript is held at the National Library of New Zealand and his journals are at the State Library of New South Wales.

Wickham, William A, *Impressions Abroad*. Adelaide: Hunkin, Ellis & King, 1931.

Wickham was born c. 1882 in New Zealand and arrived in Australia c. 1896. He was a businessman in Adelaide. This is an account of his grand tour in 1929, with descriptions of Hawai'i on his journey home.

Wilkins, William, *Australasia: A Descriptive and Pictorial Account of the Australian and New Zealand Colonies, Tasmania and the Adjacent Lands*. London: Blackie & Son, 1888.

Born in 1827 in London, Wilkins moved to Sydney to recover from bronchitis. His wife and child died on the voyage, but he arrived in Sydney in 1851 and remarried the next year. He worked as a headmaster and teacher and helped reform the state's school administration, eventually becoming a public servant. This is one of several school textbooks that were written when Wilkins was under-secretary for the Department of Public Instruction in New South Wales. It is unclear whether he had visited the Pacific Islands. This book includes a 'catalogue of educational works specially adapted for elementary and higher schools'. Wilkins died in 1892.

Wirth, George, *Round the World with a Circus: Memories of Trials, Triumphs and Tribulations*. Melbourne: Troedel and Cooper Printers, 1925.

Wirth was born in 1867 in Victoria. He joined Ashton's circus with his father and brothers in 1876, and later established Wirth's Circus. This account of a seven-week circus tour in 1888 includes a description of the journey from Sydney to New Caledonia. Wirth died in 1941.

Wood, Casey Albert, Letter, 1923–1924, MS 3526. Canberra: National Library of Australia, 1923–1924.

This is a letter to Wood's friends, describing a journey across the Pacific from Chicago to Sydney in 1923–1924. The account is in no particular order, containing descriptions of Fiji (where he stayed for six months), Tahiti, the Cook Islands, Tonga, Samoa, Hawai'i and New Zealand. Wood was an ornithologist, so there are many observations about the local fauna in his letter.

Woodburn, M Kathleen, *Backwash of Empire*. Melbourne: Georgian House, 1944.

Woodburn's background is unknown. This is an account of a holiday with her young son, Jack, to the New Hebrides on a doctor's recommendation that the climate would be good for restoring Jack's health. They travelled to Vila via Lord Howe and Norfolk Island on the *Morinda* and then lived on a coconut plantation on Erromango for several months. They likely made the journey in the 1930s, as Woodburn does not mention the Pacific War in her account. Woodburn was well educated and incorporated botanical, anthropological and linguistic observations throughout the account, as well as collected natural history specimens to take home. She also published articles in *Walkabout*.

Woodroofe, William, *There and Back: Australia to London*. London: Elliot Stock, 1915.

Woodroofe was born in 1856 in Dublin and arrived in Australia in 1876. He was a legal clerk and cordial manufacturer. This text describes a grand tour via American Samoa and Hawai'i in 1913. He died in South Australia in 1915.

Wragge, Clement Lindley, *The Romance of the South Seas*. London: Chatto & Windus, 1906.

Born in 1852 in England, Wragge was trained as a maritime navigator and moved to Australia in 1876, where he joined the South Australian survey department and studied meteorology. He founded the Meteorological Society of Australasia in 1886 and started observatories in New Caledonia, Tasmania and New South Wales. He worked as the Queensland government's meteorologist from 1887. This text is based on separate trips to New Caledonia and Tahiti c. 1893, with the intention for the former being to establish an observatory in Noumea. The text contains photographs taken by Wragge and advice that was offered to tourists who visited Tahiti. Wragge also published an *Australian Weather Guide and Almanac* (1898), as well as a short-lived serial called *Wragge: A Meteorological, Geographical and Popular Scientific Gazette of the Southern Hemisphere* (1902). Having advocated for the creation of a national weather bureau, he was bitterly disappointed in 1907 when he was not appointed head of the Commonwealth Meteorological Bureau. Wragge then moved to Auckland, before dying in 1922.

Bibliography

Abbott, John Henry Macartney. *The South Seas (Melanesia)*. London: Adam and Charles Black, 1908.

Adams, JL. 'Pearl Shelling in the Torres Strait'. *BP Magazine* 2, no. 2 (March 1930): 48.

Adler, Jacob. 'The Oceanic Steamship Company: A Link in Claus Spreckels' Hawaiian Sugar Empire'. *Pacific Historical Review* 29, no. 3 (1960): 257–69, doi.org/10.2307/3636164.

'A Famous Communard: The Adventurous Career of Louise Michel'. *The Mercury*, 27 March 1905.

Ahrens, Prue, Lamont Lindstrom and Fiona Paisley. *Across the World with the Johnsons: Visual Culture and American Empire in the Twentieth Century*. Burlington: Ashgate Publishing Co., 2013.

Akami, Tomoko. *Internationalizing the Pacific: The United States, Japan, and the Institute of Pacific Relations in War and Peace, 1919–45*. New York: Routledge, 2002.

Aldrich, Robert. *The French Presence in the South Pacific, 1842–1940*. Basingstoke: Palgrave Macmillan, 1990.

Alison, Jennifer. *Doing Something for Australia: George Robertson and the Early Years of Angus and Robertson, Publishers: 1888–1900*. Melbourne: Bibliographical Society of Australia and New Zealand, 2009.

Allan, William. *Homeward Bound, from Australia to Scotland: Impressions by the Way*. Helensburgh: Helensburgh and Gareloch Times, 1915.

Allen, Margaret. '"Innocents Abroad" and "Prohibited Immigrants": Australians in India and Indians in Australia 1890–1910'. In *Connected Worlds: History in Transnational Perspective*, edited by Ann Curthoys and Marilyn Lake, 111–24. Canberra: ANU E Press, 2006. doi.org/10.22459/CW.03.2006.

Allen, Percy S. *Stewart's Handbook of the Pacific Islands: A Reliable Guide to All the Inhabited Islands of the Pacific Ocean—For Traders, Tourists and Settlers, with a Bibliography of Island Works*. Sydney: Steward McCarron, 1920.

Anderson, J Mayne. *What a Tourist Sees in the New Hebrides*. Sydney: W.C. Penfold & Co., 1915.

Anderson, Warwick. 'Liberal Intellectuals as Pacific Supercargo: White Australian Masculinity and Racial Thought on the Boarder-Lands'. *Australian Historical Studies* 46, no. 3 (2015): 425–39. doi.org/10.1080/1031461x.2015.1071417.

Anderson, Warwick. *The Cultivation of Whiteness: Science, Health and Racial Destiny in Australia*. Carlton: Melbourne University Press, 2002.

Andrews, Malcolm. *The Search for the Picturesque: Landscape Aesthetics and Tourism in Britain, 1760–1800*. Aldershot: Scolar, 1989.

'An Ideal Wife'. *Daily Herald*, 16 March 1912. nla.gov.au/nla.news-article105221614.

Arens, William. *The Man-Eating Myth: Anthropology & Anthropophagy*. New York: Oxford University Press, 1979.

Arnold, John, and John Hay, eds. *The Bibliography of Australian Literature*. St Lucia: Australian Scholarly Publishing, 2001.

Askew, DS. 'Vanua-Lava and Its Sulphur'. *Walkabout* 1, no. 6 (April 1935): 26–7.

'A South Sea Utopia'. *Wagga Wagga Advertiser*, 7 December 1901. nla.gov.au/nla.news-article101857168.

Atkin, Charles Ager. *A Trip to Fiji via East Coast of New Zealand*. Melbourne: Massina, 1885.

AUSTLIT. 'Australian Magazines of the Twentieth Century'. www.austlit.edu.au/specialistDatasets/BookHistory/AustMag.

Australasian New Hebrides Company. *Australia and the New Hebrides*. Sydney: Australasian New Hebrides Company, 1899.

Australian Bureau of Statistics. '2112.0—Census of the Commonwealth of Australia, 1911: Volume II Part VI—Religions'. Last modified 11 November 2013, www.abs.gov.au/AUSSTATS/abs@.nsf/DetailsPage/2112.01911.

Australian Bureau of Statistics. 'A Snapshot of Australia, 1901'. www.abs.gov.au/websitedbs/D3110124.NSF/24e5997b9bf2ef35ca2567fb00299c59/c4abd1fac53e3df5ca256bd8001883ec!OpenDocument.

Australian Bureau of Statistics. 'Aboriginal and Torres Strait Islander Population'. Last modified 3 June 2010, www.abs.gov.au/ausstats/abs@.nsf/0/68AE74ED 632E17A6CA2573D200110075?opendocument.

Australian Historical Studies 46, vol. 3 (2015): 337–439.

Ballantyne, Tony. *Webs of Empire: Locating New Zealand's Colonial Past*. Wellington: UBC Press, 2012.

Ballard, Chris. 'Collecting Pygmies: The "Tapiro" and the British Ornithologists' Union Expedition to Dutch New Guinea, 1910–1911'. In *Hunting the Gatherers: Ethnographic Collectors, Agents and Agency in Melanesia, 1870s–1930s*, edited by Michael O'Hanlon and Robert L Welsch, 127–54. New York: Berghahn Books, 2000. doi.org/10.2307/j.ctt1x76fh4.11.

Ballard, Chris. 'Strange Alliance: Pygmies in the Colonial Imaginary'. *World Archaeology* 38, no. 1 (2006): 133–51. doi.org/10.1080/00438240500510155.

Ballard, Chris. 'The Art of Encounter: Verisimilitude in the Imaginary Exploration of Interior New Guinea, 1725–1876'. In *Oceanic Encounters: Exchange, Desire, Violence*, edited by Margaret Jolly, 221–57. Canberra: ANU E Press, 2009. doi.org/10.22459/oe.07.2009.08.

Banfield, Edmund James. *The Confessions of a Beachcomber*. London: T.F. Unwin, 1908.

Banivanua-Mar, Tracey. 'Cannibalism and Colonialism: Charting Colonies and Frontiers in Nineteenth-Century Fiji'. *Comparative Studies in Society and History* 52, no. 2 (2010): 255–81. doi.org/10.1017/s0010417510000046.

Banivanua-Mar, Tracey. *Violence and Colonial Dialogue: The Australian-Pacific Indentured Labor Trade*. Honolulu: University of Hawai'i Press, 2007. doi.org/10.1515/9780824865467.

Baruch, Mordecai. 'Tuamotu Archipelago: Amongst the Pearl Divers'. *Walkabout* 2, no. 3 (January 1936): 45–7.

Baume, Eric. *I Lived These Years*. Sydney: George G. Harrap & Co., 1941.

Bean, Charles Edwin Woodrow. *With the Flagship of the South*. Sydney: William Brooks, 1909.

Becke, Louis. *By Reef and Palm*. Sydney: Angus & Robertson, 1955.

Becke, Louis. *Notes from My South Sea Log*. London: T. Werner Laurie, 1905.

Bellamy, Richard Reynell. *Mixed Bliss in Melanesia*. London: John Long, 1934.

Bennett, Judith A. *Wealth of the Solomons: A History of a Pacific Archipelago, 1800–1978*. Honolulu: University of Hawai'i Press, 1987.

Bergantz, Alexis. 'French Connection: The Culture and Politics of Frenchness in Australia, 1890–1914'. PhD thesis, The Australian National University, 2015.

Berman, Russel A. *Enlightenment or Empire: Colonial Discourse in German Culture*. London: University of Nebraska Press, 1998.

Bones, Helen. 'New Zealand and the Tasman Writing World, 1890–1945'. *History Australia* 10, no. 3 (2013): 129–48. doi.org/10.1080/14490854.2013.11668484.

Bones, Helen. 'Travel Writers and Traveling Writers in Australasia: Responses to Travel Literatures and the Problem of Authenticity'. *Journeys* 17, no. 2 (2016): 74–94. doi.org/10.3167/jys.2016.170205.

'Books in Brief'. *The West Australian*, 25 August 1928. nla.gov.au/nla.news-article32218170.

Borm, Jan. 'Defining Travel: On the Travel Book, Travel Writing and Terminology'. In *Perspectives on Travel Writing*, edited by Glenn Hooper and Tim Youngs, 13–26. London: Routledge, 2004. doi.org/10.4324/9781315246970-2.

Bracken, Thomas. *The New Zealand Tourist*. Dunedin: Mackay, Bracken, 1879.

Brand, G Bell. 'Off the Beaten Track'. *BP Magazine* 1, no. 2 (1934): 69–71.

Brawley, Sean, and Chris Dixon, eds. *Hollywood's South Seas and the Pacific War: Searching for Dorothy Lamour*. New York: Palgrave Macmillan, 2012.

Bridge, Cyprian. *Some Recollections*. London: J. Murray, 1918.

Broinowski, Alison. *The Yellow Lady: Australian Impressions of Asia*. Melbourne: Oxford University Press, 1992.

Brummitt, Robert. *A Winter Holiday in Fiji*. Sydney: Methodist Book Depots, 1914.

Buckingham, Jane. 'The Pacific Leprosy Foundation Archive and Oral Histories of Leprosy in the South Pacific'. *The Journal of Pacific History* 41, no. 1 (2006): 81–6. doi.org/10.1080/00223340600652441.

Buckley, Kenneth, and Kris Klugman. *The Australian Presence in the Pacific: Burns Philp, 1914–1946*. Sydney: Allen & Unwin, 1983.

Buckley, Kenneth, and Kris Klugman. *The History of Burns Philp: The Australian Company in the South Pacific*. Sydney: Burns, Philp & Co. Ltd, 1981.

Burchett, Winston H. 'Cannibals and Talkies'. *Walkabout* 4, no. 12 (October 1938): 41–4.

Burchett, Wilfred. *Pacific Treasure Island: New Caledonia; Voyage through Its Land and Wealth, the Story of Its People and Past*. Melbourne: F.W. Cheshire, 1941.

Burchett, Wilfred. *Passport: An Autobiography*. Melbourne: Thomas Nelson, 1969.

Burns, Philp & Company, Limited. *All About Burns, Philp & Company, Limited: Their Shipping Agencies, Branches and Steamers*. Sydney: John Andrew & Co., 1903.

Burns, Philp & Company, Limited. *BP Magazine* 1, no. 1 (December 1928).

Burns, Philp & Company, Limited. *Picturesque Travel*, nos 1–5 (1911–1925).

Burton, John Wear. *The Call of the Pacific*. London: Charles H. Kelly, 1914.

Burton, John Wear. *The Fiji of To-Day*. London: C.H. Kelly, 1910.

Buzard, James. *The Beaten Track: European Tourism, Literature, and the Ways to Culture, 1800–1918*. Oxford: Clarendon Press, 1993.

Buzard, James. 'The Grand Tour and After (1660–1840)'. In *The Cambridge Companion to Travel Writing*, edited by Peter Hulme and Tim Young, 37–52. Cambridge: Cambridge University Press, 2002.

Campbell, Ian Christopher. *'Gone Native' in Polynesia: Captivity Narratives and Experiences from the South Pacific*. Westport: Greenwood Press, 1998.

Campbell, Ian Christopher. 'Savages Noble and Ignoble: The Preconceptions of Early European Voyagers in Polynesia'. *Pacific Studies* 4, no. 1 (1980): 45–59.

Campbell, Mary Baine. 'Travel Writing and Its Theory'. In *The Cambridge Companion to Travel Writing*, edited by Peter Hulme and Tim Youngs, 261–78. Cambridge: Cambridge University Press, 2002.

Cannon, Michael. 'Introduction'. In *The Vagabond Papers*, edited by Michael Cannon. Melbourne: Hyland House, 1983.

Captain Strasburg. 'Trading in the South Seas'. *Lone Hand* 1, no. 2 (November 1918): 508.

Carter, David. *Always Almost Modern: Australian Print Cultures and Modernity*. North Melbourne: Australian Scholarly Publishing, 2013.

Carter, David. '"Literary, but Not Too Literary; Joyous, but Not Jazzy": Triad Magazine, Modernity and the Middlebrow'. *Modernism/Modernity* 25, no. 2 (2018): 245–67. doi.org/10.1353/mod.2018.0018.

Carter, David. 'Transpacific or Transatlantic Traffic? Australian Books and American Publishers'. In *Reading Across the Pacific: Australia–United States Intellectual Histories*, edited by Robert Dixon and Nicholas Birns, 339–60. Sydney: Sydney University Press, 2010.

Cato, Helen D. *The House on the Hill*. Melbourne: Book Depot, 1947.

Cheeseman, Richard. *The South Sea Islands: Notes of a Trip*. Brighton: publisher unknown, 1901.

Chewings, Hannah. *Amongst Tropical Islands, or, Notes and Observations Made during a Visit of the S.S. 'Moresby' in 1899, to New Guinea, New Britain and the Solomon Islands*. Adelaide: publisher unknown, 1900.

'Chinese Problem in the South Seas'. *Pacific Islands Monthly* 3, no. 5 (December 1932): 33.

Cigler, Michael J. *The Afghans in Australia*. Melbourne: AE Press, 1986.

Cilento, Raphael. *The White Man in the Tropics: With Especial Reference to Australia and Its Dependencies*. Melbourne: H.J. Green, Commonwealth Department of Health, 1925.

Clark, Steve, and Paul Smethurst, eds. *Asian Crossings: Travel Writing on China, Japan and Southeast Asia*. Hong Kong: Hong Kong University Press, 2008.

Clarke, Robert. *Travel Writing from Black Australia: Utopia, Melancholia, and Aboriginality*. New York: Routledge, 2015. doi.org/10.4324/9781315851129.

'Clipper Yacht Elsea, for New Guinea'. *Sydney Morning Herald*, 29 September 1884. nla.gov.au/nla.news-article28369242.

Coffee, Frank. *Forty Years on the Pacific: The Lure of the Great Ocean; A Book of Reference for the Traveller and Pleasure for the Stay-at-Home*. Sydney: Oceanic, 1920.

Commonwealth of Australia. 'Japan-Born Community Information Summary'. www.homeaffairs.gov.au/mca/files/2016-cis-japan.PDF.

Cook, May. *Fijian Diary 1904–1906: A Young Australian Woman's Account of Village life in Fiji*, edited by Leigh Cook. Victoria: PenFolk Pub., 1996.

Corney, BG, J Stewart and BH Thomson. *Report of the Commission Appointed to Inquire into the Decrease of the Native Population: 1893*. Suva: Edward John March, 1896.

Corris, Peter. 'Passage, Port and Plantation: A History of Solomon Islands Labour Migration, 1870–1914'. PhD thesis, The Australian National University, 1970.

Criswick, BC. 'Coconuts and Copra'. *BP Magazine* 1, no. 4 (September 1929): 44.

Cromar, John. *Jock of the Islands: Early Days in the South Seas: The Adventures of John Cromar, Sometime Recruiter and Lately Trader at Marovo, British Solomon Islands Protectorate, Told by Himself.* London: Faber & Faber, 1935.

Crowl, Linda S. 'Politics and Book Publishing in the Pacific Islands'. PhD thesis, University of Wollongong, 2008.

Cushing, John E. *Captain William Matson (1849–1917): From Handy Boy to Shipowner.* New York: Newcomen Society in North America, 1951.

Dakin, William J. 'The Story of Nauru'. *Walkabout* 1, no. 5 (March 1935): 32–6.

David, Caroline. 'Letter to Mrs Scott, 1898'. Papers of the David Family, NLA MS 8890, Series 2, Folder 25. Canberra: National Library of Australia.

David, Edgeworth, Mrs. *Funafuti, or, Three Months on a Coral Island: An Unscientific Account of a Scientific Expedition.* London: John Murray, 1899.

Davis, William. 'Pioneering the Pacific: Imagining Polynesia in United States Literature from 1820 to 1940'. PhD thesis, The Claremont Graduate University, 2002.

Daws, Gavan. *A Dream of Islands: Voyages of Self-Discovery in the South Seas.* New York: Norton, 1980.

Daws, Gavan. *Holy Man: Father Damien of Molokai.* New York: Harper & Row, 1973.

Day, Arthur Grove. *Louis Becke.* Melbourne: Hill of Content, 1967.

Dening, Greg. *Islands and Beaches: Discourse on a Silent Land.* Honolulu: University of Hawaii Press, 1980.

Denoon, Donald. 'Pacific Island Depopulation: Natural or Un-Natural History?' In *New Countries and Old Medicine: Proceedings of an International Conference on the History of Medicine and Health*, edited by Linda Bryder and Derek A Dow. Auckland: Pyramid Press, 1995.

Denoon, Donald. Philippa Mein-Smith and Marivic Wyndham, *A History of Australia, New Zealand and the Pacific.* Oxford: Wiley, 2000.

Denoon, Donald. 'Re-Membering Australasia: A Repressed Memory'. *Australian Historical Studies* 34, no. 122 (2003): 290–304. doi.org/10.1080/10314610308596256.

Denoon, Donald. 'The Isolation of Australian History'. *Australian Historical Studies* 22, no. 87 (1986): 252–60. doi.org/10.1080/10314618608595747.

Desmond, Jane C. 'Afterword: Ambivalence, Ambiguity and the "Wicked Problem" of Pacific Tourist Studies'. In *Touring Pacific Cultures*, edited by Kalissa Alexeyeff and John Taylor, 439–50. Canberra: ANU Press, 2016. doi.org/10.22459/tpc.12.2016.31.

Desmond, Jane. *Staging Tourism: Bodies on Display from Waikiki to Sea World.* Chicago: University of Chicago Press, 1999.

Dickinson, Joseph HC. *A Trader in the Savage Solomons: A Record of Romance and Adventure.* London: H.F. & G. Witherby, 1927.

Dillon, Gerard. 'The Coco-Nut Tree'. *Walkabout* 3, no. 8 (June 1937): 27–8.

Dixon, Robert. *Prosthetic Gods: Travel, Representation, and Colonial Governance.* St Lucia: University of Queensland Press and API Network, 2001.

Dixon, Robert. 'What was Travel Writing? Frank Hurley and the Media Contexts of Early Twentieth-Century Australian Travel Writing'. *Studies in Travel Writing* 11, no. 1 (2007): 59–81. doi.org/10.1080/13645145.2007.9634819.

Dixon, Robert. *Writing the Colonial Adventure: Race, Gender, and Nation in Anglo-Australian Popular Fiction, 1875–1914.* New York: Cambridge University Press, 1995. doi.org/10.1017/cbo9781139085038.

Doorly, Gerald Stokely. *In the Wake.* London: Sampson Low Marston & Co., 1937.

Douglas, Bronwen. 'Climate to Crania: Science and the Racialization of Human Difference'. In *Foreign Bodies: Oceania and the Science of Race 1750–1940*, edited by Bronwen Douglas and Chris Ballard, 33–96. Canberra: ANU E Press, 2008. doi.org/10.22459/fb.11.2008.02.

Douglas, Bronwen. 'Conflict and Alliance in a Colonial Context'. *The Journal of Pacific History* 15, no. 1 (1980): 21–51.

Douglas, Bronwen. 'Fighting as Savagery and Romance: New Caledonia Past and Present'. In *Reflections on Violence in Melanesia*, edited by Sinclair Dinnen and Allison Ley, 53–64. Leichhardt: Hawkins Press, 2000.

Douglas, Bronwen. 'Philosophers, Naturalists and Antipodean Encounters, 1748–1803'. *Intellectual History Review* 23, no. 3 (2013): 389–91. doi.org/10.1080/17496977.2012.723343.

Douglas, Bronwen. *Science, Voyages, and Encounters in Oceania, 1511–1850.* Basingstoke: Palgrave Macmillan, 2014.

Douglas, Bronwen. 'Winning and Losing? Reflections on the War of 1878–79 in New Caledonia'. *The Journal of Pacific History* 26, no. 2 (1991): 213–33. doi.org/10.1080/00223349108572664.

Douglas, Ngaire. *They Came for Savages: 100 Years of Tourism in Melanesia*. Lismore: Southern Cross University Press, 1996.

Douglas, Ngaire, and Norman Douglas. 'P and O's Pacific'. *Journal of Tourism Studies* 7, no. 2 (1996): 2–14.

Douglas, Norman, and Ngaire Douglas. *The Cruise Experience*. Frenchs Forest: Pearson Education, 2004.

Duensing, Dawn. *Hawaiʻi's Scenic Roads: Paving the Way for Tourism in the Island*. Honolulu: University of Hawaiʻi Press, 2015.

Dunbabin, Thomas. *Slavers of the South Seas*. Sydney: Angus & Robertson, 1935.

Edmond, Rod. *Leprosy and Empire: A Medical and Cultural History*. Cambridge: Cambridge University Press, 2006.

Edmond, Rod. *Representing the South Pacific: Colonial Discourse from Cook to Gauguin*. New York: Cambridge University Press, 1997.

Ellis, Albert Fuller. *Adventuring in Coral Seas*. Sydney: Angus & Robertson, 1936.

Ellis, Albert Fuller. *Ocean Island and Nauru: Their Story*. Sydney: Angus & Robertson, 1935.

Elsner, Jas, and Joan-Pau Rubiés. *Voyages and Visions: Towards a Cultural History of Travel*. London: Reaktion Books, 1999.

'Escaped Convicts in New Caledonia'. *Sydney Morning Herald*, 27 November 1888. nla.gov.au/nla.news-article13704947.

Evans, Raymond, Kay Saunders and Kathryn Cronin. *Race Relations in Colonial Queensland: A History of Exclusion, Exploitation and Extermination*. St Lucia: University of Queensland Press, 1988.

Fabian, Johannes. *Out of Our Minds: Reason and Madness in the Exploration of Central Africa*. Berkeley: University of California Press, 2000.

Fehon, William Meeke. *Six Weeks' Excursion to the South Seas and Eastern Pacific Islands: Comprising Raratonga, Tahiti, Raiatea, Samoa and the Friendly Islands, by the New Steamer 'Waikare', 3,000 tons: (Union Steam Ship Company of N.Z., Ltd) from Sydney, 30th June, 1898*. Sydney: S.D. Townsend and Co. Printers, 1898.

'Fiji Sugar Plantation'. *Lone Hand* 4, no. 22 (February 1909).

Firth, Stewart. *New Guinea under the Germans*. Carlton: Melbourne University Press, 1982.

Fison, Lorimer. *Tales from Old Fiji*. London: Alexander Moring Ltd, The De la More Press, 1904.

Fison, Lorimer, and Alfred William Howitt. *Kamilaroi and Kurnai: Group-Marriage and Relationship, and Marriage by Elopement, Drawn Chiefly from the Usage of the Australian Aborigines: Also the Kurnai Tribe, Their Customs in Peace and War*. Melbourne: George Robertson, 1880.

Fitzpatrick, John Charles Lucas. *Notes on a Trip to New Caledonia and Fiji*. Windsor: Hawkesbury Herald, 1908.

Foster, George M. 'South Seas Cruise: A Case Study of a Short-Lived Society'. *Annals of Tourism Research* 13, no. 2 (1986): 215–38.

Fowler, Wilfred. 'The Young Dick'. *Queensland Heritage* 2, no. 1 (1969): 23–5.

Fox, Frank. *Problems of the Pacific*. London: Williams & Norgate, 1912.

Fraser, John Archibald. *Gold Dish and Kava Bowl*. London: J.M. Dent & Sons, 1954.

Freeman, Betty. *Fiji—Memory Hold the Door*. Balgowlah: B. Freeman, 1996.

Friedrichsmeyer, Sara, Sara Lennox and Susanne Zantop, eds. *The Imperialist Imagination: German Colonialism and Its Legacy*. Ann Arbor: University of Michigan Press, 1998.

Fussell, Paul. *Abroad: British Literary Travelling between the Wars*. New York: Oxford University Press, 1980.

Gaggin, John. *Among the Man-Eaters*. London: T. Fisher Unwin, 1900.

Gammage, Bill. 'Early Boundaries of New South Wales'. *Australian Historical Studies* 19, no. 77 (1981): 524–31. doi.org/10.1080/10314618108595657.

Gardner, Helen Bethea. *Gathering for God: George Brown in Oceania*. Dunedin: Otago, 2006.

Garrett, John. *To Live among the Stars: Christian Origins in Oceania*. Suva: World Council of Churches, 1982.

Gay, John J. *Through Other Lands*. Sydney: Edwards, Dunlop, 1931.

Geiger, Jeffrey. *Facing the Pacific: Polynesia and the U.S. Imperial Imagination*. Honolulu: University of Hawai'i Press, 2007.

'General News: The Labour Trade'. *The Queenslander*, 9 May 1885. nla.gov.au/nla.news-article19797950.

Gill, Walter. *Turn North-East at the Tombstone*. Adelaide: Rigby, 1970.

Gillion, Kenneth Lowell Oliver. *Fiji's Indian Migrants: A History to the End of Indenture in 1920*. Melbourne: Oxford University Press, 1962.

Goodall, Heather, Devleena Ghosh and Lindi R Todd. 'Jumping Ship-Skirting Empire: Indians, Aborigines and Australians across the Indian Ocean'. *Transforming Cultures eJournal* 3, no. 1 (2008): 44–74. doi.org/10.5130/tfc.v3i1.674.

Grant, Bruce, ed. *Arthur and Eric: An Anglo-Australian Story from the Journal of Arthur Hickman*. Melbourne: Heinemann Australia, 1977.

Grattan, Clinton Hartley. *The Southwest Pacific Since 1900, A Modern History: Australia, New Zealand, the Islands, Antarctica*. Ann Arbor: University of Michigan Press, 1963.

Great Britain, Colonial Office. *Fiji: Annual General Report for the Year 1926*. London: H.M.S.O., 1927.

Great Britain, Colonial Office. *Fiji: Annual General Report for the Year 1929*. London: H.M.S.O., 1929.

Great Britain Colonial Office, Foreign and Commonwealth Office and Ministry of Information. *Annual Report on the Social and Economic Progress on the People of Fiji, 1937*. London: H.M.S.O., 1938.

Great Britain Colonial Office, Foreign and Commonwealth Office and Ministry of Information. *Annual Report on the Social and Economic Progress on the People of Fiji, 1938*. London: H.M.S.O., 1938.

Greenwood, Justine, and Richard White. 'Australia: The World Different and the Same'. In *Routledge Companion to Travel Writing*, edited by Carl Thompson, 404–15. London: Routledge, 2016.

Griffiths, JS. 'Fiji: The Eastern Outpost of Australia'. *The Lone Hand* 12, no. 72 (April 1912): 508.

Grimshaw, Beatrice. *From Fiji to the Cannibal Islands*. London: Eveleigh Nash, 1907.

Grimshaw, Beatrice. *In the Strange South Seas*. London: Hutchinson & Co., 1907.

Grimshaw, Beatrice. 'Life in the New Hebrides'. *Sydney Morning Herald*, 25 November 1905. nla.gov.au/nla.news-article14734425.

Groves, William C. 'Life on a Coco-Nut Plantation'. *Walkabout* 1, no. 7 (May 1935): 33–6.

Grundy, Joseph Hadfield. *A Month in New Zealand; A Trip to Fiji, Tonga and Samoa*. Adelaide: Hunkin, Ellis & King, 1931.

Grundy, Joseph Hadfield. *The New Hebrides Group of Islands*. Adelaide: Hunkin, Ellis & King, 1933.

Gunga. *Narrative of a Trip from Maryborough to New Caledonia*. Maryborough: publisher unknown, 1878.

Gunson, Niel. *Messengers of Grace: Evangelical Missionaries in the South Seas, 1797–1860*. Melbourne: Oxford University Press, 1978.

Gunson, Niel. 'Paton, Francis Hume Lyall (Frank) (1870–1938)', *Australian Dictionary of Biography*. adb.anu.edu.au/biography/paton-francis-hume-lyall-frank-7976.

Hainsworth, DR. 'Exploiting the Pacific Frontier: The New South Wales Sealing Industry 1800–1821'. *Journal of Pacific History* 2, no. 1 (1967): 59–75. doi.org/10.1080/00223346708572102.

Hall, Basil. 'The Tricolour in the South Seas'. *Walkabout* 6, no. 2 (December 1939): 17–20.

Halter, Nicholas. 'Ambivalent Mobilities in the Pacific: "Savagery" and "Civilization" in the Australian Interwar Imaginary'. *Transfers* 7, no. 1 (2017): 34–51. doi.org/10.3167/TRANS.2017.070104.

Halter, Nicholas. '"Cannibals and Convicts": Australian Travel Writing about New Caledonia'. In *The Palgrave Handbook of Prison Tourism*, edited by Jacqueline Z Wilson, Sarah Hodgkinson, Justin Piché and Kevin Walby, 867–84. London: Palgrave Macmillan, 2017. doi.org/10.1057/978-1-137-56135-0_41.

Halter, Nicholas. 'Tourists Fraternising in Fiji in the 1930s'. *Journal of Tourism History* 12, vol. 1 (2020): 27–47. doi.org/10.1080/1755182x.2019.1682688.

Hanlon, David L. *Upon a Stone Altar: A History of the Island of Pohnpei to 1890*. Honolulu: University of Hawai'i Press, 1988. doi.org/10.2307/j.ctvp2n4g9.

Hassam, Andrew. *Sailing to Australia: Shipboard Diaries by Nineteenth-Century British Emigrants*. Manchester: Manchester University Press, 1994.

Hassam, Andrew. *Through Australian Eyes: Colonial Perceptions of Imperial Britain*. Carlton: Sussex Academic Press, 2000.

Hempenstall, Peter J. *Pacific Islanders under German Rule: A Study in the Meaning of Colonial Resistance*. Canberra: ANU Press, 2016. doi.org/10.22459/piugr.06.2016.

Henley, Thomas. *A Pacific Cruise: Musings and Opinions on Island Problems*. Sydney: John Sands, 1930.

Henley, Thomas. *Fiji—The Land of Promise*. Sydney: John Sands, 1926.

Henty, Stephen. 'New Caledonia'. *Walkabout* 2, no. 1 (November 1935): 29–32.

Hezel, Francis X. *Strangers in Their Own Land: A Century of Colonial Rule in the Caroline and Marshall Islands*. Honolulu: University of Hawai'i Press, 1995.

Hickson, JC. *Notes of Travel: From Pacific to Atlantic, with Description of the World's Fair at Chicago; Also Travels by Sea and Land round the World*. Parramatta: Fuller's Lightning Printing Works, 1894.

Hill, Alfred William. *A Cruise among Former Cannibal Islands, Fiji, Tonga, Samoa: A Glimpse at the Countries, People, Customs and Legends*. Adelaide: W. K. Thomas & Co., 1927.

Hilliard, David. *God's Gentlemen: A History of the Melanesian Mission, 1849–1942*. St Lucia: University of Queensland Press, 1978.

Hilliard, David. 'The South Sea Evangelical Mission in the Solomon Islands: The Foundation Years'. *The Journal of Pacific History* 4, no. 1 (1969): 41–64. doi.org/10.1080/00223346908572145.

Hirst, John. *The Australians: Insiders & Outsiders on the National Character since 1770*. Melbourne: Schwartz Publishing, 2007.

Hoare, Michael E. 'Science and Scientific Associations in Eastern Australia, 1820–1890'. PhD thesis, The Australian National University, 1974.

Hodgen, Margaret T. *Early Anthropology in the Sixteenth and Seventeenth Centuries*. Philadelphia: University of Pennsylvania Press, 1964.

Hogbin, Herbert Ian. *Experiments in Civilization: The Effects of European Culture on a Native Community of the Solomon Islands*. London: Routledge & Sons, 1939.

Holland, Patrick, and Graham Huggan. *Tourists with Typewriters: Critical Reflections on Contemporary Travel Writing*. Ann Arbor: University of Michigan Press, 1998.

Hoskins, Ian. *Sydney Harbour: A History*. Sydney: UNSW Press, 2011.

House of Representatives. *Australian Parliamentary Debates*, Vol. 6 (1901–02), 7079–7091.

House of Representatives. *Australian Parliamentary Debates*, Vol. 6 (1901–02), 7411–7412.

Howe, Kerry R. *Race Relations: Australia and New Zealand: A Comparative Survey 1770's–1970's*. Wellington: Methuen Publications, 1977.

Howe, Kerry R. 'The Fate of the Savage in Pacific Historiography'. *New Zealand Journal of History* 11, no. 2 (1977): 137–54.

Hulme, Peter. *Colonial Encounters: Europe and the Native Caribbean, 1492–1797*. London: Methuen, 1986.

Hulme, Peter. 'The Silent Language of the Face: The Perception of Indigenous Difference in Travel Writing about the Caribbean'. In *Perspectives on Travel Writing*, edited by Glenn Hooper and Tim Youngs, 85–98. London: Routledge, 2004.

Hulme, Peter, and Tim Youngs, eds. *The Cambridge Companion to Travel Writing*. Cambridge: Cambridge University Press, 2002. doi.org/10.1017/ccol05217 8140x.

Hunter, Kate. 'The Interracial Theatre of "Strip Tents" in Travelling Shows: Spaces of Sexual Desire in Southeastern Australia, 1930s–1950s'. *Journal of New Zealand Studies*, no. 14 (2013): 54–66. doi.org/10.26686/jnzs.v0i14.1747.

Ikeda, James K. 'A Brief History of Bubonic Plague in Hawai'i'. *Hawaiian Entomological Society* 25 (1985): 75–81.

Irwin, Edward Way, and Ivan Goff. *No Longer Innocent*. Sydney: Angus & Robertson, 1934.

James, John Stanley. *South Sea Massacres*. Sydney: The Australian, 1881.

Johnson-Woods, Toni. *Index to Serials in Australian Periodicals and Newspapers*. Canberra: Mulini Press, 2001.

Johnson-Woods, Toni. 'Popular Australian Writing'. In *A Companion to Australian Literature Since 1900*, edited by Nicholas Birns and Rebecca McNeer, 387–402. Rochester: Camden House, 2007.

Johnston, Anna. 'Writing the Southern Cross: Religious Travel Writing in Nineteenth-Century Australasia'. In *Travel Writing in the Nineteenth Century: Filling the Blank Spaces*, edited by Tim Youngs, 201–18. London: Anthem Press, 2006. doi.org/10.7135/upo9781843317692.012.

Johnston, Anna, and Mitchell Rolls. *Travelling Home, Walkabout Magazine and Mid-Twentieth-Century Australia*. London: Anthem Press, 2016.

Jolly, Margaret. 'Colonizing Women: The Maternal Body and Empire'. In *Feminism and the Politics of Difference*, edited by Sneja Marina Gunew and Anna Yeatman, 103–27. New York: Routledge, 1994. doi.org/10.4324/9780429039010-7.

Jolly, Margaret. 'Desire, Difference and Disease: Sexual and Venereal Exchanges on Cook's Voyages in the Pacific'. In *Exchanges: Cross-Cultural Encounters in Australia and the Pacific*, edited by Ross Gibson, 187–217. Sydney: Historic Houses Trust of New South Wales, 1996.

Jolly, Margaret. 'From Point Venus to Bali Ha'i: Eroticism and Exoticism in Representations of the Pacific'. In *Sites of Desire, Economies of Pleasure: Sexualities in Asia and the Pacific*, edited by Lenore Manderson and Margaret Jolly, 99–122. Chicago: University of Chicago Press, 1997.

Joseph, Alfred. *A Bendigonian Abroad: Being Sketches of Travel Made during a Ten Months Tour Through Europe and America*. Melbourne: Reardon & Mitchell, n.d.

Kahn, Miriam, and Sabine Wilke. 'Narrating Colonial Encounters: Germany in the Pacific Islands'. *The Journal of Pacific History* 42, no. 3 (2007): 293–97. doi.org/10.1080/00223340701691975.

Karskens, Grace. *The Colony: A History of Early Sydney*. Crows Nest: Allen & Unwin, 2010.

Keesing, Roger M. 'The Young Dick Attack: Oral and Documentary History on the Colonial Frontier'. *Ethnohistory* 33, no. 3 (1986): 268–92. doi.org/10.2307/481815.

Keesing, Roger M, and Peter Corris, eds. *Lightning Meets the West Wind: The Malaita Massacre*. Melbourne: Oxford University Press, 1980.

Kelly, John Dunham. *A Politics of Virtue: Hinduism, Sexuality, and Countercolonial Discourse in Fiji*. Chicago: University of Chicago Press, 1991.

Kirkcaldie, Rosa Angela. *In Gray and Scarlet*. Melbourne: Alexander McCubbin, 1922.

Kirkpatrick, Peter John. *The Sea Coast of Bohemia: Literary Life in Sydney's Roaring Twenties*. St Lucia: University of Queensland Press, 1992.

Kleeman, Faye Yuan. *Under an Imperial Sun: Japanese Colonial Literature of Taiwan and the South*. Honolulu: University of Hawai'i Press, 2003.

Klein, Christina. *Cold War Orientalism: Asia in the Middlebrow Imagination, 1945–1961*. Berkeley: University of California Press, 2003.

Knapman, Claudia. 'Western Women's Travel Writing About the Pacific Islands'. *Pacific Studies* 20, no. 2 (1997): 31–51.

Knapman, Claudia. *White Women in Fiji 1835–1930: The Ruin of Empire?* Sydney: Allen & Unwin, 1986.

Krauth, Nigel, ed. *New Guinea Images in Australian Literature*. St Lucia: University of Queensland Press, 1982.

Krauth, Nigel. 'The New Guinea Experience in Literature: A Study of Imaginative Writing Concerned with Papua New Guinea, 1863–1980'. PhD thesis, University of Queensland, 1983.

Kuttainen, Victoria, and Sarah Galletly. 'Making Friends of the Nations: Australian Interwar Magazines and Middlebrow Orientalism in the Pacific'. *Journeys* 17, no. 2 (2016): 23–48. doi.org/10.3167/jys.2016.170203.

Lake, Marilyn. 'Colonial Australia and the Asia-Pacific Region'. In *The Cambridge History of Australia*, edited by Alison Bashford and Stuart Macintyre, 535–59. Port Melbourne: Cambridge University Press, 2015. doi.org/10.1017/cho 9781107445758.025.

Lake, Marilyn. 'The Australian Dream of an Island Empire: Race, Reputation and Resistance'. *Australian Historical Studies* 46, no. 3 (2015): 410–24. doi.org/ 10.1080/1031461x.2015.1075222.

Lake, Marilyn. 'Historical Reconsiderations IV: The Politics of Respectability: Identifying the Masculinist Context'. *Historical Studies* 22, no. 86 (1986): 116–31. doi.org/10.1080/10314618608595739.

Lake, Marilyn, and Henry Reynolds. *Drawing the Global Colour Line: White Men's Countries and the Question of Racial Equality*. Carlton: Melbourne University Press, 2008.

Lal, Brij V. *Broken Waves: A History of the Fiji Islands in the Twentieth Century*. Honolulu: University of Hawai'i Press, 1992.

Lal, Brij V. *Chalo Jahaji: On a Journey through Indenture in Fiji*. Canberra: ANU E Press, 2012. doi.org/10.22459/CJ.12.2012.

Lal, Brij V, and Kate Fortune, eds. *The Pacific Islands: An Encyclopaedia*. Honolulu: University of Hawai'i Press, 2000.

Lamb, Jonathan. *Preserving the Self in the South Seas, 1680–1840*. Chicago: University of Chicago Press, 2001.

Laracy, Hugh. 'Beatrice Grimshaw (1870–1953): Pride and Prejudice in Papua'. In *Watriama and Co: Further Pacific Islands Portraits*, by Hugh Laracy, 141–67. Canberra: ANU E Press, 2013. doi.org/10.22459/WC.10.2013.

Latham, Linda. 'Revolt Re-Examined: The 1878 Insurrection in New Caledonia'. *The Journal of Pacific History* 10, no. 3 (1975): 48–63. doi.org/10.1080/00223347508572278.

le Couteur, Wilson. 'The New Hebrides. Development at Vila. Copra and Cotton. Aneityum Depopulated'. *Sydney Morning Herald*, 1 September 1908. nla.gov.au/nla.news-article15021942.

le Couteur, Wilson. 'The New Hebrides: Old Order and New: French Strides Forward'. *Sydney Morning Herald*, 29 August 1908. nla.gov.au/nla.news-article 15021313.

Leed, Eric J. *The Mind of the Traveler: From Gilgamesh to Global Tourism*. New York: Basic Books, 1991.

Lees, William. *Around the Coasts of Australia and Fiji Illustrated: A Handbook of Picturesque Travel and General Information for Passengers by Steamers of the Australasian United Steam Navigation Co. Ltd*. Brisbane: Robert McGregor & Coy Printers, 1916.

Lewis, Aletta. *They Call Them Savages*. London: Methuen & Co. Ltd, 1938.

Littlejohn, George Stanley. *Notes and Reflections 'on the road'*. Sydney: Swift Print, 1911.

Livingston, Kevin T. *The Wired Nation Continent: The Communication Revolution and Federating Australia*. Melbourne: Oxford University Press, 1996.

Lloyd, M. *Wanderings in the Old World and the New*. Adelaide: Vardon & Pritchard, 1901.

Louis, William Roger, and William S Livingston. *Australia, New Zealand and the Pacific Islands since the First World War*. Austin: University of Texas Press, 1979.

Lyons, Paul. *American Pacificism: Oceania in the U.S. Imagination*. New York: Routledge, 2006.

Lyons, Paul. 'Pacific Scholarship, Literary Criticism, and Touristic Desire: The Specter of A. Grove Day'. *Boundary* 24, no. 2 (1997): 47–78. doi.org/10.2307/303763.

MacCannell, Dean. *The Tourist: A New Theory of the Leisure Class*. New York: Schocken Books Inc., 1976.

Mageo, Jeannette, ed. *Cultural Memory: Reconfiguring History and Identity in the Postcolonial Pacific*. Honolulu: University of Hawai'i Press, 2001. doi.org/10.1515/9780824841874.

Marks, Ernest George. *Pacific Peril, or, Menace of Japan's Mandated Islands*. Sydney: Wynyard Book Arcade, 1933.

Marshall, Alan John. *The Black Musketeers: The Work and Adventures of a Scientist on a South Sea Island at War and in Peace*. London: William Heinemann, 1937.

Marshall, Jock. *The Men and Birds of Paradise: Journeys through Equatorial New Guinea*. London: William Heinemann, 1938.

Mason, Michele M, and Helen JS Yee. *Reading Colonial Japan: Text, Context, Critique*. Stanford: Stanford University Press, 2012.

Matson. 'About Matson: History'. www.matson.com/corporate/about_us/history.html.

Matsuda, Matt. *Empire of Love: Histories of France and the Pacific*. New York: Oxford University Press, 2005.

Matters, Charles Henry. *From Golden Gate to Golden Horn, and Many Other World Wide Wanderings: Or 50,000 Miles of Travel over Sea and Land*. Adelaide: Vardon & Pritchard, 1892.

Maude, Henry Evans. 'Review Article: Louis Becke: The Traders' Historian'. *The Journal of Pacific History* 2, no. 1 (1967): 225–7. doi.org/10.1080/00223346708572118.

McArthur, Norma. *Island Populations of the Pacific*. Canberra: Australian National University Press, 1968.

McBride, Christopher. *The Colonizer Abroad: Island Representations in American Prose from Herman Melville to Jack London*. New York: Routledge, 2004. doi.org/10.4324/9780203494400.

McCormack, Terri, et al., eds. *Annotated Bibliography of Australian Overseas Travel Writing, 1830 to 1970*. Canberra: ALIA Press, 1996.

McCormick, Peter Dodds. *Advance Australia Fair*. Sydney: Reading & Co, 1879.

McCreery, Cindy, and Kirsten McKenzie. 'The Australian Colonies in a Maritime World'. in *The Cambridge History of Australia*, edited by Alison Bashford and Stuart Macintyre, 560–84. Port Melbourne: Cambridge University Press, 2015. doi.org/10.1017/cho9781107445758.026.

McDowell, Kat. 'Copra: A Gigantic Tropical Industry'. *Sea, Land and Air* 4, no. 38 (May 1921): 97–101.

McGregor, Russell. *Imagined Destinies: Aboriginal Australians and the Doomed Race Theory, 1880–1939*. Carlton: Melbourne University Press, 1997.

McGuire, Paul. *Westward the Course: The New World of Oceania*. Melbourne: Oxford University Press, 1942.

McKay, Thomas Allan. *Seeing the World Twice 1926–1935*. Melbourne: Robertson & Mullens, 1936.

McKellar, Norman Lang. *From Derby Round to Burketown: The A.U.S.N. Story*. St Lucia: University of Queensland Press, 1977.

McLaren, Jack. *My Odyssey*. London: Jonathan Cape, 1923.

McMahon, Thomas J. 'Cocoanut Industry in the South Pacific: Its Growth and Possibilities'. *Sea, Land and Air* 4, no. 47 (February 1922): 813–16.

McMahon, Thomas. 'Lets-All-Be-Thankful Island'. *Penny Pictorial* (September 1919).

McMahon, Thomas J. 'Nauru Island', *Sea, Land and Air* 1, no. 11 (February 1919): 656–60.

McMillan, Robert. *There and Back: Or Notes of a Voyage Round the World by 'Gossip'*. Sydney: William Brooks, 1903.

Meagher, Richard Denis. *American Impressions*. Sydney: Gordon & Gotch, 1925.

Meaney, Neville. *Australia and the Wider World: A Documentary History from the 1870s to the 1970s*. Melbourne: Longman Cheshire, 1985.

Meaney, Neville. *The Search for Security in the Pacific 1901–1914*. Sydney: Sydney University Press, 1976.

Meek, Albert Stewart. *A Naturalist in Cannibal Land*, edited by Frank Fox. London: T.F. Unwin, 1913.

Meek, Ronald L. *Social Science and the Ignoble Savage*. Cambridge: Cambridge University Press, 1976.

Melvin, Joseph Dalgarno. *The Cruise of the Helena: A Labour-Recruiting Voyage to the Solomon Islands*, edited by Peter Corris. Melbourne: Hawthorn Press, 1977.

Merle, Isabelle. 'The Trials and Tribulations of the Emancipists: The Consequences of Penal Colonisation in New Caledonia 1864–1920'. In *France Abroad: Indochina, New Caledonia, Wallis and Futuna, Mayotte: Papers Presented at the Tenth George Rude Seminar*, edited by Robert Aldrich and Isabelle Merle, 39–55. Sydney: University of Sydney, 1997.

Metcalf, Bill. *From Utopian Dreaming to Communal Reality: Cooperative Lifestyles in Australia*. Sydney: UNSW Press, 1995.

Meudell, George. *The Pleasant Career of a Spendthrift*. London: Routledge, 1929.

Mickle, Alan Durward. *Of Many Things*. Sydney: Australian Publishing Co., 1941.

Miller, Edmund Morris. *Australian Literature from Its Beginnings to 1935: A Descriptive and Bibliographical Survey of Books by Australian Authors in Poetry, Drama, Fiction, Criticism and Anthology with Subsidiary Entries to 1938*. Melbourne: Melbourne University Press, 1940.

Mills, Carol. *The New South Wales Bookstall Company as a Publisher: With Notes on Its Artists and Authors and a Bibliography of Its Publications*. Canberra: Mulini Press, 1991.

Mills, Christopher. 'Briefs and Associated Papers in Cases Involving Pacific Islanders'. In Crown Solicitor's Office, Series ID 12102, Item ID 7876. Queensland: Queensland State Archives, 1884.

Mitchell, Janet. *Spoils of Opportunity: An Autobiography*. New York: Dutton, 1939.

Moblo, Pennie. 'Leprosy, Politics, and the Rise of Hawai'i's Reform Party'. *The Journal of Pacific History* 34, no. 1 (1999): 75–89. doi.org/10.1080/00223349908572892.

'Modern Utopia Planned by Tasmanians'. *Sunday Times*, 31 July 1938. nla.gov.au/nla.news-article58987760.

Moore, Clive. *Kanaka: A History of Melanesian Mackay*. Port Moresby: University of Papua New Guinea Press, 1985.

Moore, Clive. *New Guinea: Crossing Boundaries and History*. Honolulu: University of Hawai'i Press, 2003.

Moore, Clive. 'Pacific Islanders in Nineteenth Century Queensland'. In *Labour in the South Pacific*, edited by Clive Moore, Jacqueline Leckie and Doug Munro, 144–7. Townsville: James Cook Univeristy of Northern Queensland, 1990.

Moore, Clive. 'Peter Abu'ofa and the Founding of the South Sea Evangelical Mission in the Solomon Islands, 1894–1904'. *The Journal of Pacific History* 48, no. 1 (2013): 23–42. doi.org/10.1080/00223344.2012.756162.

Moore, Clive. 'The Counterculture of Survival: Melanesians in the Mackay District of Queensland, 1865–1906'. In *Plantation Workers: Resistance and Accommodation*, edited by Brij V Lal, Doug Munro and Edward D Beechert, 69–99. Honolulu: University of Hawai'i Press, 1993.

Moore, Clive, ed. *The Forgotten People: A History of the Australian South Sea Island Community*. Sydney: Australian Broadcasting Commission, 1979.

Moore, Clive, James Griffin and Andrew Griffin, eds. *Colonial Intrusion: Papua New Guinea, 1884*. Port Moresby: PNG Centenial Committee, 1984.

Mordaunt, Elinor. *Sinabada*. London: Michael Joseph, 1937.

Mordaunt, Elinor. *The Venture Book*. New York: The Century Co., 1926.

Morning Post, 31 December 1901.

Moynagh, Michael. *Brown or White?: A History of the Fiji Sugar Industry, 1873–1973*. Canberra: Pacific Research Monograph, The Australian National University, 1981.

Muckle, Adrian. *Specters of Violence in a Colonial Context: New Caledonia, 1917*. Honolulu: University of Hawai'i Press, 2012.

Muspratt, Eric. *Fire of Youth: The Story of Forty-Five Years Wandering*. London: Gerald Duckworth, 1948.

Muspratt, Eric. *My South Sea Island*. London: Martin Hopkinson Ltd, 1931.

Napier, Sydney Elliott. *Men and Cities: Being the Journeyings of a Journalist*. Sydney: Angus & Robertson, 1938.

National Centre of Biography and The Australian National University. *Australian Dictionary of Biography*. adb.anu.edu.au/.

Nelson, Hank. *Black, White and Gold: Gold Mining in Papua New Guinea, 1878–1930*. Canberra: ANU Press, 2016. doi.org/10.22459/bwg.07.2016.

Nelson, Hank. 'European Attitudes in Papua, 1906–1914'. In *The History of Melanesia*, edited by KS Inglis, 593–623. Port Moresby and Canberra: University of Papua and New Guinea and The Australian National University, 1969.

Nelson, Hank. 'Lives Told: Australians in Papua and New Guinea'. In *Telling Pacific Lives: Prisms of Process*, edited by Brij V Lal and Vicki Luker, 243–76. Canberra: ANU E Press, 2008. doi.org/10.22459/tpl.06.2008.18.

Nelson, Hank. 'Looking Black: Australian Images of Melanesians'. In *The Pacific War in Papua New Guinea: Memories and Realities*, edited by Yukio Toyoda and Hank Nelson, 144–68. Tokyo: Rikkyo University, Centre for Asian Area Studies, 2006.

Nelson, Hank. 'Our Boys up North: The Behaviour of Australians in New Guinea'. *Meanjin Quarterly* 32, no. 4 (1973): 443–41.

Newbury, Colin Walter. *Tahiti Nui: Change and Survival in French Polynesia, 1767–1945*. Honolulu: University of Hawai'i Press, 1980.

Nicoll, George Robertson. *Fifty Years' Travels in Australia, China, Japan, America, Etc., 1848–1898*. London: George Robertson Nicoll, 1899.

Nicoll, JB. 'A Cruise through Some of the Pacific Islands in 1902 by Mr and Mrs J. B. Nicoll'. In The Life and Adventures of George Robertson Nicoll, 1824–1890, MS 3292. Canberra: National Library of Australia, 1902.

Nishino, Ryota. 'Tales of Two Fijis: Early 1960s Japanese Travel Writing by Kanetaka Kaoru and Kita Morio'. *Journal of Pacific History* 49, no. 4 (2014): 440–56. doi.org/10.1080/00223344.2014.974300.

Nishino, Ryota. 'The Self-Promotion of a Maverick Travel Writer: Suzuki Tsunenori and His Southern Pacific Islands Travelogue, Nanyō tanken jikki'. *Studies in Travel Writing* 20, no. 4 (2016): 378–91. doi.org/10.1080/13645145.2016.1264356.

Nixon, A. 'Inwards Correspondence'. In Colonial Secretary's Office, Series ID 5253, Item ID 846982. Brisbane: Queensland State Archives, 1877.

Nossiter, Harold. *Southward Ho!* London: Witherby, 1937.

Obeyesekere, Gananath. *Cannibal Talk: The Man-Eating Myth and Human Sacrifice in the South Seas*. Berkeley: University of California Press, 2005.

O'Brien, Duncan. *The White Ships: Matson Line to Hawai'i, New Zealand, Australia via Samoa, Fiji, 1927–1978*. Victoria: Pier 19 Media, 2008.

O'Brien, Patty. *The Pacific Muse: Exotic Femininity and the Colonial Pacific*. Seattle: University of Washington Press, 2006.

Olcelli, Laura. *Questions of Authority: Italian and Australian Travel Narratives of the Long Nineteenth Century*. New York: Routledge, 2018. doi.org/10.4324/ 9780203709719.

Ombrello, Mark Alan. 'Monstrous Projections and Paradisal Visions: Japanese Conceptualizations of the South Seas (nan'yō) as a Supernatural Space from Ancient Times to the Contemporary Period'. PhD thesis, University of Hawai'i, 2014.

Osborne, Ernest. 'Australia and the Nauru Phosphate Deal', *Lone Hand* (August 1920): 37–8.

Osborne, E. 'Ocean Island and the Phosphate Industry'. *Lone Hand* 12 (November 1912): 42–5.

Osborne, Ernest. *Through the Atolls of the Line*. Five Dock: publisher unknown, 1900.

Paisley, Fiona. *Glamour in the Pacific: Cultural Internationalism and Race Politics in the Women's Pan-Pacific*. Honolulu: University of Hawai'i Press, 2009.

Parsons, Ronald. *A History of Australasian Steam Navigation Company and Australasian United Steam Navigation Co. Ltd*. Adelaide: publisher unknown, 1960.

Paterson, Andrew Barton. 'Banjo Paterson Ends His Story: Political Giants and "Pilgrim Fathers"'. *Sydney Morning Herald*, 4 March 1939. nla.gov.au/nla. news-article17573640.

Paterson, Andrew Barton. 'The New Hebrides: The New Pilgrims' Progress'. *Sydney Morning Herald*, 26 July 1902. nla.gov.au/nla.news-article14471684.

Paterson, Andrew Barton. 'The New Hebrides: Voyage of the Pilgrims'. *Sydney Morning Herald*, 1 July 1902. nla.gov.au/nla.news-article14468684.

Paterson, Andrew Barton. 'The Pioneers', Talks—AB Paterson, Australian Broadcasting Commission, Sydney: ABC, 1935. Series no. SP 1558/2, 629, National Archives of Australia.

Paton, Frank Hume Lyall. *Glimpses of the New Hebrides*. Melbourne: Foreign Missions Committee, Presbyterian Church of Victoria, 1913.

Paton, Frank Hume Lyall. *The Kingdom in the Pacific*. London: United Council for Missionary Education, 1912.

Paton, John Gibson. *Thirty Years with South Sea Cannibals: Autobiography of John G. Paton*, edited by James Paton. Chicago: Moody Press, 1964.

'Pearls of the Pacific'. *BP Magazine* (December 1929 – February 1930).

Pearse, Albert William. *A Windjammer 'Prentice*. Sydney: John Andrews & Co., 1927.

Pearson, Bill. *Rifled Sanctuaries: Some Views of the Pacific Islands in Western Literature to 1900*. Auckland: Auckland University Press, 1984.

Peattie, Mark R. *Nan'yo: The Rise and Fall of the Japanese in Micronesia, 1885–1945*. Honolulu: University of Hawai'i Press, 1988.

'Personalities: Henri Rochefort'. *Windsor and Richmond Gazette*, 24 August 1889.

Pesman, Ros. *Duty Free: Australian Women Abroad*. Melbourne: Oxford University Press, 1996.

Pesman, Ros, David Walker and Richard White, eds. *The Oxford Book of Australian Travel Writing*. Melbourne: Oxford University Press, 1996.

Phillips, George. *Notes on a Visit to New Caledonia*. Brisbane: Brisbane Telegraph, 1903.

Philp, John Ernest. *A Solomons Sojourn: J. E. Philp's Log of the Makira, 1912–1913*, edited by Richard Allen Herr and E Anne Rood. Hobart: Tasmanian Historical Research Association, 1978.

Pickles, Katie, and Catharine Coleborne, eds. *New Zealand's Empire*. Manchester: Manchester University Press, 2015.

Ponder, Harriet Winifred. *An Idler in the Islands*. Sydney: Cornstalk Publishing, 1924.

Powell, Sydney Walter. *Adventures of a Wanderer*. London: Jonathan Cape, 1928.

Powell, Sydney Walter. *A South Sea Diary*. London: V. Gollancz, 1942.

Powell, Sydney Walter. 'Each to His Taste'. Papers of Sydney Powell [circa 1920–1950], MS10012. Canberra: National Library of Australia.

Pratt, Mary Louise. *Imperial Eyes: Travel Writing and Transculturation*. New York: Routledge, 1992.

'Products of the Pacific Islands'. In *The Pacific Islands*, by the Australian Army Education Service. Melbourne: Army Education Service, 1942.

Quanchi, Max. 'A Name That Featured Once or Twice a Year: Not Noticing French New Caledonia in Mid-20th Century Australia'. *Journal of Pacific Studies* 29, no. 2 (2006): 195–216.

Quanchi, Max. 'Contrary Images: Photographing the New Pacific in *Walkabout* Magazine'. *Journal of Australian Studies* 27, no. 79 (2003): 77–92. doi.org/10.1080/14443050309387889.

Quanchi, Max. 'Jewel of the Pacific and Planter's Paradise: The Visual Argument for Australian Sub-Imperialism in the Solomon Islands'. *The Journal of Pacific History* 39, no. 1 (2004): 43–58. doi.org/10.1080/00223340410001684840.

Quanchi, Max. 'Norman H. Hardy: Book Illustrator and Artist', *The Journal of Pacific History* 49, no. 2 (2014): 214–33, doi.org/10.1080/00223344.2014.906298.

Quanchi, Max. *Photographing Papua: Representation, Colonial Encounters and Imaging in the Public Domain*. Newcastle: Cambridge Scholars Publishing, 2007.

Quanchi, Max. 'The Power of Pictures: Learning-by-Looking at Papua in Illustrated Newspapers and Magazines'. *Australian Historical Studies* 35, no. 123 (2004): 37–53. doi.org/10.1080/10314610408596271.

Quanchi, Max. 'Thomas McMahon: Photography as Propaganda in the Pacific Islands'. *History of Photography* 21, no. 1 (2015): 42–53. doi.org/10.1080/03087298.1997.10443716.

Quanchi, Max. 'To the Islands: Photographs of Tropical Colonies in The Queenslander'. Paper presented at the 18th Pacific History Association Conference, University of South Pacific, Suva, Fiji, 2008.

Rajkowski, Pamela. *In the Tracks of the Camelmen*. North Ryde: Angus & Robertson, 1987.

Ramsden, Eric. 'Memories of Moorea'. *Walkabout* 1, no. 8 (1 June 1935): 11–15.

Rannie, Douglas. *My Adventures among South Sea Cannibals: An Account of the Experiences and Adventures of a Government Official among the Natives of Oceania*. London: Seeley, Service & Co., 1912.

Rannie, Douglas. *Notes on the New Hebrides*. Brisbane: Royal Geographical Society of Australasia, 1890.

Rawlinson, HG. 'Indian in European Literature and Thought'. In *The Legacy of India*, edited by GT Garratt, 1–37. Oxford: Clarendon Press, 1937.

Rebell, Fred. *Escape to the Sea: The Adventures of Fred Rebell, who Sailed Single Handed in an Open Boat 9,000 Miles across the Pacific in Search of Happiness*. London: J. Murray, 1939.

Rees, Anne. 'Ellis Island in the Pacific: Encountering America in Hawai'i, 1920s–1950s'. Paper presented at the Travel, The Middlebrow Imagination, Australasia-Pacific 1918–50 Colloquium, James Cook University, Townsville, Queensland, 29 November 2013.

Reimann-Dawe, Tracey. 'Time, Identity and Colonialism in German Travel Writing on Africa 1848–1914'. In *German Colonialism and National Identity*, edited by Michael Perraudin and Jürgen Zimmerer, 21–32. New York: Routledge, 2011.

Reid, Frank. 'Isles of Pearl and Gold'. *Sea, Land and Air* 3, no. 36 (March 1921): 759–61.

Reid, Frank. 'Waters of Adventure'. *Sea, Land and Air* 4, no. 39 (June 1921): 179–81.

Rennie, Neil. *Far-Fetched Facts: The Literature of Travel and the Idea of the South Seas*. Oxford: Clarendon Press, 1995.

Richardson, Keith P. 'Polliwogs and Shellbacks: An Analysis of the Equator Crossing Ritual'. *Western Folklore* 36, no. 2 (1977): 154–9. doi.org/10.2307/1498967.

Rickard, Suzanne. 'Lifelines from Calcutta'. In *India, China, Australia: Trade and Society 1788–1850*, edited by James Broadbent, Suzanne Rickard and Margaret Steven, 64–93. Glebe: Historic Houses Trust of NSW, 2003.

Robson, Robert William, ed. *The Pacific Islands Yearbook*. 1st ed. Sydney: Pacific Publications Ltd, 1932.

Romilly, Hugh Hastings. *The Western Pacific and New Guinea: Notes on the Natives, Christian and Cannibal, with Some Account of the Old Labour Trade*. London: J. Murray, 1886.

Ross, Charles Stuart. *Fiji and the Western Pacific*. Victoria: H. Thacker, 1909.

Ross, Angus. *New Zealand Aspirations in the Pacific in the Nineteenth Century*. Oxford: Clarendon Press, 1964.

Ross, Angus, ed. *New Zealand's Record in the Pacific Islands in the Twentieth Century*. London: Hurst, 1969.

Rubiés, Joan-Pau. 'New Worlds and Renaissance Ethnology'. *History and Anthropology* 6, nos 2–3 (1993): 157–97.

Rubiés, Joan-Pau. 'Travel Writing as a Genre: Facts, Fictions and the Invention of a Scientific Discourse in Early Modern Europe'. *Journeys* 1, nos 1–2 (2000): 5–35. doi.org/10.3167/146526000782488036.

Russell, Penny. *Savage or Civilised?: Manners in Colonial Australia*. Sydney: UNSW Press, 2010.

Ryan, FI. 'Fiji Gold'. *Walkabout* 6, no. 10 (August 1940): 15–20.

Safroni-Middleton, Arnold. *A Vagabond's Odyssey: Being Further Reminiscences of a Wandering Sailor, Troubadour in Many Lands*. London: Grant Richards, 1916.

Safroni-Middleton, Arnold. *In the Green Leaf: A Chapter of Autobiography*. London: Fortune P, 1950.

Safroni-Middleton, Arnold. *Sailor and Beachcomber: Confessions of a Life at Sea, in Australia and amid the Islands of the Pacific*. London: Grant Richards, 1915.

Safroni-Middleton, Arnold. *South Sea Foam: The Romantic Adventures of a Modern Don Quixote in the Southern Seas*. London: Methuen & Co., 1919.

Safroni-Middleton, Arnold. *Tropic Shadows: Memories of the South Seas, Together with Reminiscences of the Author's Sea Meetings with Joseph Conrad*. London: The Richards Press, 1927.

Safroni-Middleton, Arnold. *Wine-Dark Seas and Tropic Skies: Reminiscences and a Romance of the South Seas*. London: Grant Richards, 1918.

Said, Edward. *Orientalism*. London: Pantheon Books, 1977.

Salesa, Damon Ieremia. *Racial Crossings: Race, Intermarriage, and the Victorian British Empire*. Oxford: Oxford University Press, 2011.

Saxby, Henry Maurice. *A History of Australian Children's Literature 1841–1941*. Sydney: Wentworth Books, 1969.

Scarr, Deryck. 'Introduction'. In *A Cruize in a Queensland Labour Vessel to the South Seas*, edited by William E Giles, 1–32. Canberra: Australian National University Press, 1970.

Scott, RJ. *The Development of Tourism in Fiji since 1923*. Suva: Fiji Visitors Bureau, 1970.

Scriver, Peter. 'Mosques, Ghantowns and Cameleers in the Settlement History of Colonial Australia'. *Fabrications: The Journal of the Society of Architectural Historians, Australia and New Zealand* 13, no. 2 (2004): 19–41. doi.org/10.1080/10331867.2004.10525182.

Seddon, Richard John. *The Right Hon. R. J. Seddon's (The Premier of New Zealand) Visit to Tonga, Fiji, Savage Island, and the Cook Islands, May 1900*. Wellington: New Zealand Government, 1900.

Seligmann, Charles Gabriel. *The Melanesians of British New Guinea*. Cambridge: Cambridge University Press, 1910.

Shanks, G Dennis, et al. 'Measles Epidemics of Variable Lethality in the Early 20th Century'. *American Journal of Epidemiology* 179, no. 4 (2014): 413–22. doi.org/10.1093/aje/kwt282.

Shapiro, Karl. *V-Letter and Other Poems*. New York: Reynal & Hitchcock, 1944.

Sharrad, Paul. 'Imagining the Pacific'. *Meanjin* 49, no. 4 (1990): 597–606.

Shineberg, Dorothy. *The People Trade: Pacific Island Laborers and New Caledonia, 1865–1930*. Honolulu: University of Hawai'i Press, 1999. doi.org/10.1515/9780824864910.

Shineberg, Dorothy. *They Came for Sandalwood: A Study of the Sandalwood Trade in the South-West Pacific, 1830–1865*. Melbourne: Melbourne University Press, 1967.

Silva, Noenoe K. *Aloha Betrayed: Native Hawaiian Resistance to American Colonialism*. London: Duke University Press, 2004. doi.org/10.1215/9780822386223.

Simpson, Colin. *Adam in Ochre: Inside Aboriginal Australia*. New York: Frederick A. Praeger, 1953.

Skwiot, Christine. 'Genealogies and Histories in Collision: Tourism and Colonial Contestations in Hawai'i, 1900–1930'. In *Moving Subjects: Gender, Mobility and Intimacy in an Age of Global Empire*, edited by Tony Ballantyne and Antoinette Burton, 190–210. Urbana: University of Illinois Press, 2009.

Skwiot, Christine. 'Itineraries of Empire: The Uses of US Tourism in Cuba and Hawai'i, 1898–1959'. PhD thesis, The State University of New Jersey, 2005.

Skwiot, Christine. *The Purposes of Paradise: U.S. Tourism and Empire in Cuba and Hawai'i*. Philadelphia: University of Pennsylvania Press, 2010. doi.org/10.9783/9780812200034.

Smith, Bernard. *European Vision and the South Pacific*. Sydney: Harper & Row, 1985.

Smith, Bernard. *Imagining the Pacific: In the Wake of the Cook Voyages*. New Haven: Yale University Press, 1992.

Smith, Vanessa. *Intimate Strangers: Friendship, Exchange and Pacific Encounters*. New York: Cambridge University Press, 2010.

Smith, Vanessa. 'Pitcairn's "Guilty Stock": The Island as Breeding Ground'. In *Islands in History and Representation*, edited by Vanessa Smith and Rod Edmond, 116–32. New York: Routledge, 2003.

Smith, Vanessa, and Rod Edmond, eds. *Islands in History and Representation*. New York: Routledge, 2003.

Smith, William Ramsay. *In Southern Seas: Wanderings of a Naturalist*. London: John Murray, 1924.

Sobocinska, Agnieszka. 'Innocence Lost and Paradise Regained: Tourism to Bali and Australian Perceptions of Asia'. *History Australia* 8, no. 2 (2011): 199–222. doi.org/10.1080/14490854.2011.11668380.

Sobocinska, Agnieszka. *Visiting the Neighbours: Australians in Asia*. Sydney: NewSouth Publishing, 2014.

Sobocinska, Agnieszka, and Richard White. 'Travel and Connections'. In *The Cambridge History of Australia*, vol. 7, edited by Alison Bashford and Stuart Macintyre, 472–93. Port Melbourne: Cambridge University Press, 2013. doi.org/10.1017/cho9781107445758.051.

Souter, Gavin. *New Guinea: The Last Unknown*. Sydney: Angus & Robertson, 1963.

Spennemann, Dirk HR. '"Vell, I don't call dot very shentlemanly gonduck": The Portrayal of Germans as Ungentlemanly South Sea Traders in Louis Becke's Short Stories'. *Pacific Asia Inquiry* 5, no. 1 (2014): 107–29.

Steel, Frances. 'An Ocean of Leisure: Early Cruise Tours of the Pacific in an Age of Empire'. *Journal of Colonialism and Colonial History* 14, no. 2 (2013): 1–12. doi.org/10.1353/cch.2013.0019.

Steel, Frances. 'Lines across the Sea: Trans-Pacific Passenger Shipping in the Age of Steam'. In *The Routledge History of Western Empires*, edited by Robert Aldrich and Kirsten McKenzie, 315–29. London: Routledge, 2013. doi.org/10.4324/9781315879499.ch21.

Steel, Frances. 'Maritime Mobilities in Pacific History: Towards a Scholarship of Betweenness'. In *Mobility in History: Themes in Transport: T2M Yearbook 2011*, edited by Gijs Mom et al., 199–204. Neuchatel: Editions Alphil, 2010.

Steel, Frances. 'Oceania under Steam: Maritime Cultures, Colonial Histories 1870s–1910s'. PhD thesis, The Australian National University, 2007.

Steel, Frances. *Oceania under Steam: Sea Transport and the Cultures of Colonialism, c. 1870–1914*. Manchester: Manchester University Press, 2011.

Steel, Frances. 'Re-Routing Empire? Steam-Age Circulations and the Making of an Anglo Pacific c1850–90'. *Australian Historical Studies* 46, no. 3 (2015): 356–73. doi.org/10.1080/1031461x.2015.1071416.

Stephens, William John. *Samoan Holidays*. Bendigo: Cambridge Press, 1935.

Stevens, Christine. *Tin Mosques and Ghantowns: A History of Afghan Camel Drivers in Australia*. Melbourne: Oxford University Press, 1989.

Stewart, Susan. *On Longing: Narratives of the Miniature, the Gigantic, the Souvenir, the Collection*. Durham: Duke University Press, 1993. doi.org/10.1215/9780822378563.

Stillman, Amy Ku'uleialoha. 'Re-Membering the History of the Hawaiian Hula'. In *Cultural Memory: Reconfiguring History and Identity in the Postcolonial Pacific*, edited by Jeannette Mageo, 187–204. Honolulu: University of Hawai'i Press, 2001.

Stillman, Amy Ku'uleialoha. *Sacred Hula: The Historical hula ala apapa*. Honolulu: Bishop Museum Press, 1998.

Stillman, Amy Ku'uleialoha, ed. *The Hula: A Revised Edition*. Honolulu: University of Hawai'i Press, 2011.

Stock, Mabel M. *The Log of a Woman Wanderer*. London: William Heinemann, 1923.

Stock, Ralph. 'On a Fijian Cocoanut Plantation'. *Lone Hand* 10, no. 59 (March 1912): 349–55.

Stock, Ralph. *The Confessions of a Tenderfoot: Being a True and Unvarnished Account of His World-Wanderings*. London: Grant Richards Ltd, 1913.

Stock, Ralph. *The Cruise of the Dream Ship*. London: William Heinemann, 1921.

Street, Brian V. *The Savage in Literature: Representations of 'Primitive' Society in English Fiction, 1858–1920*. London: Routledge, 1975. doi.org/10.4324/9781315617275.

Stuart, Annie. 'Contradictions and Complexities in an Indigenous Medical Service'. *The Journal of Pacific History* 41, no. 2 (2006): 125–43.

Sturma, Michael. *South Sea Maidens: Western Fantasy and Sexual Politics in the South Pacific*. Westport: Greenwood Press, 2002.

Sudo, Naoto. *Nanyo–Orientalism: Japanese Representations of the Pacific*. New York: Cambria Press, 2010.

Swiggum, S, and M Kohli. 'The Fleets: Matson Line 1882–1980'. The Ships List. www.theshipslist.com/ships/lines/matson.shtml.

Syvertsen, Chris. Private Record, PR01438. Canberra: Australian War Memorial, 1917–1918.

Taupo. 'Phosphate Island'. *BP Magazine* 11, no. 4 (September 1939).

Tayler, J Sinclair. 'The Isle of Submarines: A South Sea Terror'. *The Clipper*, 14 October 1905.

Taylor, George Augustine. *There!: A Pilgrimage of Pleasure*. Sydney: Building Limited, 1916.

Tcherkezoff, Serge. 'A Long and Unfortunate Voyage Towards the "Invention" of the Melanesia/Polynesia Distinction 1595–1832'. *The Journal of Pacific History* 38, vol. 2 (2003): 175–96. doi.org/10.1080/0022334032000120521.

Tench, Watkin. *A Complete Account of the Settlement at Port Jackson in New South Wales: Including an Accurate Description of the Colony; Of the Natives; And of Its Natural Productions/Taken on the Spot*. London: G. Nicoll and J. Sewell, 1793.

'The Book World: Reviews'. *The Mercury*, 30 October 1926. nla.gov.au/nla.news-article29464188.

'The Charm of Norfolk Island'. *The Pacific Islands Yearbook*, 1st ed., edited by Robert William Robson. Sydney: Pacific Publications Ltd, 1932.

'The Universal Need for "Escape"'. *Sydney Morning Herald*, 16 October 1939. nla.gov.au/nla.news-article17639412.

Thomas, Julian. *Cannibals and Convicts: Notes of Personal Experiences in the Western Pacific*. Melbourne: Cassell & Company, 1886.

Thomas, Nicholas. *Colonialism's Culture: Anthropology, Travel, and Government*. Princeton: Princeton University Press, 1994.

Thomas, Nicholas, and Richard Eves. *Bad Colonists—The South Seas Letters of Vernon Lee Walker & Louis Becke*. Durham: Duke University Press, 1999.

Thompson, Carl, ed. *The Routledge Companion to Travel Writing*. New York: Routledge, 2016.

Thompson, Carl. *Travel Writing: The New Critical Idiom*. New York: Routledge, 2011.

Thompson, Roger. *Australia and the Pacific Islands in the Twentieth Century*. Melbourne: Australian Scholarly Publishing, 1998.

Thompson, Roger C. *Australian Imperialism in the Pacific: The Expansionist Era, 1820–920*. Carlton: Melbourne University Press, 1980.

Thompson, Roger C. 'Commerce, Christianity and Colonialism: The Australasian New Hebrides Company 1883–1897'. *The Journal of Pacific History* 6, no. 1 (1971): 25–38. doi.org/10.1080/00223347108572181.

Thomson, James Park. *Round the World*. Brisbane: Outridge Printing Co., 1904.

Tichborne, Henry. *Noqu Talanoa: Stories from the South Seas by Sundowner*. London: European Mail, 1896.

Tichborne, Henry. *Rambles in Polynesia by Sundowner*. London: European Mail, 1897.

Tierney, Robert Thomas. *Tropics of Savagery: The Culture of Japanese Empire in Comparative Frame*. Berkeley: University of California Press, 2010. doi.org/10.1525/california/9780520265783.001.0001.

Title #37863 [New Zealand, Pacific Island and Canadian? Holiday], home movie. National Film and Sound Archive of Australia: c. 1928.

Title #64121 [Pacific Islands Leg of Boat Trip to U.S.; Sydney to Los Angeles by Boat], home movie. National Film and Sound Archive of Australia: c. 1927.

Tomkins, Sandra M. 'The Influenza Epidemic of 1918–19 in Western Samoa'. *The Journal of Pacific History* 27, no. 2 (1992): 181–97. doi.org/10.1080/00223349208572706.

'Tommy Tanna'. *The Clipper*, 28 December 1901. nla.gov.au/nla.news-article83085521.

'Tommy Tanna's Present Position'. *Worker*, 1 June 1901. nla.gov.au/nla.news-article70830894.

Torgovnick, Marianna. *Gone Primitive: Savage Intellects, Modern Lives*. Chicago: University of Chicago Press, 1990.

Trainor, Luke. *British Imperialism and Australian Nationalism: Manipulation, Conflict, and Compromise in the Late Nineteenth Century*. Melbourne: Cambridge University Press, 1994.

Twain, Mark. *Following the Equator: A Journey around the World*. Hartford: American Publishing Company, 1897.

University of Queensland. *AUSTLIT*. www.austlit.edu.au/.

Urry, John. *Consuming Places*. New York: Routledge, 1995.

Urry, John. *The Tourist Gaze: Leisure and Travel in Contemporary Societies*. London: Sage Publications, 1990.

Urry, John. *The Tourist Gaze*. 2nd ed. London: Sage, 2002.

USSCo. *Maoriland: Illustrated Handbook to New Zealand*. Melbourne: George Robertson & Co., 1884.

USSCo. *The All-Red Route: The Scenic Route to London*. Union Steam Ship Company of N.Z. Ltd, n.d.

USSCo. *Trip to the South Sea Islands by Union Steam Ship Company's S.S. 'Waikare': July–August, 1898*. Dunedin: J. Wilkie & Co., 1898.

Villiers, Alan John. *Cruise of the Conrad: A Journal of a Voyage Around the World, Undertaken and Carried Out in the Ship Joseph Conrad, 212 tons, in the years 1934, 1935 and 1936 by way of Good Hope, the South Seas, the East Indies and Cape Horn*. London: Hodder & Stoughton, 1937.

Walker, David. *Anxious Nation: Australia and the Rise of Asia, 1850–1939*. St Lucia: University of Queensland Press, 1999.

Walker, David, Julia Horne and Adrian Vickers, eds. *Australian Perceptions of Asia*. Kensington: UNSW Press, 1990.

Walker, David, and Agnieszka Sobocinska, eds. *Australia's Asia: From Yellow Peril to Asian Century*. Crawley: UWA Publishing, 2012.

Walton, John K. 'Histories of Tourism'. In *The SAGE Handbook of Tourism Studies*, edited by Tazmin Jamal and Mike Robinson, 115–29. London: Sage Publications, 2009. doi.org/10.4135/9780857021076.n7.

Wawn, William Twizell. *The South Sea Islanders and the Queensland Labour Trade: A Record of Voyages and Experiences in the Western Pacific, from 1875 to 1891*, edited by Peter Corris. Canberra: Australian National University Press, 1973.

Weaver-Hightower, Rebecca. *Empire Islands: Castaways, Cannibals, and Fantasies of Conquest*. Minneapolis: University of Minnesota Press, 2007.

Weir, Christine. '"Deeply Interested in These Children Whom You Have Not Seen": The Protestant Sunday School View of the Pacific, 1900–1940'. *The Journal of Pacific History* 48, no. 1 (2013): 43–62. doi.org/10.1080/00223344.2012.758921.

Weir, Christine. '"White Man's Burden", "White Man's Privilege": Christian Humanism and Racial Determinism in Oceania 1890–1930'. In *Foreign Bodies: Oceania and the Science of Race 1750–1940*, edited by Bronwen Douglas and Chris Ballard, 283–303. Canberra: ANU E Press, 2008. doi.org/10.22459/fb.11.2008.08.

Wevers, Lydia. *Country of Writing: Travel Writing and New Zealand, 1809–1900*. Auckland: Auckland University Press, 2002.

White, Hayden. 'The Fictions of Factual Representation'. In *Tropics of Discourse: Essays in Cultural Criticism*, edited by Hayden White, 121–34. Baltimore: Johns Hopkins University Press, 1978.

White, Richard. 'Armchair Tourism: The Popularity of Australian Travel Writing'. In *Sold by the Millions: Australia's Bestsellers*, edited by Toni Johnson-Woods and Amit Sarwal, 182–202. Newcastle upon Tyne: Cambridge Scholars Publishing, 2012.

White, Richard. 'Australian Journalists, Travel Writing and China: James Hingston, the "Vagabond" and G. E. Morrison'. *Journal of Australian Studies* 32, no. 2 (2008): 237–50. doi.org/10.1080/14443050802056755.

White, Richard. *Inventing Australia: Images and Identity, 1688–1980*. Sydney: Allen & Unwin, 1981.

White, Richard. *On Holidays: A History of Getting Away in Australia*. North Melbourne: Pluto Press, 2005.

White, Richard. 'The Retreat from Adventure: Popular Travel Writing in the 1950s'. *Australian Historical Studies* 27, no. 109 (1997): 90–105. doi.org/10.1080/10314619708596045.

White, Richard. 'The Subversive Tourist: How Tourism Re-Wrote Australian History'. Harold White Fellow Presentation, Canberra, National Library of Australia, 28 February 2012.

White, Richard. 'Time Travel: Australian Tourists and Britain's Past'. *Portal* 10, no. 1 (2013): 1–25.

White, Richard. 'Travel, Writing and Australia'. *Studies in Travel Writing* 11, no. 1 (2007): 1–14. doi.org/10.1080/13645145.2007.9634816.

Wilkins, William. *Australasia: A Descriptive and Pictorial Account of the Australian and New Zealand Colonies, Tasmania and the Adjacent Lands*. London: Blackie & Son, 1888.

Willmott, William E. *A History of the Chinese Communities in Eastern Melanesia: Solomon Islands, Vanuatu, New Caledonia*. Christchurch: Macmillan Brown Centre for Pacific Studies, University of Canterbury, 2005.

Wilson, Cecil. *The Wake of the Southern Cross: Work and Adventures in the South Seas*. London: John Murray, 1932.

Wilson, Rob. *Reimagining the American Pacific: From South Pacific to Bamboo Ridge and Beyond*. Durham: Duke University Press, 2000. doi.org/10.1215/9780822380979.

Wirth, George. *Round the World with a Circus: Memories of Trials, Triumphs and Tribulations*. Melbourne: Troedel & Cooper, 1925.

Wood, Casey Albert. Letter, 1923–1924, MS 3526. Canberra: National Library of Australia, 1923–1924.

Woodburn, M Kathleen. *Backwash of Empire*. Melbourne: Georgian House, 1944.

Woodhouse, Margaret, and Robert Langdon. *Pacific Islands Monthly Cumulative Index: Volumes 1 to 15 [August, 1930 to July, 1945]*. Sydney: Pacific Publications, 1968.

Woollacott, Angela. '"All This Is the Empire, I Told Myself": Australian Women's Voyages "Home" and the Articulation of Colonial Whiteness'. *The American Historical Review* 102, no. 4 (1997): 1003–29. doi.org/10.2307/2170627.

Woollacott, Angela. *Race and the Modern Exotic: Three 'Australian' Women on Global Display*. Clayton: Monash University Publishing, 2011.

Woollacott, Angela. *To Try Her Fortune in London: Australian Women, Colonialism, and Modernity*. New York: Oxford University Press, 2001.

Wotherspoon, Garry. 'The Bulletin'. *Dictionary of Sydney*. dictionaryofsydney.org/entry/the_bulletin.

Wragge, Clement Lindley. *The Romance of the South Seas*. London: Chatto & Windus, 1906.

Wynn, R, ed. *The Late Alfred Cecil Rowlandson: Pioneer Publisher of Australian Novels*. Sydney: J. Sands, 1922.

Young, John. *Adventurous Spirits: Australian Migrant Society in Pre-Cession Fiji*. St Lucia: University of Queensland Press, 1984.

Young, John MR. *Australia's Pacific Frontier: Economic and Cultural Expansion into the Pacific: 1795–1885*. Melbourne: Cassell Australia, 1967.

Youngs, Tim. *Cambridge Introduction to Travel Writing*. Cambridge: Cambridge University Press, 2013.

Youngs, Tim, ed. *Travel in the Nineteenth Century: Filling the Blank Spaces*. London: Anthem Press, 2006.

www.ingramcontent.com/pod-product-compliance
Lightning Source LLC
Chambersburg PA
CBHW040745020526
44114CB00049B/2922